SALO BARON

Salo Baron

THE PAST AND FUTURE OF JEWISH STUDIES
IN AMERICA

Edited by Rebecca Kobrin

Columbia University Press
New York

Columbia University Press
Publishers Since 1893
New York   Chichester, West Sussex
cup.columbia.edu

Copyright © 2022 Columbia University Press
All rights reserved

Library of Congress Cataloging-in-Publication Data
Names: Kobrin, Rebecca, editor.
Title: Salo Baron : the past and future of Jewish studies in America /
edited by Rebecca Kobrin.
Description: New York : Columbia University Press, [2022] |
Includes bibliographical references and index.
Identifiers: LCCN 2021044684 (print) | LCCN 2021044685 (ebook) |
ISBN 9780231204842 (hardback) | ISBN 9780231204859 (trade paperback) |
ISBN 9780231555708 (ebook)
Subjects: LCSH: Baron, Salo W. (Salo Wittmayer), 1895–1989. |
Jewish historians—United States—Biography. | Judaism—History—Study
and teaching (Higher)—United States. | Jews—History—Study
and teaching (Higher)—United States. | Columbia University. Center
of Israel and Jewish Studies.
Classification: LCC DS115.9.B37 K63 2022 (print) | LCC DS115.9.B37 (ebook) |
DDC 909/.04924007202 [B]—dc23
LC record available at https://lccn.loc.gov/2021044684
LC ebook record available at https://lccn.loc.gov/2021044685

Cover design: Julia Kushnirsky
Cover photograph: University Archives, Rare Book
and Manuscript Library, Columbia University

CONTENTS

INTRODUCTION
Salo Baron, Columbia University, and the Expansion
of Jewish Studies in Twentieth-Century America
REBECCA KOBRIN   1

Chapter One
Salo Baron's Legacy and the Shaping of Jewish Studies
Into the Twenty-First Century
JASON LUSTIG   25

Chapter Two
Organizing the Jewish Past for American Students:
Salo Baron at Columbia
BERNARD D. COOPERMAN   37

Chapter Three
Emancipation: Salo Baron's Achievement
DAVID SORKIN   81

Chapter Four
An Economic Historian Reads Salo Baron
FRANCESCA TRIVELLATO   97

Chapter Five
Salo Baron on Anti-Semitism
DAVID ENGEL   115

CONTENTS

Chapter Six
The Professor in the Courtroom: Salo W. Baron at the Eichmann Trial
DEBORAH LIPSTADT   132

Chapter Seven
Building the Foundations of Scholarship at Home: Salo Baron and the Judaica Collections at Columbia University Libraries
MICHELLE MARGOLIS CHESNER   153

Chapter Eight
From Europe to Pittsburgh: Salo W. Baron and Yosef H. Yerushalmi Between the Lachrymose Theory and the End of the Vertical Alliance
PIERRE BIRNBAUM   174

Chapter Nine
Salo Baron and His Innovative Reconstruction of the Jewish Past
ROBERT CHAZAN   192

Chapter Ten
Remembering Professor Salo Baron: Personal Recollections of a Former Student
JANE C. GERBER   207

Chapter Eleven
Recollections from the Baron Daughters
SHOSHANA B. TANCER AND TOBEY B. GITELLE   219

BIBLIOGRAPHY OF THE PUBLICATIONS OF PROFESSOR SALO WITTMAYER BARON (1895–1989)
MENACHEM BUTLER   225

ACKNOWLEDGMENTS   255

CONTRIBUTORS   259

INDEX   263

Introduction

SALO BARON, COLUMBIA UNIVERSITY, AND THE EXPANSION OF JEWISH STUDIES IN TWENTIETH-CENTURY AMERICA

REBECCA KOBRIN

On December 14, 1929, Nicholas Butler, president of Columbia University, penned a letter that altered the course of academic Jewish Studies in America. On that fateful day ninety years ago, he wrote to Dr. Salo Wittmayer Baron (fig. 0.1), a young Eastern European scholar, who was teaching at the recently established Jewish Institute of Religion.

> There has been established at Columbia University by the generous benefaction of Mrs. Nathan J. Miller, a chair of Jewish History, Literature and Institution, which it is our desire to fill by the appointment of a scholar of first rank, who will be able, because of his learning, his contacts and his point of view, to build up the strongest possible University department in this field of advanced instruction and research. . . . It is the recommendation of this committee that an invitation should be offered to you to become Professor of Jewish History, Literature and Institutions at Columbia University, from July 1, 1930 at an annual salary of $7,500 with a seat in the graduate faculty of philosophy."[1]

Baron accepted the offer, and Butler ultimately placed Baron and this chair in the Department of History.[2] These decisions not only altered the study of the Jewish past at Columbia but, as scholar Robert Liberles has noted, would "influence the growth of Jewish scholarship in universities throughout the United States for the rest of the century."³ In short, Baron's arrival at Columbia was a transformational moment: thanks to Baron, the United States, long viewed as an intellectual backwater in the Jewish world, had a top-rate scholar; and the study of Jewish history, "long relegated to Jewish institutions with limited financial and human resources," moved into "the general American university, which provided augmented resources, valuable new perspectives and challenging new questions."⁴ The explosion of Jewish studies in the American academy in the second half of the twentieth century, anchored in history, is a direct result of Butler's decision to offer the position to Baron, whose erudition, professionalism, initiative, adeptness at institution building and numerous publications set the "standard of excellence [that] almost single-handedly opened the American university to the field of Jewish studies."⁵

The coming pages seek to mark this milestone by reflecting on Baron's legacy within the context of American Jewish life, as he played an instrumental role in transforming Jewish studies in the United States through his scholarship, teaching, institution building, and mentorship both at Columbia University and far beyond its walls. To be sure, this book does not mark the first attempt to reflect on Salo Wittmayer Baron's legacy. Even while Baron was alive, his stature as a scholar, public intellectual, and communal leader prompted several publications to evaluate his scholarship, in both Hebrew and English, by enlisting leading scholars on both sides of the Atlantic.⁶ The scholarly volumes produced for him in his lifetime bespeak his influential role in shaping the academic study of Jewish history as well as the high esteem in which he was held. His very presence on the Columbia campus, as Robert Chazan notes, "added immeasurably to the arguments made for the academic seriousness of Jewish studies and Jewish history."⁷

After his death in 1989, more reflections and reevaluations of Baron's work surfaced, starting with a series of articles and a biography in 1995, along with numerous journal essays, anthologies, monographs, and popular works.⁸ Recently, new work has examined the organizations he founded that restituted stolen Jewish intellectual property or supported the developing field of Jewish studies in the United States.⁹ Many scholars have commented on Baron's formative role as scholar, public intellectual, and communal leader, but none has yet delved into how Baron used his perch in Morningside Heights to train other scholars to transform the study of the Jewish past in America.

INTRODUCTION

FIGURE 0.1. Salo Baron, circa 1934.
From the private collection of Shoshana Tancer.

Drawing on Columbia's many resources, Baron trained numerous students across several fields, produced expansive scholarly tomes, and helped build up archives and Judaica collections not only at Columbia but throughout the United States. Although several authors in this volume debate whether Baron's frameworks, concepts, insights, and arguments still hold sway for scholars in the twenty-first century, few would contest that the organizations he founded or the students he trained profoundly provided a foundation for the nascent field of Jewish studies that dramatically expanded in the latter half of the twentieth century. The questions Baron posed and the conversation he began in the American academy after his arrival at Columbia in 1930 are still discussed in some manner today. Indeed, his protégés and the students trained by those protégés constitute a critical body of scholars whose influence is felt throughout the United States: they continue to shape how students theorize, question, and narrate the evolution of Jewish history, literatures, and culture.

It seems clear that if Salo Baron had not assumed the Miller chair in Columbia University's history department in 1930, Jewish studies in the United States would look different from what we see today. The coming chapters argue that Baron, and his acceptance of this position at Columbia University, fundamentally transformed the contemporary landscape of Jewish studies in the United States. Through the following chapters, each written by a leading contemporary scholar, one can see Baron's role as a teacher, author, bibliophile, and public intellectual through new eyes. At its core, this volume highlights the unique relationship between Baron and Columbia as he used his academic base to launch individuals, institutions, and ideas that are still central to the study of the Jewish past and Jewish studies today.

All of Baron's scholarship, activism, and training of students took place against the backdrop of Columbia University's Morningside Heights campus. From this site, Baron established himself as "the dean of Jewish historians."[10] Baron's prolific output offered new frameworks in which to analyze Jews of the past across time and space. But he also founded and built many organizations and institutions that integrally shaped the study of Jewish culture and history, such as the Jewish Cultural Reconstruction Inc., founded in 1947 to collect and distribute heirless Jewish property in the American-occupied zones of Europe. He also molded the American Academy for Jewish Research. Nominated as a fellow in 1928, Baron remained active in academy affairs for six decades. Between 1940 and 1980, he served four multiyear terms as president. Even after retiring, he "continued to dominate the thinking of the Academy," as his high stature in the field and knowledge of investing provided that institution with both cachet and financial security.[11] Baron also served as president of the Conference on Jewish Social Studies (1941–54, 1963–67), which published the journal *Jewish Social Studies*, and the American Jewish Historical Society (1953–55).

In 1950, Baron created Columbia's Center for Israeli Studies, the first academic center devoted to the study of Israel's past, present, and future. Indeed, decades before any other university devoted resources to the discipline known today as Israel studies, Baron sought to create an academic center to "train students to serve as regional specialists . . . to work in finance, in journalism, in various branches of government service, and in academic research and teaching in the social sciences, in religion, and in literature . . . [by providing] a broad and well-integrated knowledge of Israel, Judaism, and the Near East."[12]

Baron was also a master at fundraising, building on the initial endowment left by the Miller family to keep Columbia at the forefront of Jewish studies as the field developed. Working hand in hand with his wife's relative, Russell Knapp, Baron helped to raise a gift of $4.3 million to establish Columbia's endowment for the Center for Israel and Jewish Studies, and he convinced others to endow new chairs in modern Hebrew literature and American Jewish history, both Baron's lifelong passions. These positions solidified Columbia as a world-class center for the study of Jewish history and literature. The Knapp family helped to collect the funds for another chair, named, in 1980, for Salo Baron himself. Baron then endowed the Salo and Jeanette Baron Prize in Jewish Studies, given every five years to the author of the best dissertation in Jewish studies at Columbia University, to ensure that Jewish studies continued to be a vital area of study at the university where he spent his career.[13] With these endowments, Baron served as "the pioneering figure" who ushered in a new era in Jewish studies at Columbia University, and ultimately the entire United States, as he demonstrated how crucial Jewish studies was for "the general university context."[14]

Although the study of Hebrew texts and Judaism had long been part of the American academy, Baron helped to permanently "move the university-based study of Judaism" in the United States "past Semitics and philology." Moreover, Baron and his work demonstrated all that could be gained by opening the "study of history in American universities to Judaic insight" as he simultaneously "promoted the development of Jewish learning in universities."[15] Baron's insistence on excavating the Jewish past both horizontally and vertically, as part of both the *long durée* of the Jewish tradition and

FIGURE 0.2. Baron and Knapp families in Canaan, Connecticut, circa 1970. Front row, from left: Salo Baron, Russell Knapp, Jeanette Baron, and Jeffrey Gitelle. Back row, from left: Dr. Gene Gitelle, Charles Knapp, and Tobey Baron Gitelle.
From the collection of Charlie Knapp.

a specific non-Jewish society, were new.[16] He is the last scholar to attempt to write a multivolume work of Jewish history that considers Jews across time and space. His presence as "a highly respected figure in one of America's pre-eminent history departments" added immeasurably to the prestige of this nascent field and was used to justify the expansion of Jewish studies through Jewish history positions at other universities.

In sum, the appointment of Salo Baron, considered at the time "the most available, suitable man,"[17] constitutes a turning point in American

Columbia University
BULLETIN OF INFORMATION

Fiftieth Series, No. 35   September 23, 1950

ANNOUNCEMENT OF THE

CENTER OF
ISRAELI STUDIES

FOR THE WINTER AND SPRING SESSIONS

1950-1951

MORNINGSIDE HEIGHTS
NEW YORK 27, N.Y.

FIGURE 0.3. Cover page, *Center of Israeli Studies, 1950–1951*, Columbia University Bulletin (Columbia University Archives).

Jewish history. This appointment transformed the United States from a backwater in the Jewish intellectual world into a center for the academic study of the Jewish past as it "radically redirected the course and growth of Jewish scholarship in American universities for the remainder of the century."[18]

TEMPLE EMANU-EL AND THE FUNDING OF MODERN JEWISH STUDIES

Baron's achievement—remaking Columbia University into a center for training scholars in a new type of Jewish studies, who would reshape Jewish studies across the country—was far from inevitable. In the 1920s, in fact, Columbia was more famous for leading the Ivy League in quotas to limit the presence of Jewish students.[19] Deans at Columbia expressed the desire to stop the "invasion of the Jewish student."[20] By many accounts, the university's student body was 40 percent Jewish in 1920.[21] Throughout the 1920s and 1930s, Columbia, along with Harvard, Yale, Dartmouth, Brown, and a host of other universities, denied the existence of quotas on Jewish students, but they all radically reworked their admissions policies to limit the number of Jews admitted from immigrant families.[22] As Columbia's Dean Herbert Hawkes explained in 1922, new admissions methods ensured that "most Jews, especially those of the more objectionable type," would not be granted admittance,[23] as immigrant Jews were "undesirables" who should not be allowed to attend Columbia College, "no matter what their record in the very important matter of As and Bs."[24] By 1934, Columbia University's Director of Admissions Frank H. Bowles was able to report that of the entering freshman class, 58 percent were Protestants, 25 percent Catholics, and 17 percent Jews.[25]

So why, as it sought to limit the number of Jewish students, did Columbia University in 1929 establish a new chair dedicated to the history of Jewish culture, civilization, and literatures? The answer lies somewhere between Columbia's firm commitment to the separation of its academic studies from its admission policies and the university's desire to raise funds. Baron's arrival in 1930, through the support of an endowment by Linda Miller, was part of a larger effort undertaken by members of New York City's Temple Emanu-El to make the study of Jewish life and literature into a respected academic pursuit. This prominent synagogue, whose members were among the city's financial elite, had long seen itself as leading American Jewry.[26]

To combat rising discrimination in American higher education, the leaders prodded their members to use the money at their fingertips to establish the study of Jews on par with any other academic discipline in the American academy. While these donors from Temple Emanu-El hoped their generosity would alter Jews' place in the university, Nicholas Butler at Columbia saw their gifts as an easy way to tap into the wealth of New York to fortify the university's endowment.

This symbiotic relationship between New York's wealthy Jewish elite and Columbia University long predated Baron's arrival and had begun with the appointment of Temple Emanu-El's rabbi, Dr. Richard Gottheil, to the Gustav Gottheil Lectureship in Semitic Languages in 1886. Gottheil, along with other members of Temple Emanu-El's rabbinic and lay leadership, led the philanthropic effort to lay the foundation for a new type of Jewish scholarship throughout American higher education.[27] Gottheil's appointment coincided with the temple's donation of rare Jewish books and manuscripts to Columbia's library collection, which made the school's collection one of "the largest in the country."[28]

Gottheil's association with Columbia should not obscure the ways in which Baron's appointment was a turning point for Jewish studies in the United States. Although Hebrew has long been studied in American universities, in keeping with the initial mission to train ministers, one should not confuse the study of Hebrew with an interest in Jewish history. Early American "enthusiasm for the study of the biblical text or Hebrew" did not reflect American elites' interest in the life and texts of contemporary Jews in America or in Europe.[29] By the end of the nineteenth century, an explosion in "Oriental studies" at several American universities coincided with an increased interest in studying post-Biblical Jewish texts. Between 1886 and 1902, five scholars were appointed to American university posts devoted to studying Jewish literature beyond the Bible: Richard Gottheil at Columbia (1886), Cyrus Adler at Johns Hopkins (1888), Morris Jastrow at the University of Pennsylvania (1892), Emil G. Hirsh at Chicago (1892), and William Rosenau at Johns Hopkins (1902).[30] All these men were placed in Semitics departments, as post-Biblical Jewish life and literature were usually considered branches of Semitics, never seen—as Baron insisted they be—as part of European or other regional histories or literatures. No one was placed in a history department.

But these scholars laid the foundation for Baron's appointment, which ultimately came to fruition thanks to Gottheil's successor, Rabbi Hyman

Enelow. Rabbi Enelow constantly pushed the wealthy members of Temple Emanu-El to advocate for the establishment of university-based chairs in Judaica. He firmly believed that the proliferation of such chairs would promote a greater academic acceptance of Jews in America. By placing scholars who promoted studying Jewish texts and the Jewish past at the highest levels in America's esteemed academic research institutions, this group sought to secure a place for Jews in the American mind. For example, Enelow arranged for congregant Lucius Littauer to endow a chair promoting Jewish scholarship at Harvard University. Littauer was convinced by Enelow, writing about his "conviction that the proper . . . study and exposition of the character, influence, literature and philosophy of the Jewish religion—involve a profound knowledge of original Hebrew sources and materials that would require of its Professor a particularly authoritative knowledge of Hebrew and Hebrew literature."[31] When Harvard appointed Harry Wolfson, a close friend of Littauer, as the Nathan Littauer Professor of Hebrew Literature and Philosophy in 1925, Littauer provided for a full professor's salary of $6,000 for three years, to be followed by a $150,000 endowment.[32]

Rabbi Enelow was similarly instrumental in enabling the Miller endowment for the Nathan Miller Chair in Jewish History, Literature and Institutions at Columbia University. Enelow encouraged Mrs. Linda Miller to create and dedicate a chair to the memory of her husband, prompting others to note that Linda Miller might "not be a name known to many [but should be recognized as] . . . the greatest patroness of learning, literature and art in the history of American Jewry thus far."[33] Born in 1877 in Wheeling, West Virginia, Miller was not drawn to traditional charity work like other women of her class. She loved learning and scholarly pursuits and soon became a devoted follower of Rabbi Enelow, who often spent time at her home in New Rochelle. Appreciating the importance of Jewish texts, Miller and her philanthropic legacy made possible the donation of Rabbi Enelow's massive collection of 20,000 volumes, including 1,100 manuscripts, to the Jewish Theological Seminary. The extensive correspondence among Nicholas Butler, the search committee, and Miller illustrates not only how involved she was in the search but also how enthusiastically committed the representatives of Columbia were to making this pioneering chair a success from the outset.

To be sure, Enelow's instrumental role in setting in motion the Miller gift differed from his role in arranging the Littauer chair, as he believed that he would be Miller's chosen candidate. He hoped to follow in Gottheil's shoes and combine his rabbinic parsonage at Temple Emanu-El with a university position. Although he was among those considered, in the end, Columbia was committed to finding someone who would be a recognized scholar of Jewish texts and history and whose research would be of interest to those outside the field.[34] Linda Miller wrote dozens of letters to both Butler and the search committee, as she appreciated the importance of this position. In the end, though, Columbia would not let her choose and offered the position to the scholar they considered "the most suitable man," the European-trained Salo Baron, who would become the first professor of Jewish history in the United States.[35] Ultimately, then, Baron's influence was made possible by the combined efforts of a determined donor, a Columbia University administration seeking to place itself at the vanguard of academic Jewish study and curry favor with the wealthy Reform Jewish community of New York City, and an ambitious scholar. When these three forces combined, history was made.

SALO BARON: "THE MOST SUITABLE MAN" FOR THE MILLER CHAIR

So how did Salo Wittmayer Baron, a scholar from Eastern Europe who had only recently arrived in the United States, become "the most suitable man" for Columbia's Nathan Miller chair? And how did Baron reshape the study of Jewish history at Columbia and the larger field of Jewish studies over the following fifty-six years? Few in Tarnów, a city of the former Polish-Lithuanian Commonwealth absorbed into the Habsburg Empire in 1795, would have guessed that Salo Baron, born in 1895, would radically alter studies of the Jewish past in the United States. Born to an educated and wealthy banking family, Baron received a rigorous training in Hebrew and Judaic studies. As a result of his family's wealth and class, Baron spoke German at home, but he also picked up Yiddish and the vernacular Polish spoken by the masses of Jews and non-Jews who populated his hometown. In 1914, the bright and ambitious Baron ventured to Vienna, where he would earn three doctorates from the University of Vienna, in philosophy (1917), political science (1922), and law (1923) while simultaneously receiving a rabbinic ordination from Vienna's Israelitisch-Theologischen Lehranstalt rabbinical seminary.

FIGURE 0.4. Portrait of Salo Wittmayer Baron, 1918, taken shortly after receipt of his first doctorate in philosophy.
From the private collection of Shoshana Tancer.

Baron's rapid acquisition of several graduate degrees bespeak his brilliance and intellectual ambition, which faced formidable obstacles as a result of the politics of interwar Austria. In Vienna, even a scholar as talented as Baron could not become a university professor of Jewish history, and he was forced to find employment at the Judisches Padagogium (Jewish Teachers College). A 1926 invitation of Rabbi Stephen S.

INTRODUCTION

Wise to teach at his new Jewish Institute for Religion (JIR), an innovative rabbinic seminary seeking to surmount the denominational divides already prominent among American Jews, brought Baron to New York. In his time at the JIR, which prided itself on its distinguished faculty, Baron taught a series of courses. At the same time, outside the classroom, he produced scholarship that offered radical new visions for the conceptualization and study of Jewish history, most notably his 1928 *Menorah Journal* article, "Ghetto and Emancipation: Shall We Revise the Traditional View?"[36] The importance of this article for both launching his career and shaping the academic study of Jewish history in the United States is dealt with at length by several authors in this volume.

Significantly, Baron ends this article with a charge to future Jewish historians, declaring that "it is time to break with the lachrymose theory of the pre-Revolutionary woe and to adopt a view more in accord with historical truth."[37] With this sentence, he launched his vision of the centrality of Jewish history to Jewish studies while simultaneously making a name for himself in the United States through a journal aimed at intellectually engaged laypersons who were not exclusively part of the academy. With this article, one sees that from the outset of Baron's career in the United States, he considered himself an intellectual who spoke to the public and a figure with deep awe for the American experiment.

BARON, AMERICAN JEWISH STUDIES, AND JEWISH STUDIES IN AMERICA

The articles assembled in this volume touch on various areas of Baron's impact, but his impact on not only the study of Jewish history in the United States but American Jewish history as its own legitimate field is particularly notable. As historian Hasia Diner pointed out, Baron saw himself as "an American."[38] This self-identification speaks to his deep love for his newly adopted home in the United States, which began from the moment he arrived and shaped his activities at Columbia University and beyond. Baron's steadfast dedication to the study of American Jewry surfaces vividly in his numerous essays in which Baron performs mental gymnastics to locate a usable past for American Jewry.[39] Seeing the writing of American Jewish history as akin to a community-building project, Baron rarely critiqued Jewish life in the United States with the same rigor he applied to Jewish life in Europe. Thus, Baron's critiques of emancipation, the voluntary nature of Jewish life, and integration into the modern world, which he aimed at the West generally—both Europe and the United States—in the 1930s grows muted as he studies Jewish life in the America in later decades.

It is little coincidence that Columbia University was the premier site for the study of American history in the mid-twentieth century, and although Baron never produced a substantial monograph on American Jewish history, he did continually write about it. As historian Eric Goldstein has noted, Baron suspended his critical thinking and strategies for analysis in these essays on the American Jewish past, appearing as though "he was arguing with himself and trying to convince himself of the great future for Jewish life in America."[40]

Despite the fact that Baron did not produce an independent monograph on Jewish life in the United States, his training of students fundamentally altered the path of the field. From the moment he arrived at Columbia, Baron's impact was immense, as he trained many in the first generation of Jewish studies scholars who would bring the teaching of Jewish studies to campuses across the country. Baron not only guided students through coursework but also played an integral role in the selection of their dissertation topics, which reflected what he saw as fruitful and interesting. Baron's protégés spanned disciplines, from history to sociology and literature, but all recognized the central role he played in their training and the questions they asked. As Joshua Trachtenberg wrote in his 1939 dissertation, one of the first completed under Baron's mentorship, "Professor Salo W. Baron not only conveyed significant comments about the content and style of the paper, but he suggested the topic as well."[41]

Regardless of the field, Baron exerted notable influence on the graduate students he mentored in his office and in the seminar he convened in his dining room by pushing them to select topics he deemed important for the development of the field. As influential sociologist Marshall Sklare similarly stated in his pioneering 1953 dissertation on the development of Conservative Judaism, he was led to this topic, which is essential to understanding American Jewish life, by Baron."[42] Even after retiring, Baron continued to shape a generation of scholars who filled departments of Jewish studies nationwide. As Yaffa Eliach relates in her 1973 dissertation, already a decade past Baron's retirement, "My sincere gratitude goes to Professor Salo W. Baron, Professor Emeritus of Jewish History, Columbia University and dean of Jewish historians, who read this dissertation and offered constructive criticism and suggestions."[43] As Abraham Duker summed up, working with Baron was a life-changing event for his students: "To Professor Salo W. Baron my esteemed teacher and sponsor," began his dissertation, "I owe much not only for help in the choice of the subject, the facilitation of an extensive research trip and a year of research, his skillful guidance and persistent urging, but also for the knowledge and insight in Jewish history and historical interpretation that I have gained from studying under him and associating with him."[44]

Through this close mentoring, Baron shaped a generation of scholars who ventured across the United States to influence how undergraduate and graduate students theorized, conceptualized, and thought about Jews and Jewish history. Their impact on the growing field of Jewish studies cannot be emphasized enough. Indeed, just one of Baron's students, Yosef Yerushalmi, trained dozens of students at his posts at both Harvard University and Columbia, schooling them in the questions raised by Baron and the methodologies he employed to address those issues. The map in figure 0.5 illustrates where in the United States Baron's students and those who studied under them can be found. More work needs to be done to examine this network as future scholars query how Baron shaped Jewish studies in the United States by training and inspiring so many students who passed through Columbia's campus.

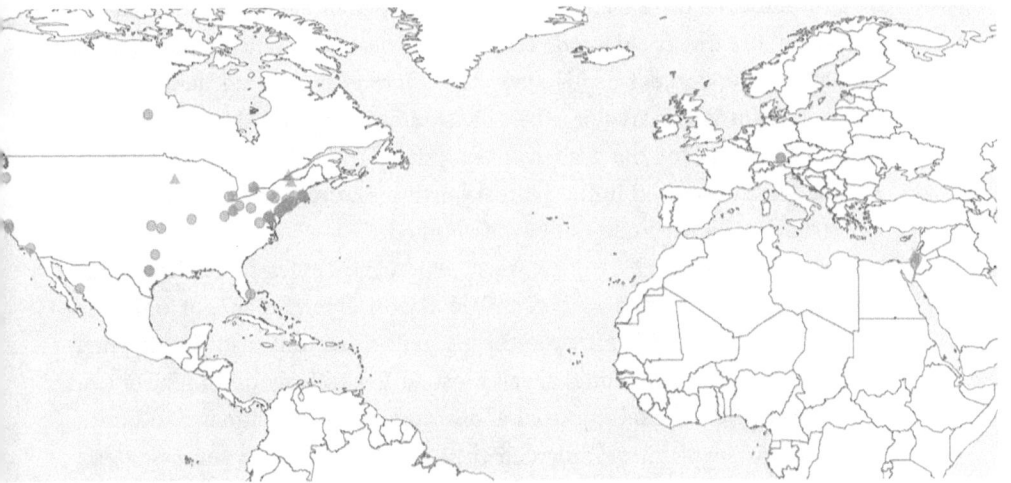

FIGURE 0.5. Map of the networks of students trained by Salo Baron and his students and where they taught.

In its interrogation of Baron's legacy as a scholar, public intellectual, mentor, and figure central to the history of Columbia University, this volume opens with fresh reevaluations of his work by leading scholars. In the opening chapter, Jason Lustig examines how scholars in the twenty-first century are still shaped by Baron's conceptualizations and theories. His "enduring legacy," as Lustig argues, is that "he was not merely offering scholarly publications but creating an entire field. And in doing so, he was by necessity a figure not just of scholarship but of history."[45]

Bernard Cooperman next discusses the various Jewish intellectual and American academic contexts in which Salo Baron was forced to operate on assuming his position at Columbia. Cooperman places Baron in his appropriate scholarly and social contexts so that readers can appreciate the forces shaping his life and scholarship over the five decades that followed. David Sorkin explores Baron's revolutionary new take on the process of emancipation, not only for Jews but for European history as well. As Sorkin comments, Baron made clear that "emancipation was, then, not a discrete phase of European Jewish history with a terminal destination; instead, it was a continuing process integral to the modern world."[46]

In contrast to Sorkin's insight that Baron saw Jewish history as a prism through which to gain new insights into European political history, Francesca Trivellato observes that in the realm of economic history, Baron remained "mute" on "the historiographical battles that were being waged outside of Jewish studies." David Engel then explores Baron's deployment of anti-Semitism as an analytical category, which Engel argues was set for Baron as early as 1912 and "remained rather consistent despite radical changes in the context of his analysis."[47] Baron's unshifting definition of anti-Semitism is remarkable when considered alongside the fact that the hallowed centers for the academic analysis of the Jewish past in Central Europe were destroyed in the years following Baron's arrival at Columbia, a destruction Baron could not have fathomed.

But from his perch in New York, where he tirelessly published his scholarship and trained students, Salo Baron emerged as not only the most important Jewish historian of his generation but also a renowned public intellectual who could speak most authoritatively on the European Jewish past. After Israel captured and brought Adolf Eichmann to Israel, the new Jewish country "intended this trial to be both a successor and a counterweight to the Nuremberg proceedings . . . [as there] the tragedy of the Jews, though on the docket in the context of 'crimes against humanity,' was, essentially, a sidebar," as Deborah Lipstadt explores.[48] Israel had hoped that witnesses like Baron "would help the world grasp the immense loss that not just individual Jews but the entire Jewish people had suffered."[49] Baron's testimony at the Eichmann trial made him into a defining public intellectual of the twentieth century in a way "few historians were capable of, a historical *tour de force.*" In short, there was "virtually no aspect of Jewish life upon which he did not touch. He described a uniquely vital, thriving, and creative community, one that reveled in the new, even as it embraced its rich past. It was a masterful and sweeping summary of Jewish life" in Europe.

Although his testimony at Eichmann's trial made Baron a household name, his vision of Jewish history—in which he recognized "the extraordinary impact European Jewry had on the societies in which they lived"— played an integral role in his building Columbia's Judaica manuscript and book collection. As Michelle Chesner, the Norman Alexander Librarian for Jewish Studies at Columbia University, points out, though we know of Baron's critical role in saving Nazi-looted Jewish books, manuscripts, and Judaica from postwar Europe through the Jewish Cultural Reconstruction Project, "less well known, however, is the outsized impact that Baron had on the collections" at Columbia, which "ensured the library's place as a one of the most important Judaica collections in the United States."[50] This chapter fills a lacuna in understanding Baron's impact on the study of the Jewish past, as, along with his scholarship, he is central to "the history of Judaica collections in the United States in the twentieth century [which] has yet to be fully written." Indeed, when this history is written, "Salo Baron will feature prominently within it . . . [because] over the course of more than thirty years as a professor at Columbia, Baron was actively involved in building library collections for research and scholarship in the field that he shaped in America, that of Jewish history."[51]

The final section probes what, from the vantage point of American Jewish history, might be Baron's greatest achievement in shaping Jewish studies in the United States: training dozens of students to pursue the study of Jewish history through his prism. Baron advised and trained dozens of the most of the significant Jewish historians of the next generation, including his first successor in the Miller Chair, Gerson D. Cohen, who later became chancellor of the Jewish Theological Seminary of America. His teaching, questioning, and mentoring of students saw his interpretation of the Jewish past become "the reigning approach within the field throughout the United States, and had major influence in European and Israeli academic circles as well."[52] One could argue that his students, or students trained by his protégés, are key to understanding the development of Jewish studies programs in the United States, as these individuals placed Jewish history, rather than study of the Bible or post-Biblical Jewish texts, at the center of Jewish studies in the postwar period.

Pierre Birnbaum opens this section with an examination of Baron's legacy in conjunction with that of his student Yosef Yerushalmi. In 1980, Yerushalmi, then at Harvard, moved back to Columbia to become the first Salo Wittmayer Baron Professor of Jewish History and to direct the Center for Israel and Jewish Studies. As Birnbaum reflects in his chapter, Yerushalmi and his work must be seen in conversation with the big questions raised by Baron and his lifetime of work. As Birnbaum argues, Baron's "integrationist" approach to analyzing Jewish history heralds a rethinking of how the Jewish past should be researched, narrated, and taught both within and outside the academy. This chapter reflects on how Yerushalmi's oeuvre, in particular his paradigm-shifting *Zakhor*, extends Baron's arguments and frameworks against the "lachrymose" view of the Jewish past. However, Birnbaum notes, the two scholars diverged as well, most noticeably on the importance of studying American Jewish history and appreciating what America offered Jews. As Birnbaum argues, Yerushalmi's contempt for American Jewry "was so different from Baron's visions . . . that Yerushalmi wrote that 'nowadays, the Diaspora is no more in Babylon than in Alexandria.'"[53] Yerushalmi claims that he can "almost" call himself an Israeli and lives in the United States only because of circumstances and not ideology, a perspective firmly at odds with Baron's view of the centrality of the United States to the Jewish past and present.

As Birnbaum reflects on the scholarly conversation between Baron and Yerushalmi, the next two chapters, by Robert Chazan and Jane Gerber, two of Baron's doctoral students, demonstrate how he mentored and shaped a generation of Jewish historians. "It was Prof. Baron's custom to invite his graduate students who were working on their dissertations to convene every week at his home on Claremont Avenue. We sat around the dining room table and reported on where we were on our work."⁵⁴ Both Chazan and Gerber recall these weekly events and how Baron made sure he was up to date and able to follow his students' progress or lack thereof. At the same time, Gerber's chapter speaks to the difficulty women faced in the academy, as the entire company expected her to help serve and clean up at these weekly meetings at Baron's apartment, but Baron also offered unflinching support to ensure her success in the field. Indeed, Baron seems to have been sensitive to some of the challenges of living in a patriarchal world from an early age, adopting his maternal grandparents' surname, Wittmayer, as his middle name before leaving Tarnów to pursue his education. He made this choice in order to ensure that the name would not vanish from the world because his maternal grandparents had only daughters. Despite the ongoing patriarchal expectations at the graduate student dinners, Gerber emphasizes that Baron respected, encouraged, and supported women in their scholarly pursuits.

FIGURE 0.6. Salo and Jeanette Baron, circa 1975.
From the private collection of Shoshana Tancer.

INTRODUCTION

Such support of women in the academy existed not just in the realm of Jewish history. As Charlie Knapp, whose parents endowed the chair at Columbia in American Jewish history, recalled,

> My mother was the daughter of a concert violinist who gave up her public career when she married my grandfather. . . . After my mother graduated Barnard in 1947, and married my father in 1949 and, reading between the lines of the way she told the story, must have hinted that she was looking forward to the life of a housewife when Salo intervened and suggested that she should not waste her education and clear abilities and should pursue graduate studies. She received her MA (history) and Ph.D. (French literature) from Columbia where she taught for a couple of years until moving to Hunter College's Romance Language Department where she stayed until her retirement in the early 1990s. She published over 50 books during her lifetime and was always one of the most popular professors.[55]

Salo Baron might have encouraged women to pursue their careers in the academy, but his career owed much to his wife, who served him in so many capacities that one family member called her "his secret weapon."[56] The final chapter, penned by his daughters, Shoshana Tancer and Tobey Gitelle, brings to life the man that they knew only as their father and recognizes that his prodigious scholarly output was made possible by one primary collaborator: a PhD candidate in the Economics Department at Columbia, whose dissertation researched the Jewish bankers of Europe. American-born Jeanette Meisel (1911–85) became Baron's wife in 1934 and must be seen, as his daughters argue, as indispensable to Baron's success. It is no coincidence that the only bibliography of all of Baron's writings, ranging from the scholarly world to the popular press, was assembled by Jeanette Baron. This volume closes with Menachem Butler's expansion of her bibliographic work and a full bibliography of Salo Baron's writings.

The arrival of Baron at Columbia University reshaped the academic study of Jewish history in the United States for much of the twentieth century. To be sure, his scholarship was most important to him, and evaluations of that work constitute much of this volume. Although few read it today, Baron's *Social and Religious History of the Jews* boldly sought to update the work of nineteenth- and early twentieth-century

INTRODUCTION

predecessors Heinrich Graetz and Simon Dubnow by providing a synthetic, global history of Jewish life. Whereas Graetz's and Dubnow's political agendas shaped their narratives, Baron hoped to show how the tools of social science, contextualizing the Jewish past politically, religiously, and socially, would shed light not only on Jews but on other societies as well. Baron's linguistic reach enabled volumes remarkable for their range and rigor of scholarly apparatus.

But he did not merely shape the world through his scholarship. Baron amassed collections for others to use to engage the past and devoted himself to educating the world on all that the Jewish community had lost in the twentieth century. Both of these achievements were embodied in the students he trained, who left, and continue to leave, an imprint on the United States as they spread Baron's understanding and methodologies to Jewish studies programs throughout the country. There are few places where scholars trained by Baron or his disciples cannot be found. In this way, the conversation that Baron started can be seen as continuing to this day.[57] Baron's deep belief in the power of Jewish history to both create and sustain Jewish community is the lesson that keeps being told. Indeed, this is one of Baron's most lasting legacies, as he himself eloquently explained: "For those of us who believe in the divine guidance of history—and Judaism has, in my opinion, pioneered along the lines of historical, as well as ethical, monotheism—the divine will has often revealed itself through historical processes. More than thirty years ago I insisted that 'the interpretation and reinterpretation of the history of the people, a kind of historic Midrash, to serve as a guidance for the future.'"[58] Just as Midrash—the ancient Jewish commentary on the Bible—captured the efforts of ancient rabbis to respond to contemporary problems and crafts new stories by connecting new Jewish realities and the unchanging biblical text, so, too, did the engagement of Salo Baron with the Jewish past shape his world along with the Jewish future in the United States.

NOTES

1. Nicholas Butler to Salo Wittamayer Baron, December 14, 1929, Central Files, Columbia University Archives and Columbiana Library (hereafter abbreviated CUF), Mrs. Nathan Miller file.
2. Laurence Balfus, "Jewish Studies at Columbia University" (master's thesis, Columbia University, 2000), 44.

INTRODUCTION

3. Robert Liberles, *Salo Wittmayer Baron: Architect of Jewish History* (New York: New York University Press, 1995); Paul Ritterband and Harold S. Wechsler, *Jewish Learning in American Universities: The First Century* (Bloomington: Indiana University Press, 1994), 150
4. Robert Chazan, "Jewish History in American Academia: The Roles of Salo Baron," in *The Enduring Legacy of Salo W. Baron*, ed. Hava Tirosh-Samuelson and Edward Dabrowa (Kraków: Jagiellonian University Press, 2017), 167
5. Ismar Schorsch, "The Last Jewish Generalist," *AJS Review* 18, no. 1 (1993): 39.
6. Saul Lieberman, ed. *Salo Wittamayer Baron: Jubilee Volume on the Occasion of His 80th Birthday* (Jerusalem: American Academy for Jewish Research, 1974). Vol. 3 has the title *Sefer ha-yovel li-khevod Shalom Baron li-melot lo shemonim shana*.
7. Chazan, "Jewish History in American Academia," 168.
8. There are truly too many works devoted to Baron to mention all, but several noteworthy ones include Robert Liberles, "Salo Baron and the Development of Jewish Studies," *Jewish Studies* [מדעי היהדות] no. 30 (1990): 37–42; Robert Chazan, "The Historiographical Legacy of Salo Wittmayer Baron," *AJS Review* 18, no. 1 (1993): 29–37; David Engel, "Salo Baron's View of the Middle Ages in Jewish History: Early Sources," in *Studies in Medieval Jewish Intellectual and Social History: Festschrift in Honor of Robert Chazan*, ed. David Engel, Lawrence W. Schiffman, and Elliot R. Wolfson (Leiden: Brill, 2012); E. Carlebach, D. Sorkin, A. Teller, and D. Engel, "Symposium: Rethinking Salo Baron in the 21st Century," *AJS Review* 38, no. 2 (2014) 417–41; Susannah Heschel and Arthur Hertzberg, *Writing a Modern Jewish History: Essays in Honor of Salo W. Baron* (New Haven, CT: Yale University Press, 2006); and Tirosh-Samuelson and Dabrowa, *The Enduring Legacy of Salo W. Baron*. Also see *AJS Review* 39, no. 1 (2015), which published a symposium on Baron. Several monographs address Baron's role in creating various organizations, such as the Jewish Cultural Reconstruction Inc. (JCR). See Elisabeth Gallas, *A Mortuary of Books: The Rescue of Jewish Culture After the Holocaust* (New York: New York University Press, 2019); and Jason Lustig's soon-to-be-published *A Time to Gather: Archives and the Control of Jewish Culture* (New York: Oxford University Press, forthcoming).
9. Gallas, *A Mortuary of Books*; and Gish Amit, "The Largest Jewish Library in the World: The Books of Holocaust Victims and Their Restitution Following World War II," *Dapim* 27, no. 2 (2013): 107–28.
10. Liberles, "Salo Baron and the Development of Jewish Studies," 37.
11. Robert Chazan, "Salo Wittmayer Baron (1895–1989)," *Proceedings of the American Academy for Jewish Research* 58 (1992): 12
12. "Center for Israeli Studies," *Columbia University Bulletin* 50, no. 35 (September 1950): 2.
13. "Baron Directs Newly Formed Israel Center," *Columbia Spectator* XCV, no. 3 (September 29, 1950).
14. Chazan, "Jewish History in American Academia," 168.
15. Ritterband and Wechsler, *Jewish Learning in American Universities*, 151.
16. Frederick E. Greenspahn, "The Beginnings of Judaic Studies in American Universities," *Modern Judaism* 20, no. 2 (May 1, 2000): 209–25.
17. Butler to J. I. R Board of Trustees Chairman Julian Mack, December 21, 1929.

INTRODUCTION

18. Balfus, "Jewish Studies at Columbia University," 2.
19. There is a large historiography on this topic. See H. Wechsler, *The Qualified Student: A History of Selective College Admission in America* (New York: Wiley, 1977); Marcia Graham Synnott, *The Half-Opened Door: Discrimination and Admissions at Harvard, Yale, and Princeton, 1900–1970* (Westport, CT: Greenwood, 1979); Jerome Karabel, *The Chosen: The Hidden History of Admission and Exclusion at Harvard, Yale, and Princeton* (Boston: Houghton Miffflin, 2005); and Dan Oren, *Joining the Club: A History of Jews and Yale* (New Haven, CT: Yale University Press, 1985).
20. Paul W. Kingston and Lionel S. Lewis. *The High Status Track: Studies of Elite Schools and Stratification* (Albany, NY: State University of New York Press, 1990), 82
21. Wechsler, *The Qualified Student*, 79.
22. Synnott, *The Half-Opened Door*.
23. Synnott, *The Half-Opened Door*, 18.
24. Wechsler, *The Qualified Student*, 166
25. Synnott, *The Half-Opened Door*, 18; Kingston and Lewis, *The High Status Track*, 79
26. Ronald B. Sobel, "The History of New York's Temple Emanuel: The Second Half Century" (PhD diss., New York University, 1980).
27. Sobel, "The History of New York's Temple Emanuel."
28. Columbia University Libraries, "History of Jewish Studies Collections at Columbia," https://library.columbia.edu/libraries/global/jewishstudies/historyjsc.html.
29. Arnold Band, "Jewish Studies in American Liberal Arts Colleges and Universities," *American Jewish Yearbook* 67 (1966): 5. Also see Abraham I. Katsh, *Hebrew in American Higher Education* (New York: New York University Bookstore, 1941); Katsch, *Hebrew Language, Literature and Culture in American Institutions of Higher Learning* (New York: Payne Educational Sociology Foundation, 1950);and Katsch, "Hebraic Studies in American Higher Education: An Evaluation of Current Trends," *Jewish Social Studies* 21, no. 1 (January 1959).
30. Band, "Jewish Studies in American Liberal Arts Colleges and Universities." 6.
31. Paul Ritterband and Harold S. Wechsler (hereafter abbreviated to Ritterband et al), *Jewish Learning in American Universities* (Indiana University Press, 1994), 120.
32. Balfus, "Jewish Studies at Columbia University," 17-18.
33. Ruth Sapin Hurwitz, "Linda Miller, a Memoir," *Menorah Journal* (Autumn 1937).
34. The search committee was composed of Richard Gottheil, V. Williams Jackson, professor of Indo-Iranian Languages; James T. Shotwell, professor of History; Virginia C. Gildersleeve, professor of English and dean at Barnard College; Herbert E. Hawkes, professor of Mathematics and dean at Columbia College; Robert H. Fife, Gebhard Professor of Germanic Languages and Literature; William Linn Westerman, professor of Ancient History; and Herbert W. Schneider, assistant professor of Philosophy, in order to ensure appointment of a recognized scholar. But the inclusion of Robert M. MacIver, professor of Social Science; Raymond C. Knox, chaplain of the University; and Henry Sloan Coffin, president of the Union Theological Seminary was to make sure that the selected scholar would be of interest to non-Jews as well.
35. Nicolas Butler to Julian Mack, December 21, 1929.
36. Salo Baron, "Ghetto and Emancipation: Shall We Revise the Traditional View?" *Menorah Journal* 14 (1928): 6, 515-26.
37. Baron, "Ghetto and Emancipation," 6, 526.

38. Hasia Diner, "Salo Baron: An American," in Tirosh-Samuelson and Dabrowa, *The Enduring Legacy of Salo W. Baron*.
39. Indeed, his *Steeled by Adversity* is often read as a secondary source, but I think it is most enlightening to see it as a primary source by a scholar trying to push American Jews to view their own past in new ways (*Steeled by Adversity: Essays and Addresses on American Jewish Life*, ed. Jeannette Meisel Baron, Philadelphia: Jewish Publication Society, 1971).
40. Eric Goldstein, correspondence with author, April 6, 2021.
41. Joshua Trachtenberg, "Jewish Magic and Superstition: A Study in Folk Religion" (PhD diss., Columbia University, 1939).
42. Marshall Sklare, "Conservative Judaism: A Sociological Analysis" (PhD diss., Columbia University, 1953), 2.
43. Yaffa Eliach "Jewish Hasidim, Russian Sectarians Non-Conformists in the Ukraine, 1700–1760" (PhD diss., City University of New York, 1973).
44. Abraham Duker, "The Polish Jewish Emigration and the Jews: Studies in Political and Intellectual History" (PhD diss., Columbia University, 1956).
45. Jason Lustig, "Salo Baron's Legacy and the Shaping of Jewish Studies Into the Twenty-First Century," this volume.
46. David Sorkin, "Emancipation: Salo Baron's Achievement," this volume.
47. David Engel, "Salo Baron on Anti-Semitism," this volume.
48. Deborah Lipstadt, "The Professor in the Courtroom: Salo W. Baron at the Eichmann Trial," this volume.
49. Lipstadt, "The Professor in the Courtroom."
50. Michelle Margolis Chesner, "Building the Foundations of Scholarship at Home: Salo Baron and the Judaica Collections at Columbia University Libraries," this volume.
51. Chesner, "Building the Foundations of Scholarship at Home," .
52. Michael Stanislawski. "Salo Wittmayer Baron: Demystifying Jewish History," *Columbia Magazine*, January 15, 2005, https://magazine.columbia.edu/article/salo-wittmayer-baron-demystifying-jewish-history.
53. Pierre Birnbaum, "From Europe to Pittsburgh: Salo Baron and Yosef Yerushalmi Between the Lachrymose Theory and the Vertical Alliance," this volume.
54. Menorah Rothenberg, email correspondence with author, November 22, 2020.
55. Charlie Knapp, email correspondence with author, December 6, 2020.
56. Charlie Knapp, interview by author, December 8, 2020.
57. Eric Goldstein, conversation with author, April 6, 2021.
58. Baron, *Steeled by Adversity*, 568.

Chapter One

SALO BARON'S LEGACY AND THE SHAPING OF JEWISH STUDIES INTO THE TWENTY-FIRST CENTURY

JASON LUSTIG

Salo Baron is rightly venerated as one of the leading Jewish studies scholars of his generation—he produced the last great synthesis of Jewish history, his eighteen-volume *Social and Religious History of the Jews* (1952–83). And he helped to build the field of Jewish studies in the United States in institutional and intellectual terms. His 1929 appointment at Columbia University is widely regarded as a watershed moment in the history of modern Jewish studies, indicating a certain acceptance of the field at the university, and his tenure ushered in an era of renewed growth, as Baron's students and the students of his students helped to establish Jewish studies across North America.[1] But what is his significance today, looking back from our vantage point of the twenty-first century, decades since his passing in 1989? If Baron was critical in the shaping of Jewish studies across the course of the twentieth century, what is his legacy in terms of shaping Jewish studies into the twenty-first?

This chapter approaches this question by suggesting that we separate the ways in which Salo Baron has been remembered as a master of Jewish history and his actual place within the history of twentieth-century Jewish life. For instance, it is unquestioned that Baron was not actually the first university professor of Jewish studies in the United States.[2] Nevertheless, Baron's wide veneration, in contrast to his contemporaries, such as Harry Wolfson at Harvard, who have mostly fallen into relative obscurity (especially in the shadow of Baron and his accomplishments), points out how his image within historical memory—particularly among those who find themselves among his intellectual and professional descendants—may have overshadowed his role as an actor of history. If we want to understand Baron's legacy, we must distinguish between the way in which he and his work has been elevated to a scholarly and intellectual pantheon in historians' collective memory, and how he played a role as an active figure of history itself.³

The matter at hand is that Baron, as a figure of history, can be subjected to the same historical forces and intellectual frameworks that we might apply to any other historical subject. There is no doubt that his scholarship was and remains incredibly consequential, shaping both medieval and modern Jewish historiography. Nevertheless, much of Baron's scholarship and its primacy actually falls within the realm of memory—which is to say that with the exception of his essay "Ghetto and Emancipation," few directly interact with his research. Baron stands tall in the mind of most Jewish historians for two factors: first, as the last in a line of scholars to try his hand at writing a truly monumental history of the Jews by himself, thereby representing an image of an older form of historical scholarship—but which few actually read; and second, through the frame of "Ghetto and Emancipation," which set the terms of much scholarship on medieval and modern Jewish history over the last century, particularly the rejection of the lachrymose history of the Jews—and which is universally read in Jewish studies graduate training but which for all but a few scholars subsequently becomes a general point of reference rather than a specific piece with which to interact in an intense, productive fashion. By contrast, some of Baron's most lasting contributions were through his actual historical activity, certainly in view of his efforts to rebuild Jewish life after the Holocaust. With the rise of the study of contemporary history, and particularly the history of the post-Holocaust era, Baron comes to the forefront not just as a historical scholar but as a historical actor.

To fully interrogate the interplay between the Baron of memory and the Baron of history, it will be useful to highlight three aspects of his legacy and how they come together to shape his impact, from the perspective of the twenty-first century. First, Baron's scholarly legacy is most certainly secured by his efforts to produce the last and latest monumental history of the Jews and the ways he set the field's intellectual contours and agenda, even an "ideology," if an academic field might be said to have one. Second, Baron seeded the field of Jewish studies across the United States through the proliferation of his students, and students of his students, who have populated the field of Jewish studies up to current times. In this respect, Baron is not dissimilar from Leopold von Ranke (1795–1886), who shaped historical study by setting new methodological standards, primarily by dramatizing the study of archives as the center of the modern scholarly persona, and also how his students spread across Germany and around the world, bringing his model of the history seminar to new shores, including the United States.[4] Nevertheless, Ranke's place in the field of history is very much within the realm of memory: in the past generation, scholars have underlined the fact that Ranke was by no means the first to use archives, and, as Georg Iggers famously noted, the image of Ranke in the American academy was filtered through the lens of those students who worked with him and brought his model back to the United States.[5]

We might understand Baron as holding a similar position within Jewish studies, where he shaped the field through his students, and also holds a critical position within memory rather than history itself. These two components of Baron's legacy—how he set the intellectual contours of Jewish studies and helped to propel its growth in the United States over the course of his career—lead directly to a third element: that Baron was a critical figure of public history, particularly in the aftermath of the Holocaust, when he played an important role in the rebuilding of Jewish culture through his work in Jewish Cultural Reconstruction, as president of the American Jewish Historical Society (AJHS), and also in the trial of Adolf Eichmann.

Baron's work as a scholar, teacher, and public figure were not isolated elements of his career. Instead, they were crucially intertwined. The twinned successes and failures of his *Social and Religious History*, for instance, stand at the nexus of the achievements and challenges of twentieth-century Jewish studies as a whole. That is to say, his eighteen-volume history charts the expansion of the field through the 1950s to 1980s, which took place partly due to his efforts to produce new generations of scholars who took posts across the country. And, indeed, he saw himself as a watchful eye over the field, periodically offering his reflections on its growth.[6] This expansion, however, actually doomed his historical project to failure, because there became just too much scholarship for any one person to synthesize in a single stroke.[7] Moreover, we can read Baron's

Social and Religious History as an attempt to bring Jewish history before a wide public, inasmuch as it emerged from a set of ten public lectures, and also that he built an edifice for scholarship—which were also key characteristics of his public historical work, which centered on the building up of institutions of historical scholarship, such as the AJHS, or creating the possibility for future research through salvaging Jewish books and other cultural materials looted by the Nazis.

We should not downplay, by any measure, Baron's scholarly contributions, which were varied, diverse, and immense. He was, in some fashion, a "universal Jewish historian," as one person put it, being a figure who could comment and reflect on any aspect of Jewish history, usually without notes.[8] But the truth is that now, a generation after the publication of Baron's final works, most people do not read his scholarship, with the exception of his famous essay "Ghetto and Emancipation." Baron's *Social and Religious History*, like Dubnow's *Weltgeschichte* and Graetz's *Geschichte der Juden*, is a monument to Jewish history that sits on the bookshelf rather than being an actively utilized resource. That is, Baron's specific scholarly findings have been largely surpassed. To some extent, this to be expected. When Yosef Hayim Yerushalmi taught his sequence of courses on Jewish history at Columbia, for instance, he relied extensively on Baron's synthesis. For the course on medieval Jewish history, Baron's *Social and Religious History* was Yerushalmi's basic textbook, and in his lectures on early modern and modern Jewish history, he also read excerpts from it in class.[9] Today, however, Baron's general outlook is useful, but his research has entered a new phase. Although his *Social and Religious History* does present a useful synthesis, however dated it may be, it is not read as an up-to-date scholarly resource. Instead, it is now part of the historiographical literature, reflecting Baron's general shift from an actor in history to a figure who is to be studied.

These days, Baron's scholarly legacy is not measured in terms of the specific findings of his research. But his general outlook still sets the terms of debate at the heart of academic Jewish studies, with three major tendencies: first, his analysis of medieval Jewish life, with his opposition to the so-called lachrymose history of the Jews; second, his focus on the power of history within Jewish religion and culture; and, third, his synthetic approach to Jewish history. Here, the clear starting point is with his 1928 essay, "Ghetto and Emancipation," which remains at the heart of many courses in both modern and medieval Jewish history.[10] It offered a general reorientation of the debate on the relationship between modern Jewish life and what came before, part of a much broader social discourse on the nature of modernity in which figures like Simon Dubnow looked to the idea of the ghetto, and of emancipation, as critical components of understanding the nature of Jewish life within the possibilities of emancipatory countries.[11]

This question—whether considered by Baron or the many others who approached it—was not only a matter of historical inquiry; it also had profound ramifications for present-day matters. What did it mean to be a Jew in the modern world? What was the purpose of emancipation, and had it succeeded in its purported aims? The entire Jewish social discourse of the nineteenth and twentieth centuries, from 1789 to 1945 and beyond, turned on the crux of this question, and it stood at the heart of debates about Jewish integration and acculturation, the need for nationalism—whether Zionist, Diasporist, or otherwise—and the question of the nature of the Jewish community. In many respects, we can read the works of Dubnow and Heinrich Graetz through this lens, too, with their own consideration of Jewish history over the course of recent centuries offering ammunition for their own critiques of religious reform (for Graetz) or the calls for Diaspora nationalism (for Dubnow).

Baron's analysis of the medieval period in contrast with modern Jewish life has led to an underlying assumption of modern Jewish studies, an almost reflexive rejection of the lachrymose conception of Jewish history and the undermining of the claim that emancipation was a universal good.[12] This might be called an ideology of modern Jewish studies, with scholars playing the role of emphasizing that Jewish history was not merely a parade of tragedies, in contrast with popular memory. Even with recent critiques of such a "neo-Baronian" school, "Ghetto and Emancipation" has had an outsized impact in scholarly terms, especially when we consider that it was written for a nonscholarly audience.[13] The essay's impact is further compounded by its brevity and concision, which makes it appropriate for assignment to undergraduates, as it succinctly and concisely draws together the major thesis that would underline all of Baron's work over the course of his career.

Less widely recognized, perhaps, is the connection between Baron's synthesis of Jewish history and Yerushalmi's work on history and memory, which itself might be read as in conversation with the work of his own teacher. Baron opened both editions of his *Social and Religious History*, in 1937 and 1952, with an emphasis on the historical nature of Judaism. "The Jewish religion," he wrote, "has been from the very beginning and in the progress of time has increasingly become a *historical* religion, in permanent contrast to all *natural* religions."[14] This argument—and it is a compelling one—was that in the development of the Jewish religion, one finds numerous examples of traditions and practices that were transformed from a previous meaning tied to nature to ones that were imbued with the meaning of historical events. Baron thereby emphasized the importance of history in shaping Jewish culture. However, when Yerushalmi penned *Zakhor: Jewish History and Jewish Memory* a generation later, it is difficult to read that text and not see it as a repudiation of his teacher's own perspective: Baron emphasized that Jewish culture and religion were based in historical experiences, but Yerushalmi stressed that it was not history but historical *memory* that has been the dominant force in Jewish culture.[15] In this respect, we can see another example of how Baron's legacy helped to set the terms of debate within Jewish studies over the past century, about both the nature of medieval and modern Jewish life and the question of the role of history in Judaism and Jewish cultures.

A third—but by no means necessarily final—instance of the influence of Baron's scholarly approach has been through his own synthetic approach to Jewish history. He embodied a sense of the study of all of Jewish history, however one defines it. His *Social and Religious History* manifested this most specifically, in a kind of catholic or universal approach to Jewish history that attempted to bring everything under one umbrella. Baron, of course, was not the first scholar to take this approach, and we can trace its origin to the holistic conception of Jewish history espoused by the earliest scholars of modern Jewish studies in the nineteenth century.[16] However, it is notable that Baron spread this ethos specifically in the context of Jewish studies in the United States through his own network of students, and especially through Yerushalmi and his students. Nevertheless, in recent years, there has been a certain resistance against this notion of Jewish history as a unified field, as scholars increasingly place various Jewish histories within their specific context rather than Jewish history as a whole.[17]

Altogether, the key point to underline is that Baron certainly has had a major part to play in terms of the *memory* of modern Jewish studies and the self-conception of scholars as they think about their own field.

However, the majority of his research has been surpassed, and his most important influence has been in shaping the contours of the field itself; his notion of Judaism's historical nature has been repudiated by the school of memory-focused scholarship of the past half-century; and his idea of the universal, all-encompassing Jewish history has also found itself the subject of critique. To say that Baron shaped the contours of the field, though, is by no means a small contribution. But such a reassessment places it in context.

When we understand Baron as a figure of history and not just a towering scholarly master, his historical importance becomes clearer. Because, ultimately, Baron was an active player in the events of his own lifetime; he was not limited to the library and lecture hall but had a wider calling. This can be illustrated, for instance, by his efforts to publish in popular venues, including his constantly examined "Ghetto and Emancipation," as well as his involvement in groups such as the AJHS in the 1940s and 1950s.[18] It is certainly true that Baron was one of a number of scholars, alongside Jacob Rader Marcus of Hebrew Union College and Harvard's Oscar Handlin, who looked down on the AJHS as a society of amateurs, and he hoped to professionalize the field of American Jewish historical studies.[19] Nevertheless, we should see Baron's work at the AJHS as an effort to build the edifice of Jewish studies and reach a wide public. He understood the importance of the tercentenary of American Jewish life, commemorated in 1954, and helmed the AJHS that year.

Perhaps the most important element of Baron's work in his own time, which has been an area where Baron's star has risen most rapidly in recent scholarship, has been in the area of restitution and other cultural programs of the post-Holocaust era. In the 1940s, Baron played a critical role in the formation of Jewish Cultural Reconstruction and, through it, contributing to the broad effort to rebuild Jewish culture after the Holocaust. As early as August 1940, he ruminated on what the reconstruction of Jewish life might look like, but he considered the possibility that Jewish culture might be reestablished in Europe itself after the war.[20] Within just a few short years, Baron and his colleagues in the United Kingdom and in Mandate Palestine all settled on the consensus that Jewish life must be rebuilt elsewhere, and he committed himself to the process of locating looted and scattered Jewish cultural treasures and applying them toward this broader effort at strengthening Jewish life.[21] Baron leveraged those platforms and tools at his disposal toward this aim, including the academic journal *Jewish Social Studies*, which published inventories of looted property.[22] Baron was an instrumental public face of the project, and he has thus played the part of protagonist in the proliferating studies subject on the reconstruction of Jewish life after the Holocaust.[23]

Baron's role in the story of Jewish Cultural Reconstruction reflected his wider work to establish the material basis of Jewish scholarship through bibliographic work and also collecting and publishing archival sources, manuscripts, and other historical materials. It is not coincidental that Baron, in the inaugural issues of *Jewish Social Studies*, published bibliographic guides to new work in Jewish studies, and he also commented on Cecil Roth's *Magna Bibliotheca Anglo-Judaica* (1937), saying that he hoped others would produce bibliographic guides on other Jewish countries.[24] Additionally, he spoke actively of the need to document American Jewish life and argued that there should be regional archives around the United States.[25] And he also helped to publish volumes of historical records, which served to make these materials available for teaching and research.[26] Altogether, Baron was directly involved in the process of making available the materials of Jewish history—which is both a scholarly contribution and also part of the broader historical activities of this moment, in the aftermath of the Holocaust, when Jews sought to grasp the materials of their past and recreate the edifices of Jewish scholarship and culture more broadly.

Baron's place in this history is notable because it highlights a great through line in his career, his part in the shift of the Jewish cultural epicenter from Europe to new shores. This movement was especially notable in the aftermath of the Holocaust, about which Baron was particularly outspoken on the tremendous and tragic cultural shift that had thrust American Jewry into the center of worldwide Jewish culture.[27] But he also represented this movement in terms of his own biography, beginning as he did in Galicia and making his way to the United States, bringing with him European learning and its pedigree, as well as the movement of cultural goods themselves. In this respect, Baron's work was just one part—but an instrumental one—of a much bigger process in the building of Jewish cultural resources in America and Israel/Palestine.

To give one parallel example, Hebrew Union College (HUC) had long brought European scholars to train its "American rabbis for American Israel," a project that can be viewed from the early years of the institution in which the college imported European professors in the effort to bring refugee scholars in the 1930s.[28] After World War II, HUC leaders such as Nelson Glueck spoke publicly of the need to draw on the American scholarly community for "our teachers and teachers of our teachers."[29] This represented a broader realization that American Jewry needed to be self-sufficient, to no longer rely on Europe as a cultural, intellectual, and scholarly wellspring. Baron's work to rescue looted property was part of this cultural reorientation, speaking to the movement of both cultural material, scholars, and other cultural resources that would power the growth of both the United States and the state of Israel as centers of Jewish scholarship.

Altogether, the arena of the restitution of looted Jewish cultural property and Jewish cultural reconstruction—both the institution that Baron headed and the general project—indicates a merging of his work to build the edifice of Jewish studies in the postwar era and the emergence of Baron as a figure of history, not just of scholarship. That is, Baron's efforts to locate Nazi-looted Jewish property, and relocate it specifically to institutions where it could be put to use, has helped to make the materials of Jewish history available for research even today. In many ways, this speaks to Baron's enduring legacy: he was not merely offering scholarly publications but creating an entire field. And in doing so, he was by necessity a figure not just of scholarship but of history.

Baron was cognizant that his institutional activity was of great importance. In the recollection of Robert Liberles, Baron frequently returned in interviews to his organizational activity rather than his scholarship.[30] He understood his position as a figure of history, acting at a momentous point in modern Jewish history, during the era of the Nazi regime and in the aftermath of the Holocaust. Ultimately, much of this work to create the edifices of Jewish scholarship after World War II falls into the realm of both institutional work and scholarship—but we should recognize them as part of the realm of history, not of memory.

This chapter has highlighted how we might consider Baron as part of the development of contemporary Jewish history. Baron's legacy is certainly scholarly, but in many respects, those contributions have been more in the realm of memory, as he is a figure on whom scholars have projected their own sense of how Jewish scholarship has developed in the United States. If we see him as a creature of his time, that is not to diminish his work, which in many ways offers a timeless monument to a lifetime of scholarly achievement. Instead, it highlights the ongoing process in which towering scholars of past generations shift from the arena of the scholarly discourse to considering their important roles in the development of modern Jewish history itself.

NOTES

1. Arnold Band, "Jewish Studies in American Liberal-Arts Colleges and Universities," *American Jewish Year Book* 67 (1966): 1–30.
2. Frederick E. Greenspahn, "The Beginnings of Judaic Studies in American Universities," *Modern Judaism* 20, no. 2 (May 1, 2000): 209–25. Also see Paul Ritterband and Harold S. Wechsler, *Jewish Learning in American Universities: The First Century* (Bloomington: Indiana University Press, 1994).
3. This shift is evident in scholarship published in recent years, including a number of memorial volumes, among which are Susannah Heschel and Arthur Hertzberg, *Writing a Modern Jewish History: Essays in Honor of Salo W. Baron* (New Haven, CT: Yale University Press, 2006); and Hava Tirosh-Samuelson and Edward Dabrowa, eds., *The Enduring Legacy of Salo W. Baron* (Kraków: Jagiellonian University Press, 2017). Also see *AJS Review* 39, no. 1 (2015), which includes papers from a symposium on Baron.
4. Georg Iggers and James M. Powell, eds., *Leopold von Ranke and the Shaping of the Historical Discipline* (Syracuse, NY: Syracuse University Press, 1990); David Telman, "Clio Ascendant: The Historical Profession in Nineteenth-Century Germany" (PhD diss., Cornell University, 1993).
5. Kasper Eskildsen, "Leopold Ranke's Archival Turn: Location and Evidence in Modern Historiography," *Modern Intellectual History* 5, no. 3 (2008): 425–53; Philipp Müller, "Ranke in the Lobby of the Archive: Metaphors and Conditions of Historical Research," in *Unsettling History: Archiving and Narrating in Historiography*, ed. Sebastian Jobs and Alf Lüdtke (Frankfurt: Campus Verlag, 2010), 109–25; and Georg Iggers, "The Image of Ranke in American and German Historical Thought," *History and Theory* 2, no. 1 (1962): 17–40.
6. Salo W. Baron, "Emphases in Jewish History," *Jewish Education* 11, no. 1 (April 1939): 8–39; Baron, "Newer Emphases in Jewish History," *Jewish Social Studies* 25, no. 4 (1963): 235–48; Baron, *The Contemporary Relevance of History: A Study in Approaches and Methods* (New York: Columbia University Press, 1986).
7. See Michael Stanislawski, "Salo Wittmayer Baron: Demystifying Jewish History," *Columbia Magazine*, January 15, 2005.
8. Lloyd P. Gartner, "Salo Baron, Universal Jewish Historian," *Jewish Historical Studies* 42 (2009): 173–88.
9. Yosef Yerushalmi, "Medieval Jewish History. Syllabus and Readings," Columbia University RBML MS 1581 10/17; Yerushalmi, "Early Modern Jewish History: From Spanish Expulsion to French Emancipation," Spring 1981, Columbia University RMBL MS 1581 10/11; Yerushalmi, "Lecture Notes," Columbia University RBML MS 1581 10/6.

10. Salo Baron, "Ghetto and Emancipation: Shall We Revise the Traditional View?," in *The Menorah Treasury: Harvest of Half a Century*, ed. Leo W. Schwarz (Philadelphia: Jewish Publication Society, 1964), 50–63.
11. See discussion in recent works: David Sorkin, *Jewish Emancipation: A History Across Five Centuries* (Princeton, NJ: Princeton University Press, 2019); Daniel B. Schwartz, *Ghetto: The History of a Word* (Cambridge, MA: Harvard University Press, 2019).
12. Robert Chazan, "A New Vision of Jewish History: The Early Historical Writings of Salo Baron" *AJS Review* 39, no. 1 (2015): 27–47; Adam Teller, "Revisiting Baron's 'Lachrymose Conception': The Meanings of Violence in Jewish History," *AJS Review* 38, no. 2 (November 2014): 431–39.
13. David Engel, *Historians of the Jews and the Holocaust* (Stanford, CA: Stanford University Press, 2010); David Engel, "Crisis and Lachrymosity: On Salo Baron, Neobaronianism, and the Study of Modern European Jewish History," *Jewish History* 20, nos. 3–4 (December 2006): 243–64.
14. Salo Baron, *A Social and Religious History of the Jews* (New York: Columbia University Press, 1937), I:4–5; also 2nd ed, I:4.
15. Yosef Hayim Yerushalmi, *Zakhor: Jewish History and Jewish Memory* (Seattle: University of Washington Press, 1996).
16. David N. Myers, "The Ideology of Wissenschaft Des Judentums," in *History of Jewish Philosophy*, ed. Oliver Leaman and Daniel H. Frank (New York: Routledge, 1997), 706–20.
17. See, for example, David A. Hollinger, "Communalist and Dispersionist Approaches to American Jewish History in an Increasingly Post-Jewish Era," *American Jewish History* 95, no. 1 (March 2009): 1–32; Lila Corwin Berman, "Jewish History Beyond the Jewish People," *AJS Review* 42, no. 2 (November 2018): 269–92.
18. Beth Wenger, "Salo Baron and the Vitality of American Jewish Life," in *Enduring Legacy*, 259–71.
19. Jason Lustig, "Building a Home for the Past: Archives and the Geography of American Jewish History," *American Jewish History* 102, no. 3 (2018): 375–99.
20. Salo Baron, "Reflections on the Future of the Jews in Europe," *Contemporary Jewish Record* 3, no. 4 (July–August 1940): 355–69.
21. See Salo Baron, "The Spiritual Reconstruction of European Jewry," *Commentary* 1 (December 1, 1945): 4–12.
22. Commission on European Jewish Cultural Reconstruction, "Tentative List of Jewish Cultural Treasures in Axis-Occupied Countries," *Jewish Social Studies* 8, no. 1 (1946): 1–103; Commission on European Jewish Cultural Reconstruction, "Tentative List of Jewish Publishers of Judaica and Hebraica in Axis-Occupied Countries," *Jewish Social Studies* 10, no. 2 (1948): 1–56; and Commission on European Jewish Cultural Reconstruction, "Addenda and Corrigenda to Tentative List of Jewish Cultural Treasures in Axis-Occupied Countries," *Jewish Social Studies* 10, no. 1 (1948): 1–16.
23. See, among many, Elisabeth Gallas, *A Mortuary of Books: The Rescue of Jewish Culture After the Holocaust* (New York: New York University Press, 2019); Elisabeth Gallas et al., eds., *Contested Heritage: Jewish Cultural Property After 1945* (Göttingen: Vandenhoeck & Ruprecht, 2020); Shir Kochavi, "Salvage to Restitution: 'Heirless' Jewish Cultural Property in Post-World War II" (PhD diss.,

University of Leeds, 2017); Ayaka Takei, "The Jewish People as the Heir: The Jewish Successor Organizations (JRSO, JTC, French Branch) and the Postwar Jewish Communities in Germany" (PhD diss., Waseda University, 2004); Jason Lustig, "Who Are to Be the Successors of European Jewry? The Restitution of German Jewish Communal and Cultural Property," *Journal of Contemporary History* 52, no. 3 (July 1, 2017): 519–45; Dana Herman, "Hashavat Avedah: A History of Jewish Cultural Reconstruction, Inc." (PhD diss., McGill University, 2008); Katharina Rauschenberger, "The Restitution of Jewish Cultural Objects and the Activities of Jewish Cultural Reconstruction, Inc.," *Leo Baeck Institute Year Book* 53 (2008): 191–211; and Rena Lipman, "Jewish Cultural Reconstruction Reconsidered: Should the Jewish Religious Objects Distributed Around the World After WWII be Returned to Europe?," *KUR. Kunst und Recht, Journal für Kunstrecht, Urheberrecht und Kulturpolitik* 4 (2006): 89–93.

24. Salo W. Baron, "Jewish Social Studies, 1938–39: A Selected Bibliography," *Jewish Social Studies* 2, no. 3 (1940): 305–88; Baron, "Jewish Social Studies, 1938–39: A Selected Bibliography (Concluded)," *Jewish Social Studies* 2, no. 4 (1940): 481–605; Baron, review of Cecil Roth, *Review of Magna Bibliotheca Anglo-Judaica. A Bibliographical Guide to Anglo-Jewish History*, *Jewish Social Studies* 2, no. 1 (1940): 97–99.
25. Salo Baron, "American Jewish History: Problems and Methods," *Publications of the American Jewish Historical Society* 39 (September 1949): 221–23.
26. Joseph L. Blau and Salo W. Baron, *The Jews of the United States, 1790–1840: A Documentary History* (New York: Columbia University Press, 1963).
27. See, for example, Salo W. Baron, "American Jewish Scholarship and World Jewry," *American Jewish Historical Quarterly* 52, no. 4 (1963): 274–82.
28. Michael A. Meyer, *Hebrew Union College–Jewish Institute of Religion: A Centennial History, 1875–1975* (Cincinnati: HUC Press, 1976); Michael A. Meyer, "The Refugee Scholars Project of the Hebrew Union College," in *Judaism Within Modernity: Essays on Jewish History and Religion*, ed. Michael A. Meyer (Detroit: Wayne State University Press, 2001), 345–61; and Jason Lustig, " 'Mere Chips from His Workshop': Gotthard Deutsch's Monumental Card Index of Jewish History," *History of the Human Sciences* 32, no. 3 (July 2019): 49–75.
29. Nelson Glueck, "Our Seminaries," *CCAR Year Book* 59 (1949): 303–4.
30. Steven J. Zipperstein and Robert Liberles, "A Conversation About Salo Baron Between Robert Liberles and Steven J. Zipperstein," *Jewish Social Studies* 1, no. 3 (1995): 68–69.

Chapter Two

ORGANIZING THE JEWISH PAST FOR AMERICAN STUDENTS

Salo Baron at Columbia

BERNARD D. COOPERMAN

To say that academic historical knowledge is socially constructed is neither to denigrate it nor to deny its "objectivity" and truth. Rather, it is to acknowledge that how historians envision their task—how they go about writing what they write—changes over time. I take it for granted that historians themselves can be studied historically—that how they frame their narrative changes with circumstances and their intended audience. Of course, historians respond to new discoveries and take advantage of new techniques thus to see "better" events that were already considered well understood. But beyond this, they frame altogether new questions, reconsidering the sufficiency of older causal chains in light of new critical theories and more recent social consensus. And as they address an audience that is itself the product of a specific time and space, they seek to convince in the terminologies that their students and readers will understand. To properly understand what a particular historical account was intended to mean, therefore, we have to understand the specific anxieties and ambitions of both the historian and the audience. Only in this way can we catch the connotations of the words and phrases used.

This chapter is about Salo Baron, a young man who, in early 1930, was appointed to the new Nathan Miller Chair in Jewish History, Literature and Institutions at Columbia University. The paper is an attempt, so to speak, to get inside Baron's head, though I hasten to add that my ambition is in no way psychohistory. I cannot claim the psychological training that such a task would demand. Nor have I had real access to Baron's inner thoughts and impressions. The autobiography to be entitled "Under Three Civilizations" on which Baron was working remained unfinished at the time of his death.[1] A series of interviews that Baron granted in the summer of 1987 provide useful details on which I will draw throughout the chapter, but they offer only limited insights into Baron's personal feelings, trepidations, or aspirations.[2] The admiring interviewers—first, his student and eventual successor at Columbia, Zvi Ankori, and then American writer and editor Chaim Potok—rarely challenged the nonagenarian or pushed him in directions he seemed not to want to go. Moreover, though at least one of his students attested that Baron could give voice to strong opinions about some of his colleagues,[3] he seems by temperament to have been personally formal and reserved, a point emphasized several times by his daughter.[4]

If this chapter is not about Baron's inner life, neither is it yet a detailed investigation of his historiographical theories or methods, a task that must wait for a separate study. Baron's enormous output was characterized by a multiplicity of perspectives and great facility at synthesis based on his unique mastery of a vast number of sources in many languages. As Cecil Roth noted in an encyclopedia entry in 1957, all of this placed Baron "in the line of the greatest Jewish historians of all times."[5] But they also make it very difficult to pick out particular topics as representative of a method or approach. Baron's goal was not the promotion of a specific interpretive approach; he aimed at comprehensiveness itself. The subject of our investigation is how Baron understood comprehensiveness, why he aimed to be all-inclusive, and how the effort at encyclopedic coverage shaped what became his life's work.

We shall use a biographical framework not to get at the man but in the belief that the stages of Baron's academic life each contributed to the task he undertook, to why his work came out as it did, and to what he meant to tell his contemporaries. I am trying to sketch what Baron brought with him in 1926 when, while maintaining his apartment in Vienna, he undertook to face the academic and intellectual challenges of New York City, and then in 1930, when he accepted—again, not without some reservation—a newly endowed position at Columbia. I am trying to understand the challenges that he faced in opting, at that time and in that place, for an American academic career first in a rabbinic school and then in a secular university. We shall be examining his moment in time in the academy, how he conceived of his task there, and how his approach and achievement fit in with—and helped to shape—an American academic discipline that he is often credited with creating.[6] That was a halcyon era for professionalized historical studies in American universities as our own is not; but even now, when it has become common to bemoan "the death of the humanities," there is much of significance to learn from this man who devoted himself to humanistic study.[7]

I

The young man who took the job at Columbia was himself the product of rapid shifts in the landscape of Jewish intellectual activity. We are used to analyzing Jewish modernization in terms of a binary that contrasts tradition (particularistic behaviors, dress, food, and language, all informed by religious belief) with modernity (comportment based on increasing acculturation to "modern" values and norms drawn from the outside society). But that is far too simple a dichotomy. Born to a wealthy, traditional, and broadly cultured family in the Galician city of Tarnów in 1895, Baron was exposed as a child and youth to a complex, changing, and increasingly divided Jewish intellectualism. His maternal grandfather, Hirsch Wittmayer, to whom the young boy was deeply attached and with whom he identified strongly, was a wealthy businessman. Baron remembered himself at the age of six accompanying the old man to early-morning prayers. On the way, Hirsch would stop at his store before his employees arrived and put his hand into the cashbox, grabbing some coins without counting them so he could hand them out, again without counting, to the beggars who gathered around the synagogue. This same grandfather objected strenuously when his daughter and son-in-law opted for new styles of education for their daughter, Baron's older sister Klara Gisele.

Baron's father, Elias, on the one hand, was the president of the Jewish *kehila*, a staunch supporter of the religious institutions of the town and active in their administration, and a representative to the organizing conference of Agudat Israel. And yet, he was also reputed to have, before his marriage at age nineteen, translated Schiller into Volapük, the international language project that would soon be largely replaced by Esperanto. Baron's mother, though traditionally pious, was also interested in secular literature.

Baron credits her with teaching him how to purchase works of western literature from mail-order catalogues sent from Germany. When her children decided to learn English using the popular Langenscheidt distance-learning method, she eagerly joined in.

But there are also clear indications of reactionary pressures within this world. Baron remembers being taunted by children his own age when it was accidentally revealed that he was attending the gymnasium even if only to sit for the examinations. When Baron's sister married a university-trained lawyer (a *doktor*), her father was publicly shamed in the *kloyz* and forced to leave an institution that he had supported and led for years—no matter that the new son-in-law was himself fully observant and came from a distinguished rabbinic family.

To say that there was competition and tension over claims to intellectual and religious authority in the Jewish world in which Baron was born and raised is, of course, nothing new. The Haskalah—the Jewish "Enlightenment"—had been spreading its rationalist message for over a century, and the politics of imperial Galicia had allowed for the growth of a class of educated Jewish professionals and well-off merchants who valued western education. By the time Salo Baron attended the Jagiellonian University in nearby Kraków, the Jewish community of his native Tarnów (roughly 15,000 Jews, some 41 percent of the city's population in 1910) had already produced close to 300 graduates.[8] At the same time, traditional Talmudic learning also flourished in the city, and Hasidic groups were growing and multiplying there as well, as in Galicia generally. Tension, animosity, and rivalry were inevitable.

A sense of the dynamic in the town can be gleaned from the life of the self-described *ilui* (that is, child prodigy Talmudist), Mordechai David Brandstätter (1844–1928), who moved to Tarnów from a nearby village. He found the atmosphere there depressing. Fourteen years old and just married, the boy was expected to continue his studies in the bigger town, but he was disappointed by the people he met. "The scholars I found there," he recalled, "were all as dry as potsherds and without a drop of heartfelt emotion or softness of soul. They were Talmudic scholars without knowledge or insight and enthusiastic fanatic Hasidim with false empty visions." Brandstätter was gradually driven to search for new intellectual avenues, and he would go on to gain a measure of fame as a writer of satiric short stories about the Jewish world he had encountered. Among the local Hasidim, however, he was reputed a confirmed *apikoros* (heretic) who smoked his cigar and drank his beer while studying Talmud on Yom Kippur, the Day of Atonement. The hostility embarrassed the old man; according to contemporary figures from the literary world who had seen him in Tarnów, he actually lived a completely traditional life there, only changing into western dress when he traveled. In an autobiographical note written on the occasion of his seventieth birthday, Brandstätter was careful to emphasize a more pacific vision of his daily interactions:

> I despised them in my heart, but openly I behaved towards them with friendliness. . . . I sometimes made fun of these Hasidim, their ideas and their companies, but I never argued with them and did not do battle against them. In my heart I didn't hate them. On the contrary, even though I mocked their foolishness, I liked their good qualities. In these they far excelled over our newly enlightened brethren. At least they knew the Torah on which I had been raised, whereas the enlightened ones in the town didn't know it, had never heard [of it], and didn't want to know or hear anything about it.[9]

By the time of Baron's adolescence, Brandstätter had become a figure of significant wealth, status, and political power in Tarnów, and the young Baron clearly admired him. (The admiration seems to have been mutual. When, in 1913, Baron began studying for rabbinic ordination in Kraków, Brandstätter encouraged the project and offered to use his own position as head of the community to arrange for Baron's future appointment as Tarnów's rabbi.) It might not be surprising, then, that one of the first articles the teenage Baron published was a laudatory review of Brandstätter's work for the Hebrew-language Warsaw journal *Ha-Tzefira*, written in conjunction with the communal celebration of the old man's seventieth birthday in May 1914. From his youth, Baron had been raised in the dual-identity tradition of his idol: for example, he, too, had dressed traditionally in Tarnów but changed to western clothes when his family vacationed at Czech spas like Carlsbad or Marienbad. Baron took it for granted—or perhaps we should say, he wanted to believe—that the balance was sustainable and that it was possible to be critical of certain elements within the community without being a traitor to its core values. In his article, therefore, he emphasized that despite his satirical representations, the old man had felt true "love for all Israel."[10]

Baron and Brandstätter may have liked and admired each other, but they came from very different eras, and the chronological gap between them had also witnessed a tectonic shift in the bases, location, and extent of Jewish knowledge. For one thing, the older man had no formal education outside of his rabbinic study, no access to what might be termed secular or non-Jewish education. He had acquired his extra-Talmudic knowledge only through a slow and difficult personal journey of exploration and discovery. Brandstätter's memoir rings with more than a touch of insecurity about his educational limitations and literary abilities. He had studied German with an elderly Moravian Jew, a refugee from Proßnitz (modern Prostějov, Czech Republic) who had settled in Tarnów. Unfortunately, the man was a "pedantic" teacher whose textbooks were the limited stock of Jewish religious works translated into German by reformers like Max Emanuel (Mendel Bri) Stern and Ludwig Phillipson that he had brought with him. Only slowly had Brandstätter picked up enough to translate into Hebrew a German article on Jewish involvement in the crucifixion of Jesus.

Matters were quite different for the young Salo Baron. For his schooling, alongside intensive study with his live-in Talmudic tutor, Baron was registered as an externist (that is, a private student who did not attend classes in person but sat for examinations) at a local Polish gymnasium. He studied classics as well as mathematics and the physical sciences. He learned modern languages like German and French while also developing real affection for the Polish language, history, and literature. He was proud of how well he did in the examinations for the *matura*, the prerequisite for university admission.

In light of all this, it is interesting to see how Brandstätter imagined what the experience of attending a university would have been. In the 1872 story, "The Oppressor of the Jews from the Town of Grieleb" ("*Tzorer ha-Yehudim me-Ir Grieleb*"), for example, we are struck by his naive enthusiasm. The tale is replete with the stylized plot devices typical of the era: secret identities revealed, frustrated but upright young men and women searching for enlightenment; and—in order to resolve all plot tangles—the *deus ex machina* of children promised in marriage, separated and lost, only to rediscover each other and achieve happiness. Studying at university is one of these plot devices, called on to explain apparent inconsistencies. At one point, for example, the town governor—the story's hero—portrays his own university education to a local Jewish teenager. The governor-hero (who at this point is assumed to be a gentile) explains his familiarity with Jewish texts and sources by saying that he had been friendly with Jewish students during his own university years. It was they who had introduced him to the purity of the Hebrew language and the idealistic Hebrew literature of its modern writers. A little later the same hero, now revealed to be a Jew himself, explains that he had built on his own university experience to gain a posting as governor of a heavily Jewish area in order to help carry out the modernization and education of his co-religionists. The point, then, is that Brandstätter, who himself, as mentioned, had had no university experience, presented it as a benign opportunity for Jews to widen their horizons, make true friendships with non-Jews, and gain access to government postings. As the young Baron read these stories, in other words, he would not only have absorbed the positive value of an enlightened Judaism; he was also being socialized into the notion that a university education was neither unusual for Jews nor culturally, religiously, or personally threatening.

Access to non-Jewish education was not all that had shifted in the half-century between Brandstätter and Baron. The substance of Jewish knowledge itself had also expanded radically. Jewish content and, indeed, the very language in which that content was expressed had been transformed. Brandstätter had had to develop mastery of the new Hebrew—a point that is easy to overlook nowadays, when Hebrew is a rich, living language with an enormous literature on every level and millions of speakers who can take for granted the inner logic of their mother tongue. Brandstätter, however, had to build on the staccato Hebrew-Aramaic blend of Talmudic study that, when it proved insufficient for elaborate communication, could be supplemented with flexible Yiddish. He had to acquire the mechanisms of continuous literary narrative in Hebrew and then use them to read and write about new topics, concepts, and images. Literary creativity required, as Hayim Nahman Bialik would put it, "inventing the *nusach*"—that is, building a library of words and images, phrasing, allusions, and linguistic rhythms through which meaning could be expressed and nuanced.[11] Brandstätter described how he first became aware of the possibility of narrative prose in Hebrew only when a more sophisticated friend lent him a few medieval texts with narrative sections and pointed out similar passages in traditional works. Then, on a business trip to Warsaw, the young man encountered Jewish bookshops filled with the wealth of recent Hebrew literature then being produced for a burgeoning audience. His account of another business trip, this time to Vienna, makes clear his uncertainty and genuine trepidation as he began to dream of joining this new world. He gathered up his courage to make the "pilgrimage" to the one-room apartment of Peretz Smolenskin, to that holy place in the Fourth District where his hero ate, slept, and edited the maskilic periodical, *Ha-Shahar*. He was astonished when the great man accepted a story for publication and then continued to encourage his work.

Here again, Salo Baron's education had been quite different. Along with his Talmudic studies and secular studies, he had studied Hebrew with Yosef Umansky, an advocate of the Zionist-oriented *heder metukan* approach to Jewish education that saw contemporary Hebrew language and literature as key to national revival. In interviews, Baron often referred back to this beloved teacher, emphasizing how Umansky had opened him up to the world of contemporary Hebrew literature and turned him from someone who identified with Polish nationalism into a confirmed (cultural) Zionist.[12]

In summary, if we imagine the eighteen-year-old Salo Baron, we see not only a brilliant high-schooler well prepared to enter the outside non-Jewish world of scholarship and letters. We also see a young man for whom Jewish learning itself has become new, with new content, new demands, and new ambitions. These are what excited the young man who would register at the University of Vienna, provocatively listing his native language as Hebrew.[13]

II

Though there was talk of Baron, clearly an excellent student, training as an engineer to manage the oil fields that his father had inherited[14] or as a medical doctor, it was probably always clear that the teenager would devote himself to some aspect of what would come to be called Jewish studies. The field was then changing in content and emphases, and Baron's training would reflect these shifts. Certainly from the point of view of a career, Baron began with the idea of obtaining "a good *smikha*"—that is, ordination from a prominent rabbinic scholar. It had been toward this end that Baron's father arranged for his son, newly matriculated, to study in Kraków in preparation for an examination from Joseph Engel, a Tarnów native who then headed the larger city's rabbinic court.[15] At the same time, Baron took advantage of his weekly commutes to Kraków to enroll in courses at the Jagiellonian University; he signed up for the same courses his older sister had taken the year previous. (Baron admitted that he had not excelled in these courses because he had invested most of his time in his demanding Talmudic and halakhic studies.)

But it seems fairly clear that this was merely a stopgap; Baron's academic ambition was directed toward Vienna. His plans may well have been set several years before, when he had accompanied his father on a summer vacation to Carlsbad. By chance they had taken a place in the same house as Rabbi Samuel Hirsch Margulies, then chief rabbi of Florence and head of the *Collegio Rabbinico* there.[16] The elder Baron became friendly with the Galician-born and German-trained Margulies and asked him for advice about his son's academic career. Margulies, reflecting his own experience, recommended that after finishing his *matura*, the boy spend a year at each of several universities (an academic pattern then common in Austria), ending up in Florence, where Margulies would take him on as a student at the *Collegio Rabbinico Israelitico* and also arrange for him to complete his doctorate at the University of Florence. Whether that was, in fact, Baron's plan we do not know for certain. At least in part because of the outbreak of World War I, Baron would remain in Vienna for the following twelve years.

In Vienna, Baron enrolled in the *Israelitisch-theologische Lehranstalt*, the city's modern rabbinical school established in 1893.[17] There he joined some twenty-five other students distributed over the school's five- to six-year program who formed, he later remembered, a close-knit and engaged community.[18] The school was under the active direction of Rabbi Adolf (Aryeh) Schwarz, a brilliant scholar who devoted his life to opening up the texts and methodologies of classic and medieval *halakha*.[19] Like comparable colleges in Metz/Paris, Padua/Rome/Florence, Breslau, Berlin, Budapest, and London, the Vienna school was charged with training new generations of rabbis who could give appropriate voice to Jewish values. They would act as dignified representatives of the community to the outside society as well as—and here I stress—to the Jews themselves.[20] Some accounts have emphasized the apologetic purpose of these schools. Writing about his own school in Vienna, for example, Baron emphasized "a dramatic controversy over the Talmud between an anti-Jewish Prague professor, August Rohling, and a staunch defender of Jewish rights, Joseph Samuel Bloch." It was this, he suggested, that motivated wealthy Jewish philanthropists to finance the school, a tactic through which to respond to the increasing anti-Semitic rhetoric of the era.[21]

But the Lehranstalt was more than a school for apologetics or an answer to anti-Semitism. For both the faculty and the donors who footed the bills, it was part of a multi-local effort to put *Wissenschaft des Judentums*, the flowering scientific and critical approach to Jewish scholarship, on solid institutional footing.[22] Structurally, these schools were a reflection of Jewish demographic growth, increasing urbanization, and expanding wealth—all of which allowed for, and required, organizing the training of a more sophisticated religious leadership at every level. As intellectual institutions, these schools were the locus of Jews' developing aspirations for their own ever-expanding cultural heritage. As the young Harry Austryn Wolfson would put it a few years later, Jewish intellectual treasures were "scattered all over the world and rotting in the holds of libraries." It was the task of Jewish scholarship to "unearth . . . these buried treasures . . . begging and pleading to be freed, like so many prisoners held in captivity. We have the means to free them, to disenchain them, to bring them to light."[23] Long-forgotten manuscripts were carefully deciphered and systematically examined, and the Jewish legal, theological, spiritual, and hermeneutic legacy was continually enriched and enlarged. (The discovery of the astonishing wealth in the Cairo Geniza is only the best-known example of what was going on in libraries all over Europe where Jewish manuscripts had been accumulating unstudied for centuries.) The thrust of the effort was philological and textual, as critical methodologies developed in other fields were now applied to Jewish texts. Hundreds and, soon, thousands of books and journals in Hebrew and the main European languages were turned out, a dizzying cascade of knowledge that demanded institutions like the Vienna Lehranstalt, where these books could be available and students could be given the basic categories through which to appreciate and assess the new knowledge.

How did the young Baron and his classmates experience this scholarly agenda now presented to them in formal lectures with written papers, examinations, and degrees? What was their classroom experience? How did they react to the expanding bibliography? We can get a feeling of the day-to-day atmosphere from the memoir of Abraham J. Brawer, who attended

ORGANIZING THE JEWISH PAST FOR AMERICAN STUDENTS

the Lehranstalt just a few years earlier. After discussing the great gaps in preparatory Talmudic training between the students from the Lithuanian, Galician, and Polish east on the one hand and those from the Czech lands, those who had grown up in Vienna proper, and the boys from Hungary who had been educated at a gymnasium on the other, Brawer went on to describe the required Talmud class given by the rector, Rabbi Schwarz himself:

> During my first year . . . I prepared daily. . . . Nevertheless, for the most part I didn't understand the questions the lecturer raised, as he sat behind piles upon piles of books from which he would read, quote, and compare textual variants that, obviously, the students did not have before them. There was a servant who would carry in many volumes and place them on the lectern when the lecturer entered the room. In addition, the rector would regularly ring for him . . . to bring yet more volumes from the library. . . . Often the lecture was, in fact, an investigation of the sources and a working out of scientific theories carried on aloud in front of the students. Most—and sometimes all—of us were unprepared to understand the flow of the analysis.[24]

Brawer's memoir, with its ironic humor, may be intentionally overstating the limitations of a diaspora education for his Israeli readers half a century after the events. Baron talks about the experience in only the most serious and positive tones. For him it was an intellectual challenge to which he rose eagerly. In one of the interviews he gave in 1987, Baron spoke of one of his favorite teachers, the polymath Avigdor (Victor) Aptowitzer.[25] The latter, a Galician like Baron and himself an alumnus of the Lehranstalt, taught a broad range of Rabbinics—*halakha, midrash,* hermeneutics, medieval Talmudic commentary, and even philosophy and kabbalah. Baron recalled for his interviewer a paper he had written for Aptowitzer—a Hebrew translation of the introduction to the Zohar from the original medieval Aramaic. This was a considerable undertaking in itself: the original fills twenty-eight pages in the closely printed standard edition. Baron was proud of the result and regretted that he had no copy, as the paper was lost when the Nazis closed the school soon after the Anschluss. But what is revelatory is that Baron, in describing the project, adds that, of course, in preparation he had read the entirety of the Zohar. This was just a few years before Gershom Scholem began working on his

Munich dissertation (a critical edition and German translation of *Sefer ha-Bahir*), and the field of Jewish mysticism presented an attractive area of new scholarly research.[26] But when the interviewer, Zvi Ankori, asks Baron whether he undertook this arduous task because he was attracted to the doctrines of kabbalah, the latter quickly says no. He was just interested in knowing what this difficult and important work contained. He was, he says, never attracted to the mystical ideas of the book itself; he had undertaken the task simply because he wanted to know about this significant part of the Jewish heritage.

One other consideration helps us to understand Baron's experience as a student at the Lehranstalt. When he entered the school, he was religiously observant. He admits to his interviewers, somewhat elliptically, that he was intensely "Orthodox" at the time, and reports that he would take on voluntary fasts for himself trying to sway the Divine, for example, to help Allenby in the battle for Jerusalem. He seems already to have been a little embarrassed at his own piety (or perhaps at his credulous application of traditional pietistic techniques to such worldly concerns), for when his father unexpectedly visited in Vienna on the day of his self-imposed fast, young Baron went to great lengths to hide what he was doing from the older man.

In 1920, after completing his course of studies at the Lehranstalt, Baron was ordained with the right to both teach and judge (*yore yore, yadin yadin*), thus fulfilling his father's dream.[27] But for some reason that he does not make clear, soon after Baron simply lost interest in intense personal religion. It may be that in this, Baron was influenced by some of his teachers at the Lehranstalt; there were at least a few who were known no longer to accept traditional beliefs about, for example, the divine origin of the biblical text.[28] More generally, even among the members of his rabbinical program, the rubrics of Jewish identity were becoming variegated, and intellectual authority was determined not by personal belief or ritual observance but by the depth and breadth of one's knowledge. Whatever the specific cause, so far as we can tell from his writings, this was not a wrenching experience for Baron. He makes no mention of soul-searching or personal angst—simply a shift in orientation from medieval texts to cotemporary demographic and political history. There is no sense that history served him, in the well-known phrasing of Baron's student Yosef Hayim Yerushalmi, as faith for a "fallen Jew."[29] Rather, in his years at the Lehranstalt, the intense academic intellectualism that already drove him during his teen years seems simply to have flowered, becoming its own satisfaction and the basis of his long and dedicated career. In America, Baron was not actively engaged in religious circles; his daughter remembers their family as "definitely secular Jews" who were not members of any synagogue. Within the family, she reports, Sabbath regulations were respected only pro forma when visiting more observant acquaintances from the Jewish Theological Seminary faculty.[30]

The Lehranstalt and the other schools like it were, for the most part, professional schools. The students in Vienna were working toward a rabbinical diploma that would allow them to serve in congregations or at least to work as licensed teachers of religion around the empire. But the schools were also an organizational structure that constituted the world of Wissenschaft des Judentums, each institution a vital node in a broad and growing network of Jewish scholarship. Students and teachers not inclined to community service could move from one European city to another and eventually to Palestine or the United States, building their careers and expanding the new academic culture.

To give only a few examples, Abraham Brawer, the boy whom we encountered in Talmud class, published his doctorate in 1910 (see later in this chapter) and then moved to Palestine, where he had a distinguished career as a geographer and educator. One of his teachers at the Lehranstalt, Adolf Büchler (nephew of the famously peripatetic medievalist Adolf Neubauer) had studied rabbinics in Budapest and Breslau, obtained his PhD from the University of Leipzig, and served as professor of Jewish history at the Vienna Lehranstalt, where he had taught the young Brawer, from 1893 to 1906. Büchler then moved to London to direct Jews' College. Brawer's study partner, Harry Torczyner (Naftali Zvi Tur-Sinai), went from the Lehranstalt to Berlin's Hochschule für die Wissenschaft des Judentums and then to Palestine and Hebrew University. The list can be easily extended. Baron fits well with this devoted group of intellectuals not only because he shared their background and scholarly interests but also because he already saw himself as what we might call a Jewish cosmopolitan. He was attracted to the possibility of international travel, and when he completed his training, he would be able to choose among positions in Jerusalem, Florence, and New York.

Like all of his rabbinical school classmates, Baron was simultaneously pursuing a degree at the University of Vienna. He completed two separate academic doctorates there in 1920 and 1922 and obtained a law degree the following year. The latter suggests that Baron was seeking to guarantee his future livelihood; in an interview, he also recalled taking courses in what today we would call the business school but stopped because he hadn't enjoyed them. He also told an interviewer that he practiced law in Vienna at least part time between 1923 and 1926. One suspects, nevertheless, that the law degree was more than a professional move, and it may give us a useful key to a shift in Baron's academic interests. A law degree was a way for the young man to gain the training and credentials he needed to operate in an area of international relations that he increasingly saw as crucial to the future of the Jewish people—namely, the negotiation of Jewish minority rights within the state systems that had emerged out of the imperial collapse following World War I.

Though he was a declared Zionist from his teen years, Baron seems not to have been attracted by the organizational or political activities associated with that movement in Vienna. His Zionism was cultural and expressed itself especially in efforts to support the use of Hebrew in speaking and in writing. While a student he had helped to organize and lead general Jewish organizations like the *Zentralverband der jüdischen Jugendgruppen Österreichs*, which was dedicated to the cultural development of all Jewish students in Austria. When asked by an interviewer whether he had enjoyed the famous bar-hopping (*knappes*) of student life in the Viennese capital, he dismissed the question, mentioning only that one night each week, he and his fellow students from the Lehranstalt and the Semitics Department at the university had met to use their Hebrew in discussions of literature and the politics of the day.[31] What engaged Baron in these years was not working for a Herzlian Jewish state or even for mass Jewish settlement in Palestine. What attracted him was working for Jewish minority rights that would everywhere include state recognition of Jews' autonomous cultural institutions.[32] With his law degree in hand, Baron was able to follow up on his political convictions by serving as a representative of the Austrian League of Nations' Union at the General Assembly of the International Federation of the League of Nations' Unions and for two years serving on its Representative Council, where he consistently advocated for Jews' minority rights.[33]

The relation between the state and the fate of the Jewish people was also the focus of Baron's historical studies at the university. For his first doctorate, he worked with August Fournier, who had written extensively on the Congress of Vienna.[34] Baron wrote his thesis on *The Jewish Question at the Congress of Vienna*, mining the rich archives of Vienna to trace the interrelation between the allocation of state power among the various German political entities and the redefinition of the civil position of Jews within them.[35] This was the beginning of his life-long effort to tie the dynamics of the Jewish experience to the broader contexts of the surrounding nations.

In his second doctorate, Baron moved from the practicalities of negotiating power to the theory of the state itself. A nationalist himself, Baron was attracted to what he considered a crisis in the internationalist thinking of socialism after World War I. He took for his entry point the political theories of Ferdinand Lassalle,[36] the fiery, Jewish-born political agitator and nationalist whose speeches and pamphlets lay behind the organization of the German Socialist Party. Baron worked on the thesis under distinguished jurist Hans Kelsen, author of the 1920 Austrian Constitution (and a converted Jew from Prague) and probably more directly under Professor Carl Grünberg, an "orthodox" Marxist (and also of Jewish origin) who held a chair in economic history at Vienna and would soon leave to become the founding director of the Institut für Sozialforschung, later referred to simply as the Frankfurt School. As he worked on Lassalle, Baron was not unaware of his subject's Jewish background, and he wrote an article, "Ferdinand Lassalle the Jew," which offered an insightful analysis of the complexity of Jewish identity denied, a paper that can still be read with pleasure today. "Lassalle's problem was not that he was a Jew," he wrote. "Rather it was that he had stopped being a conscious Jew without doing so in his subconscious." This almost psychological enquiry was not germane to the dissertation, and Baron published it separately—and in Hebrew.[37]

Baron was by no means the only Lehranstalt student whose university studies focused on legal and political history rather than philology and religion. Even Brawer, whose memoir of Adolf Schwarz's Talmud class at the Lehranstalt we have already cited, chose to write his dissertation (1910) on the history of Galicia in 1772, the year that area became an Austrian province. At the same time, he also wrote a separate Hebrew article to explore the emperor's attitude toward his new Jewish subjects.[38] In preparing for his book on Habsburg Jewry, William O. McCagg came across several more unpublished dissertations by Jewish doctoral students in Vienna who opted to mine the rich Viennese archives and explore the legal, social, and economic history of Jewish communities in imperial lands.[39] It might surprise some readers to learn that Raphael Mahler was also enrolled at the rabbinical college and in the university's Semitics Department in these years, writing a dissertation in 1922 on social aspects of the idea of progress. It is tempting to imagine the two young men arguing as they drank coffee in a student cafeteria—Baron, the conservative believer in state power and the rule of law who would soon be known as an admirer of medieval corporatism, and Mahler, a confirmed Marxist who would call for reversing the nationalistic orientation of modern Jewish historiography in favor of appropriate emphasis on "social antagonisms, class struggle and social opposition within the community."[40] Though apparently such coffee breaks never occurred, there is no doubt that the Lehranstalt students of the 1920s were inflamed by an ever more varied set of political ideologies and were increasingly focusing their university studies on political, legal, and social history rather than the more traditional linguistic, philological, and religious topics of the past.[41]

What must have been a lively student community devoted to historical scholarship would inevitably soon disperse. Some would make their way to Palestine. Others, like Mahler, became part of the exciting rebirth of a nationalist Polish school of Jewish historians especially in Warsaw.[42] Baron was not yet ready to leave Vienna. From 1919, he held the position of professor of Jewish history at the new *Paedagogium*, or Teacher's Institute, founded by the city's dynamic Rabbi Tzvi Peretz Chajes. This allowed him time to finish his university studies and publish his theses. Each of his books and articles and his related political work were adding to his reputation, and he began to receive job offers: from Florence to head up the Collegio that he had heard about years before from Rabbi Margulies; from Jerusalem, where an Institute for Jewish Studies opened in December 1924; from Breslau, famously home to Heinrich Graetz, where a new chair had been established; and from New York, where the nascent Yeshiva University was beginning to build a faculty. And it was at this point that Stephen S. Wise came to Vienna to attend the World Zionist Congress and succeeded in convincing Salo Baron to take the leap, come to New York, and teach Jewish history at the Jewish Institute of Religion (JIR). The year was 1926.

III

When Salo Baron arrived in the United States, his academic identity, his sense of the intellectual challenge and purpose of Jewish studies, had been built up slowly through mastery of successive layers of knowledge. The intense rabbinics of his youth had been nuanced through the critical textual and philological discipline of his college years. The exciting dream of breathing new life into Hebrew had engaged his nationalistic pride and shaped his reading and writing. And all this had been integrated with broad mastery of secular culture—that is, the languages, literatures, and methods that he imbibed and argued over with his high school examiners in Tarnów and with his professors at the University of Vienna. Most saliently, he had become convinced that a Jewish history written from exclusively Jewish sources was no longer sufficient.

Institutionally, America might have seemed to present a situation similar to what he already knew in Vienna: he would be teaching at a Jewish rabbinical school, and his students would be young men who were also expected to master what was taught on the "outside." But what must have surprised Baron was his students' lack of preparation, not only when it came to European languages but even when it came to Jewish knowledge, not only the intricacies of traditional texts but, even more so, the vast scholarly literature that was appearing. He was soon convinced that as a teacher, his main task would be to give generations of American Jewish students the tools they needed to join the sophisticated debates that had evolved in Europe.[43] Almost from the start, therefore, he called on his colleagues to create an "advanced studies" track at JIR that would allow students to do more than professional rabbinical preparation. His colleagues were skeptical and grudgingly agreed if he would be in charge of it. To his frustration, however, their pessimism had been justified; there was no demand, especially once the Great Depression made the economics of more years in school simply unrealistic for students. It would only be with his transfer to Columbia University in 1930 that Baron would be able to devote himself to more purely academic graduate education. Making this possible for students was the task that would shape the rest of his career.

What ultimately lay behind Baron's move to Columbia were the determined efforts of an elite and prosperous Reform Jewish community associated with Temple Emanu-El. In 1927, when it was built, Emanu-El's new building at Fifth Avenue and 65th Street was the largest synagogue structure in the world and could boast that it held more worshippers than St. Patrick's Cathedral, ten blocks to the south. What interests us here is the fact that the wealth of this congregation was dedicated not just to an edifice. Over many decades, the synagogue's rabbis and members had sought to raise the profile of Jewish studies in the city, an ambitious effort that grew naturally from their own commitment to a highly intellectual and spiritual understanding of Jewish identity and culture.[44]

Among the many distinguished figures who led Temple Emanu-El in those years, we can mention Gustav Gottheil (rabbi from 1873 until his retirement in 1899). After obtaining his doctorate from the University of Jena and studying under Moritz Steinschneider and Leopold Zunz in Berlin, Gottheil had led a Reform Jewish congregation in Manchester, England, before he was called to New York. Historians have credited him with impressive and wide-ranging contributions to both Jewish and the general spiritual life of that city, but what interests us in the present context is that under his leadership, the temple embarked on an ambitious effort to build a Jewish studies program at Columbia. They endowed a professorship in Semitic studies in 1887, donated a treasure trove of forty-five rare Hebrew manuscripts and twenty-five hundred printed works to the Columbia library in 1892,[45] and endowed the Gustav Gottheil Lectureship in Semitic Languages in 1903 in honor of the seventy-fifth birthday of their by then rabbi emeritus. Gustav's son Richard chose not to follow his father into the pulpit; instead, he opted for a life of scholarship. After graduating from Columbia, he studied for his doctorate in Berlin and then returned to New York, where, perhaps not surprisingly, he was the first incumbent of Columbia's chair in rabbinic literature, the endowed professorship mentioned earlier. From 1889, he was head of the university's enlarged Semitics program, stubbornly holding onto the position until his death.

Richard Gottheil published widely not only on ancient Semitic languages and literatures but also on medieval Jewish (especially Sephardic) history, Geniza texts, Jewish genealogy, and Zionism. He was also a major contributor, as both writer and field editor, to the *Jewish Encyclopedia* (1906), a monument to Jewish scholarship in its time and testimony not only to Gottheil's own erudition but to the ambitious agenda that had been set out for Jewish studies and, increasingly, to the realization of that goal specifically in the United States.[46] Gottheil also made important bibliographical contributions to several fields, serving as director of the Oriental Division of the New York Public Library from 1897 and helping to shape that institution's important research collection.[47] At Columbia he trained several generations of young scholars in Semitic languages and rabbinics, including future luminaries as different from each other as Joseph Hertz (1894)[48] and Stephen Wise (1902). Hertz, on the day after he graduated from Columbia, became as well the first ordained graduate of the Jewish Theological Seminary (though Orthodox rabbis had to be "imported" from the Lower East Side to actually examine him for *smikha*) and was appointed, from 1913, chief rabbi of the British Empire. Wise, on the other hand, was ordained by Adolf Jellinek in Vienna and served in so-called liberal synagogues in New York. After turning down the offer of the rabbinical position at Temple Emanu-El, Wise went on to establish the Free Synagogue.[49] It was from that base that Wise established the Jewish Institute of Religion next door. Gottheil served on the Institute's board.[50]

When Salo Baron came to New York, Temple Emanu-El was led by Rabbi Hyman Enelow, a dynamic and inspiring figure in the development of Liberal Judaism in America and a tireless advocate for the importance of sophisticated Jewish education and learning. Enelow, himself a dedicated student of medieval Jewish ethical literature, was horrified by what he saw as the "idolatry of sociology" then in vogue and warned the graduating class of Hebrew Union College in 1912 to focus instead on the spiritual concerns of Judaism: "The God of Israel is more than any fortuitous interest of the hour." Reflecting, perhaps, his own educational experience (he had spent several years at the University of Chicago before training for the rabbinate in Cincinnati), Enelow convinced several of the wealthiest members of his congregation to donate funds for chairs of Jewish studies programs at leading American universities, first Lucius Littauer at Harvard (1925) and then Linda Miller at Columbia (1929).[51]

In retrospect, these endowments for Jewish studies at secular universities have been treated as radical innovations; as we have seen, however, they were much more the continuation of a lengthy process in the development and institutionalization of the field in Europe and America. At least in the case of the gift to Columbia, we can also trace the changing emphases in Jewish studies that we first saw in Vienna now working themselves out in institutional terms. The lengthy correspondence over the gift between Mrs. Miller (very much under the influence of Enelow) and

President Butler highlight the religious and cultural values of the community as opposed to the new approach represented by Baron. Miller was herself a devoted student of Hebrew and medieval Hebrew poetry, and in years past, she and her husband had been major supporters in the development of the library collection at the Jewish Theological Seminary.[52] Salo Baron was definitely not the candidate she would have preferred for the chair, especially because she perceived him as a Jewish nationalist, the very antithesis of the spiritual Judaism she wanted to promote.[53] After a lengthy search effort, the position was finally offered to Ismar Elbogen in Berlin. When he ultimately refused for personal reasons, he recommended Baron as the best candidate. The stage was set for the next step in Baron's career. And here we will see one more indication of how he had come to conceive his field.

Once at Columbia, Baron made it clear that he wished to teach specifically in the Department of History and not in the expected departments devoted to Oriental languages or to philosophy and religion.[54] It is tempting to speculate about his motives in this: did Baron see the history department as more prestigious or as closer to "mainstream" in the university curriculum? Was he trying to avoid the compartmentalization that he had encountered in Vienna? There is yet another possibility: perhaps Baron was merely trying to carve out his own academic turf away from the authority of Richard Gottheil? The latter had, as we have seen, long dominated Jewish studies at Columbia. He was one of the original members of the search committee for the Miller chair and had asserted then his assumption that "of course, the Chair will be in the department of Oriental languages and literatures."[55] Baron, however, made it clear to President Butler at their first meeting that he would have none of that. Whatever his personal considerations, however, the move to the Department of History was also central to Baron's own vision of the task of the Jewish historian. It was time, he argued, to go beyond a consideration of "internal factors" as if "the dominant trends determining . . . Jewish developments originate and disappear . . . only within the Jewish people as a separate entity. As if it were possible completely to isolate any community or individual from the rest of the world and deny any external influences upon it!"[56] Baron was convinced that the time had come to write the history of the Jews not as a subject apart but within the broader flow of social events and forces. Thus, although from the start he would teach courses devoted specifically to Hebrew texts and literature, his ambition as a historian was always to highlight the broader context that determined Jews' fate, within which they acted and to which they contributed. In this he was reflecting, in his own way, the orientation that had inspired him and his fellows at the University of Vienna.

For its part, Columbia's Department of History was none too pleased with the idea and at first voted to reject both Baron and the Miller chair. It is tempting to assume that this was simply an expression of knee-jerk animosity toward Jews and Jewish studies, along the same lines as the hostility famously repeated about Columbia's Department of English. That narrative, associated with the so-called New York Jewish intellectuals, focused on candidates' self-perception and emphasized their immigrant origins, their precocious youthful intellectualism, the anti-Semitism they overcame, and their own personal alienation from the Jewish community and religion.[57] But Salo Baron did not carry the emotional burden of growing up the poor child of uprooted immigrants in lower-class neighborhoods of New York. Certainly, he was not unmoored from his own Jewish roots. In the interviews he gave in 1987, Baron treated his initial rejection matter-of-factly and had nothing but praise for President Butler, whom he remembered as genuinely interested in Jewish history.

Though it cannot be said that Jews, even years later, were especially welcome in the Department of History,[58] the faculty's initial objection to Baron in 1930 probably had less to do with narrow ethnic hostility and more to do with their perception of how Jewish studies as a field fit in with what they considered their discipline. They argued that the department had no courses in Christian or Islamic civilization. A professor of Jewish civilization and institutions logically belonged either in the Philosophy Department or in Semitics. President Butler was, however, a determined administrator, and he found a way to satisfy Baron's demand. He turned to history department chair Carlton Hayes, himself a Europeanist whose work focused especially on the history of nationalism, and who in later years would serve as U.S. ambassador to Spain and eventually be elected president of the American Historical Association. Carlton Hayes was also a convert to Catholicism and famously devoted much of his professional energy to raising the level of Catholic historical scholarship in America and to legitimizing the place of Catholic and Christian civilization in the general curriculum. Baron's interest in integrating the history of the Jews into broader history thus fit perfectly with Hayes's own ambitions about including Catholic civilization into that same curriculum.[59] Together, Hayes and Butler managed to push through the appointment. Baron's coming can be seen as part of a general shift in the orientation of the American historical profession. Years later, Baron would wryly remember being invited to his first department faculty meeting, when his colleagues "looked him over," as he did them. Anyone familiar with academic politics will appreciate the tension in the room; here was a candidate and an endowed chair being imposed on an academic community.

The friction might have stemmed from another consideration as well. These years marked, we must remember, a high point in the development of the American academic discipline of history,[60] and at Columbia in particular, there seems to have been considerable debate and tension within the faculty. Columbia had just revamped the college core curriculum, replacing introductory departmental courses in philosophy, history, economics, and government with CC (contemporary civilization) A and B—intensive seminars that challenged students to study and discuss social problems and ideology. On another level, the "New History," promoted by Charles Beard and James Harvey Robinson, had left an indelible mark even after those scholars had left to establish The New School for Social Research.[61] Strong voices were urging emphasis on outreach and teaching. Baron would have immediately encountered other recent hires like Allan Nevins, several times winner of the Pulitzer Prize, who had come to Columbia after distinguishing himself as a journalist and writer of popular history. Nevins (who never bothered to earn a PhD) famously attacked the pedantry of the academic historians he encountered and urged them to write in a more accessible style for a larger, popular audience.[62]

Another new colleague, Jacques Barzun, came from a different background. He was raised near Paris, where his parents had moved in the highest intellectual circles of French modernism, and then accompanied his parents to America (his father served in the French diplomatic corps). Barzun had graduated Columbia as valedictorian of the class of 1927 and immediately begun to teach for the Department of History there while pursuing his doctorate. Thoroughly elitist in his approach to knowledge, Barzun would nevertheless devote his life's work to exposing college students to great books and ideas. As teacher and administrator, he would shape Columbia's undergraduate curriculum, not least in his forty-year teaching collaboration with Lionel Trilling in the General Honors Course and then in Humanities A (HumLit), the core of Columbia's liberal arts curriculum.[63]

How did such colleagues with their emphasis on new concepts of history and new ways of teaching undergraduates see or influence Baron? If we are to judge from his personal recollections and from the courses he taught, Baron was not drawn to innovation in classroom format, but he was certainly aware of the need for improved teaching methodologies. As we have noted, already at JIR, Baron had sought to establish an "advanced" program for students who had completed their rabbinical training. Now he would try this at Columbia. But could it work? Baron was worried. When, in a casual conversation in 1929, George Alexander Kohut offered to use his influence to put forward Baron's candidacy for the Columbia position, Baron replied that he could not imagine that there would be any students interested in his courses considering that there were no jobs.[64] Later, after he had spoken to President Butler, Baron went to lunch with a number of faculty members and repeated his worries. When one of the professors remarked that if there were no students, he would be able to sit in his room and write books, Baron protested that he was too young to retire. But he stuck to his plan. Once he was hired, Baron aimed his teaching at research-oriented and sophisticated levels; no undergraduate could enroll in his classes, he boasted to an interviewer, without written permission from him and from the dean.[65] Perhaps to his own surprise, his worries proved unfounded. Years later, Baron could still remember his relief when he found no less than twenty-three students waiting for him in his first class in Fayerweather Hall.

Baron's story about his first class at Columbia does not end there. Getting student bodies into the classroom was not yet enough. How to teach at the advanced level Baron believed appropriate? After the class, a student approached him, obviously puzzled. "You mentioned two books in your lecture, Professor. An Old and a New Testament. What are those?" Astonished at the young man's ignorance, Baron asked the young man what he was studying at the university. "Chemistry" came the reply. "So why are you taking my course?" "I was interested in the topic," came the reply. When Baron later told this story, he laughed and stressed that the young man had studied hard, received the highest grade in the class, and gone on to a professorial career in his chosen field.

But what had become, for Baron in retirement, a well-polished humorous anecdote must have seemed, in the 1930s, a serious and intimidating challenge. He came to realize that he would not just be training professional rabbis and academic scholars; he was to present Jewish history to interested generalists. But how to bridge the abysmal ignorance of his students and give them not only information but also the tools with which to learn? Baron believed that the key lay in exposing them to the bibliographic wealth that, as we have seen, scholars—generalists as well as those working on Wissenschaft des Judentums—were accumulating.[66] The challenge might not be automatically obvious in our own day of the internet, online encyclopedias, and instant access to a seemingly endless supply of scanned books and articles. But in 1920s New York, the challenge was concrete. At JIR, where he was formally appointed librarian, and then at Columbia, where President Butler and he agreed that he would devote his first semester to book purchasing, Baron set himself assiduously to the task of building up a working library for students. Even that was not enough. The solution was not just to have books available on the library shelves. Equally important, teachers had to provide navigation guides for students about to set sail. And here we find, I think, the heart of Baron's ambition and the key to the structure of his *chef d'ouevre*.

The impossibility of keeping up with publications in their field has preoccupied Jewish (and other) scholars since biblical times.[67] By the twentieth century, even a relatively new and small field like Wissenschaft des Judentums had been inundated by the volume of studies published in many places and many languages. Listing and describing the new books, and then the journal articles, integrating them all into the cumulative library, and keeping everything organized and usable within shifting categories of scholarly discourse became itself a cardinal task of Jewish scholarship. Thus, in addition to the famous bibliographies of manuscripts and rare printed books based on the library collections now in university and national libraries, Jewish scholars began to publish magazines listing and reviewing current publications in the field.[68] In 1923, for example, when scholars answered the call from Hayim Nahman Bialik to produce a new journal that would provide "an academic basis and scientific preparation" for the Hebrew reading community, it went without saying that each issue would include a list of titles recently received. But granted the recent disruption of the war years, the first issue also had to include a full bibliography of books published between 1914 and 1918 arranged according to academic field.[69]

Of course, the bibliographic challenge was by no means limited to Jewish studies. Departments of history all across the United States had gone about addressing the task. A quick glance at the American Historical Association's 1931 *A Guide to Historical Literature*[70] spotlights the pedagogic task before Baron. That volume lists literally thousands of books and articles, each briefly reviewed by one of scores of scholars from all over the country. Whole sections of the book are devoted to the history of specific countries or to topics such as Christianity and Mohammedanism [sic], but for the history of the Jewish people and religion, there is no separate section and only a tiny number of entries. The only bibliographic aid mentioned for Judaica is the list of the holdings of the New York Public Library prepared before World War I by Richard Gottheil and Joshua Bloch.[71] Baron had defined this as the central obstacle for any research in Jewish studies when he was at JIR, and now he set out to make academic historical study of the Jews and Judaism possible by producing a bibliographic handbook for his own field that would rival—and, indeed, outdo—the AHA guide. He did this by himself, unaided by research assistants. It is in this sense that Robert Liberles was undoubtedly correct when he labeled Baron "the architect of Jewish history."

Baron erected the scaffolding and constructed the building by becoming a creature of libraries, and of Columbia's Butler library in particular. As Michael Stanislawski, the current holder of the Miller Chair in Jewish History, wrote for Columbia's alumni magazine,

> For nearly 60 years, Professor Salo Baron could be seen daily in the stacks of Butler Library, researching his epoch-making *Social and Religious History of the Jews*. When he was in his late 80s, and the *History* was in its 16th or 17th volume but had reached only the early modern period, Baron was often asked if he would get to the twentieth century. He always responded that he had a deal with the Creator: he would not be taken from this world before his life's work was completed.[72]

Though he also engaged in archival work, especially at the start of his career, it was the pursuit of bibliographic comprehensiveness that lies at the very heart of Baron's historical oeuvre. It shaped his approach to every topic and dictated what and how he wrote.

The first edition of the *Social and Religious History* was planned as a single volume based on the Schermerhorn Lectures, the ten-lecture series he had been invited to give when he took the position at Columbia. But the book kept expanding; the original publisher rejected what had become a weighty set of three volumes, one of which was nothing but 171 pages of footnotes, 121 pages of bibliography, and a 99-page index, all printed in a far smaller type size than the body of the text in the first two volumes. What Baron ended up proudly presenting to readers was a guide to all the available literature. Whatever he planned when he first gave the lecture series, by the time he composed the book, Baron did not want to produce a popular summary of Jewish history. Such a task he would leave to his sometime rival, Cecil Roth. That scholar, in addition to his vigorous academic research and publishing in several fields, worked assiduously at teaching young American Jews in summer institutes and writing for the popular market. Roth had managed to produce a one-volume popular history in 1936, the year before Baron's work appeared. Roth's *Short History of the Jewish People* was enormously successful (by the standards of books in Jewish history); it would go through several revisions and be republished many times over the coming half century and more.[73] Baron had a different goal in mind. Having structured an overall narrative of Jewish history from biblical times to the present—that is, having told a story—Baron now used the publication of *Social and Religious History* to elaborate and discuss his arguments, using the footnotes to demonstrate how he had arrived at his generalizations, and to introduce interested readers to the "state of the field." The footnotes are more than bibliographical lists. Rather, they are reasoned discussions with the reader about the intimacies and logic of historical thinking. For each topic, they lay out the issues at stake and show the reader how to think through the problem.

Let me give one example chosen more or less at random. At the start of "The Status of 'Infidels,'" his four-page treatment of the situation of Jews under Islam (I: 315–19), Baron manages to include references to rulings attributed to the Prophet, individual rulers, and specific schools of Muslim jurisprudence over the centuries, and he brings lengthy citations from medieval texts with brief parenthetic mentions of their bibliographical sources. He generalizes that (a) under Islam, Jews were better off than under Christianity; (b) legal discrimination existed but "actually affected life only to a minor extent" because "many of these laws were rarely carried out, and influential Jews or Christians always found means of evading the others"; and (c) "nevertheless, there is no doubt that in the period of the caliphate, more poignantly than ever before, the Jews felt themselves disparaged as 'infidels.' . . . The foundations were then laid for the ghetto, the badge and the oath *more judaico*. But"—and now he reassures his reader— (d) "in the oriental mode of life, as well as in the popular view, these signs of segregation never possessed the degrading character which they assumed in Christian Europe in the later Middle Ages."

Read now, almost a century after Baron penned this section, we are struck by how much our own terminology and categories of historical analysis have changed. His "orientalism," his essentialized characterization of the mentality of the Islamic world, grates on our ear when he tells us that the "erotically minded Orient" frequently allowed for "free sexual relationships between Muslims and Christians." This problem is compounded when we read his rather naive assurance about the effectiveness of rabbinic rule when he adds in a note that of course, "the rabbis seemed to have kept [such sexual activities] out of Jewish life with much greater efficacy" (III: 77n3).

So what do we have here? Following the demands of his mission—to survey *all* of Jewish history—Baron has been forced to overgeneralize with simplistic characterizations of entire societies over many eras and in many lands. He has opted for the ethnographic rhetoric of his time. He has had not only to oversimplify; in this densely written combination of erudition and generalization, he has had to carefully, as the Yiddishism would have it, "dance at two weddings." He presented Islam as more tolerant than Christianity and as the ultimate source of later Christian intolerance.

But let us now turn to the footnotes. It is there that we learn what lies behind Baron's narrative. We will look at only one of the three notes to this section. It consists of eighty-five lines in a tiny typeface (III: 76n2). In it Baron explains that the political situation of Jews under Muslim domination is still obscure. He emphasizes that historical change and geographic dispersion inevitably means that generalizations are weak. He recommends further reading, referring his readers, for example, to five volumes of a journal published in Hyderabad, India, and he admits that "much detailed research will still be needed . . . to reconcile the frequently contradictory evidence." He explains the difficulty of assessing the origins and significance of the Pact of Omar, surveys what had been done in many different works on the political and legal status of Jews in various countries, and goes

FIGURE 2.1. Jewish historians in the office of the Jewish Section at an international historical congress, Warsaw, 1933: (left to right) Ignacy Schiper, Abraham Duker, Emanuel Ringelblum, Raphael Mahler, Salo W. Baron, Me'ir Halevi, Majer Bałaban, M. Stein, and an unidentified participant.
From the archives of the YIVO Institute for Jewish Research, New York.

on to list the work then available about Jews living outside the caliphate—in India, for example. There are even treatments of the Falashas and the Khazars. In other words, Baron's *Social and Religious History* is actually two books: one narrative and one scholarly. It is in the footnotes that the timbre of Baron's scholarly achievement is to be most clearly viewed.

To focus on footnotes and bibliography is in no way is to minimize Baron's accomplishment. I can report from personal experience that working on some small and, even to my mind, specialized or even arcane theme, if I glance at Baron's remarks on the topic and at his footnote, I will not only find a rich treasure trove of references that I haven't yet seen but will also realize that he had understood the ins and outs of the scholarly debate in a comprehensive and illuminating manner that is still enlightening. Arthur Hertzberg, one of Baron's students, reported the same sense of astonishment at Baron's erudition and grasp of issues. He described devoting a year to preparing to work on his dissertation topic, but when he went to discuss his topic with Baron, the latter easily added considerable further information of which Hertzberg had not been aware.[74]

Baron began his scholarly publishing career as a modernist with two books on nineteenth-century topics. While he worked on the three-volume *History*, he managed also to publish at least twenty-two studies in four languages. These ranged from scholarly book reviews to a detailed overview of the violent attacks against Jews in Damascus (1860), from studies of Renaissance and modern Jewish historiography to reports and historicizing contextualizations of current Jewish affairs. In the following years he would maintain this pace of publishing, producing articles as well as pathbreaking books on topics such as the structure of Jewish communities down to the end of the eighteenth century[75] and *The Russian Jew Under Tsars and Soviets* (1964).[76] But at least from 1952, Baron became ever more focused on a single project: revising the global history of the Jewish people that he had begun almost inadvertently when he first came to Columbia. He spent almost forty years producing no less than eighteen volumes covering everything from the biblical to the Talmudic, the medieval to the early modern. Ironically, he would never manage to cover modern Jewish history, the period with which he had begun his scholarly career.

Baron was enormously proud of his accomplishment, remarking in the introduction to volume 13 (1969) that rumors had reached his ears from as far away as Australia that he employed a team of researchers. All the work, he insisted, was his own, his only helpmate his wife, Jeannette, who had first come to him for advice on her dissertation topic and had stayed on to become his wife and editor. In prefaces to various volumes, he insisted as well that he had actually read every one of the thousands of sources he cited. In the introduction to volume 3 of the first edition, for example, he goes out of his way to emphasize that he had "made use of all publications here listed." Self-consciously, he had marked with a dagger (†) the "twenty monographs which were inaccessible to him, but which he nevertheless wish[ed] to bring to the reader's attention."[77] In such scrupulous honesty one can feel his awareness of, and pride in, what he had accomplished. And yet, there was an implicit limitation to this magnificent accomplishment. Baron's astonishing erudition turned a life-long project to summarize and contextualize the history of the Jews into a *bibliographie raisonée*, a reference work that became simply too big to be consumed and, moreover, was fated to be out of date as soon as it was published.

Baron was aware of the bibliographical challenge. In July 1940, he devoted issue 3 of volume 2 of a journal he had established and edited,

Jewish Social Studies, to an eighty-three-page bibliography of more than 3,500 works that he felt were relevant to the social history of the Jews and that had appeared in 1938–39 (that is, after the first edition of the *Social and Religious History* appeared). That bibliography was then republished in 1941 as a stand-alone volume, accompanied in best Baronian fashion by additions and an index. It was apparently intended as the first in a regular series, although the experiment would never be repeated.[78] Even so, Baron would never let go of the dream, as the enormous and never-completed second edition of the *Social and Religious History* demonstrates. Arthur Hertzberg reported that when Baron and his wife had asked him to continue the project, he—that is, Hertzberg—had protested that he did not have the erudition—indeed, that no one did.[79]

Baron's effort to organize all of the Jewish past would be taken over by databases and search engines, by computerized and connected library catalogues, by databases of scanned journals and out-of-copyright books, by RAMBI and HebrewBooks.org and academia.edu. The explosion of knowledge of which we are the beneficiaries and the victims today has not trivialized but expanded and built upon Baron's project. Inevitably, the advantages of new tools and methods of bibliographic retrieval have meant that something was also lost. They are no longer the product of a single astonishing intellectual. Our databases are repositories rather than guides, and we have lost something in that. But there seems to have been no choice. The age of the printed, cumulative list would seem to be over, whether we are speaking about the AHA's guide or Baron's *Social and Religious History*, not because these weren't astonishingly good but simply because there is always too much more to be included!

Among the several accolades on Salo Baron's tombstone, we read that he was the "founder of modern Jewish Studies." This is at least a problematic statement; as we have seen, the field was constructed by a range of scholars in many different parts of the world. Even when we focus on Columbia itself, the assertion ignores the foundational efforts of Richard Gottheil. Even the claim emphasized in university publications that Baron held the first chair in Jewish history at a secular university is true only in the technical sense that Harry Wolfson's position at Harvard, established four years earlier, was officially dedicated to "Hebrew Literature and Philosophy" rather than "Jewish History, Literature and Institutions." Still, Baron does have a claim to a foundational role, first through the many students whom he trained over the years, and perhaps even more so through his magnum opus, the eighteen volumes of the *Social and Religious History of the Jews*. When Baron's biographer, Robert Liberles, called him the "architect of Jewish history," it was surely because of this monumental academic project. Even though the book remained unfinished, it has earned Baron the title of founding father, the scholar who single-handedly made Jewish studies accessible within the broad expanse of western historical studies.

Baron's accomplishment can be appreciated if we step outside the realm of Jewish studies for a moment and consider a tale of such historical projects in another society. In his 1983 novel, *Silent House*, Nobel laureate Orhan Pamuk has provided us with two memorable but depressing pictures of modern historical studies.[80] Pamuk, a member of the Columbia faculty who, I am told, has a brother who is a historian, speaks of two Turkish scholars facing modernity. First there is Selahattin Bey, an exiled and alienated encyclopedist who seeks to enlighten his countrymen by translating for them accounts of the glorious march of scientific progress and giving them a broader context for their cultural specificity. And then there is his son Faruk, an alcoholic academic historian who endlessly copies details from forgotten archival documents into a notebook. The work of both men is ultimately futile. The pages of the father's encyclopedia are burned by his widow as heretical and threatening; Faruk's notebook ends up being discarded by a teenage vandal. I mention Pamuk's novel here to remind us that the modernizing intellectual exercise of academic history is never guaranteed success. But working within the institutional framework of Columbia University, Salo Baron did succeed in laying a strong foundation for both an academic field and for the public enthusiasm that has sustained it for decades.

Even though Baron chose to study the past, his historical oeuvre—the *Social and Religious History of the Jews* as well as the many other articles and journals he produced over the years—was never mere nostalgia. His work was a series of consciously molded and acute responses to current intellectual and pedagogical challenges. In his magnum opus, Baron was seeking to address the questions and problems of his time and place. Our needs have changed and our conception of knowledge and authority have evolved. It is not yet clear what tools we have developed to address the altered circumstances of learning. People today speak of the academic humanities being in crisis. Salo Baron's unceasing efforts reveal just how much work has always been required to turn the records of the past into meaningful narratives for the future.

NOTES

1. The working files for the autobiographical project are currently stored with the rest of Baron's papers in the library at Stanford University, marked as Boxes 579 and 580. A section was published as a "keepsake" to mark the acquisition of Baron's library and archive by Stanford: *Under Two Civilizations: Tarnów, 1895–1914; Selected from the Memoirs of Salo Wittmayer Baron* (Stanford, CA: Stanford University, 1990). Baron also contributed "A Memoir of My Library" as an introduction to David L. Langenberg, ed., *Of Many Generations: Judaica and Hebraica from the Taube-Baron Collection* (Stanford, CA: Stanford University Libraries, 1989), 17–21, reprinted in *Tablet* magazine, September 8, 2015 (https://www.tabletmag.com/sections/arts-letters/articles/a-memoir-of-my-library). No doubt the large collection of Baron's correspondence and records preserved at Stanford would yield a great deal more information. See, for example, Zachary M. Baker, "The Landscape of Jewish Studies, 1930–55; Gleanings from Salo W. Baron's Correspondence," in *The Enduring Legacy of Salo W. Baron*, ed. Hava Tirosh-Rothschild and Edward Dąbrowa (Kraków: Jagiellonian University Press, 2017), 227–43. Historian Robert Liberles's *Salo Wittmayer Baron, Architect of Jewish History* (New York: New York University Press, 1995) remains the outstanding effort to reconstruct Baron's work, life, and career based on direct study of archival materials, interviews with the historian, and careful evaluation of his publications.

    On the genre of historians' autobiographies and the problematics of interpreting them, see the enlightening explorations by Jeremy D. Popkin, "Historians on the Autobiographical Frontier," *AHR* 104, no. 3 (June 1999): 725–48; and "History, Historians, and Autobiography Revisited," *a/b: Auto/Biography Studies* 32, no. 3 (2017): 693–98.

2. I would like to thank Dr. Eitan Lev Kensky, Reinhard Family Curator of Judaica and Hebraica Collections at Stanford, as well as the digital archival staff there for their help in accessing both sets of videos and helping me understand what is available. The Potok interviews were conducted as part of an oral history project sponsored by the American Jewish Committee. Audio cassettes are stored at the New York Public Library (https://catalog.nypl.org/record=b14998587~S98); I thank Dr. Lyudmila Sholokhova, Curator of the Dorot Jewish Collection, for help in locating them. I have relied on these tapes for a sense of Baron's self-understanding but have not cited them directly, in part because I have not had access to the originals. Moreover, it is not always clear how much of what is said is a reflection of the interviewers' assumptions. Ankori, for example, had his own memories of Tarnów. His father, Aazik Wróbel, was the live-in tutor for the teenage Baron over many years, and Ankori himself was born in Tarnów in 1920, six years after Baron had left, and grew up there until leaving for Palestine in 1937. See Zvi Ankori, *Chestnuts of Yesteryear: A Jewish Odyssey* (Jerusalem: Gefen, 2003). Ankori's own strongly Zionist terminologies further intrude to shape the questions and prompts he uses with his teacher. On the other hand, Chaim Potok's questions reflect an American Jewish set of assumptions, and Baron, visibly tired during much of the interview, sometimes seems able to respond only very briefly, not fully explaining why Potok's terms or questions were misplaced or misguided.

3. Arthur Hertzberg, "Salo W. Baron and the Writing of Modern Jewish History: Speculations in Honor of His Centennial," in *Writing a Modern Jewish History: Essays in Honor of Salo W. Baron*, ed. Barbara Kirshenblatt-Gimblett (New York: Columbia University Press, 2006), 10–24:11.
4. Shoshana Baron Tancer, "The Baron Family: A Personal Perspective," in *Enduring Legacy*, 39–45. I thank Ms. Tancer and her sister, Tobey Baron Gitelle, for sharing memories of their father.
5. Cecil Roth, "Shalom Baron," *Ha-Enziklopedia ha-Ivrit* 9 [in Hebrew] (1958), coll. 519–20.
6. It is not difficult to find exuberant encomia about Baron's centrality to the establishment and shaping of the field of Jewish historical studies in America. See, for example, Michael T. Ryan, ("creator of the discipline of Jewish Studies in America"), "Preface," in *Of Many Generations*, 9; Hava Tirosh-Samuelson, ("the most prominent Jewish historian in the twentieth century"), "Editor's Introduction; A Tribute to Salo W. Baron," in *Enduring Legacy*, 9; Liberles, *Baron, Architect of Jewish History*. For a discussion of the "iconic" status of Baron's view of Jewish history, see David Engel, "Crisis and Lachrymosity: On Salo Baron, Neobaroniansm, and the Study of Modern European Jewish History," *Jewish History* 20 (2006): 243–64. But also see Engel's "Salo Baron and Poland: The Limits of Influence," in *Enduring Legacy*, 191–99.
7. Theodore S. Hamerow, "The Professionalization of Historical Learning," *Reviews in American History* 14, no.3 (September 1986): 319–33, a chapter in the author's more comprehensive work of *Reflections on History and Historians* (Madison: University of Wisconsin Press, 1987). How such professionalization was related to the move of Jewish studies from the context of rabbinical seminaries into secular universities is one of the underlying questions of our exploration.
8. The data are taken from Rachel Manekin, "Being Jewish in *Fin de siècle* Galicia: The View from Salo Baron's Memoir," in *Enduring Legacy*, 81–98, an excellent introduction to the cultural complexity of the Galician Jewish world in which Baron grew up. On Jews at the university, see also in the same volume, Edyta Gawron, "Salo W. Baron at Jagiellonian University," 69–80.
9. Zvi Scharfstein, the future "entrepreneur" of Hebrew teaching in the United States, moved to Tarnów to teach Hebrew in the years preceding World War I. There he bonded with Brandstätter, and he reports that the two spent many wonderful hours together. In 1914, Scharfstein was recruited to prepare a biographical sketch of the older man for the community festivities in honor of Brandstätter's seventieth birthday (the occasion that was presumably also the inspiration for Baron's article cited in the next note). At Scharfstein's request, Brandstätter jotted down some autobiographical notes which survived the war, made their way to New York, and were eventually published in the New York Hebrew-language journal, *Ha-Doar* under the title, *Mi-Toldot Hayyai* (vol. 12, 134–35, and vol. 20, 364–65). The same journal also published columns of aphorisms and quips by the now elderly, and somewhat passé, Galician writer, under the title "Kismim" (vols. 18–32). Brandstätter's notes offer a wonderful case study in the various strands of learning and experience that created the small-town Galician *maskil* of his era and deserve to be translated.

10. *Ha-Tzefira*, Warsaw, nos. 94 and 95, (April 24–25, 1914). On Brandstätter's life, see *Yivo Encyclopedia of Jews in Eastern Europe*, https://yivoencyclopedia.org/article. aspx/Brandstetter_Mordekhai_David, accessed July 20, 2021, as well as the entry in the Hebrew Wikipedia, s.v. Baron also contributed to a lengthy obituary about the author, "*Al Kever* Mordekhai David Brandstetter *z.l.*," *Ha-Do'ar* 8, no. 28: 440–41. Recent literary scholarship on Brandstätter is surveyed in Avner Holtzman, "Mordekhai David Brandstetter: A *Maskil* Beyond His Time," *Studia Judaica* 35 (2015): 9–33, translated in Holtzman's Hebrew collection, *Ad Halom: Tahanot ba-Sifrut ha-Ivrit* (Jerusalem: Carmel, 2016), 30–47.
11. Hayim Nahman Bialik coined the phrase to describe the contribution of Sholom Yankev Abramowitch (Mendele Mokher Seforim) to the development of modern Hebrew literature. "Yotzer ha-Nusah," https://benyehuda.org/read/6964, accessed July 21, 2021.
12. In later years Baron made a point, whenever he was in Israel, of paying a personal visit to the elderly scholar. Joseph Umansky (1860–1965) is nowadays best remembered for his series of learned studies of Talmudic authorities (*Hakhamei ha-Talmud* [Tarnów, 1929 and 1931; Jerusalem, Mosad Ha-Rav Kuk, 1949–52). But at the time, he was known for establishing a number of the new type of schools, first in Ukraine and later in Galicia. He weathered World War I in Vienna and then returned to Tarnów until he left for Palestine in 1934. On Umansky, see https://isheiisrael.wordpress.com/2021/01/05/רבי-יוסף-אומנסקי/, accessed July 21, 2021. The *heder me-tukan* (improved elementary school) approach to Jewish education was associated with the Zionist excitement in eastern Europe from the end of the nineteenth century. On the politics and curriculum of the *heder metukan* approach (or, as it was referred to by its ultra-Orthodox opponents, using the Ashkenazic pronunciation, the *heder mesukan* [חדר מסוכן]), see Yossi Goldstein, "*Ha-Heder ha-Metukan be-Rusiya ke-Vasis le-Ma'arekhet ha-Hinukh ha-Tziyonit*," *Iyunim be-Hinukh* 45 (1986): 145–67, https://lib.toldot.cet.ac.il/pages/sub.asp?author=2259. Zvi Scharfstein who, as we mentioned, had come to Tarnów to teach modern Hebrew, summarized simply: "The nationalist movement created the *heder ha-metukan* that spread quickly throughout Russia and Poland, introducing new procedures and a new spirit, enlivening the Hebrew language in the mouths of thousands of students." *Ha-Heder be-Hayyei Ameinu* [*The Heder in the Life of the Jewish People*] (New York: Shiloh, 1943; 2nd ed. Tel-Aviv: Elisha, 1951), 224.
13. On Baron's linguistic identity and its relation to the nature of Jewish nationalist self-expression in the Galician context, see Marsha Rozenblit, "A Zionist Who Spoke Hebrew: Salo Baron in Vienna," in *Enduring Legacy*, 99–114. More generally, see Joshua Shanes, *Diaspora Nationalism and Jewish Identity in Habsburg Galicia* (Cambridge: Cambridge University Press, 2012).
14. On the background to this industry and Jewish participation in it, see Valerie Schatzker, *The Jewish Oil Magnates of Galicia: A History 1853–1945* (Montreal: McGill-Queen's University Press, 2015).
15. On Rabbi Joseph Engel, and the dynamics of his positions in Tarnów and Krakow, see the extensive biographical essay by his grandson, David Morgenstern, published together with Engel's *She'erit Yosef* (Tel Aviv: 1980)
16. Samuel Hirsch (Scemuel Zevi) Margulies, a graduate of the Breslau Jewish *Hochschule* and of the University of Leipzig in philosophy and Semitics, was at first

ORGANIZING THE JEWISH PAST FOR AMERICAN STUDENTS

a controversial choice when he was appointed rabbi of the modernizing Jewish community of Florence in 1890. See Lionella Viterbo, "La nomina del rabbino Margulies: Un 'excursus' nella Firenze ebraica di fine ottocento," *La Rassegna Mensile di Israel*, ser. III, vol. 59, no. 3 (September-December 1993): 67–89. But the power of his personality and the influence of his spiritual leadership were not to be doubted, especially from 1899, when the Collegio Rabbinico Italiano was transferred to the city on the Arno and reopened there under his direction. His rigorous academic methodologies and spiritual influence left a lasting impression on a generation of young Italian Jewish intellectuals. Elizabeth Schächter, *The Jews of Italy, 1848–1915* (London: Vallentine Mitchell, 2011), chap. 6, "A Jewish Renaissance," 206–30.

17. On the Vienna seminaries as well as the various attempts that led up to their establishment, see Peter Landesmann, *Rabbiner aus Wien: Ihre Ausbildung, ihre religiösen und nationalen Konflikte* (Vienna: Böhlau Verlag, 1997). Still useful is N. M. Gelber, "Toldot Beit ha-Midrash le-Rabanim be-Vina," in *Mosdot Torah be-Eyropa be-Vinyanam u-ve-Hurbanam* [Jewish Institutions of Higher Learning in Europe, Their Development and Destruction], ed. S. K. Mirsky (New York: Ogen Publishing House of the Histadruth Ivrith of America, 1956), 715–30. The older Vienna Beit Hamidrasch, established by rabbi and scholar Adolf Jellinek in 1863, was still functioning when Baron came to Vienna, but with limited financial resources, it was unable to attract more than a handful of students.

18. The size of the student body can be gauged by consulting the school's *Jahresberichte*, or annual reports (https://catalog.hathitrust.org/Record/100608880) which list the students as well as their place of origin (the overwhelming majority were from Galicia). During the war years, lists include students who were unable to attend classes because they had been caught behind enemy lines. *Sefer ha-Zikaron le-Veit ha-Midrash le-Rabanim be-Vina* (Jerusalem: Reuben Mass, 1946), lists 335 students (including 200 from Galicia), 72–82.

19. The Hungarian-born Schwarz (1846–1931) was a graduate of the Breslau *Jüdisch-theologisches Seminar*, where he had reportedly been the favorite pupil and then close friend of its founding principal, Zechariah Frankel. A prolific author, Schwarz made important contributions to the textual and methodological study of early rabbinic *halakha* as well as to the methodology underlying Moses Maimonides's code, the *Mishneh Torah*. On Schwarz, see the relevant entry in *Encyclopaedia Judaica*, ed. Michael Berenbaum and Fred Skolnik, 2nd ed., (2007), as well as Meir Waxman, "Prof. Aryeh Schwarz" [in Hebrew], in *Hokhmat Yisrael be-Ma'arav Eyropa*, [I], ed. Simon Federbusch (Jerusalem: M. Nyuman, 1958), 482–490.

20. Jacob Mann, "Modern Rabbinical Seminaries and Other Institutions of Jewish Learning," *Yearbook of the Central Conference of American Rabbis* 35 (1925): 295–310 provides a useful overview of when and why these schools were established. The schools of western and central Europe are part of the same network of scholarship as similar institutions in major centers in the United States, a point that is only now being investigated. See *From Breslau to Jerusalem: Rabbinical Seminaries Past, Present and Future* [in Hebrew], ed. Guy Miron (Jerusalem: Schechter Institute of Jewish Studies and Leo Baeck Institute, 2009). The government-sponsored schools in tsarist Russia displayed a somewhat different dynamic; see, for example, Michael Stanislawski, *Tsar Nicholas I and the Jews: The Transformation of Jewish Society in Russia 1825–1855* (Philadelphia: Jewish Publication Society, 1983), 103ff.

21. Salo Baron, "*Israelitisch-theologische Lehranstalt*," in *Encyclopedia Judaica* 2, 10, 754–55; the article was written for the first edition of that encyclopaedia (1972). Baron was proud of the school whose alumni, he stressed, "serve in high positions in the rabbinate and schools of higher learning in Europe and the U.S. as well as in Israel." See also his *A Social and Religious History of the Jews* (New York: Columbia University Press, 1937), II, 258–59 and n30 *ad loc*.
22. On Wissenschaft generally, see Ismar Schorsch, *From Text to Context: The Turn to History in Modern Judaism* (Hanover: Brandeis University Press, 1994). For the specific issues driving the field when Baron began his studies, see Paul Mendes-Flohr, "*Wissenschaft des Judentums* at the Fin-de-Siècle," in *Jewish Historiography Between Past and Future: 200 Years of* Wissenschaft des Judentums, ed. Paul Mendes-Flohr, Rachel Livneh-Freudenthal, and Guy Miron (Berlin: Walter de Gruyter, 2019), 163–79. (The volume grew out of a conference held in Israel in 2018. Videos of the introductory presentations and several of the papers are available on YouTube at "200 Years of Wissenschaft des Judentums: Historiography, Ideology and the Challenge of a Usable Past," https://www.youtube.com/watch?v=D2nYw3afcH0). Still to be explored is the complex cultural interplay between the work of the faculties' "intellectual specialists" and the ambitions of the "laity"—the boards of directors and donors who supported these schools. For a fascinating glimpse into this for Berlin, see Christoph Schmidt, "A Voyage in the Enchanted House: A Family History from the Personal Perspective," *Jewish Historiography Between Past and Future*, 127–61.
23. "The Needs of Jewish Scholarship in America," *Menorah Journal* 7 (1921): 28–35. Writing just after the devastation and dislocation of World War I, Wolfson had become convinced that only American Jewry was in a position to accomplish the task, but the scholarly task that he described was, *mutatis mutandis*, already outlined by Leopold Zunz a century earlier in his *Etwas über die rabbinische Litteratur* (Berlin: Maurersche Buchhandlung, 1818), the pamphlet generally credited with initiating Wissenschaft des Judentums. (A partial translation by James Redfield is available in *Classic Essays in Early Rabbinic Culture and History*, ed. Christine Hayes [New York: Routledge, 2018], 27–42.) Quoting here specifically from Wolfson (whose career overlapped with Baron's at several points) is meant to highlight the continuity of Wissenschaft's focus on textual study. Although Baron will, as we shall see, move in a different direction, he never lost sight of the importance of the codicological and bibliographical study in which he was trained. See, for example, D. S. Loevinger on the distinguished codicologist and bibliographer Arthur Zachariah Schwarz, son of Baron's teacher Adolf Schwarz; *Hokhmat Yisrael be-Ma'arav Eyropa*, [II], ed. Simon Federbusch (Jerusalem: M. Nyuman, 1963), 257–64; and Baron's own preface to the expanded edition of the younger Schwarz's *Die hebräischen Handschriften in Österreich (ausserhalb der Nationalbibliothek in Wien)*, vols. IIa and IIb (New York: American Academy for Jewish Research, 1973), vii–ix.
24. Avraham Yaakov Braver, *Zikhronot Av u-Vno* (Jerusalem: 1966), here quoted from the excerpt in Asaf Yedidya, *Batei Midrash Nusah Ashkenaz: Zikhronot shel Bogrei ha-Seminarim le-Rabanim be-Germaniya u-ve-Ostria* [*Ashkenazi Batei Midrash: Memoirs of Graduates of Rabbinical Seminaries in Germany and Austria*] (Jerusalem: Carmel, 2010), 306. Brawer (1884–1975), a native of Lwow (Lemberg), attended the Lehranstalt between 1905 and 1909, where he was a classmate of,

ORGANIZING THE JEWISH PAST FOR AMERICAN STUDENTS

among others, future linguist and biblical scholar Harry Torczyner (Naphtali Zvi Tur-Sinai). While still a teenager in Lwow, Brawer was part of the circle of budding eastern Galician Hebraists that met at the home of Eliezer Meir Lifshitz, a future noted educator in Palestine and Israel. That circle included Zionist writer and social critic Joshua Rader-Feldmann (Rabbi Binyamin), future Nobel laureate Shmuel Yosef Czaczkes (Shai Agnon), and linguist Hanokh Distenfeld (later, Yalon); Brawer's memorial note for Lifshitz as "Man, Teacher, and Principal" in *Ha-Tzofeh* (July 6, 1956): 5.

25. Aptowitzer, a Galician from Tarnopol who studied at the University of Vienna and the Lehranstalt from 1899, served Baron as a personal model and mentor. In the memorial note that Baron wrote (with Michael Higger) for the *Proceedings of the American Academy for Jewish Research* 13 (1943): xii–xiii, his admiration for his teacher's abilities, kindness, and fortitude are clear. Indeed, there are suggestions that during the years of Baron's study there, the Lehranstalt found itself in somewhat tenuous circumstances. Baron records that it was Aptowitzer's dedication to his alma mater that saved it, because in 1915, the scholar had turned down an attractive offer from Hebrew Union College in Cincinnati in order to help the Viennese institution stay afloat.

26. George Y. Kohler has helped to put twentieth-century scholarship on kabbalah into better context in his *Kabbalah Research in the Wissenschaft des Judentums (1820–1880): The Foundation of an Academic Discipline* (Berlin: De Gruyter Oldenbourg, 2019). See especially "Epilog—the Years 1894–1907." On Scholem's early turn to mysticism see David Biale, *Gershom Scholem: Kabbalah and Counter-History*, 2nd rev. ed. (Cambridge, MA: Harvard University Press, 1982), 28–34, and David N. Myers, *Re-Inventing the Jewish Past: European Intellectuals and the Zionist Return to History* (New York: Oxford University Press, 1995), 155–57.

27. In 1942, a ceremony was held at New York's Congregation Shearith Israel to mark the four hundred fiftieth anniversary of the arrival of Jews in North America. The congregation's rabbi, David de Sola Pool, expressed some compunction at allowing Baron to speak from the pulpit on the grounds that the professor was not ordained. Baron "happily" assured the rabbi, as he put it, "that I was the recipient of a formal ordination from the Jewish Theological Seminary of Vienna which actually included the characteristic words *yore yore, yadin yadin* (He may teach and judge)." Baron, "Reply to Professor Abraham Karp's Address," *American Jewish History* 71, no. 4 (June 1982): 497. The year of Baron's ordination is shown in the interview Baron gave to Professor Dora Askowith when he was appointed at Columbia; "Teaching Jewish History," *Jewish Tribune* (February 14, 1930): 2–3.

28. See, for example, the observations of Abraham Brawer about Professor Heinrich Tzvi Müller, who was then teaching at both the Lehranstalt and the University of Vienna; Yedidya, *Batei Midrash*, 307.

29. Yosef Hayim Yerushalmi, *Zakhor: Jewish History and Jewish Memory* (Seattle: University of Washington Press, 1982), 86. This phrase, which has been picked up and emphasized in many treatments of Yerushalmi's work, has taken on, I believe, far greater existential, cultural, and explanatory force than even Yerushalmi meant for it. It implies, as well, a sharp rupture of identity far more intense than might have actually been experienced by most Jews, including those intellectuals devoted to Jewish historical study.

30. There was inevitably gossip within the intimate world of Jewish studies in New York City about the level of Baron's personal religious observance and speculation about whether, for example, he daily donned phylacteries. See *Communings of the Spirit: The Journals of Mordecai M. Kaplan, Volume 1: 1913–1934*, ed. Mel Scult (Detroit: Wayne State University Press, 2001–20), vol. I, entry for April 10, 1932, 474. (My thanks to Daniel Cedarbaum, executive director, Mordecai M. Kaplan Center for Jewish Peoplehood, for this reference.) For the comments of Baron's daughter, Shoshana Tancer, I draw from her personal correspondence with me, November 29, 2020, as well as from her presentation, "The Baron Family," 39–45.
31. Rozenblit, "A Zionist Who Spoke Hebrew," 107. When interviewed by Ankori, Baron jokingly complained that he was constantly drafted by his fellows to hold office in the various Zionist clubs they formed. His active roles in "Theologia" (the student organization of the Lehranstalt) and "Hatechijah" (the Zionist student association in Vienna) is confirmed by newspaper announcements in the contemporary Viennese Jewish press—for example *Dr Blochs Oesterreichische Wochenschrift* available at http://sammlungen.ub.uni-frankfurt.de/cm/id/3020846.
32. Baron's insistence on state support as necessary for Jewish cultural survival is an important, and underappreciated, element in his famous 1928 article, "Ghetto and Emancipation: Shall We Revise the Traditional View?" *Menorah Journal* 14 (June 1928): 515–26. On this, see my "Reframing Time to Save the Nation: The Jewish Historian as Cultural Trickster," in *Chronologics*, ed. Barbara Mittler et al. (Heidelberg: Heidelberg University Publishing, forthcoming).
33. See Askowith, "Teaching Jewish History."
34. Fournier was then in ill health (he died in 1920), but he was very supportive of his young student and sponsored him for membership in the university's Historical Institute. Baron remembered the appointment fondly because it had provided not only a stipend but also a warm library in which to work and read otherwise banned foreign newspapers during the difficult years of the war.
35. *Die Judenfrage auf dem Wiener Kongress* (Vienna: Löwit Verlag, 1920). One cannot help thinking of the famous joke about the biology professor who assigned his class a research project on the elephant. The Jewish student wrote about "The Elephant and the Jewish Question." This joke, which makes no sense to my students nowadays, was ubiquitous in the earlier twentieth century for good reason: it evoked Jews' overwhelming concern about their unstable legal, political, and social status and assumed that every academic investigation, no matter how distant, would be turned in that direction. An enlightening discussion of the joke's not-trivial implications for constitutional practice in the United States introduces the 1994 Harris Lecture given by Professor Martha Minow at the Indiana University School of Law-Bloomington, published as "The Constitution and the Subgroup Question," *Indiana Law Journal* 71, no. 1 (Winter 1975): 1–25.
36. *Die Politische Theorie Ferdinand Lassalles* published as volume 2 of the *Archiv für Geschichte des Sozialismus und der Arbeiterbewegung* (Leipzig: C. L. Hirschfeld, 1923), a publication series directed by Baron's teacher, Grünberg.
37. Salo Baron, "Ferdinand Lassalle the Jew," *Ha-Tekufah* 23 (1925): 347–62.
38. *Galizien: wie es an Österreich kam: eine historisch-statistische Studie über di inneren Verhältnisse des Landes im Jahre 1772* (Leipzig: Freytag, 1910); "Ha-Keysar Yosef ha-Sheni vi-Yehudei Galitziya," *Ha-Shiloah* 23 (1910). The book was translated

into Hebrew and published, together with the article and two other studies on the Frankist movement that appeared in *Ha-Shiloah*, 33 and 38 (1918 and 1921) in *Galitziya vi-Yhudeha: Mehkarim be-Toldot Galitziya ba-Me'a ha-18* (Jerusalem: Mosad Bialik, 1956).

39. William O. McCagg, *A History of Habsburg Jews, 1670–1918* (Bloomington: Indiana University Press, 1989), 277f, mentions Helene Kohn, "*Beiträge zur Geschichte der Juden in Österreich unter Kaiser Joseph II*" (1919); Leib Weissberg, "*Die Judenemanzipation und die österrischische Reichsverfassung von 1849*" (1921); Menasche Josef Friedler, "*Die galizischen Juden vom wirtscharftlichen, kulturellen und staatbürgerlichen Standpunkt, 1815–48,*" (1923); and Rudolf Leitner, "*Die Judenpolitik der österreichischen Regierung in den Jahren 1848–1859,*" (1924). I have not been able to determine whether any of these writers were simultaneously students at the Lehranstalt. McCagg's list shows that the pattern would continue during the early 1930s.

40. Mahler's call is quoted from the introduction to his *A History of Modern Jewry 1780–1815* (New York: Schocken, 1971), xi.

41. In the paper he contributed to *Sefer Refael Mahler* (*Studies in Jewish History Presented to Professor Raphael Mahler on his Seventy-Fifth Birthday*), ed. Sh. Yeivin (Merhavia, Israel: Sifriat Poalim, 1974), 78, Baron notes that the two men had "first met at the International Congress of Historical Sciences at Warsaw in 1933."

42. On this development, see most recently Natalia Aleksiun, *Conscious History: Polish Jewish Historians Before the Holocaust* (Liverpool: Littman Library of Jewish Civilization in association with Liverpool University Press, 2021).

43. Salo Baron, "The Study of Jewish History," *Jewish Institute Quarterly* 4, no. 2 (January 1928): 7–14 summarizes the advice he gave to students in these early years of his teaching the United States. See also his recommendations for student research, cited in note 66.

44. They might have been responding as well to the efforts by more traditionally observant Jews to expand the "Jewish Theological Seminary and Scientific Institution" in these years. The focus on introducing Jewish studies at a secular university like Columbia nevertheless highlights a significant difference between the American and European models for the study of religion.

45. "The People in the Books: Hebraica and Judaica Manuscripts from Columbia University Libraries," https://exhibitions.library.columbia.edu/exhibits/show/hebrew_mss/scholars/nyda_1963_002_01873.

46. Shuly Rubin Schwartz, *The Emergence of Jewish Scholarship in America: The Publication of the* Jewish Encyclopedia (Cincinnati: Hebrew Union College Press, 1991). On the growth of nineteenth-century Jewish studies and Wissenschaft des Judentums, see above, note 22.

47. Paul Ritterband and Harold Wechsler, *Jewish Learning in American Universities: The First Century* (Bloomington: Indiana University Press, 1994), 85ff., treats Gottheil's active role in the politics of establishing Jewish studies in the United States and at Columbia. His part in establishing the Miller Chair and bringing Baron to Columbia is treated in chap. 7, 150–71. On Gottheil's scholarship and teaching, see the memorial minute by Joshua Bloch, *Journal of the American Oriental Society* 56, no. 4 (December 1936): 472–79, accompanied by the nine-page

"Selected Bibliography" of Gottheil's writing prepared by his assistant at the New York Public Library, Ida Pratt (480–89). The "Biographical Sketch" by Louis Newman prepared for the *American Jewish Year Book* 39 (1937 [for 5698]): 29–46, is especially useful in providing a sense of Gottheil's activities with students and outside of academe. A festschrift prepared to honor Gottheil's seventieth birthday was never published because of the economic collapse of the Great Depression. Gottheil's papers are stored at the American Jewish Archives; see the finding aid at http://collections.americanjewisharchives.org/ms/ms0127/ms0127.html, accessed July 21, 2021. Francis Kelsey's careful preface to *Fragments from the Cairo Genizah in the Freer Collection*, ed. Richard Gottheil and William H. Worrell (New York: Macmillan, 1927), v–vi, provides a sense of the challenges to Jewish studies and the difficulties of collaborative scholarship in this era.

48. Hertz, who immigrated to the United States at age twelve, received his undergraduate training at New York City College. His Columbia doctoral dissertation, *The Ethical System of James Martineau*, appeared as vol. 1, no. 3, of the series "Columbia College Contributions to Philosophy, Psychology and Education" (1894). On Hertz, see Harvey Warren Meirovich, *A Vindication of Judaism: The Polemics of the Hertz Pentateuch* (New York: Jewish Theological Seminary, 1998), especially chap. 1; Derek Taylor, *Chief Rabbi Hertz: The Wars of the Lord* (London: Vallentine Mitchell, 2014); and the brief article by Benjamin J. Elton, "A Bridge Across the Tigris: Chief Rabbi Joseph Herman Hertz," *Conversations* 21 (Winter, 2015): 67–81, https://www.jewishideas.org/article/bridge-across-tigris-chief-rabbi-joseph-herman-hertz, accessed July 21, 2021.

49. Wise refused the offer of the pulpit at Temple Emanu-El because its board would not promise him the liberty to speak as he wished on contemporary issues. His refusal "to be muzzled" was covered in detail in the *New York Times*, January 7, 1906, 5.

50. The tale of Stephen Wise's educational career provides a fascinating window on the dynamics of Jewish intellectualism in New York City in those years. Wise entered City College at age thirteen but switched to Columbia in his senior year to study with Richard Gottheil. Subsequently, he spent three years in Vienna studying with (and serving as secretary to) the city's great rabbi and Wissenschaft scholar Adolf Jellinek. Ordained and still only nineteen, Wise returned to New York and was appointed assistant, and soon senior, rabbi of New York's Temple Bnai Jeshurun. In addition to his heavy workload there, he also managed to take courses with Gottheil and received his doctorate in 1902. Melvin I. Urofsky, *A Voice That Spoke for Justice: The Life and Times of Stephen S. Wise* (Albany: State University of New York Press, 1982), chap. 1, "Goodly Beginnings," treats, among other things, the debate over whether Wise had plagiarized his doctoral dissertation on *The Improvement of the Moral Qualities: An Ethical Treatise of the Eleventh Century* (published as *Columbia University Oriental Studies* vol. 1, New York: Columbia University Press, 1902), as well as the scholarly reaction to the work. See also Mark A. Raider, "Stephen S. Wise and the Urban Frontier: American Jewish Life in New York and the Pacific Northwest at the Dawn of the 20th Century," *Quest* (October, 2011). http://www.quest-cdecjournal.it/focus.php?id=225. In the New York City of those years, Jewish studies were an intimate and personal affair. Note, for example, that Wise and Joseph Hertz studied together as teenagers, taking private lessons from

Rabbi Alexander Kohut alongside the latter's son, George Alexander Kohut. On the founding of the Jewish Institute of Religion, see also *Challenging Years: The Autobiography of Stephen Wise* (New York: G. P. Putnam's Sons, 1949), chap. 8.

51. David Philipson, "Hyman Gerson Enelow," *American Jewish Year Book* 36 (1934–35): 33–53.
52. Israel Davidson, ed., *Essays and Studies in Memory of Linda R. Miller* (New York: Jewish Theological Seminary of America, 1938). This book was, as Cyrus Adler commented in his foreword, "the first volume in memory of a Jewish woman among the many memorial volumes ever brought together." It was Miller's generosity that also made possible the publication of Davidson's monumental *Thesaurus of Mediaeval Hebrew Poetry*.
53. Liberles, *Baron, Architect of Jewish History*, deals with the correspondence extensively. See especially the letter of December 20, 1929, which he published in full (82). Miller expresses her frustration over Baron and his nationalist views: "Of course, Zionism is dead, but the doctrine of the ethnic Jew goes on to express itself in further dangerous forms." This doctrine, she believed, "was the most dangerous to Judaism as a spiritual force in the world."
54. What follows here is based on Baron's own account of his coming to Columbia as told to Zvi Ankori in 1987. Liberles, in *Baron, Architect of Jewish History*, 88–93, while acknowledging Baron's version, tells the story differently, based on his reading of correspondence he found in the Columbia University Archives. In that version, Baron was initially unclear as to the university department where the position should be located and, at least at one point, thought that he was being offered to be alone in a one-person department. As my interest in this chapter is to trace the development of Baron's own view of the nature and purpose of Jewish studies at Columbia, I have opted to follow his version of events.
55. Quoted by Liberles, *Baron, Architect of Jewish History*, 64.
56. Baron saw this as the primary limitation of the magnificent historical opus of Heinrich Graetz. The quote is taken from "Graetz and Ranke: A Methodological Study," a revised translation of Baron's early essay, "Graetzens Geschichtsschreibung," *Monatsschrift für Geschichte und Wissenschaft des Judentums* 62 (1918): 5–15, and republished together with a translation of his article in the German *Encyclopaedia Judaica* 7 (1931), 645–52, as "Heinrich (Hirsch) Graetz, 1817–1891" in his collected *History and Jewish Historians: Essays and Addresses*, compiled by Arthur Hertzberg and Leon A. Feldman (Philadelphia: Jewish Publication Society, 1964), 263–275:271. The original German read,

    Graetz . . . will sie auch lediglich aus sich selbst erklären. Die die jüdische Entwicklung bestimmenden herrschenden Tendenzen entstehen bei ihm und vergehen nur innerhalb des jüdischen Volkes als eines abgesonderten Ganzen. Als ob wirklich irgend eine Gemeinschaft so wie eine Einzelperson ganz von der übrigen Welt abgeschlossen, keinen irgendwie gearteten Einfluß von derselben empfangen würde! (8–9)

57. The engaged brilliance of these young people was caught sympathetically in Mark Van Doren's "Jewish Students I Have Known," *Menorah Journal* 13, no. 3 (1927): 264–68. The difficulty of gaining a faculty appointment and then tenure is emphasized in Diana Trilling's "Lionel Trilling, a Jew at Columbia," *Commentary* 67, no. 3

(March 1979): 40–46. The narrative was repeated and utilized over and over in memoirs by the next generation. See, for example, Carolyn G. Heilbrun, *When Men Were the Only Models We Had: My Teachers Barzun, Fadiman, Trilling* (Philadelphia: University of Pennsylvania Press, 2002) and Anne Fadiman, *The Wine Lover's Daughter: A Memoir* (New York: Farrar, Straus and Giroux, 2017).

58. The maverick medievalist Norman F. Cantor would record in his memoirs being invited to join the department in 1960 by then chair Richard B. Morris. The latter, son of a Brooklyn rabbi and "a Jew who got things done" was, Cantor is careful to emphasize, also "the first full-blooded Jew . . . to teach in the Columbia History Department" "aside from the holder of an endowed chair in Jewish history [that is, Baron]." *Inventing Norman Cantor: Confessions of a Medievalist* (Tempe: Arizona Center for Medieval and Renaissance Studies, 2002), 75–76.

59. Baron mentions Hayes's Catholicism in his 1987 interview with Ankori but without explaining its implications for the appointment. Hayes summarized his view of the central, positive role of Christianity in his 1954 lectures, published as *Christianity and Western Civilization* (Stanford, CA: Stanford University Press, 1954). Nowadays, his confident assertions about terms such as *liberty* and *progress* might strike the reader as naive; see the review by John Kamerick in *Catholic Historical Review* 41, no. 2 (July 1955): 195–96. His effort to reframe the current rhetoric about the relative significance of Catholicism and Protestantism in European history was his extremely popular textbook, *Political and Social History of Modern Europe* (New York: Macmillan, 1916; reprinted often). As much as the book reflected the principles of the New History that he had imbibed from Charles Beard and James Harvey Robinson during his studies at Columbia, it was also a critique of the prevailing denigration of pre-Reformation Catholicism and what he considered an overly positive presentation of the Protestant Reformation. Hayes associated nationalism, then the greatest threat to civilization, with Protestantism that itself had challenged the Catholic universalist tradition. On the complicated role Hayes played in developing the field of Catholic historiography, see Patrick Allitt, "Carlton Hayes and His Critics," *U.S. Catholic Historian* 15, no. 3 (Summer 1997): 23–37. It is relevant to mention that Hayes was also active, over the opposition of most Catholic bishops in the United States, in the National Conference of Christians and Jews, serving as its first Catholic cochairman from 1928 to 1946. While serving as U.S. ambassador to Spain, Hayes is also credited with saving a large number of Jewish refugees; see Emmet Kennedy, "Ambassador Carlton J. H. Hayes's Wartime Diplomacy: Making Spain a Haven from Hitler," *Diplomatic History* 36, no. 2 (2012): 237–60; and John P. Willson, "Carlton J. H. Hayes, Spain, and the Refugee Crisis, 1942–1945," *American Jewish Historical Quarterly* 62, no. 2 (December 1972): 99–110.

60. Hamerow, "The Professionalization of Historical Learning"; and, more generally, Peter Novick, *That Noble Dream: The "Objectivity Question" and the American Historical Profession* (Cambridge: Cambridge University Press, 1988).

61. I rely here on Judith Friedlander, *A Light in Dark Times: The New School for Social Research and Its University in Exile* (New York: Columbia University Press, 2019), especially chap. 3.

62. In 1938, Nevins famously tried to convince the American Historical Association to sponsor a popular journal; his narrow failure reportedly left him frustrated and angry. He would eventually help to found the Society of American Historians and

the widely distributed magazine, *American Heritage*. His view of his "dry-as-dust" colleagues was encapsulated in his famous essay, "What's the Matter with History?" *Saturday Review of Literature* (February 4, 1939): 3–4, 16, an argument that has had its own history.

63. On Barzun, see "Jacques Barzun," November 10, 2010, https://www.youtube.com/watch?v=pjyDg2hncE0; and Columbia News, October 25, 2012, https://news.columbia.edu/news/columbia-icon-jacques-barzun-dies-after-extraordinary-life-intellectual-leadership. In Barzun we hear a passionate belief in the function of scholarship to correctly identify great ideas and to pass them on through engaged writing and teaching. Barzun's call for "scholars with a knack for organizing materials [to] freely turn to writing textbooks" may well have influenced Salo Baron in how he would shape his life's work as we shall see.

64. On George Alexander Kohut, a rabbi, educator, and activist on behalf of Jewish studies, see Alexander Marx's article in *American Jewish Year Book* 36 (1934–35 [for 5695]): 54–64; and Stephen S. Wise, "George Alexander Kohut," in *Jewish Studies in Memory of George A. Kohut*, ed. Salo W. Baron and Alexander Marx (New York: Alexander Kohut Memorial Foundation, 1935), ix–xi.

65. I have not been able to check enrollment lists at Columbia (or, later, at the Jewish Theological Seminary) to see what this might have meant in practice. Baron's daughter Shoshana Tancer reports that his focus on graduate students is what allowed her father to concentrate his teaching in two contiguous days per week and spend the rest of his time writing; "The Baron Family," 41.

66. Salo W. Baron, "Research in Jewish History," *Jewish Institute Quarterly* 4, no. 4 (May 1928): 1–7. Baron saw the need to link schools of Jewish studies to large universities exactly because only such institutions could provide the necessary research libraries. See, for example, his "Jewish Studies at Universities: An Early Project," *Hebrew Union College Annual* 46 (1975): 357–76.

67. Ecclesiastes 12:12: "The making of many books is without limit." The challenge to the medieval Jewish intellectual is clear in the commentaries to this verse of authorities such as Solomon ben Isaac (RaSHI), and Obadiah Sforno as they struggle to acknowledge the problem while not giving in to its possibly defeatist implications.

68. We can mention as two examples Moritz Steinschneider, *Hebräische Bibliografie* (1859–1882) and Moïse Schwab, *Répertoire des articles relatifs à la littérature juives parus dans les périodiques, de 1665 à 1900* (1914–1923, edited and republished as *Index of Articles Relative to Jewish History and Literature Published in Periodicals, from 1665 to 1900* [New York: Ktav, 1972]).

69. Ismar Elbogen, Y. N. Epstein, and N. Torczyner, eds., *Dvir: Ma'asaf-Et le-Hokhmat Yisrael* (Berlin: Dvir and Jüdischer Verlag, 1923–24). The invitation letter from Bialik and the response of the editors are an excellent guide to the ambitions of the field at the time. Note that Epstein and Torczyner had both been at the Lehranstalt in Vienna.

70. William Henry Allison, Sidney Bradshaw Fay, Augustus Hunt Shearer, and Henry Robinson Shipman, eds., *A Guide to Historical Literature* (New York: Macmillan, 1931). By way of comparison and to show the impact of the work done by Professor Baron and several generations of Jewish historians who built upon his legacy, see the most recent iteration of the guide, the third edition, edited by Mary Beth Norton and Pamela Gerardi (almost 27,000 entries dealing especially with material

published between 1961 and 1992; New York: Oxford University Press, 1995). This volume includes twenty pages devoted to Jewish history prepared by Professor David Ruderman.

71. *List of Works Relating to the History and Condition of the Jews in Various Countries* (New York: New York Public Library, 1914).
72. Michael Stanislawski, "Salo Wittmayer Baron: Demystifying Jewish History," Columbia Magazine, January 15, 2005, https://magazine.columbia.edu/article/salo-wittmayer-baron-demystifying-jewish-history.
73. *A Short History of the Jewish People B.C. 1600–A.D.1935* (London: Macmillan, 1936). In 1930, on the eve of starting the job at Columbia, Baron told Dora Askowith of Hunter College that in his opinion, the "best book for a general survey of the total past of the Jewish people is still Graetz, preferably in German." The one-volume history by Max L. Margolis and Alexander Marx, *A History of the Jewish People* (Philadelphia: JPS, 1927), he considered "too short a treatment and . . . too compact a collection of facts to be handled easily by the inexperienced student."
74. Hertzberg, "Salo Baron and the Writing of Modern Jewish History," 11.
75. *The Jewish Community: Its History and Structure to the American Revolution* (Philadelphia: Jewish Publication Society of America, 1942).
76. Salo W. Baron, *The Russian Jew Under Tsars and Soviets* (New York: Macmillan, 1964).
77. Salo Baron, *A Social and Religious History of the Jews, Vol. 13: Late Middle Ages and Era of European Expansion, 1200–1650—Inquisition, Renaissance, and Reformation*, 2nd ed. (New York: Columbia University Press, 1969), v–vi. In a similar vein, Baron also explained that because he was dealing with a later historical period, the amount of bibliography had expanded enormously and he hadn't been able to read a few of the titles he cited.
78. *Bibliography of Jewish Social Studies* (New York: Conference on Jewish Relations, 1941).
79. Hertzberg, "Salo Baron and the Writing of Modern Jewish History," 23.
80. The English translation was published by Knopf in 2012.

Chapter Three

EMANCIPATION
Salo Baron's Achievement

DAVID SORKIN

Salo Baron wrote about emancipation throughout his career. He devoted his first book to a significant chapter of emancipation, the Congress of Vienna, and continued to address the subject, publishing an extended lecture on ethnic minority rights toward the end of his life.[1] It was a subject that patently preoccupied him; indeed, in his scholarship on the modern period, it was perhaps the subject that concerned him most. It is therefore not surprising that among his contemporaries he offered the most conceptually inclusive and geographically comprehensive understanding of emancipation. He endeavored to free himself from the two prominent *parti pris* positions of his day: namely, the emancipationist and the nationalist.

Heinrich Graetz (1817–91), the preeminent Jewish historian of the second half of the nineteenth century, cast emancipation in messianic terms of redemption: "The [French] Revolution was a judgment which in one day atoned for the sins of a thousand years.... A new day of the Lord had come 'to humiliate all the proud and high, and to raise up the lowly.' For the Jews, too, the most abject and despised people in European society, the day of redemption and liberty was to dawn after their long slavery among the nations of Europe."[2]

In stark contrast, Simon Dubnow (1860–1941), the foremost historian of the early twentieth century, understood emancipation as degradation through assimilation: "The emancipated Jews of western Europe... demanded their liberty not as free men but as slaves; their appeal for equal rights came with timidity and obsequiousness; they thought that civic rights required the sacrifice of their souls and the offering up of the holy treasures of their nation.... 'Assimilation' of this kind was ... nothing but a change in the form of servitude, the substitution of inner for external humiliation."[3]

Baron also adamantly rejected ideologically constrained, mono-causal explanations. Moreover, he disaggregated emancipation from the other subjects with which historians had conventionally associated it, such as Haskalah, religious reform, social mobility, acculturation, and, above all, as Dubnow illustrates, "assimilation." He thereby delineated emancipation as an independent subject of scholarly investigation.[4]

In this chapter, I first explore Baron's contribution to the study of emancipation by treating his writings over some six decades.[5] Although he elaborated various aspects at different times, his understanding of emancipation remained fundamentally the same. A chronological argument tracing the development of his ideas is therefore inappropriate. I also evaluate the problematic aspect of some of his terminology.

AMBIGUITY

First and foremost, Baron accentuated the essential ambiguity of emancipation, its disadvantages alongside its advantages, its stupendous losses as well as its tremendous gains. He questioned one-dimensional accounts of emancipation, especially the integrationist historians' unalloyed celebration (e.g., Graetz) and the nationalist historians' unrelieved castigation (e.g., Dubnow). Baron sought a third way between those extremes.

His quest for an alternative interpretation was already apparent in his book on the Congress of Vienna. He provided a compelling answer to the congress's failure to grant Jews equality throughout central Europe. A uniform emancipation was linked to German unification. The two causes shattered on the same rock of German state particularism. The small German polities strenuously resisted Prussian and Habsburg attempts at domination. The congress was unable to tame the fissiparous impulses that had plagued the Holy Roman Empire for centuries.[6]

At the same time, Baron made clear the congress's achievements. Paid advocates such as Carl August Buchholz (1785–1843), who represented the Jews of the Hanseatic cities (i.e., Lübeck, Hamburg, and Bremen), and the Viennese Jewish bankers and their wives who entertained and lobbied the diplomats, succeeded in bringing the legal status of the Jews onto the congress's agenda as an independent issue rather than a mere codicil to the question of German unity.[7] Buchholz specifically advocated for a uniform treatment of the Jews' rights against the prerogatives of any individual polity. In fact, he often did so in opposition to the myopic Jewish representatives of individual Jewish communities.[8] Baron further stressed the congress's success in maintaining equality in numerous polities and the moral triumph of making the "Jewish question" a "European question."[9]

Baron published "Ghetto and Emancipation" in 1928. The decade following the close of World War I was a rare moment that, if it did not soften the Jews' ideological dividing lines, may have cooled some of the antagonists' tempers. English (Lucien Wolf) and American (Louis Marshall) emancipationist intercessors had aided Jewish nationalists to achieve international recognition of national minority rights in east central Europe's successor states, and the English intercessor subsequently monitored them.[10] With the charter of the Balfour Declaration in hand and the British Mandate in place, Zionists thought to expand the Jewish Agency and the larger settlement project to enlist non-Zionists.[11] At the same time, emancipationists' fear that Zionism would arouse accusations of dual loyalty and thereby undermine their citizenship in the Diaspora had not occurred. Was Baron inspired by these seemingly propitious developments?

In his now canonical essay, Baron subverted the emancipationist, nationalist, and Reform bipolar, black-and-white versions of Jewish history in which the new dispensation of emancipation replaced the "extreme wretchedness" of the middle ages.[12] Baron argued that prior to emancipation, the Jews had been a "privileged minority" whose legal status was comparable to that of "city burghers" and whose poorest members enjoyed a higher standard of living than the vast majority of the surrounding population (*villeins*). Indeed, he treated the legal status of direct subjection to the emperor, "serfs of the chamber" or *servi camerae*, as embodying that privilege. He used David Hume's categories to characterize that status as "civil subjection" compared with the peasants' "domestic slavery."[13] Conclusive proof of that "privileged" position for Baron was the fact of population increase: the number of Jews rose far more rapidly than the general population both before and after emancipation.[14]

At the same time, Baron highlighted what Jews lost in making the transition from an "ethnic organism" to a "confession." They were divested of their "internal autonomy," which gave them "a full, rounded life . . . under a corporate governing organization" and which "contributed in large part toward the preservation of Jewry as a distinct nationality."[15] Jews now began to consider themselves as a religion, or "confession," rather than a national group. They also found themselves subject to such onerous "equal duties" as military service.

Baron stressed that these developments were perhaps unavoidable given that emancipation was "a necessity even more for the modern State than for Jewry."[16] As the state dismantled corporations in order to bring the entire populace under the jurisdiction of one uniform legal system, the Jews could not remain an exception separated by a distinct corporate status that legislated internal autonomy.

EAST-WEST DIVIDE

In writing about emancipation, Baron discarded the cliché of the east-west divide that impaired so much of the scholarship then and, it is worth emphasizing, continues to do so to this day. He offered the most geographically comprehensive account, extending from England in the west to Russian in the east. In addition, he incorporated the New World colonies. Transcending the supposed east-west divide was essential to his third way between the emancipationist and the nationalist positions.

One could plausibly propose that in this regard, his own geographical origins informed his historical imagination. Baron was a native of Galicia, a region whose political emancipation (1868), which followed from the creation of the Dual Monarchy, aligned its Jews with the "West."[17] The social and economic structure of that impoverished province, however, which the Habsburg Empire had intentionally kept backward by deliberately locating industrial development elsewhere, aligned the Jews with the "East." In the terms of the east-west divide, here was the anomaly of an emancipated "eastern" European community.

Galicia's peculiar situation produced a remarkable harvest of intellectuals and artists in general and historians in particular. Moses Schorr (1874–1941) was born in Przemysl; Meyer Balaban (1877–1942), Philip Friedman, and Natan Gelber (1891–1966) hailed from Lwow; Raphael Mahler and Artur Eisenbach from Nowy Sącz; Emanuel Ringelblum from Buczacz; and Ignazy Schiper (1884–1943) and Baron from Tarnów. These historians benefited from a strong Jewish textual education combined with the provinces' Polonized schools, including a rigorous gymnasium and multilingual humanist education. Those aspiring scholars had the option of attending any number of outstanding universities: Lvov or Cracow in Galicia itself, Vienna in the imperial capital, or, after World War I, Warsaw.[18]

Born in 1895 into an "enlightened" Hasidic family of wealthy bankers and businessmen, Baron studied as an external student at a gymnasium in Tarnów but mostly had private tutoring to prepare for his exams. He attended the University of Cracow for about a year, leaving just ahead of the advancing Russian army. Alongside tens of thousands of other Galician refugees, he made his way to Vienna, where he spent a dozen years (1914–26).[19] In Vienna he received degrees in history (1917), political science (1922), and jurisprudence (1923) while also studying Judaica at the *Israelitisch-Theologischen Lehranstalt*.[20]

David Engel has shown that Baron's "lachrymose theory" could well have been indebted to some of the Polish historians of the pre–World War I era who questioned the "regnant negative image of the Middle Ages" and the unmitigated celebration of the modern state.[21] Baron could have encountered this scholarship either in gymnasium or during his studies in Cracow.

In his 1937 *A Social and Religious History of the Jews*, Baron argued for a tripartite division of Europe. He summarized: "The progress of Emancipation was . . . slow and full of sudden reversals . . . it may be asserted that Western European Jewry was emancipated in the eighteenth, Central European Jewry in the nineteenth, and the East European Jewish masses in the twentieth century."[22] For Baron, the "protracted struggle for emancipation in Germany (including Austria) . . . [made it] the classical laboratory for the Jewish question in the nineteenth century."[23] He divided Europe between those countries that made a "fresh start" in their policies toward Jews: England, the Low Countries, and France (he included the United States) and the "old monarchies" in central and eastern Europe that preserved established patterns: namely, Germany, Austria-Hungary, and Russia.[24] In the central European states of Germany, Austria-Hungary, and Italy, the progress of emancipation kept pace with that of democracy:

both challenged "vested interests," and emancipation also faced "inveterate animosities."[25] Baron insistently pointed out that the vast majority of Europe's Jews, those concentrated in tsarist Russia though also in the Ottoman Empire, still did not enjoy legal equality at the beginning of the twentieth century.[26]

LEGAL AND SOCIAL HISTORY

Baron understood emancipation as a legal and an extralegal process. Perhaps because he had taken degrees in law, history, and political science in Vienna, he was acutely aware that one should not equate paper legislation with an actual historical condition. He understood that it was insufficient to evaluate the Jews' prescribed legal status without examining their lived situation. That is, one had to determine if and in what manner legal changes were implemented and the precise impact(s) of such changes.

Baron provided examples of the extremes. He argued that in the American colonies, the Jews' situation, frequently better than that of Catholics or dissenting Protestants, often exceeded the legal one. In contrast, the Minority Rights Treaties that guaranteed the Jews' equality, which Poland had signed at the Versailles Peace Conference, brought few benefits to the Jews' parlous position in the interwar period. Nevertheless, he recognized that "once adopted, [law] becomes a social force."[27]

CAUSALITY

Baron promoted a multicausal explanation of emancipation. While he held that emancipation had been a necessity for the state, he also recognized the significance of a range of other factors. This was especially the case as he argued that "social," "economic," and "intellectual" emancipation had preceded political emancipation. European Jewry grew in numbers from its lowest point in 1648 to its greatest in 1937. It expanded geographically to Holland, Belgium, and England and the colonies and, with the partitions of Poland to the Austrian interior, Hungary and Russia's southern provinces. With "geographical expansion" came an "intensification of Jewish economic life."[28] He asserted that it was imperative to consider the "totality of forces" to understand "the halting historic progression toward Jewish equality of rights."[29] He attributed significance to capitalism, the

Enlightenment, and the Haskalah (beginning in Italy and Holland, not Germany).[30] One of his more memorable lines is "To find the beginnings of Jewish enlightenment in Mendelssohn, is a curious misjudgment, due mainly to the provincialism of German Jewish historiography."[31]

MINORITY RIGHTS

Baron argued that for the half century from the 1890s to 1940, Jewish leaders were preoccupied with a novel expansion of emancipation qua individual equal rights: namely, the collective equality known as "national minority rights." Minority rights aimed to preserve and foster the Jews' "ethnic identity" above and beyond equal rights.[32]

The idea of national minority rights had first emerged in the multinational Habsburg Empire. During the debates of the 1848 Revolution, some representatives of the minority peoples laid claim to their own language and heritage as well as to political representation.[33] By the end of the nineteenth century, national minority rights had grown to have two complementary forms. As cultural rights they designated "the rights of minority peoples who wished to cultivate their own culture and control their schools, welfare agencies and other communal institutions," and, where possible, to "collect a proportionate part of government expenditures." As political rights they denoted "quotas in political elections" organized according to "electoral *curias*."[34]

Jewish political parties adopted these ideas in the first decade of the twentieth century. The socialist Bund adopted national minority rights by 1901–3; the Zionists, in 1906 (at Helsingfors, the program of "work in the Diaspora" known as "*Gegenwartsarbeit*").[35] Baron pointed to the "League for the Attainment of Equal Rights for the Jewish People in Russia" (March 1905), which, "short-lived but for a time quite influential," promoted "a combination . . . of equality and national self-determination."[36]

These ideas came to fruition after World War I. The Soviet Union, as "part of a complete revamping of the established order," allowed Jews to have their own Yiddish grammar and secondary schools and their own judiciary but also to occupy some municipal administrations (*soviets*) wherever they constituted the majority of a town's population.[37]

In consequence of the concerted advocacy of multiple Jewish delegations, the Paris Peace Conference imposed cultural national minority rights, including provisions for government subsidies, on the newly independent successor states, beginning with Poland and including Czechoslovakia, Yugoslavia, Romania, Greece, Austria, Bulgaria, Hungary, and Turkey.[38]

Yet national minority institutions and rights did not last long. The USSR began to dismantle those specifically Jewish institutions from the early 1930s. The successor states, with one or two notable exceptions (e.g., Czechoslovakia), reneged on their paper commitments and repeatedly violated Jews' rights.[39] After World War II, the idea of national minority rights disappeared in the frenzied endeavor to establish "human rights."[40]

INTERNATIONAL GUARANTEES

Baron argued for the insufficiency of emancipation legislated by individual states. During and after emancipation, there was an exponential growth of violence against Jews. Jews had fared better in multinational empires and "nationalities-states" than in "nation-states." Nation-states often succumbed to virulent nationalism and, in the interwar period, violated and subverted the safeguards of "national minority rights." For those reasons, Baron looked to the guarantee of international law and an international organization capable of enforcing such law.[41] He dated the origins of such international guarantees to the 1814 treaty between the Netherlands and the allies, which established equality of all inhabitants.[42] Here, again, he may have been influenced by trends in Polish scholarship.

Some of the same Polish historians of the pre–World War I era who questioned the "regnant negative image of the Middle Ages" and celebration of the modern state had also argued that the modern state had destroyed the international order and undermined the medieval ideal of the "welfare of all."[43] Traumatized by Poland's dismemberment, those historians had clearly recognized the deficiencies of the modern state unrestrained by an enforceable international order.

Baron had first pointed to the need for international order in his book on the Congress of Vienna, which he wrote during a period when he experienced a singular degradation of his own political status. He had been a citizen of the multinational Austro-Hungarian Monarchy. The successor Austrian nation-state refused to recognize his claim to citizenship. During his years in Vienna, he was officially "stateless": Austria considered him a "Polish" national. Baron found himself dependent on the caprice of bureaucrats who could refuse to issue even a temporary passport that would enable him to visit his family during vacations. He was able to resolve the issue only with outside intervention. When the well-connected Stephen Wise hired Baron to teach at the Jewish Institute of Religion in New York, he secured Baron an Austrian passport as well as an American visa.[44]

TERMINOLOGY

Baron's achievements with regard to emancipation are incontrovertible. The key respect in which I am critical is that he did not succeed in developing a terminology and conceptual framework consistent with his rigorous analysis. He employed anachronistic terms and concepts. I will consider two related examples.

First, he treated Holland as a case of "fundamental equality minus a few disabilities."[45] It is a misnomer to speak of Holland. One should speak here, rather, of Amsterdam. Other cities, whether in Holland or other provinces, prohibited Jews: Groningen did not admit Jews until 1711, Utrecht until 1789, and Deventer only in the 1790s.[46] In addition, "equality" presupposed that there was no charter granting specified privileges. Yet, other Dutch cities did issue charters: Alkmaar, 1604; Haarlem, 1605; and Rotterdam, 1610.[47]

The special position of Amsterdam Jewry derives from the fact that it was the first Jewry to settle in western Europe without a charter. The Jewish resettlement of western Europe from the 1550s, beginning with the Italian cities (Ancona, Venice, Livorno) and continuing up the Atlantic seaboard (Bordeaux, Hamburg), had rested on charters. Jews were treated as a merchant colony and, like other merchant colonies, negotiated for and received a charter. Charters granted privileges, often extensive, as in the case of the famous "Livornina" (1593), which could be construed as forms of parity with other burgher groups. By definition, a charter could not vouchsafe "equality": a society based on charters had no uniform legal status that could serve as a standard of equality.

Amsterdam was a civil society in the making. It did not issue charters to any merchant groups. Rather, it subjected all merchants to a uniform commercial law and created a single court to adjudicate all cases of marine insurance.[48] Amsterdam's government was struggling to determine how to govern—and maintain social control and discipline in—a multiconfessional city. Calvinism was the "public," albeit not the established church; it represented a minority of the populace. Yet all religions aside from Calvinism had to be excluded from, or have only strictly regulated access to, public space. For example, until 1796, Catholics prayed in so-called attic churches (*schuilkerken*), which were not public—that is, visible from the street—but were an open secret.

In some respects the city's treatment of Jews became a template for other groups: the Jews exercised internal authority vested in a lay leadership, maintained fixed boundaries vis-à-vis other religious groups, and, perhaps above all, took responsibility for their own poor.[49] Among the various non-Calvinist confessions, only Jews and Lutherans, who were seen as wealthy merchants of foreign origin, were allowed to erect public ecclesiastical buildings beginning in the 1630s.[50]

Yet one should not overlook the novel and inchoate nature of the Jews' position. The community was, in Daniel Swetschinski's formulation, a "voluntary religious association governed, in part, as a mercantile community."[51] Jews paid municipal and state taxes as individuals, not collectively. The Jews' organization had the status of the "Jews' church" (*Jodenkerck*). The *Mahamad*'s authority rested on unresolved ambiguities: it arrogated to itself a vast array of powers that the municipal government neither deputed not disputed. It looked to Venice as its mother community, yet Venice's status was fundamentally different, as it was based on charters. The status of individual Jews was similarly unresolved. Jews could acquire municipal citizenship from 1597, but it was not heritable, so they remained "permanent first-generation immigrants." They were not admitted to the guilds and had no access to administrative, legal, or military posts.[52] In the hierarchy of religious groups, their burgher membership was less than that of the Calvinists yet not entirely comparable to that of Catholics and other dissenters who were restricted to private worship but eligible to join the guilds.

It would be wrong to assume that there was an established equality from which the Jews were excluded by a few "disabilities." There was a religiously defined hierarchy of differentiated "burgher" statuses. Jews were included in that hierarchy; they belonged to an emerging civil society. They were being accorded basic civil rights: residence and most occupations, religious freedom, and juridical standing. They paid their taxes as individuals and as individuals were subject to the local courts.

EMANCIPATION

Where one can speak of Jews gaining equality is in the Dutch colonies. In Dutch Brazil (1645), Surinam (1665), Nova Zeelandia (1657), and Cayenne (1659) they were recognized as equal to the "native born" or other colonists—but in charters, as the colonies were established and governed through charters.

The second example of terminological difficulty is England, which Baron characterized as a case of "equal citizens subject only to such disabilities as arose indirectly from the existing legislation." Here again the formulation presupposes or posits a preexisting equality. It is more precise to characterize the situation of the first Jews in England after 1655, following Todd Endelman's formulation, as a "statutory vacuum": they tested their legal standing empirically, on a case-by-case basis, largely through the courts but sometimes through direct intervention in Parliament or at court.[53] Their status gradually came to resemble that of Protestant dissenters. It is no surprise that the first purpose-built synagogue in London, Bevis Marks (1699–1701), was designed by a Quaker architect, had the façade of a dissenting chapel, and was located on a lane rather than a public street.

Here again, Jews were being included in a nascent civil society: they appeared to have freedom of residence and occupation (except where excluded by an oath, as in the case of becoming a freeman of the City of London). Individuals paid their own taxes. The community, the *Mahamad*, arrogated to itself the same powers as its mother community in Amsterdam and on a similarly ambiguous foundation, as this was a historically unprecedented voluntary community. Moreover, the English colonies also granted equality in charters, following either the Dutch precedent or the privileges the Dutch had extended to Jews.[54]

These terminological problems inhere in the study of emancipation, as it appears to be innately or, by definition, teleological; that is, it leads to the predetermined goal of equality. Baron himself testified to this innate teleology in using such phrases as the "progress of emancipation" or "the halting historic progression toward Jewish equality of rights."[55] It is thus difficult to avoid applying a retrospective terminology such as "fundamental equality minus a few disabilities."

Yet Baron did offer at least one means to escape the quandary of teleology. He reconsidered emancipation's endpoint. Reflecting on Europe's virtually continent-wide abrogation of emancipation in the interwar period, he speculated, "One should not be surprised, indeed, if historians of the future would date the beginnings of real Jewish emancipation not with 1787 or 1790 or even 1848, but rather with the first postwar year of 1946."[56] Baron recognized that the Holocaust had not put an end to emancipation and that the postwar world opened a new era of it. Postwar regimes reinstated equal rights and endeavored, with varied success, to restore expropriated property and pay reparations.[57]

Emancipation was, then, not a discrete phase of European Jewish history with a terminal destination; instead, it was a continuing process integral to the modern world. If we were to embrace Baron's suggestion, the history of emancipation need not be written teleologically.

Avoiding teleological history is precisely what historians should attempt to do, however difficult. Rather than peering backward through the long-distance telescope of a desired equality, we should peer forward by putting a microscope to the multiple situations in which Jews found themselves and functioned, many of which resist easy definition because they were unprecedented, fluid, or mercurial. After all, Jews in seventeenth-century Amsterdam and London would not have measured their status against an abstract goal of equality. We need to recover, by defining precisely, the pertinent categories and concepts of the time in order to integrate them into a comprehensive account of emancipation.

Baron successfully removed many of the formidable obstacles that precluded the careful study of emancipation as well as pioneering many of the most productive approaches. He treated it separately from the associated issues that prevented a precise understanding. He thereby established emancipation as an autonomous subject of serious historical research.

NOTES

This is a revised and expanded version of a paper first delivered at the Association for Jewish Studies Conference, on a panel organized by the American Academy for Jewish Research, and subsequently published as, "Salo Baron on Emancipation," *Association for Jewish Studies Review* 38, no. 2 (November 2014): 423–30.

1. *Die Judenfrage auf dem Wiener Kongreß: Auf Grund von zum Teil ungedruckten Quellen dargestellt* (Vienna: R. Löwit, 1920); *Ethnic Minority Rights: Some Older and Newer Trends* (Oxford: Oxford Centre for Postgraduate Hebrew Studies, 1985).
2. Heinrich Graetz, *History of the Jews*, 6 vols. (Philadelphia: Jewish Publication Society, 1895), 5:429–30.
3. Simon Dubnow, *Nationalism and History: Essays on Old and New Judaism*, ed. Koppel Pinson (New York: Atheneum, 1970), 110–12.

4. This is in sharp contrast to the monograph that has dominated the subject among English-language readers for the past four decades, Jacob Katz, *Out of the Ghetto: The Social Background of Jewish Emancipation, 1770-1870* (Cambridge, MA: Harvard University Press, 1973). In a book of twelve chapters, Katz devoted four to causes, three to religious consequences, two to social and demographic factors, and one to the legal process. Katz concentrated on three countries (France, Prussia, and the Habsburg Empire), treated England and Holland only in passing, and excluded eastern Europe.
5. I rely on the following publications by Baron: *Die Judenfrage auf dem Wiener Kongreß*; the classic essay, "Ghetto and Emancipation: Shall We Revise the Traditional View?" *Menorah Journal* 14, no. 6 (1928): 515-26; the chapter "Emancipation" in the second volume of his *A Social and Religious History of the Jews*, 3 vols. (New York: Columbia University Press, 1937), 2:224-45, 260-61; the chapter in his account of the modern period, "The Dynamics of Emancipation" in *Great Ages and Ideas of the Jewish People*, ed. Leo Schwarz (New York: Modern Library, 1956), 315-37; his most concentrated account of emancipation, "Newer Approaches to Jewish Emancipation," *Diogenes* 29 (Spring 1960): 56-81; *Ethnic Minority Rights*; and *From an Historian's Notebook: European Jewry Before and After Hitler* reprinted from *American Jewish Year Book* 63 (1962).
6. *Die Judenfrage auf dem Wiener Kongreß*, 72-117; "Dynamics of Emancipation," 326-27. For a recent account of particularism see Michael Hundt, *Die Modernmächtigen deutschen Staaten auf dem Wiener Kongress* (Mainz: Zabern, 1996).
7. *Die Judenfrage auf dem Wiener Kongreß*, 147. For recent scholarship see Michael Hundt, "Die Vertretung der jüdischen Gemeinden Lübecks, Bremens und Hamburgs auf dem Wiener Kongreß," *Blätter für deutsche Landesgeschichte* 130 (1994): 143-90; and Glenda Sluga, "'Who Hold the Balance of the World?' Bankers at the Congress of Vienna, and in International History," *American Historical Review* 122, no. 5 (December 2017): 1403-30.
8. *Die Judenfrage auf dem Wiener Kongreß*, 51-70.
9. *Die Judenfrage auf dem Wiener Kongreß*, 206.
10. Mark Levene, *War, Jews, and the New Europe: The Diplomacy of Lucien Wolf, 1914-1919* (London: Littman Library, 1992), 161-302; M. M. Silver, *Louis Marshall and the Rise of Jewish Ethnicity in America: A Biography* (Syracuse: Syracuse University Press, 2013), 345-77; and Carole Fink, *Defending the Rights of Other: The Great Powers, the Jews, and International Minority Protection, 1878-1938* (Cambridge: Cambridge University Press, 2004), 283-94.
11. *Trial and Error: The Autobiography of Chaim Weizmann*, 2 vols. (Philadelphia: Jewish Publication Society, 1949), 2:304-14; Silver, *Louis Marshall and the Rise of Jewish Ethnicity in America*, 497-516.
12. "Ghetto and Emancipation," 525. Similarly, "Dynamics of Emancipation," 316-17; "Newer Approaches to Jewish Emancipation," 65-8.
13. "Ghetto and Emancipation," 518; "Dynamics of Emancipation," 316-17; "Newer Approaches to Jewish Emancipation," 67-68.
14. "Ghetto and Emancipation," 521-22.
15. "Ghetto and Emancipation," 519-20; "Dynamics of Emancipation," 317-18; "Newer Approaches to Jewish Emancipation," 68-69.
16. "Ghetto and Emancipation," 524; "Dynamics of Emancipation," 317; "Newer Approaches to Jewish Emancipation," 57; *From an Historian's Notebook*, 16.

17. The Galician Diet voted to enact equality in 1868. See *Die Debatten über die Judenfrage in der Session des gallizischen Landtages vom J. 1868* (Lemberg, 1868). On emancipation in Galicia, see Filip Friedmann, *Die Galizischen Juden im Kampfe um ihre Gleichberechtigung (1848-1868)* (Frankfurt: Kauffmann, 1929), 179-81; and Rachel Manekin, *Yehudei Galitsia veha-Huka ha-Austrit: Reshita shel Politika Yehudit Modernit* (Jerusalem: Zalman Shazar, 2015), 47-54.
18. Antony Polonsky, "Artur Eisenbach and Polish-Jewish History," in *The Emancipation of the Jews in Poland, 1780-1870*, Artur Eisenbach (Oxford: Blackwell, 1991), xv-xvii; and Natalia Aleksiun, "Polish Jewish Historians Before 1918: Configuring the Liberal East European Jewish Intelligentsia," *East European Jewish Affairs* 34, no. 2 (Winter 2004): 41-54. For Emanuel Ringelblum, see Samuel D. Kassow, *Who Will Write our History? Rediscovering A Hidden Archive from the Warsaw Ghetto* (Bloomington: Indiana University Press, 2007).
19. David Engel, "Crisis and Lachrymosity: On Salo Baron, Neobaronianism, and the Study of Modern European Jewish History, *Jewish History* 20 (2006): 259-63.
20. Robert Liberles, *Salo Wittmayer Baron: Architect of Jewish History* (New York: New York University Press, 1995), 22-25.
21. David Engel, "Salo Baron's View of the Early Middle Ages in Jewish History: Early Sources," in *Studies in Medieval Jewish Intellectual and Social History: Festschrift for Robert Chazan*, ed. David Engel et al. (Leiden: Brill, 2012), 299-315.
22. *Social and Religious History of the Jews*, 2:228. Similarly, "Newer Approaches," 57-64; "Dynamics of Emancipation," 321-37. In *The Russian Jew under Tsars and Soviets* (New York: Macmillan, 1964), Baron discusses emancipation for Alexander II's reign ("Whiff of Liberalism"), 46-50. The book has no entry for emancipation in the table of contents or index.
23. *Social and Religious History of the Jews*, 2:239; "Dynamics of Emancipation," 326-27. He called Germany the "public forum for a discussion of 'the Jewish question,'" in *From an Historian's Notebook*, 17.
24. "Newer Approaches," 57-64; "Dynamics of Emancipation," 326-27.
25. "Newer Approaches," 64.
26. *Social and Religious History of the Jews* 2:245; "The Jewish Question in the Nineteenth Century," *Journal of Modern History* 10, no. 1 (1938): 60; "Dynamics of Emancipation," 334-335; "Newer Approaches," 81; *From an Historian's Notebook*, 15.
27. "Dynamics of Emancipation," 320; "Newer Approaches," 75.
28. *Social and Religious History of the Jews* 2:164-80.
29. "Newer Approaches," 80.
30. For capitalism, beginning with mercantilism, see *Social and Religious History of the Jews* 2:175-90; for the Enlightenment, 2:202-204; and for the Haskalah, 2:210-223. For capitalism and the Haskalah, see "Newer Approaches," 76-78.
31. *Social and Religious History of the Jews* 2:204.
32. *Ethnic Minority Rights*, 3-4. "Ghetto and Emancipation," 526; "The Jewish Question in the Nineteenth Century," 61; *Social and Religious History of the Jews*, 2:242-43; "Dynamics of Emancipation," 333; "Newer Approaches," 74-75; *From an Historian's Notebook*, 15-16.
33. *Ethnic Minority Rights*, 3-6. For the term's origins, see Kai Struve, "'Nationale Minderheit'—Begriffgeschichtliches zu Gleichheit und Differenz," *Leipziger Beiträge zur jüdischen Geschichte und Kultur* 2 (2004): 233-58. The Habsburg Constitutional

Committee's first session discussed the issue of nations lacking representation (*nicht vertretenen Völker*). See Anton Springer, ed., *Protokolle des Verfassungs-Ausschusses im Oesterreichischen Reichstage, 1848–1849* (Leipzig: Hirzel, 1885), 9–11.
34. *Ethnic Minority Rights*, 3–4.
35. *Ethnic Minority Rights*, 10.
36. "Dynamics of Emancipation," 333. After the 1905 Revolution, all the major Jewish political parties, including the emancipationists or liberals, embraced national minority rights under the league's auspices. See Simon Rabinovitch, *Jewish Rights, National Rites: Nationalism and Autonomy in Late Imperial and Revolutionary Russia* (Stanford, CA: Stanford University Press, 2014), 77–78, 104, 110–13, 135.
37. *Ethnic Minority Rights*, 11, 13; *From an Historian's Notebook*, 23.
38. *Ethnic Minority Rights*, 13–18.
39. "Newer Approaches," 74.
40. *Ethnic Minority Rights*, 22–33.
41. "Newer Approaches," 80–81; "The Jewish Question in the Nineteenth Century," *Journal of Modern History* 10 (March 1938): 64–65. He discussed his personal experience of the League of Nations and United Nations in *Ethnic Minority Rights*, 20–22.
42. *A Social and Religious History of the Jews*, 2:238.
43. Engel, "Salo Baron's View of the Early Middle Ages in Jewish History," 299–315.
44. Engel, "Crisis and lachrymosity," 259–63.
45. "Newer Approaches," 59.
46. Jonathan Israel, *The Dutch Republic: Its Rise, Greatness and Fall, 1477–1806* (Oxford: Clarendon, 1995), 658.
47. Daniel M. Swetschinski, *Reluctant Cosmopolitans: The Portuguese Jews of Seventeenth-Century Amsterdam* (London: Littman Library of Jewish Civilization, 2000), 48.
48. Amsterdam refused to issue charters to the various merchant groups that applied for them: "the urban government made every effort to secure the freedom of individual merchants to trade in the products and markets of their choice. A separate legal status clearly did not fit this policy. Instead, the city magistrate determined that the person and goods of all merchants should be treated equally in equal circumstances." See Oscar Gelderblom, *Cities of Commerce: The Institutional Foundations of International Trade in the Low Countries, 1250–1650* (Princeton, NJ: Princeton University Press, 2013), 40. For marine insurance, see Francesca Trivellato, *The Promise and Peril of Credit: What a Forgotten Legend about Jews and Finances Tells Us about the Making of European Commercial Society* (Princeton, NJ: Princeton University Press, 2019), 22–23.
49. Peter van Rooden, "Jews and Religious Toleration in the Dutch Republic," in *Calvinism and Religious Toleration in the Dutch Golden Age*, ed. R. Po-Chia Hsai and H.F.K. Van Nierop (Cambridge: Cambridge University Press, 2002), 132–47.
50. Joke Spaans, "Religious Policies in the Seventeenth-Century Dutch Republic," in Hsai and Van Nierop, *Calvinism and Religious Toleration in the Dutch Golden Age*, 81.
51. Swetschinski, *Reluctant Cosmopolitans*, 187.
52. Swetschinski, *Reluctant Cosmopolitans*, 24–25.

53. Todd Endelman, *The Jews of Britain, 1656–2000* (Berkeley: University of California Press, 2002), 36.
54. Yosef Haim Yerushalmi, "Between Amsterdam and New Amsterdam: The Place of Curaçao and the Caribbean in Early Modern Jewish History," *American Jewish History* 2 (December 1982): 188. For an account of Amsterdam and London as the first nascent civil societies in which Jews lived see, David Sorkin, *Jewish Emancipation: A History Across Five Centuries* (Princeton, NJ: Princeton University Press, 2019), 17–33.
55. *Social and Religious History of the Jews*, 2:228; and "Newer Approaches," 80.
56. "Dynamics of Emancipation," 336.
57. Sorkin, *Jewish Emancipation*, 309–19.

Chapter Four

AN ECONOMIC HISTORIAN READS SALO W. BARON

FRANCESCA TRIVELLATO

During the winter of 1926, shortly after he had been hired at the Jewish Institute of Religion in New York City, Salo W. Baron taught a class on the economic history of the Jews in the Middle Ages, among a few other courses he offered that term.[1] Half a century later, twelve years after his retirement from Columbia University in 1963, he contributed several sections to a slim textbook titled *Economic History of the Jews*, which to this day stands virtually alone in the genre.[2] These two moments bracket Baron's consistent, if muddled, engagement with a subject that has long been framed by hoary stereotypes about Jewish economic prowess and that, for historical and historiographical reasons, most economic historians have relegated to the margins.

Baron's writings on the economic history of Jews oscillate between, on the one hand, an emphasis on the effects of oppression and the glorification of Jews' mercantile skills (during premodern times) as well as their excellence at capitalistic entrepreneurship (after the Industrial Revolution) on the other. Overall, Baron's work represents an internalist approach to the study of the economic history of the Jewish people that shies away from carrying out systematic comparisons, both across Jewish groups and with other groups living in the same time and region, even as it commends the value of such comparisons.[3]

For an economic historian like me, with a keen interest in the roles of Jews and Christian images of Jews in the development of commercial society in premodern Europe, reading Baron today produces a sense of dissonance. This dissonance stems from the fact that, generationally, Baron belonged to a cohort of scholars who revolutionized the economic history of premodern Europe and succeeded in moving it to the center of the academic discipline. They were so successful that historians of the Renaissance or the French Revolution had to grapple with economic arguments in their fields as a matter of course to an extent that they do not today. Steeped as he was in a different scholarly tradition, Baron, however, remained insulated from these currents. As a result, his examination of Jews' economic roles was not always the most up to date.

Interestingly, among the figures who shepherded the renewal of economic history in Europe during the interwar period, several were Jewish—almost all more secular than Baron, though also, if only because of the tragic events of the mid-twentieth century, committed to bringing Jewish topics to the mainstream of the profession. Born in 1895, Baron led a particularly long life, passing away in 1989 at the age of ninety-four. But he was only nine years younger than Marc Bloch (1886–1944), the cofounder of the French journal *Annales* with Lucien Febvre; seventeen years younger than Gino Luzzatto (1878–1964), a notable Italian Jewish socialist, antifascist, and towering figure in economic and medieval history; and four years older than Michael Postan (1899–1981), who was born in Bessarabia and fled to the United Kingdom after the October Revolution, where he became professor of economic history at the University of Cambridge and where, alongside his wife, the older and more established scholar Eileen Power, he devoted his energy to editing *The Economic History Review* and the volumes on the Middle Ages of *The Cambridge Economic History of Europe*.

Although these authors and their colleagues wrestled with Werner Sombart's major work, *Der moderne Kapitalismus* (Modern Capitalism), of which no full translation in English exists to this day, they dismissed his 1911 *Die Juden und das Wirtschaftsleben* (The Jews and Economic Life)—an account of Sephardi Jews' domination of the sixteenth-century European commercial expansion that stressed their ostensible financial dexterity—the evidentiary and analytical standards of which did not meet those of the profession.[4] By contrast, Baron continued to take *Die Juden und das Wirtschaftsleben* seriously. As I show, these different points of departure account for the dissonance between the treatment of the economic history of Jews, especially in the premodern period, at the hands of Baron and his contemporaries outside of the field of Jewish history beginning in the 1920s.

ECONOMIC THEMES IN THE WORK OF SALO W. BARON

As many have observed, Baron was still a very young man when, in 1928, he wrote his most widely read and consequential piece, "Ghetto and Emancipation." In the ghetto, he claimed, "the Jews might live in comparative peace, interrupted less by pogroms than were peasants by wars, engaged in finance and trade at least as profitable as most urban occupations, free to worship, and subject to the Inquisition only in extreme situations."[5]

As part of his deeply revisionist view of the medieval and early modern periods, he also celebrated the economic conditions in the ghetto: "Despite all the restrictions placed on his activities, it is no exaggeration to say that the average Jewish income much surpassed the average Christian income in pre Revolutionary times." As proof of this uncorroborated statement, Baron asked rhetorically, "is it not remarkable that the most typical ghetto in the world, the Frankfort *Judengasse*, produced in the pre-Emancipation period the greatest banking house of history?"[6] Even his justly admiring biographer Robert Liberles calls this passage "flippant."[7]

Baron's indictment of interwar capitalism in the same essay struck a more realistic chord than his idealized view of the pre-emancipation ghetto. He described the capitalism of his own days as "medievalism on a higher plane." "Liberal *laissez faire*"—he continued—"is being more and more supplanted by a system of great trusts, protectionism, Fascism, Sovietism. Growing dissatisfaction with democracy and parliamentarianism has brought about a movement back to a modified medievalism." From Baron's perspective, there were a few positive signs amid these frightening trends. "That Reform and Zionism have both begun, though timidly and slowly, to reconsider the Jewish Middle Ages is encouraging.... With other national minorities the Jews claimed and are claiming, not without success, the equilibrium between their full rights as citizens and the special minority rights they think necessary to protect their living national organism from destruction and absorption by the majority, a process that has often proved to be harmful both for the absorber and the absorbed."[8]

Baron regarded unfettered capitalism and liberalism as sworn enemies of organized Jewish life—a theme to which he would return with vengeance in a later piece.

This early essay foreshadows a twin tendency in all of Baron's subsequent approaches to the topic: an optimistic view of Jews' economic positions in the premodern period and a politicized treatment of twentieth-century political economies and ideologies.

Whereas both the first (1937) and expanded (1952–80) editions of *A Social and Religious History of the Jews* are sprinkled with sections on Jews' economic activities, only in the second volume of the first edition is the theme discussed in a sustained fashion.[9] There, Baron describes Jews' rapid alienation from agriculture with the rise of feudalism in Europe. Stressing persecution and vexing taxation as factors leading Jews into the monied economy, he also consistently singles out the economic sphere as one in which the most affluent among Jews, whether as tax collectors or merchants, carved out a space for themselves within the oppressive Christian societies in which they lived. Tackling head-on Sombart's theory of Jews' pivotal role in the development of modern capitalism, he refutes Sombart's notion that the most advanced financial instruments had antecedents in rabbinic law and, more generally, that "the Jews were the fathers of modern capitalism" during the medieval commercial revolution.[10] He nevertheless makes an exception for "the Spanish-Portuguese refugees, Jewish and Marranos"—that is, the protagonists of Sombart's *Die Juden und das Wirtschaftsleben*—who "throughout the sixteenth and seventeenth centuries settled in all western lands." However, for Baron, "the most spectacular rise of the Jews under capitalism came in the first half of the nineteenth century," when "under the leadership of the Rothschild family of Frankfurt, London, Paris, Vienna, and, temporarily, Naples, the Jewish bankers and industrial entrepreneurs secured a position unrivaled in Jewish history."[11]

Moreover, when he moves from socioeconomic analysis to philosophical considerations of Jews' involvement in the economy, Baron finds common cause with Sombart. He agrees that Jews' "peculiar ethnic and religious experiences ... gave them further advantages. Their whole history had molded mind and outlook, conscious and unconscious attitudes, in a manner suitable to modern capitalism." Their historical detachment from agriculture and identification with the bourgeois spirit of urban life had produced "the artificiality of all Jewish existence, the consequent prevalence of speculative thinking, as against peasant concreteness."[12] Baron is therefore ready to conclude that "capitalism, in essence 'artificial,' based upon an exchange of abstract values, represented the most abstract and irrational of values, viz., money, found the Jews ready to carry its implications to the logical extreme."[13]

It is perplexing that in the mid-1930s, as conspiracy theories regarding Jews' alleged rootless cosmopolitanism and dominance of international finance were growing ever more menacing, Baron did not perceive the potential problem that designating Jews as the epitomes of abstraction could engender. In a seminal text of 1946, Jean-Paul Sartre would argue that in the anti-Semitic trope about Jews' love for money, "money often assumes the abstract form of shares of stock, checks, bank deposits."[14] For traditional anti-Semites, Sartre added, these are not legitimate forms of property, in the way in which objects, land, and other tangible possessions are, and contribute to the subversion of social order.

In 1942, in the middle of World War II, Baron published two very different pieces addressing the economic status of Jews in medieval Europe and in the contemporary United States, respectively. In "The Jewish Factor in Medieval Civilization," he aimed to persuade European medievalists to be more receptive of all aspects of Jewish history, including its economic ones. He relied on a then recent volume by Walter Fischel on Jews in Medieval Islam to insist that during the High Middle Ages, Jews arriving in Europe from the Middle East introduced new methods of trade and possibly new types of commercial paper instruments, playing "a role far in excess of their numbers."[15] Mindful that "much material, particularly outside of Germany, still awaits thoroughgoing investigation," Baron nonetheless reaffirmed that "in the local trade of the growing centers north of the Alps and Pyrenees the Jews *must have* performed certain *pioneering* services" in the distribution of both luxury and cheap goods.[16] As we will see, by 1942, leading economic historians of the European Middle Ages had in fact already put most of these claims behind them. Unfamiliar with that literature, Baron listed Jewish advancements in various economic areas, hiding behind the requisite cautionary call for the need to conduct additional research not only on Jewish moneylending but also on Jews' involvement in the slave/captive trade.

In the second of his 1942 pieces, Baron compared the advantages of socialist and capitalist systems for the Jewish people, but the outcome of his inquiry was predetermined. He asked, "Are not the Jews bound to lose out with every weakening of the capitalist system of production, even if such weakening be not necessarily combined with the disappearance of civil liberties, civic equality and, generally, of political democracy?"[17] The question was little more than rhetorical. Having described Sombart's *Die Juden und das Wirtschaftsleben* as a "brilliant, though undisciplined, treatise," he recalled that authors such as Hermann Wätjen and Herbert Bloom had "reduced [it] to its proper proportions"—as if empirical correction was all Sombart's misguided framework of analysis required.[18] His homage to Sombart was even more unnecessary since Baron was unequivocal in noting, correctly, that there was no "conclusive evidence for the oft-asserted great influence of post-biblical Judaism on the emergence of the 'capitalist spirit' and the modern commercial techniques."[19] In fact, as he conceded, Baron's real concern was with "the influence of modern capitalism on the Jew and his destiny,"[20] or the opposite of Sombart's question about Jews' influence on modern capitalism, and the piece soon turned into a lament for the consequences of materialism and individualism for Jewish life. Baron never doubted the superiority of capitalism over socialism for the Jews as individuals, but he conceived assimilation and secularism as threats to Jews as a collective. Needless to say, these were not the issues that anguished economic historians outside of the field of Jewish history, no matter how directly touched they were by (or sensitive to) the dramatic events that were unfolding before their eyes.

In 1945, asked to contribute to a volume in honor of the leading Talmudist and giant figure in American conservative Judaism Louis Ginzberg, Baron wrote about the nineteenth-century German rabbi Levi Herzfeld (1810–84), who, together with Ludwig Philippson (1811–89), had been among the early advocates of reform within Judaism and the author of a history of Jewish trade in antiquity. Baron called Herzfeld "the founder of the new discipline of Jewish economic history."[21] The subject and the tenor of this tribute encapsulate what I described as Baron's muddled engagement with economic history. The Columbia professor appreciates Herzfeld's view that the best response to the rising anti-Semitism that followed the economic crisis of 1873 in Germany was "a solid factual history of Jewish commerce," which could show that "it was not 'native predisposition' but historic circumstances which induced the Jewish people to engage in commerce."[22] In this respect, published in 1879, Herzfeld's study was a prescient antidote to Sombart's 1911 distorted and essentialized portrait of Jews' superior economic skills.

Baron also hailed Herzfeld for "his keen sensitivity . . . for the interrelations between Jewish and general history," which he judged to be far greater than that of all his contemporaries, Heinrich Graetz's included.²³ He was right, but this insight, no more than his praise of Herzfeld's critique of Jews' innate economic prowess, formed little more than a cameo. However laudatory, Baron's remarks did not inspire him to follow in the German rabbi's footsteps.

As late as 1961–62, in an account of modern Jewish history that he prepared for the trial of Adolf Eichmann by the Israeli court in Jerusalem, Baron called Sombart "the leading German student of the rise of modern capitalism" in the twentieth century. While acknowledging Sombart's proclivity for hyperbole and his double-edged admiration for Jews, he proceeded by citing or summarizing several of his dubious claims.²⁴ Baron alluded to what he called the Jewish "domination" (in quotation marks) of the liberal professions in the 1930s and emphasized the anti-Semitic backlash that it provoked.²⁵ He also stressed, on multiple occasions, the Jewish presence among both the upper echelons of international finance and industry and the anticapitalist socialist and trade unionist leaders, hardly concealing his lack of sympathy for the latter. Based on intuition rather than data, Baron estimated that during the interwar period, the occupational profile of the Jews and the rest of the population converged for the first time, "not so much because the Jews have changed as because the Western world has become increasingly 'Jewish' in its economic structure."²⁶ Yuri Slezkine's 2004 *The Jewish Century* tacitly built on this intuition.²⁷

If we now turn to the two premier economic journals published in Britain and France during the time when Baron's career was taking off, the dissonance to which I alluded at the onset of this chapter—between his conception of economic history and the development of the field among historians of premodern Europe, and especially between his views of Sombart and theirs—will become clear.

THE ECONOMIC HISTORY REVIEW

The first issue of the British journal *The Economic History Review* appeared in January 1927; the two editors-in-chief were Ephraim Lipson (1888–1960), born in Sheffield to a lower-middle-class Jewish family and a specialist of the economic history of modern England, and Richard Henry Tawney

(1880–1962), the great socialist scholar of the nexus between religion and capitalism, who questioned both Weber and Sombart. A keyword search for "Jews" and "Jewish" in the journal's digital archives for the years 1927–50 yields forty-eight entries between stand-alone articles, book reviews, and short notices. Not a huge number, but—and this is my point—a series of influential contributions that come from outside the inner circle of Jewish history and could have prodded Baron to discard Sombart's perspective and consider more grounded views of Jews' roles in European economic history.

In the opening issue of the new journal, Tawney himself included a review of the French historian Henri Sée, whose *Les Origines du capitalisme moderne* he called "a masterpiece of lucidity and compression."[28] Like most scholars of his generation, Sée engaged with Sombart's major work, *Der moderne Kapitalismus*, disputing its depiction of the Middle Ages as a precapitalist epoch; he also downplayed significantly the role for Jewish merchants and financiers. The journal's second issue featured a survey of "Recent Work in German Economic History (1900–1927)," which credited two groundbreaking studies by Jewish economic historians—Georg Caro's "comprehensive book" and Moses Hoffmann's volume on Jewish financial occupations—with demonstrating that "there is a great deal of opposition to Sombart, who assigned to the Jews a place of exceptional importance in the development of capitalism."[29] Baron cited both of these German Jewish authors, Caro and Hoffmann, in passing; the attention devoted to them by the *EHR* is an indication of the respect that they commanded even outside of the field of Jewish history and, more generally, of the possibility of convergence between Jewish and economic historians.

Opening his 1933 bibliographical essay on "medieval capitalism," Postan clarified that although any serious discussion of the subject of capitalism remained indebted to Karl Marx, "it is Werner Sombart, rather than Marx, who must be regarded as the originator and sponsor of the ideas that have been agitating the students of medieval capitalism for the last thirty years."[30] Postan illustrated how, for Sombart, the Middle Ages constituted "the non-capitalist or 'pre-capitalist' epoch *par excellence*" and discussed those scholars who challenged this theory, notably Henri Pirenne, the aforementioned Sée, Lujo Brentano, Georg von Below, N. S. B. Grass, Heinrich Sieveking, as well as (in the English context) Frank Hyneman Knight and Sylvia Thrupp, not to mention a number of more specialized authors.[31] Postan concluded, appropriately, that "the combined effect of these studies has been to destroy the ancient view of the paucity of productive credit in the Middle Ages, and to reveal the organic part which credit played in medieval trade. This revelation has removed medieval economy further still from Sombart's pre-capitalist style, but it has not solved the further problem as to whether medieval credit itself possessed anything resembling the 'capitalist structure of finance.'"[32]

The next point that Postan tackled most concerned Baron. He noted that "the problem of Jewish finance and its contribution to the rise of capitalism, made fashionable again by Sombart's study on the subject, produced a whole avalanche of literature, mostly polemical." Postan estimated that "the full and authoritative story of Jewish finance in the Middle Ages still remains to be written," again singling out the works of Caro and Hoffman as the most reliable to date and aligning himself with the critics of Sombart who contested "his view of the Jews as caretakers and purveyors of the capitalist spirits in the non-capitalist Middle Ages."[33] A year later, in 1934, Harvard economic historian Abbott Payson Usher put it simply: "some have believed that the Jews played an active and important part in the maintenance of banking throughout the early Christian period, but recent studies indicate that the development of banking among the Jews began at a relatively late date."[34]

For our purposes, these interventions are reminders that while Baron was at work on the second volume of the first edition of *A Social and Religious History of the Jews*, the most reputable economic historians of Europe had settled their scores with Sombart, especially with regard to Jews' economic roles in the Middle Ages, and did not consider his views in *Die Juden und das Wirtschaftsleben* as worth the attention that Baron was lending them.[35]

THE FRENCH *ANNALES*

In 1926, Bloch and Febvre founded the *Annales d'histoire économique et sociale*, better known simply as *Annales*, which marked a watershed moment in European and world history writing. Abandoning the traditional emphasis on politics and diplomacy, they launched "a periodical of economic and social history" that sought to overcome academic specializations.[36]

In the early issues of *Annales*, the question of Jews' economic roles in the Middle Ages is largely treated by omission, in the sense that space is devoted to the advocates of the commercial revolution of the Middle Ages who put Italian and Flemish merchant bankers on a pedestal, including Pirenne and Armando Sapori.³⁷ In 1929, distinguished Marxist historian Henri Hauser discussed the role of "pre-capitalist banking" with regard to its Florentine, Genoese, Sienese, and "Lombard" protagonists in the Middle Ages, the Fugger and Welser in the sixteenth century, and the Amsterdam *Wisselbank*, the Bank of England, and the Huguenots in the seventeenth century, with no mention of Jews.³⁸

Other contributions, however, took Sombart to task explicitly for its exaggerated views of Jews' determining role in jump-starting Europe's transition to a capitalist economy. Historian André-É. Sayous passed away without having published a monograph but having refuted Sombart's thesis concerning Jews' place in the development of Western capitalism on the basis of extensive archival research in Genoa, Marseille, and Barcelona. A prolific author of articles and book chapters, Sayous was also a close collaborator of *Annales*. In 1932, Febvre praised his "critique of Sombart," whom he described as possessing the dubious talent of bringing his readers along (*"un entraîneur d'hommes"*).³⁹ In 1937, the journal featured a piece by the still young but already authoritative medievalist Roberto Lopez, whose title alone, "Aux origines du capitalisme génois," left little doubt about its content.⁴⁰

By the mid-1930s, in short, like *The Economic History Review*, *Annales* had also sided with those specialists in the economic history of the European Middle Ages who had put to rest Sombart's view of the Jews as the only capitalist vanguards in a feudal society. The articles it published on the development of early European capitalism were substantial, had a profound impact on current and later scholarship, and could have informed Baron on some of the subjects of his magnum opus. The general import of the French historiographical debate on the origins of modern capitalism would appear even more robust if we included monographs as well—not only the 1926 landmark study by Sée but also Hauser's companion book from a Marxist perspective.⁴¹

Moreover, *Annales* could not be faulted for ignoring Jewish topics altogether. In 1930, the journal reviewed the French translation of a study of the land problem in Mandatory Palestine by Abraham Granovsky, which had first been published in Hebrew and German. The reviewer was renowned sociologist Maurice Halbwachs, who would die in Buchenwald in 1945. Born into a Christian family, Halbwachs grew closer to Judaism after his marriage to Yvonne Basch, daughter of Victor (a noted Dreyfusard, Zionist, and president of the *Ligue des droits de l'homme*) and herself a prominent figure in the feminist and pacifist movements. In 1927, he traveled to Egypt, Palestine, and Lebanon to gather material for a study of sociology of religions, which appeared in 1941, after the promulgation of the Vichy anti-Jewish legislation, as *La Topographie légendaire des Evangelies en Terre sainte*.[42] This research surely led to his being tapped to write the 1930 review, in which Halbwachs offered a balanced summary of the conflict between the Zionist supporters of land collectivization and private property, but in the end, he expressed skepticism toward the meager achievements that the Jewish National Fund, headed by Granovsky, who advocated collectivization, had accomplished in its first twenty-six years of existence.[43]

In 1939, under the rubric "Jewish problems," *Annales* reviewed three different but important volumes: Léon Berman's history of Jews in France from its origins to the present (here the reviewer put the accent on emancipation and the Crémieux decree of 1870); a work published by the World Jewish Congress on Jews' then current economic condition (with praise for the statistical data assembled by YIVO concerning the Polish case); and a demographic and onomastic study of the Jews of North Africa compiled by the chief rabbi of Algeria, Maurice Eisenbeth, which drew on both community and public statistics and thus offered a more accurate picture and higher population figures than those appearing in French censuses.[44] In the aftermath of the war, *Annales* reviewed a French translation of a Yiddish manual of Jewish history written by Simon Dubnov for elementary schoolchildren, a novel study of Jews in France under Napoleon, and an important volume published by the Centre of Contemporary Jewish Documentation, which detailed the anti-Semitic propaganda mobilized by the French state under the Vichy regime (1940–44).[45]

CONCLUSION

The responsibility that fell on Baron's shoulders with his appointment as the first holder of a Jewish history chair in a secular institution of higher education in the United States was enormous. Hailing from Galicia, he achieved more than any Jewish academic in North America before him. His voracious and ever-expanding erudition, however, never strayed too far from the blueprint of his early training; even once he entered the temple of the secular university in New York City, his interest in the historiographical battles that were being waged outside of Jewish studies was rather subdued. Or at least this was the case for his attitude toward economic history and the debates that unfolded in the pages of journals such as *The Economic History Review* and *Annales*.

In 1939, then still in his mid-forties, Baron remarked, "so far neither the Marxist nor the other economic interpreters of Jewish history have succeeded in producing a general synthetic work on the entirety of Jewish experience." Although he admitted that the contributions of some economic historians of the Jewish past were "undoubtedly of great value," he found them to be "fragmentary explanations of certain phases of Jewish history."[46] Oddly, for all his dislike of the dominance of ideas over practices in the tradition of Jewish history writing—the "theocratic view of history"[47] that he spent his life rebuffing—he never considered seriously the possibility that a more in-depth examination of economic life and institutions could add to his project.

The easiest explanation for this lack of interest lies in his early education and personal penchants, but it extends to a broader ambiguity that encompasses his work. In principle Baron stated that "the historical explanations of the Jewish past must not fundamentally deviate from the general patterns of history which we accept for mankind at large or for any other particular national group." But he also maintained that a "*socio-religious* approach" was most suited to the study of Jewish history because, compared with economics, community, and other social factors, religion was "the most conspicuous place at least in the consciousness of the Jews throughout the three and a half millennia of their existence."[48]

These are difficult premises from which to pursue a comparative economic history. These considerations also lend some valence to Jacob Neusner's criticism of Baron for assuming that "a single group, with a continuous, linear history, formed also a cogent and distinct economic entity, with its own, continuous, linear, economic history." In Neusner's view, it is not possible to describe "the Jews' history as one cogent history, their economics as an economy, and their 'philosophy' or even theology as a single system everywhere sustaining a single 'Judaism,'" and only once these assumptions are dispensed with, can "the analytical work ... begin."[49]

With greater sympathy and sensitivity, Liberles pinpoints the unresolved tension at the heart of Baron's work and personality and thus helps us to understand some of the paths not taken by this eminent scholar, including in his approach to Jewish economic history. He reiterates Baron's "conviction that Jewish history was no more unique than the history of any other social group and that it must be described and exploited using the same norms as used elsewhere in the historical profession."[50] But Liberles also notes that Baron's belief in the transhistorical interrelation between Jews and Judaism led him to assert "the legitimacy of the religious factor in history" and to join "forces with Max Weber and in a sense with Werner Sombart as well."[51] Upon assuming the Miller Chair in Jewish History, Literature, and Institutions at Columbia University, Baron apparently wished that it be located in either the religion or Semitic languages department, whereas the university president insisted it be housed in the Department of History. Baron's desire for autonomy may have accounted for his preference as much as, if not more than, a disciplinary rift. In any case, the university ultimately prevailed and Baron embraced the opportunity to be part of the Department of History.[52]

That was in 1930. Ninety years later, the same history department is home to the Salo Wittmayer Baron Professorship, and Jewish history is more and more represented across the historical profession, at least in North America. Still, the study of the economic life of past Jewish societies remains for the most part confined to a separate subfield, which does not place a great premium on comparison and maintains a certain fixation with Sombart, at least in certain academic quarters.[53] My hope is that the remarks in this chapter will soon begin to sound like ancient history, as those interested in exploring the manifold facets of Jews' interactions with the economic sphere are finding it increasingly natural to be in dialogue with a broader range of scholarly approaches than Baron did.

NOTES

1. Robert Liberles, *Salo Wittmayer Baron: Architect of Jewish History* (New York: New York University Press, 1995), 33.
2. Salo W. Baron, Arcadius Kahn, et al., *Economic History of the Jews*, ed. Nachum Gross (Jerusalem: Keter, 1975). The same year another brief synthesis appeared: Marcus Arkin, *Aspects of Jewish Economic History* (Philadelphia: Jewish Publication Society of America, 1975). The pioneering work by Russian-born University

of Chicago economist Arcadius Kahn on Eastern European Jewish immigrants to the United States was collected posthumously as Kahn, *Essays in Jewish Social and Economic History* (Chicago: University of Chicago Press, 1985). Only a decade ago were the writings of Nobel laureate Simon Kuznets on Jewish economic history first assembled in two volumes: *Jewish Economies: Development and Migration in America and Beyond*, ed. Stephanie Lo and E. Glen Weyl (New Brunswick, NJ: Transaction, 2011–12).

3. A partial exception is the paper that Baron read to the Annual Meeting of the American Historical Association in December 1936, published as Salo W. Baron, "The Jewish Question in the Nineteenth Century," *Journal of Modern History* 10, no. 1 (1938): 51–65. It contains a survey of economic and demographic data about the Jewish population in Europe and Russia, including some comparisons with analogous trends among local Christian inhabitants, and is framed for a nonspecialized audience.

4. Werner Sombart, *Der moderne Kapitalismus*, 2 vols. (Leipzig: Duncker & Humblot, 1902); Sombart, *Der moderne Kapitalismus*, 3 vols., 2nd ed. (Munich: Duncker & Humblot, 1916–28). A partial English translation appeared as Sombart, *Economic Life in the Modern Age*, ed. Nico Stehr and Reiner Grundmann (New Brunswick, NJ: Transaction, 2001). See also Werner Sombart, *Die Juden und das Wirtschaftsleben* (Leipzig: Duncker & Humblot, 1911); Sombart, *The Jews and Modern Capitalism*, trans. M. Epstein (London: T. F. Unwin, 1913). Luzzatto did more than others to bring Jewish and general economic history into dialogue with each other. In spite of his reservations about the book's overall thesis, he translated an abridged edition of *Der modern Kapitalismus* into Italian: Sombart, *Il capitalismo moderno: Esposizione storico-sistematica della vita economica di tutta l'Europa dai suoi inizi fino all'età contemporanea*, trans. Gino Luzzatto (Florence, 1925); Luzzatto, "L'origine e gli albori del capitalismo: A proposito della seconda edizione del 'Capitalismo moderno' di Werner Sombart," *Nuova rivista storica* 6 (1922): 39–66, reprinted in Luzzatto, *Dai servi della gleba agli albori del capitalismo: Saggi di storia economica* (Roma-Bari: Laterza, 1966), 485–527. A few years prior, however, Luzzatto had already made plain his criticisms of Sombart's *Die Juden und das Wirtschaftsleben*: Gino Luzzatto, "Rassegna: Pubblicazioni di storia economica-sociale," *Nuova rivista storica* 3 (1919): 632–46.

5. Salo Baron, "Ghetto and Emancipation: Shall We Revise the Traditional View?" *Menorah Journal* 14, no. 6 (1928): 515–26, at 523–24.

6. Baron, "Ghetto and Emancipation," 523.

7. Liberles, *Salo Wittmayer Baron*, 45.

8. Baron, "Ghetto and Emancipation," 526.

9. Salo Wittmayer Baron, *A Social and Religious History of the Jews*, 3 vols. (New York: Columbia University Press, 1937); Baron, *A Social and Religious History of the Jews*, 2nd ed., 17 vols. (New York: Columbia University Press, 1957–80).

10. Baron, *Social and Religious History of the Jews* (1937), 2:177.

11. Baron, *Social and Religious History of the Jews* (1937), 2:183.

12. Baron, *Social and Religious History of the Jews* (1937), 2:176.

13. Baron, *Social and Religious History of the Jews* (1937), 2:177.

14. Jean-Paul Sartre, *Anti-Semite and Jew* (New York: Schocken, 1995, originally published 1946), 126.

15. Salo W. Baron, "The Jewish Factor in Medieval Civilization," *Proceedings of the American Academy for Jewish Research* 12 (1942): 1–48, at 18 and 18n29, citing Walter J. Fischel, *Jews in the Economic and Political Life of Mediaeval Islam* (London: Royal Asiatic Society, 1937) as well as Baron, "The Economic Views of Maimonides," in *Essays on Maimonides: An Octocentennial*, ed. Salo Wittmayer Baron (New York: Columbia University Press, 1941), 127–264.
16. Baron, "The Jewish Factor in Medieval Civilization," 19 (emphasis added) and 19n30.
17. Salo W. Baron, "Modern Capitalism and Jewish Fate," *Menorah Journal* 30, no. 2 (1942): 116–38, reprinted in *History and Jewish Historians: Essays and Addresses by Salo W. Baron*, ed. Arthur Hertzberg and Leon A. Feldman (Philadelphia: Jewish Publication Society of America, 1964), 43–64, at 47.
18. Baron, "Modern Capitalism and Jewish Fate," 47. Here Baron lifts his phrasing concerning Sombart's treatment of Jews and capitalism verbatim from his preface to Baron, *A Social and Religious History of the Jews* (1937), 1:v. The references are to Hermann Wätjen, *Das Judentum und die Anfänge der modernen Kolonisation: Kritische Bemerkungen zu Werner Sombarts "Die Juden und das Wirtschaftsleben"* (Berlin: W. Kohlammer, 1914); Wätjen, *Das holländische Kolonialreich in Brasilien: Ein Kapitel aus der Kolonialgeschichte des 17. Jahrhunderts* (Haag: Martinus Nijhoff, 1921); and Herbert I. Bloom, *The Economic Activities of the Jews in Amsterdam in the Seventeenth and Eighteenth Centuries* (Williamsport, PA: Bayard, 1937). Two years later, Baron mentioned Wilhelm Roscher, Max Weber, and Lujo Brentano among Sombart's "disciples as well as opponents" and singled out Levi Herzfeld for his efforts to collect statistics about Jews' economic activities: Baron, "Emphases in Jewish History," *Jewish Social Studies* 1, no. 1 (1939): 15–38, at 23.
19. Baron, "Modern Capitalism and Jewish Fate," 48.
20. Baron, "Modern Capitalism and Jewish Fate," 48.
21. Salo Baron, "Levi Herzfeld: The First Jewish Economic Historian," in *Louis Ginzberg: Jubilee Volume on the Occasion of His Seventieth Birthday; English Section* (New York: American Academy for Jewish Research, 1945), 74–104, reprinted in Baron, *History and Jewish Historians*, 322–43, at 325. Rabbi Levi Herzfeld, *Handelsgeschichte der Juden des Alterthums* (Braunschweig, Germany: J. H. Meyer, 1879).
22. Baron, "Levi Herzfeld," 327, 334.
23. Baron, "Levi Herzfeld," 334.
24. Salo W. Baron, "European Jewry Before and After Hitler," *American Jewish Year Book* 62 (1962): 3–53, at 9.
25. Baron, "European Jewry Before and After Hitler," 10.
26. Baron, "European Jewry Before and After Hitler," 12.
27. Yuri Slezkine, *The Jewish Century* (Princeton, NJ: Princeton University Press, 2004), includes several ambivalent references to Sombart. Detailed studies of Jewish occupational structures tell a more complicated story. For example, on interwar Hungary, see Mária M. Kovács, "Interwar Antisemitism in the Professions: The Case of the Engineers," in *Jews in the Hungarian Economy 1760–1945: Studies Dedicated to Moshe Carmilly-Weinberger on his Eightieth Birthday*, ed. Michael K. Silber (Jerusalem: Magnes, 1992), 237–44.
28. R. H. Tawney's review of Henri Sée, *Les Origines du capitalisme moderne (Esquisse historique)* (Paris: Armand Colin, 1926), in *The Economic History Review*

(hereafter *EHR*) 1, no. 1 (1927): 156–59, at 157. See also Henri Sée, *Modern Capitalism: Its Origin and Evolution*, trans. Homer B. Vanderblue and Georges F. Doriot (New York: Adelphi, 1928).

29. Georg Brodnitz, "Recent Work in German Economic History (1900–1927)," *EHR* 1, no. 2 (1927): 322–54, at 335. Also see Georg Caro, *Sozial- und wirtschaftsgeschichte der Juden im Mittelalter und der Neuzeit*, 2 vols. (Leipzig: Gustav Fock, 1908–20); Moses Hoffmann, *Der Geldhandel der deutschen Juden während des Mittelalters bis zum Jahre 1350* (Leipzig: Duncker & Humblot, 1910).
30. Michael Postan, "Studies in Bibliography: I. Medieval Capitalism," *EHR* 4, no. 2 (1933): 212–27, at 212.
31. Postan, "Studies in Bibliography," 212.
32. Postan, "Studies in Bibliography," 216.
33. Postan, "Studies in Bibliography," 216.
34. Abbott Payson Usher, "The Origins of Banking: The Primitive Bank of Deposit, 1200–1600," *EHR* 4, no. 4 (1934): 399–428, at 402.
35. This is not to say that economic historians dispensed with other aspects of Sombart's work. After the publication of a critical review of *Der moderne Kapitalismus*, Sombart was offered ample space for a reply by the *EHR* editors. See Werner Sombart, "Theory and Economic History," *EHR* 2, no. 1 (1929): 1–19.
36. [Marc Bloch and Lucien Febvre], "À nos lecteurs," *Annales d'histoire économique et sociale* (hereafter *AHES*) 1, no. 1 (1929): 1–2. Having changed its name to *Annales d'histoire sociale* from 1939 to 1941 in order to escape censorship, the publication was registered as *Mélanges d'histoire sociale* in 1943–44, but reverted to its original title in 1945. Note that Bloch opposed these name changes before being killed by the Nazis and Febvre behaved very insensitively toward his Jewish colleague; see Philippe Burrin, *France Under the Germans: Collaboration and Compromise*, trans. Janet Lloyd (New York: New Press, 1996), 317–23. The epistolary exchanges between Febvre and Bloch on this matter do not appear among the letters between the two that Febvre published in a volume devoted to the memory of the deceased cofounder in 1945: "Marc Bloch: Témoignages sur la période 1939–1940; Extraits d'une correspondence intime," *Annales d'histoire sociale* 8, no. 1 (1945): 15–32. In 1946, the journal, now directed by Fernand Braudel, acquired the name by which it is best known, *Annales: Économies, Sociétés, Civilisations*, which it kept until 1994, when it became *Annales: Histoire, Sciences Sociales*. The way in which the journal is digitized for the period before 1939 does not allow for keyword searches, so I based the survey discussed in the body of the text on my reading of the tables of contents.
37. For example, Henri Pirenne, "L'instruction des marchands au moyen âge," *AHES* 1, no. 1 (1929): 12–28. The book review section also devoted numerous pages to the urban history of the Middle Ages, with the assessment of studies by Pirenne, Sapori, Pierre Lavedan, and others.
38. Henri Hauser, "Réflexions sur l'histoire des banques à l'époque moderne (de la fin du XVe à la fin du XVIIIe siècle)," *AHES* 1, no. 3 (1929): 335–51. In a short review of a journal article by J. G. van Dillen on the *Wisselbank* of Amsterdam (founded in 1609), Febvre praised the author for his sobriety and statistical data, as well as his comparisons with the public banks of Venice, Genoa, Lyon, and Antwerp. Lucien Febvre, "La banque d'Amsterdam," *AHES* 1, no. 3 (1929): 444–45. Van Dillen

would go on to write extensively about Jews' contributions to Amsterdam's stock market, curbing excessive estimates of their supposed predominance. For example, see van Dillen, "De economische positie en betekenis der Joden in de Republiek en in de Nederlandse koloniale wereld," in *Geschiedenis der Joden in Nederland*, ed. Hendrik Brugmans and A. Frank (Amsterdam: van Holkema and Warendorf, 1940), 561–616.

39. Lucien Febvre, "Une critique utile: Les origines du capitalisme moderne à Gênes et W. Sombart," *AHES* 4, no. 15 (1932): 318–19. The review referred to Sayous, "*Der moderne Kapitalismus* de W. Sombart et Gênes aux XIIe et XIIIe siècles," *Revue d'histoire économique et sociale* 18, no. 4 (1930): 427–44; and "Les Juifs," *Revue économique internationale* 24, no. 3 (1932): 491–535. See also Sayous, "Dans l'Italie à l'intérieur des terres: Sienne de 1221 à 1229," *AHES* 3, no. 10 (1931): 189–206. A full bibliography can be found in André-E. Sayous, *Structure et évolution du capitalisme européen, XVIe-XVIIe siècles*, ed. Mark Steele (London: Variorum Reprints, 1989), xiii–xxiv.

40. Roberto Lopez, "*Aux origines du capitalisme génois*," *AHES* 9, n. 47 (1937): 429–54, which includes Sayous among its references (453). A year later, in 1938, Lopez fled Italy upon the proclamation of the so-called Racial Laws.

41. Sée, *Les Origines du capitalisme moderne*; and Henri Hauser, *Les Débuts du capitalisme* (Paris: Félix Alcan, 1927).

42. Annette Becker, *Maurice Halbwachs: Un intellectuel entre guerre mondiales 1914-1945* (Paris: Angès Viénot, 2003), 271–90.

43. Maurice Halbwachs, "Propriété individuelle ou propriété collective: Le problème palestinien," *AHES* 2, no. 6 (1930): 270–71; and review of Abraham Granovsky, *Les problèms de la terre en Palestine* (Paris: Rieder, 1928). Born in the Russian Empire in 1924, Granovsky (later Granot in Hebrew) immigrated to Jerusalem in 1922 and became one of the signatories of the Israeli declaration of independence in 1948 and a member of the Knesset.

44. Léon Berman, *Histoire des Juifs de France des origines à nos jours* (Paris: Lipschutz [1937]); *La Situation économique des Juifs dans le monde* (Paris: Congrès juif mondial, Département économique, 1938); Maurice Eisenbeth, *Les Juifs de l'Afrique du Nord: Démographie & onomastique* (Alger: Imprimerie du lycée, 1936). Paul Leulliot reviewed the first two and René Lespès the latter in *Annales d'histoire sociale* 1, no. 1 (1939): 108–11.

45. Simon Dubnov, *Précis d'histoire juive, des origines à 1934*, trans. Isaac Pougatch (Paris: Pyoum, 1946); Robert Anchel, *Napoléon et les Juifs* (Paris: Les Presses universitaires de France, 1928); Jacques Polonski, *La Presse, la propagande et l'opinion publique sous l'occupation* (Paris: Éditions du Centre de documentation juive contemporaine, 1946). Paul Leulliot reviewed the first two titles and Maurice Baumont gave an account of the latter: "Judaisme," *Annales: Économies, Sociétés, Civilisations* 2, no. 4 (1947): 497–99.

46. Baron, "Emphases in Jewish History," 23. He also lamented the paucity of studies of Jewish economic thought. I have excised this topic from my chapter for reasons of space.

47. Baron, "Emphases in Jewish History," 26.

48. Baron, "Emphases in Jewish History," 27–28, 35 (emphasis in the original).

49. Jacob Neusner, "Jews in Economies and the Economics of Judaism: The Case of Salo W. Baron," appendix to his *Why Does Judaism Have an Economics? The Inaugural Saul Reinfeld Lecture in Judaic Studies at Connecticut College, April 13, 1988* (New London, CT: Connecticut College, 1988), 21–28, at 26 and 28.
50. Liberles, *Salo Wittmayer Baron*, 124.
51. Liberles, *Salo Wittmayer Baron*, 142.
52. Liberles, *Salo Wittmayer Baron*, 88–93.
53. A book like Maristella Botticini and Zvi Eckstein, *The Chosen Few: How Education Shaped Jewish History, 70–1492* (Princeton, NJ: Princeton University Press, 2012), for example, won the 2012 National Jewish Book Award. It not only takes Sombart as one of its legitimate sources, but it also lends itself to the kind of criticism that Neusner leveled against Baron (see note 49).

Chapter Five

SALO BARON ON ANTISEMITISM

DAVID ENGEL

Salo Baron was the author of the entry entitled "Anti-Semitism" in each annual printing of the *Encyclopedia Britannica*'s fourteenth edition between 1962 and 1973.[1] This article contained Baron's most comprehensive statement on the subject to date and at the time the only one devoted exclusively to it.[2] In the opening sentence, Baron declared that "anti-Semitism, consisting of hostile expressions or actions against Jews, has been a more or less constant feature of Jewish life in the Diaspora."[3] This sentence appears to have offered the closest approximation of a definition of the term in any of his voluminous writings.

At first glance, the definition seems extraordinarily broad. Numerous scholars before and since have endeavored to restrict use of the term in various ways, so that it would designate something more specific than "*all* forms of hostility towards Jews and Judaism throughout history, . . . extending . . . to all times and places regardless of specific circumstances, differences between historical epochs and cultures, or other factors that might give the term more specificity and critical sharpness."[4] Baron, by contrast, made no explicit effort "to define cut-off points which define *essential* antisemitism"[5] or to distinguish the phenomenon from "the normal, xenophobic prejudice which has prevailed between ethno-religious groups during virtually every period of history."[6] On the contrary, much of the "anti-Jewish feeling" that he included within the scope of his discussion was not, as he represented it, significantly different from hostility faced by "other minorities"; it originated in "the general factors creating antagonisms among groups, such as the dislike of the different, the search for scapegoats in periods of crisis and the tendency to generalize the shortcomings or transgressions of individuals and to attribute them to the entire group." To be sure, Baron noted, these factors "have been aggravated in the case of Jews by the heritage of religious hatreds and folkloristic superstitions," causing antagonism "sometimes" to take on "a specific character owing to the extraordinary situation and outlook of the Jewish people."[7] However, in theory at least, his presentation did not explicitly exclude "hostile expressions or actions against Jews" that were not so "aggravated" or that lacked such a "specific character" from consideration under the rubric of "antisemitism".

In practice—in the actual manner in which Baron used the word, in the senses he actually attached to it and the referents he employed to convey them—the matter was more complicated.

In the relatively short space allocated to him, Baron hardly could have hoped to discuss the full range of "hostile expressions or actions against Jews" in all times and places. He might have represented that range by suggesting a typology of hostility, dividing his article into sections offering salient examples from different times and places of verbal smears, repulsive visual imagery, exclusionary legislative measures, violent attacks, social ostracism, unfavorable literary and linguistic figures, antagonistic sermons and ideological screeds, interpersonal conflicts in which the Jewishness of one of the opponents was mentioned, and the many additional sorts of "hostile expressions or actions against Jews" that have been recorded over the centuries. But he did not choose this approach. He chose instead to present a unified historical narrative, from pre-Christian antiquity through World War II, extrapolated from and exemplified by a set of data points representing only a single type. Those data points appear to have recommended to him, de facto, a far narrower conception of "antisemitism" than the initial sentence of his article on the subject suggests.

Baron did not articulate the type's delimiting features. However, on the basis of his subsequent narrative, these can fairly be characterized as false or misleading statements about Jews as a collective offered in the context of political debates or clashes over resources. Thus, Baron explained, the political ambitions of Haman in the Book of Esther, the efforts of the Seleucid ruler Antiochus IV to Hellenize Judea in the second century BCE, and friction among local leaders, imperial authorities, and the Jewish community of Alexandria during the first century CE generated a series of charges about the Jews' religion, culture, and collective character aimed at justifying their opponents' actions. Those charges—alleging, *inter alia*, Jewish separatism, disloyalty, barbaric rituals, inborn cowardice, and fundamental misanthropy—"were taken over by the apologists of the nascent Christian church" for use in conflicts in which both Jews and Christians were persecuted by pagan rulers and in which each endeavored to undermine the other in the oppressors' eyes.[8] Christian scripture, he observed, added to them two new accusations: one concerning "the specific Jewish 'sin' of having crucified Christ"; the other "that Jews misinterpreted materialistically (i.e., literally) the Old Testament passages foretelling the coming of the Messiah."[9] Once Christians assumed hegemony in the Roman Empire, those older and newer charges together underwrote "a long series of legislative enactments . . . designed to lower the status of the synagogue and its worshipers, to segregate Jews from believing Christians and to curtail Jewish religious self-determination[:] . . . the Jew was declared a permanent alien and wanderer who, because of his repudiation of Christ, . . . was to be maintained in a status of legal and social inferiority and removed from close social contact with believers."[10] Later in the middle ages, when Christians began to challenge the position of Jews in European commerce, some church leaders figured Jews as parasitic exploiters, no doubt in order to justify restrictions on Jewish economic activity. Jews' economic competitors themselves also invented calumnies of their own, identifying Jews with the devil and charging them with ritual murder,[11] to support their demands for expulsion and segregation.

The era following the Peace of Westphalia, when, according to Baron, "freedom of religion began to be increasingly accepted as a dominant principle of public law," witnessed a shift in the emphasis of false charges about Jews "from the religious to the political and socio-economic issues."[12] Evidently Baron meant that political efforts to prevent application of the new principle, along with its corollaries of "the idea of mutual toleration" and "equality of rights," to Jews tended less and less to justify their positions on the basis of purported features of the Jewish religion, turning increasingly to accusations that Jews habitually exploited the peasantry or formed a state within a state. Nevertheless, he stressed, "the various clerical parties" that were among the most notable opponents of Jewish civic equality "used these arguments to rationalize their old religious antagonisms without incurring the odium of religious intolerance."[13] At the same time, however, "the newly arising socialist parties . . . effectively employed them in their agitation against the established order."[14] "As a consequence of the widespread ruin brought about by the financial crisis of 1873," Baron noted, the same arguments became the basis for a new political movement. The movement appeared first in recently unified Germany, where "ancient prejudices provided a welcome scapegoat for sufferers from the depression" in a manner that appeared to benefit "conservative and ultramontane" elements.[15] However, the movement soon split in two after a radical faction, proclaiming a "theory of nationality" inspired by G. W. F. Hegel and propagated by journalist Wilhelm Marr of Hamburg, castigated Christianity along with Judaism as "not compatible with the theological and ethical conceptions of the Germanic peoples."[16] The schism between Christian and anti-Christian factions, in which each party remained at more or less equal strength, condemned the movement in Germany to failure. In neighboring Austria, by contrast, the anti-Christian argument met with little purchase, permitting those whose opposition to Jewish civic equality allowed for appeals to explicitly Christian motifs to gain somewhat greater political traction. Certain elements in France also found it expedient "to make use of the teachings of German antisemitism in party politics," in a manner that left "permanent scars on French public life."[17] And in Russia, "landowners who had been hurt by the [1861] emancipation of the serfs" were aided in their quest to dominate the government by "a nationalist and reactionary agitation" that drew on motifs from "medieval anti-Semitism" and contemporary "German anti-Semitic teachings" to generate "an explosion" of violence against Jews in 1881.[18]

The twentieth century marked a new chapter in Baron's narrative. Now the ancient canard of disloyalty was transfigured into a charge of Jewish "internationalism." The accusation served several different interests: groups seeking to curb mass migrations between states, nationalists promoting their own imperial commercial blocs over global free trade, monarchists worried by the growing strength of liberal political movements that appeared to transcend state borders, and capitalists of all stripes frightened by the communist triumph in Russia. The Nazi movement in Germany managed to combine warnings about a purported worldwide Jewish conspiracy, epitomized in the *Protocols of the Elders of Zion*, with assertions propagated earlier in Germany by all manner of opponents of Jewish civic equality in a way that "appealed both to the underprivileged masses and to the élite of aristocrats, former army officers and bureaucrats displaced by the revolution."[19] The coalition of these elements brought the Nazis to power. The Nazis also found a way to utilize their particular combination of falsehoods as "an instrument of German foreign policy."[20] The result, Baron declared, was "a tragic deterioration of the position of Jews far beyond the German frontiers," culminating in the death of "perhaps six out of every seven Jews found in the [Nazi-]occupied areas."[21]

Baron's encyclopedia entry thus told a story about the creation and expansion of a reservoir of antagonistic collective representations of Jews on which certain historical actors in various places and times found it expedient to draw in order to advance interests or to vindicate political positions.[22] Though he made no explicit statement concerning why he chose this particular set of referents for an article entitled "Anti-Semitism" (out of the broader range of "hostile expressions or actions against Jews" to which the term might be applied), in fact he employed the word fairly consistently throughout to signify the reservoir itself, together with the set of political arguments and governmental actions that he believed had drawn on it over the centuries. Moreover, Baron presented the reservoir mainly as the product of fairly ordinary, real-world political and economic struggles in which at least some Jews were demonstrably implicated; in his telling, it served as a source of *justification* for "hostile expressions or actions against Jews" more than as a *motivation* for them. The people who propagated the falsehoods that formed the data points on which he hung his narrative seem to have done so, in his telling, not so much out of sincerely held conviction or emotion but for altogether instrumental reasons. They knew that their statements were not true, but the ends they sought rendered their mendacity proper and even praiseworthy in their own minds. Sometimes they may have inspired belief among their audience, but in his article, Baron did not examine the reasons they succeeded when and where they did. His sole hint concerning his approach to this question made reference to common psychosocial phenomena characteristic of majority-minority interactions in general, not to any special hatred purportedly reserved for Jews alone.

In short, what Baron called "antisemitism" seems rather like what early eighteenth-century Scottish satirist John Arbuthnot called "political lying." Jews, to be sure, were "antisemitic" political lies' sole target, but only the choice of target distinguished "antisemitism" from that universally practiced "noble and useful art . . . such as serves for a model of education for an able politician" anywhere and everywhere.[23]

Neither in the encyclopedia article nor anywhere else did Baron explain why he chose to represent "antisemitism" in this fashion, instead of concentrating, say, on the activities of the late-nineteenth century German movement with which the term was originally associated, as had the entry on the same subject in the *Encyclopedia Britannica*'s eleventh edition.[24] Consequently, his thinking can only be surmised. Nevertheless, the full corpus of Baron's writings offers insight into how his understanding of the term and its referents may have developed.

The word "antisemitism" did not figure noticeably in Baron's scholarly writing before the appearance of the first edition of his *Social and Religious History of the Jews* in 1937 or in articles of a more publicistic or policy-oriented nature before 1930.[25] Its lone appearance before that date came in one of his earliest journalistic pieces, a commentary on the 1912 boycott of Jewish businesses in Congress Poland, published in five installments of the Kraków Hebrew-language weekly *Hamicpe* in February and March 1913, when he was a mere seventeen years old. In that set of articles, Baron referred to several Polish political figures as "antisemites," clearly on account both of their support for the boycott and of their advocacy for limitations on Jewish civic and political rights in the Polish lands.[26] In one place he spoke of "the antisemitic current" (*haZerem haAntishemi*) within the Polish Progressive Democratic Party (*Stronnictwo Postępowo-Demokratyczne*), whose veteran leader, Aleksander Świętochowski, "a famous liberal, has now changed his tune and is placing himself against the Jews" by joining the boycott movement.[27] And in the article's penultimate sentence he used the word "antisemitism" (*antishemiyut*) as a synonym for "the antisemitic propaganda" (*haTa'amulah haAntishemit*) being disseminated by boycott advocates.[28]

It seems noteworthy, in light of his observations half a century later, that Baron's description of that propaganda made no reference to use of motifs from an earlier era. Its terms, as he presented it, were drawn entirely from the contemporary context. Moreover, the propaganda that Baron reviewed and undertook to refute did not attack the Jewish religion. Nor did it ascribe to all Jews, everywhere and at all times, any insidious cultural characteristics. Instead, it propagated falsehoods about the history and current behavior of *Polish* Jews, claiming that Jews consistently fail to demonstrate proper gratitude for the action of fourteenth-century Polish King Kazimierz III (the Great), who had "saved them during their time of trouble and kindly taken them in while throughout Europe they were being persecuted";[29] express hatred toward the Polish nation; refuse to identify with it; and withhold financial support from Polish cultural institutions. The reason the "antisemites" spread such lies in support of their boycott call, Baron explained, was entirely political: to punish Jews for their vote in the recent election to the Fourth Russian State Duma, which had helped to defeat the candidacy of the boycott's leader. "They are speaking baseless libels about the Jews only . . . in order to build themselves up by destroying them [i.e. the Jews]."[30] Moreover, he declared, "they themselves . . . see that their words have no basis in reality."[31] They nevertheless expected their lies to bring political benefit, he surmised, because by "pouring out their wrath upon the weak Jews," they could promise the many "Poles who in recent years . . . have become merchants, opened shops, and begun to compete with their Jewish neighbors . . . the spoils that will come from robbing the Jews of their livelihood."[32] In short, one of the central referents in Baron's latter-day understanding of the word "antisemitism"—false or misleading statements about Jews offered in the context of political struggles or of clashes over resources—appears to have found expression already in his youth.

The second central referent—the reservoir of antagonistic collective representations of Jews on which political actors could draw to justify their positions—became evident only a quarter century later, in the first edition of Baron's classic *Social and Religious History of the Jews*, published in 1937.[33] There, for the first time, Baron used the expression "classical anti-Semitism" to designate phenomena in the Greco-Roman world bearing "comparison with the various shades of modern Jew-baiting" that he had observed in Poland and Romania.[34] Then, as later, most of the referents subsumed by the phrase were arguments aimed at ending "the favorable legal status of the strong Jewish minority granted by the imperial laws of the Ptolemies or the Romans," which were resented by "the ever-so-noisy and quarrelsome citizenry of a Graeco-Oriental municipality."[35] Also, as he had claimed regarding similar arguments advanced during the Polish boycott campaign of 1912, here, too, Baron ventured that "much of the inflammatory material in vogue in anti-Jewish propaganda was the product of conscious fabrication."[36] Those two observations evidently led him to formulate, for what appears to have been the first time, a theoretical generalization about "anti-semitism" in the abstract: "As always in anti-Semitism, the vital force [behind ancient anti-Jewish propaganda literature] was resentment of the alien character of the Jews."[37] Indeed, Baron made it clear that his conception of "classical anti-Semitism" had been formulated with his own era firmly in mind: "To general denunciations of Jewish aloofness [in antiquity] were added a quantity of attacks on Jewish customs and beliefs, many of which have a quite modern sound. From the disparagement of Jewish 'contributions to civilization' to the discovery of an offensive odor emanating from Jewish bodies; from cheap witticisms about circumcision and abstention from pork to allegations of 'atheism' or donkey worship, almost every note in the cacophony of medieval and modern anti-Semitism was sounded by the chorus of ancient writers."[38]

Baron also noted another feature of such calumnies, one born of conditions specific to the ancient world that nevertheless allowed the denunciations and attacks eventually to transcend the circumstances of time and place:

> In view of the "classical" reverence for tradition, with its undistinguishable [sic] maze of mythology, folklore and actual history, it was necessary to prove that Judaism had been corrupt from the beginning. Hence the oriental Hellenists proceeded to retell the history of the Jews in an unfavorable light. They dwelt especially upon the period of Israel's origin, upon the personality and the age of Moses. Seizing upon the story told about half a century after Alexander by Manethon, an Egyptian priest-historian, concerning the expulsion of the Hyksos from Egypt, they interpreted the biblical Exodus as an expulsion motivated by the fear that the Jews would contaminate the people of the country with leprosy. Thus Manethon's innocuous statement grew into a legend, repeated and amplified by one writer after another. It was finally adopted as historical truth by most Graeco-Roman historians.[39]

Here, it seems, was the first adumbration of a reservoir of disparaging falsehoods about Jews, available to each generation for use and expansion according to its particular cultural predilections and political needs.

Baron enumerated the falsehoods whose origins he placed in antiquity in a single eight-page section of the first volume of the *Social and Religious History*, to which he gave the heading "classical anti-Semitism." The work contained no comparable section entitled "medieval anti-Semitism." In fact, unlike in his encyclopedia article from the 1960s, Baron does not appear in 1937 to have regarded the middle ages as a time in which the reservoir of available calumnies expanded notably. To be sure, he noted that "it was in medieval Europe that the Jews became the 'Wandering Jew,'" but the context of the observation makes clear that he referred not to a hostile image but to a political fact: "nowhere else [than in medieval Europe] did the practice of *expulsion* become a prominent factor in the relations between Jew and Gentile."[40] More noteworthy for him in the Christian middle ages than the calumnies themselves, it seems, were the range and frequency of *actions* toward Jews that the lies supported. Before that era, he wrote, "anti-Semitism [i.e., in Baron's usage, false or misleading statements about Jews] had existed in one guise or another wherever Jews lived in dispersion, . . . but nowhere else than in medieval Europe did persecutions follow in such quick succession, assume such universal character, or have such lasting effects."[41] That sentence marked one of the few appearances of the word "antisemitism" in his chapters on the middle ages. Significantly, although he described extensively the various sorts of persecutions to which medieval European Jews were subjected—not only expulsions but also restrictions on economic activity and residence, popular violence, religious disputations, and the Inquisition—he does not appear to have employed the word to characterize any interaction between Jews and Christians before the sixteenth century. "Antisemitism" continued to refer to representations, not acts.

From the sixteenth century on, by contrast, Baron noted a renewed proliferation of invidious representations. "An examination of the anti-Semitism of the post-emancipation era reveals many relatively new features," he argued, pointing to a set of "new accusations and arguments" concocted by leaders of the masses in response to the increasing entry of Jews into socioeconomic sectors that previously had been closed to them. Some new features, such as figuring Judaism as "one of the incurable diseases," were already evident in the aftermath of the expulsion from Spain, as an expression of "the popular reaction to the Neo-Christians," whose economic activity could not be delegitimized by appeals to falsehoods about the Jewish religion. In Baron's view, a straight line connected this charge to the "racial anti-Semitism" of the nineteenth and twentieth centuries.[42] Others surfaced later, especially after Jews had begun, as part of the emancipation process, to become prominent in the liberal professions and in the cultural life of their surrounding societies. Thus, Baron observed, whereas in earlier eras Jews had been castigated for their unwillingness to meld with other peoples, now "precisely the opposite accusation was hurled. They are corrupting the nation by insidiously boring from within! Not lack of western education, but domination over national arts, sciences and letters, became the avowed reason for opposition."[43]

Accordingly, "modern anti-Semitism" received its own section heading, as "medieval anti-Semitism" had not.[44] For Baron the modern era was marked not only by new falsehoods but also by the emergence of new organizations whose purpose was to spread the falsehoods across the globe. Still, however, in his view, those organizations continued to disseminate both old and new slanders not out of belief in or commitment to any consistent set of ideas but for instrumental reasons alone:

> The very term "anti-Semitism" became a source of strength to those who gathered under it. Without positive connotation, it could easily conceal the divergence among the different trends. There was, in fact, not one anti-Semitic movement, but many. It included those who wanted the elimination of Jewish competition in the economic field; those who wished to destroy the Jews as capitalists; those seeking revenge on Jewish leaders of socialism; those who believed in racial purity, and the superiority of their own race over all others; those demagogues who detected in the excitation of popular anger against the Jews a means of personal political aggrandizement; and those who sought to deflect popular resentment of their own misgovernment into other channels. Such an omnibus term could easily cover a multitude of motives and impulses. As time went on, however, the inconsistencies of anti-Semitic ideology and the diversities of interest frequently came to the fore, and interminable dissensions followed.[45]

The motifs of "modern anti-Semitism" were thus, for Baron, more varied than those of "classical anti-Semitism." Nevertheless, both sets shared at least one common feature: they consisted of falsehoods about Jews disseminated in the context of struggles for political or economic hegemony. As for the middle ages, however, Baron generally refrained from employing "antisemitism" to characterize hostile expressions or actions against Jews in which such a struggle was not evident. There were, for example, instances of social exclusion of Jews that were supported, he thought, by attitudes rooted not in the stock reservoir of anti-Jewish representations but in a different set of behavioral conventions:

> In western social life alone certain irrational impulses or inveterate habits delayed the desired amalgamation [of Jews]. In America, especially, the lack of a landed gentry and titles of nobility, and the prevalent political democracy, led to rigid social exclusiveness among the plutocratic families; more rigid, indeed, than anywhere in Europe. Judge Hilton's refusal, in 1877, to admit to his Grand Union Hotel in Saratoga Springs, Joseph Seligman, to whom President Grant had a few years before offered the post of Secretary of the Treasury, was an early instance of such social fastidiousness. . . . In Europe many a wealthy Jewess succeeded in purchasing a poor, but titled, husband, thus forcing "society" to accept her, along with him. In the happy days of liberalism, the Jewish question seemed to be solving itself through these assimilatory processes.[46]

This analysis was not part of Baron's discussion of "modern anti-Semitism", which focused only on the political, not on the social, arena. The exclusion of an important Jewish political figure from a private hotel in the United States was instead, for Baron, no more than a bit of backsliding in the course of a historical process that tended overall toward social integration, not substantially different from any other expression of social snobbery aimed at defending an outmoded class structure. Without the explicit support of false statements about Jews in general, beyond the conviction that Mr. Seligman did not belong to the class to which the hotel catered, this act evidently did not qualify as "antisemitic" in Baron's lexicon.

In short, Baron's understanding of the word "antisemitism" appears to have changed little between 1912 and 1937, his formative years as a historian. Throughout this interval, he used the word to designate a sort of specifically *political* lying about Jews, lying undertaken to justify actions aimed at adding to or preserving the political or economic power of the liars. Whereas initially he had focused on lies concerning particular Jewish communities in specific times and places, during the 1930s, he appears to have been more concerned with lies that were supposed to apply universally to all Jews across time and space. Nevertheless, he does not appear to have regarded universal applicability as a necessary condition for employing the word. The existence of such universally applicable charges and their appearance in an identifiable chronological sequence, however, provided him with a set of data points on which he constructed his encyclopedic historical survey of "anti-Semitism" in the 1960s.

That Baron fashioned his 1960s historical survey out of materials first assembled during the 1930s and earlier indicates that his use of the term was hardly affected by the Nazi Holocaust.[47] Thus, when Robert Servatius, lead defense attorney for SS-Obersturmbannführer Adolf Eichmann, to whose 1961 trial in Jerusalem Baron was summoned as an expert witness on Jewish history, asked him on cross-examination to "detail the reasons for this negative attitude, for this struggle against the Jewish people," Baron answered in terms he had formulated before the war:

> Many theories have been offered as to the source of anti-Semitism and its development. . . . [Fundamental is] the hatred of the Jews as being of a different kind, that is to say what is occasionally called in English the "dislike of the unlike;" the strange was something that was not liked. For this they also found many different intellectual explanations: for example the Jews were too dominant in economics, they lent money on interest, they took control of cultural affairs, etc. All kinds of justifications. But this was the basic factor, that evidently the hatred arose solely because of this difference between the majority and the minority, and they wanted to justify it somehow. They justified it by using one argument or another.[48]

Baron had spoken of "dislike of the unlike" in 1937 as a "psychological factor" that helped lies propagated by antisemites make inroads into the broader society.[49] Following his response to Servatius, the presiding judge asked him to explain again "what were the motivations of anti-Semitism." Baron reemphasized the phrase: "The answer is, dislike of the unlike," adding, "There were also special factors in each country. This was economic jealousy, people who did not like their competitors who were Jews, whether in the professions or in business."

These replies were delivered impromptu; Baron had not prepared to answer the question in advance. That under such circumstances he would, off the cuff, frame the historic "struggle against the Jewish people" as a set of "arguments" used to "justify" "economic jealousy" born of "dislike of the unlike" and the "difference between the majority and the minority" may indicate, perhaps, that these associations were foremost in his mind whenever he heard and spoke the word "antisemitism." In fact, in a 1975 lecture at Columbia University on "Third World and Other New Attitudes Toward the Jew," Baron surveyed "rationalizations for antisemitism" through the ages, concluding that "dislike of the unlike" had bred "endless combinations" of arguments drawn from a central stock of disingenuous justifications that fell in and out of favor depending upon changing political and economic circumstances.[50] The arguments themselves, not their practical expression, formed the core of his presentation.

Thus, although some deviations are evident from time to time, his use of the word in his writings over a fifty-year period appears largely consistent with such an understanding. Although Baron's only formal definition of the word theoretically encompassed all hostile expressions or actions against Jews, in practice he restricted its scope to false arguments about Jews employed as *justifications* for actions by members of a majority undertaken to advance their interests against those of a Jewish minority living among them.

Others, of course, have understood the word and the limits of its referents differently. Baron's usage does not comport with the delimitations and features suggested more recently by David Berger, Ben Halpern, Gavin Langmuir, Bernard Lewis, Deborah Lipstadt, or Robert Wistrich, to name but a few.[51] This divergence does not mean that Baron's understanding was more or less correct than others.[52] "Antisemitism" has no tangible referents in nature, whose presence or absence in a suspected manifestation offers a vehicle for differential diagnosis, as it were. It signifies instead an analytical category created by human beings for various purposes, whose boundaries vary with the categorizers and their aims. The boundaries of Baron's category appear to have been set implicitly during the first forty years of his life as he analyzed specific aspects of Jewish life in the past and in his own day. Subsequently they remained rather consistent despite radical changes in the context of his analysis.

NOTES

1. These were the final twelve years of the fourteenth edition of *Encyclopedia Brittanica*; a redesigned fifteenth edition replaced it in 1974. Baron's initial four-page article was expanded to ten pages for the 1967 printing. See Jeannette Meisel Baron, "A Bibliography of the Printed Writings of Salo Wittmayer Baron," in *Salo Wittmayer Baron Jubilee Volume* (Jerusalem: American Academy for Jewish Research, 1974), English Section, 1:1–37, nos. 350, 414. The citations that follow are from the expanded 1967 version (hereafter cited as *EB*).
2. The only other discrete piece of writing in which Baron addressed the subject directly was his foreword to a 1942 collection of essays entitled *Essays on Antisemitism*. In it he proclaimed "the need of further, more detailed and even more searching investigations" of "the history of antisemitic movements," noting that "there are . . . large areas" in that history "where even the preliminary accumulation of documentary evidence is still sadly lacking." However, he offered no thesis of his own on the topic beyond some general observations on the dangers facing Jews of his own day. Salo W. Baron, "Foreword," in *Essays on Antisemitism*, ed. Koppel S. Pinson (New York: Conference on Jewish Relations, 1942), x. He subsequently published an article entitled "Changing Patterns of Antisemitism," which followed the approach outlined in the encyclopedia entry. See below, n. 50. I recall hearing Baron claim, in his later years, that he had written the entry on antisemitism in the prospectus (*Probeheft*) for the German-language *Encyclopedia Judaica*, whose first ten volumes were published in Berlin between 1928 and 1934, before the Nazi rise to power ended the project. However, I have been unable to corroborate either my own recollection or the existence of such an article by Baron. His bibliography lists no such publication. The actual entry "*Antisemitismus*" in the encyclopedia in question was credited to Dr. E. Jacob of Saarbrücken.
3. *EB*, 81.
4. Robert S. Wistrich, *Antisemitism: The Longest Hatred* (New York: Schocken, 1991), xvi. A proper survey of the full range of definitions in the scholarly literature is a desideratum. Meanwhile, see the observations in Kenneth L. Marcus, *The Definition of Anti-Semitism* (New York: Oxford University Press).
5. Ben Halpern, "What Is Antisemitism?" *Modern Judaism* 1 (1980): 253.
6. Wistrich, *Antisemitism*, xviii.
7. *EB*, 81–82.
8. *EB*, 82.
9. *EB*, 82.
10. *EB*, 82.
11. Baron posited that "the foundations for recurrent ritual murder accusations against both Jews and early Christians" had been laid in Seleucid times, but "from the 12th century . . . the ancient ritual murder accusation appeared with greater frequency" (*EB*, 82).
12. *EB*, 82.
13. *EB*, 82.
14. *EB*, 82–83.
15. *EB*, 83.
16. *EB*, 83.

17. *EB*, 83. The phrase "the teachings of German anti-Semitism" appears here to have signified the full set of false accusations concerning Jews disseminated by the new political movement that crystallized after 1873 more than any coherent ideology, whose existence Baron's emphasis on the split within the movement along ideological fault lines tacitly denied. Such a reading is consistent with Baron's usage of "anti-Semitism" throughout the article.
18. *EB*, 83.
19. *EB*, 85.
20. *EB*, 85.
21. *EB*, 86.
22. Although the narrative effectively ended in 1945, the entry continued with a geographical survey of the ways in which arguments that drew on the reservoir proved or failed to prove politically effective in various countries before and after World War II. Evidently Baron did not perceive any significant twentieth-century additions to the reservoir itself beyond the charge of "internationalism."
23. [John Arbuthnot], "Proposals for Printing a Very Curious Discourse . . . Entitled [sic] . . . The Art of Political Lying," *Miscellanies* 2 (2nd ed., 1733), 244.
24. Lucien Wolf, "Anti-Semitism," in *The Encyclopedia Britannica: A Dictionary of Arts, Sciences, Literature and General Information*, 11th ed. (Cambridge: Cambridge University Press, 1910), 2:134–46.
25. For details, see note 33.
26. For the full text of the entire article, see David Engel, "Tsa'ir miGalitsiyah al haHerem haAnti-Yehudi bePolin haKongresa'it: MiKitvei haNe'urim shel Shalom (Salo) Baron," *Gal-Ed* 19 (2004): 29–55 (Hebrew pagination). The word "antisemite" appears on 36, 37, 42, 43, 44, 45, 48, 49, 50, and 53. In one of these locations (42), he counted his principal interlocutor in the article, Kraków-based journalist Antoni Chołoniewski, as being "among the antisemites" on the same grounds.
27. Engel, "Tsa'ir miGalitsiyah al haHerem haAnti-Yehudi bePolin haKongresa'it," 44.
28. Engel, "Tsa'ir miGalitsiyah al haHerem haAnti-Yehudi bePolin haKongresa'it," 55.
29. Engel, "Tsa'ir miGalitsiyah al haHerem haAnti-Yehudi bePolin haKongresa'it," 37.
30. Engel, "Tsa'ir miGalitsiyah al haHerem haAnti-Yehudi bePolin haKongresa'it, 42. On the political episode in question, see, *inter alia*, Stephen D. Corrsin, *Warsaw Before the First World War: Poles and Jews in the Third City of the Russian Empire 1880–1914* (Boulder, CO: East European Monographs, 1989), 89–104.
31. Engel, "Tsa'ir miGalitsiyah al haHerem haAnti-Yehudi bePolin haKongresa'it," 42.
32. Engel, "Tsa'ir miGalitsiyah al haHerem haAnti-Yehudi bePolin haKongresa'it," 43–44.
33. Salo Wittmayer Baron, *A Social and Religious History of the Jews* (New York: Columbia University Press, 1937) (hereafter cited as *SRH1*). It is noteworthy that the word did not appear in Baron's two signal works of the interval: his study of the Jewish question at the Congress of Vienna (Salo Baron, *Die Judenfrage auf dem Wiener Kongreß, auf Grund von zum Teil ungedruckten Quellen dargestellt*, Vienna: R. Löwit, 1920) and his essay on Jewish understandings of the middle ages and the modern era (Salo Baron, "Ghetto and Emancipation: Shall We Revise the Traditional View?" *Menorah Journal* 14, no. 6 [1928]: 515–26), in which he inaugurated his critique of the "lachrymose theory of pre-Revolutionary woe." In the work on the Vienna Congress, he noted that "die nationale-religiöse Verklärung

[des Zeitalters der Reaktion] schloß die Juden als einen Fremdkörper von der Gesellschaft aus, und die historische Schule forderte anstatt der Verbesserung der Lage der Juden die Aufrechterhaltung aller Beschränkungen" (179), but he evidently did not require the word "antisemitism" to describe either this situation or the "Hep-Hep-Bewegung" of 1819, which, he claimed, issued from it.

In a brief study of the condition of Romanian Jewry undertaken for the American Jewish Congress (Salo Baron, *The Jews of Roumania*, New York: American Jewish Congress, 1930), he used the word to refer to propaganda against Jews carried on by A. C. Cuza, founder in 1922 of the National Christian Union (*Uniunea Națională Creștină*), one of whose aims was to protect "the economic, political, and cultural interests of the Rumanians against the Jews by all legal means," and Corneliu Zelea-Codreanu, who, five years later, established the League of the Archangel Michael (*Ligiunea Arhanghelului Mihail*), a political pressure group *cum* paramilitary organization that promised, *inter alia*, to end peasant "slavery to the Kikes" (Keith Hitchens, *Romania 1866–1947*, Oxford: Clarendon, 1994, 403; Irina Livezeanu, *Cultural Politics in Greater Romania: Regionalism, Nation Building, and Ethnic Struggle, 1918–1930*, Ithaca, NY: Cornell University Press, 1995, 290). Codreanu had begun his political career in 1922, when, in cooperation with Cuza, he organized the Association of Christian Students (*Asociația Studenților Creștini*). Baron called university students the "chief anti-Semitic propagandists in the country" (8), but he noted that "a year or two after graduation they forget all about it" (9). Students were attracted to Codreanu's message, he claimed, mainly out of boredom: "A large part of these students comes unsatisfactorily prepared, and having no interest in studies they spend their time and energy, in absence of university sports, in Jew-baiting or actual Jew-beating" (9). Baron also observed that Codreanu's political rival, Iuliu Maniu, of trying to co-opt the same group by using public funds to support fraternities that excluded Jews and attacked them. It appears, then, that in this pamphlet, Baron used "antisemitism" to refer not only to political propaganda inimical to Jews but also to violence against Jews instigated for political purposes by people other than the actual perpetrators, who did not necessarily possess any lasting personal animus toward Jews. Moreover, both the propaganda and the violence sprang from circumstances particular to Romania at the time.

34. *SRH1*, 1:143, 146. For Baron's observations on Romania, see the previous note.
35. *SRH1*, 1:147.
36. *SRH1*, 1:148.
37. *SRH1*, 1:147.
38. *SRH1*, 1:149.
39. *SRH1*, 1:150.
40. *SRH1*, 2:27. Emphasis in the original. Even the blood libel, he declared, was of ancient origin; it "had long been forgotten in western Europe," but "in the twelfth century it suddenly reappeared." "From that time on, this accusation, amplified by many a detail, . . . served as the most vigorous stimulus for popular hatred in the West." Consistent with his notion of libels as a reflection and product of clashing intergroup interests, he speculated that "apart from religious prejudice, economic factors, such as the competitive appetites of the Christian burghers, doubtless played a significant role" in its revival. *SRH1*, 2:33–35.

41. *SRH1*, 2:33–35.
42. *SRH1*, 2:63.
43. *SRH1*, 2:298.
44. *SRH1*, 2:285–98.
45. *SRH1*, 2:296.
46. *SRH1*, 2:284–85.
47. This lack of influence is consistent with his post-Holocaust writing in general. See David Engel, *Historians of the Jews and the Holocaust* (Stanford, CA: Stanford University Press, 2010), 64–69.
48. The Nizkor Project, "The Trial of Adolf Eichmann," Session 13, accessed July 27, 2021, http://www.nizkor.com/hweb/people/e/eichmann-adolf/transcripts/Sessions/Session-013-02.html.
49. *SRH1*, 2:288.
50. The lecture was published a year later: Salo W. Baron, "Changing Patterns of Antisemitism: A Survey," *Jewish Social Studies* 38, no. 1 (1976): 5–38.
51. Wistrich, *Antisemitism*; Halpern, "What Is Antisemitism?"; David Berger, *Persecution, Polemic, and Dialogue: Essays in Jewish-Christian Relations* (Boston: Academic Studies Press, 2010), 3; Gavin Langmuir, *Toward a Definition of Antisemitism* (Berkeley: University of California Press, 1990), 311–52; Bernard Lewis, *Semites and Anti-Semites* (New York: W. W. Norton, 1986), 81; and Deborah E. Lipstadt, *Antisemitism Here and Now* (New York: Schocken, 2019), 14–16.
52. Noting this fact does not preclude calling into question Baron's understanding of specific historical incidents. It is possible that, *according to his own criteria*, certain incidents that he excluded from the category "antisemitism" ought to be included, or vice versa. However, there is no basis for judging the criteria themselves right or wrong.

Chapter Six

THE PROFESSOR IN THE COURTROOM
Salo W. Baron at the Eichmann Trial

DEBORAH LIPSTADT

In 1961, west Jerusalem was, despite being the capital of the fledgling state of Israel, a somewhat sleepy city. The Knesset was then housed in a mandate-era building at the edge of the downtown commercial district, at the intersection of Ben Yehuda Street and King George Way. A few blocks west, in the direction of what were then some of the city's older but seedier neighborhoods—they have long since been gentrified—was a brand-new cultural center, whose theater, transformed into a courtroom, would be the site of Israel's legal proceedings against Adolf Eichmann, one of the chief operating officers of the Holocaust. It was aptly named Beit Ha'am, House of the People, because, though it was Israel that was prosecuting the case, in reality, it was being brought in the name of the entire Jewish people, including those who had suffered and perished at Eichmann's and his compatriots' hands as well as those who remained alive but had to live with the consequences of what had been lost. As one observer expressed it on the opening day, "there is an entire people standing before the judges today: a dead people which is no less powerful for it."[1] For all intents and purposes, this was to be the "Jewish Nuremberg," with the defendant standing trial not just for what he did but what had been done by the regime he had so fully and proudly served.

Eichmann had been captured—or, more accurately—kidnapped by Israeli operatives in Argentina in May 1960. In the immediate postwar period, he hid in northern Germany posing as a farmworker. Then, when his name was mentioned at Nuremberg, he decided it was too risky to remain in the country. With the help of other Nazis and their sympathizers, including those in the hierarchy of the Roman Catholic Church, he escaped to Buenos Aires.

Eichmann's presence there was not the deep secret it has often been portrayed to be. The CIA, Argentinian police officials, German embassy personnel, and German expats who had settled in Argentina, many of whom anticipated a resurrection of National Socialism, all knew he was there. He regularly met with the expats in order to describe, with no sense of remorse, what he did during the war. (His presentations were recorded, and some of the transcripts were entered as evidence in the trial.) However, those who knew his whereabouts had no interest in revealing them or capturing him. Consequently, he lived a relatively undisturbed, though modest, life for well over a decade. His wife and children joined him there. The children kept the Eichmann name and regularly renewed their passports at the German embassy.

Then Israel, tipped off by some German officials, including Fritz Bauer, a German Jew who, after being incarcerated in a concentration camp in the 1930s for being a socialist, had escaped to Sweden, where he spent the rest of the war. Now the attorney general of the state of Hesse, he was appalled at the ability of leading Nazis to escape legal reckonings and decided, with the quiet support of other officials, that if Germany refused to act, Israel would. When Eichmann's presence in Argentina was confirmed for Prime Minister David Ben-Gurion, he could have recommended that he be "done in." His unexplained death would well have served as an alert to other leading Nazis that they should not sleep soundly in their beds. Instead, Ben-Gurion ordered that Eichmann be captured and brought to Israel to stand trial.

The day after Eichmann landed at Israel's Lod airport, Ben-Gurion entered the Knesset chambers and, in a short announcement that, despite its terseness, caused an immense national and international reaction, informed the Knesset that Eichmann was in Israel sitting in a jail awaiting trial. In moments, the news reverberated throughout Israel. In a transparent effort to avoid international opprobrium, Ben-Gurion claimed—but no one believed—that the Israelis who found him were acting independently and that Eichmann had voluntarily agreed to come to Israel for a trial.

The news, "*Eichmann b'yadaynu*" (Eichmann is in our hands), was telegraphed throughout Israel. In the days following, it was front-page news worldwide.

Israel intended this trial to be both a successor and a counterweight to the Nuremberg proceedings. There, the tragedy of the Jews, though on the docket in the context of "crimes against humanity," was, essentially, a sidebar.[2] The atrocities against them were certainly not ignored, but they were addressed within the entire panoply of German war crimes against civilian populations. Many peoples had suffered. Many had been starved, tortured, and even murdered. Jews had been targeted. Possibly because they did not fully grasp the consequences of what had happened, prosecutors did not tell the court that the persecution that Jews had faced was the realization of a German plan to annihilate the Jewish people. To make matters worse, the prosecution at Nuremberg decided to bring very few victims to testify, particularly Jewish victims, who, some among them thought, were too emotional and whose testimony would not be entirely trustworthy.

Israel intended this trial to be different. This time, the Jewish tragedy would be front and center. It would not be subsumed by other misdeeds the Nazis committed. A charge, omitted at Nuremberg, would be added to those brought against Eichmann: crimes against the Jewish people. It would be the first charge in the indictment. Moreover, this time the victims' story would be told in its entirety. For the prosecution there were two sets of victims. One, quite naturally, was the individuals who had been murdered or suffered horrendous physical and social deprivation. But there was another, more all-encompassing, set of victims. The Jewish people, as a multifaceted collective, had sustained an irreplaceable loss. Entire communities, together with their extensive educational, philanthropic, social, political, recreational, and professional institutions and organizations, were gone. The populations that had created, nurtured, and sustained them were no more. When the trial opened in Jerusalem in 1961, fifteen years after the tragedy, some European Jewish institutions had been rebuilt. But they were barely even a pale shadow of what had once been. The contours of what had been wiped off the face of the map needed to be laid before the court.

It was in this context that Professor Salo W. Baron entered into these landmark judicial proceedings. From a forensic perspective, his testimony describing the world that was gone was intended for the court; that is, the judicial tribunal that would adjudicate Eichmann's fate. However, as with virtually everything else at this trial, the intended target was far more expansive. It included more than the couple of hundred people who lined up each day hoping to be admitted to the "audience" sitting in the theater *qua* courtroom. It also extended beyond the Israeli population, many of whom walked around during the months of the trial with transistor radios glued to their ears. This was the first trial to be video recorded for television. (There were audio recordings of Nuremberg, which only recently have been melded with some of the video recordings. Only limited portions of the Nuremberg proceedings were filmed.[3]) In the Eichmann trial, the video recording was conducted by a television company and copies flown out each evening to Europe and the United States. When the Israeli government agreed to this arrangement, it was doing so, as Gideon Hausner expressed it, so that "the whole world could watch."[4] They hoped that the witnesses, among them Baron, would help the world grasp the immense loss that not just individual Jews but the entire Jewish people had suffered.

Before the proceedings could even be scheduled or witnesses such as Baron could be asked to testify, there were a host of structural challenges that had to be resolved. In "normal" circumstances, there would have been no question as to who would serve as prosecutor, defense attorney, or presiding judge. This being a criminal proceeding, the attorney general would designate the lawyer most knowledgeable about prosecuting such crimes. The defense attorney would be chosen by the accused, and the presiding judge would be the president of the district court in which the trial was being held. He would designate the other two members of the tribunal. The trial would have been held in the small, rather dingy courtrooms at Jerusalem's Russian Compound.

But this was no ordinary trial. After a bitter political fight over who would serve as attorney general, and after the top two candidates had withdrawn, Hausner was appointed to the post. He was a commercial lawyer with no experience in criminal law, so no one expected him to take on such a high-profile war crimes trial. Other lawyers in his office and government officials assumed he would designate someone else. But he insisted on prosecuting the case himself.

If the trial was to avoid the appearance of a Soviet-style "show" trial, and if Eichmann was to be given, as Ben-Gurion insisted would be the case, a fair hearing based on international law, he needed an attorney who would wage a vigorous and substantial fight on his behalf. Most Israeli lawyers insisted that they would never defend him. A few, however, volunteered to do so. Despite their antipathy toward Eichmann, they believed that in a democratic system, even a Nazi war criminal had to have legal representation. However, Israeli authorities feared for such a lawyer's well-being. The Israeli public, a vast number of whom were either survivors or had lost immediate family members in the Holocaust, might vent their anger on an Israeli who appeared to rally to a Nazi's side. Some German lawyers volunteered to take on this role. Most of them were rejected, apparently because they were either highly incompetent or had been members of the Nazi Party.

At the suggestion of Eichmann's family, the Israeli justice minister chose Robert Servatius. Though Servatius had never joined the Nazi Party, he had defended Nazis who had been tried at Nuremberg. There remained, however, two additional problems regarding his participation. Who would pay his fee? Generally, Germany paid legal costs when one of its citizens was tried by a foreign court for war crimes. Germany, however, intent on distancing itself from Eichmann, refused to pay. It argued that, because Eichmann had fled Germany and lived abroad under an alias, it bore no responsibility for him. The Eichmann family also refused to pay. Recognizing that Eichmann had to have a proper defense, Israel agreed to cover the costs. Yet there was still another obstacle. In order to represent a defendant, an attorney had to be a member of the Israeli bar. Justice Ministry officials asked the Knesset to enact legislation regarding capital cases, which this was, to permit a lawyer who was not a member of the bar to represent a client. The law was passed.

Equally pressing was the question of who should preside. Israel has no juries, so a three-person tribunal would adjudicate the case. One among them would be the presiding judge. Judge Binyamin Halevi, president of the Jerusalem district court, could have designated himself—and was apparently anxious to do so—as presiding judge. However, in 1954, Halevi had presided over the trial of Rudolf Kastner. Kastner, a Hungarian Jew, had been the one who, in 1944, engaged in what became known as the "blood for goods negotiations" with Eichmann. Kastner facilitated the escape of a trainload of Hungarian Jews. However, many Hungarian Jews did not consider him a hero because, they claimed, he failed to alert hundreds of thousands of other Jews to the fact that deportation to Auschwitz meant almost certain death. After the war, he emigrated to Israel, where a Hungarian Jew whose family had been murdered accused him of "vicariously murdering" Hungarian Jews. Kastner sued him for libel and lost. In his decision, Halevi described Kastner as having "sold his soul to the devil [*Satan*]."[5] Given that the "devil" with whom he negotiated was Eichmann, it would be hard to consider Halevi an impartial judge. Once again, the Knesset resolved the matter by enacting a law stipulating that in capital cases, a supreme court judge had to preside. That judge, Moshe Landau, would be joined on the three-person tribunal by a judge from the district and one from another district. Halevi appointed himself, which was not surprising.

As for location, the Russian Compound courtrooms were totally inadequate for a trial that the world press was clambering to attend. One of Ben-Gurion's assistants, Teddy Kolleck, suggested Beit Ha'am. The theater was transformed into a courtroom. (On the day before the trial, Judge Moshe Landau visited the site and asked that the red carpet be removed so that there would be no question that this was now a courtroom.)

With the technical matters in place, the prosecution began to design its case. Hausner, involved in other state matters, began to prepare for the case only in January 1961, three months before the trial was scheduled to begin. He sequestered himself in a Tel Aviv hotel and began to "consume" the Nuremberg trial documents at the rate of a volume a day.[6] Hausner believed that although Nuremberg had been a forensic success, it had "failed to reach the hearts" of the public. Prosecutors there, in a desire for "efficien[cy] and simpl[icity]," had relied on a "few witnesses and films of concentration camp horrors, interspersed with piles of documents." Just like his predecessors at this war crimes trial, he, too, could have "secured a conviction" by letting the documents and the archives "speak." But Ben-Gurion and Hausner wanted more than just one man's conviction. They wanted to impress on the world the immensity of the Jewish people's loss. They needed not just the written word but "a *living* record of gigantic human and national disaster."[7] Hausner, at the suggestion of Rachel Auerbach, a survivor of Ringelblum's *Oyneg Shabes* group of the Warsaw ghetto, decided to rely on witnesses as well as documents.[8]

Hausner made what would become a controversial and legitimately criticized forensic decision. In addition to witnesses who directly encountered Eichmann and could report on his specific activities, he introduced an array of witness who would describe aspects of the Holocaust with which Eichmann had no connection. These actions had also been included in the indictment, which charged Eichmann with the "implementation" of the Final Solution, including exterminating Jews in Poland at death camps, shootings in the USSR by the *Einsatzgruppen*, forcing Jews to be sterilized and have abortions, compelling the victims to live in conditions that were "likely to bring about their physical destruction," and causing thousands to die in forced labor camps, ghettos, and transit camps. He was also charged with crimes against non-Jewish victims, including Roma and Sinti (Gypsies), Polish non-Jews, and a host of other civilians.[9]

Bureau 06 was the special police investigatory body created to prepare the materials on which the indictment against Eichmann would be based. As the evidence mounted, members of the bureau, together with Justice Ministry officials, began to discuss the prosecution's need for a witness who could depict for the court what had been destroyed.[10] They did not think this would be a terribly onerous task. In contrast to the witnesses who had to tell horrific stories of what happened to them and their loved ones, this witness, the organizers believed, would have a much more straightforward assignment. Severely underestimating what Baron would devote to his testimony, they thought all that was required was the "presentation of a compilation of speeches, articles, books and other publications."[11] Even that, however, required the right person.

Bureau 06 members considered and rejected a number of candidates, some because they were too young, unimpressive, or imprecise in their rendition of facts.[12] Ultimately, two names remained on the list: Salo Baron and Yaakov (Jacob) Robinson. Benjamin Eliav, the Israeli consul general in New York, who would be the one to reach out to Baron to inquire about his interest in serving, was told to wait until Robinson made up his mind. Robinson had served as a special adviser on Jewish matters to Justice Robert Jackson at the Nuremberg trials. He was also involved in a panoply of international criminal law and human rights battles in the decades before and after 1945. He had assisted Israel at the United Nations. Consequently, he was the Israelis' first choice. Though he initially demonstrated some interest in accepting the position, Robinson eventually declined. He was helping Hausner prepare the international arguments of the case and believed he could not handle both jobs simultaneously.

(Though he often sat next to Hausner at the trial, he became even more closely connected to the trial when he wrote an extensive and detailed historical critique of Hannah Arendt's harsh evaluation of the trial.)[13] That left Baron.

Eliav, informed that Robinson had declined, turned to Baron, who apparently was unaware that he was not Israel's first choice.[14] Baron accepted at once. One might have assumed that this would be a straightforward task for Baron, who by then had achieved a singular position in the field of Jewish history, one that his biographer would rightfully describe as "the architect of Jewish history" and who would legitimately be credited with having professionalized the field of Jewish history in the United States.[15] But that was not so. Arthur Herzberg, who did his graduate work at Columbia under Baron's tutelage, recalled that "he had never seen Baron as anxious as he was when preparing" for his testimony.[16]

Once Baron agreed to serve as a witness, Hausner began to send him instructions concerning what the prosecution needed. In a confidential letter, Hausner asked him to depict the critical historical events that had preceded the Holocaust and the feelings of Jews who had survived at the end of the war. Hausner wrote that "it is important to prove the Nazi intention to annihilate the Jewish people, and therefore it is vital for the trial to present documentation that will expose the national and cultural value of the Jewish centers that were destroyed in the Holocaust."[17]

Baron arrived in Israel at the end of March. The instructions kept coming. While waiting for his turn to testify, he met with Ben-Gurion, who also told him what he anticipated Baron's testimony would accomplish. After their meeting, Ben-Gurion described his expectations in his diary: "It is important to make clear to our youth [and also to the world] the magnitude of the qualitative loss, resulting from the extermination of six million, and therefore [we must] describe the spiritual character of the Jewry that was exterminated, [and we must] present (Jewry's) outstanding personalities, [such as] Einstein, Bialik, Dubnow, etc." Hausner and Robinson, who, as adviser on international matters, was concerned about foreign affairs, asked him to avoid any comments that might harm Israel's relations with other countries. The impact of the trial on Israel's foreign relations was of major concern to Ben-Gurion. (One of the few specific requests Ben-Gurion made to Hausner, after reading the text of his opening statement, was that he change all references to Germany to

Nazi Germany in order to avoid the impression that he was attacking Adenauer and the postwar Federal Republic of Germany, from whom Israel was anxious to purchase arms.)[18]

But this was not their only request of Baron. Hausner and Robinson asked that he not include too many details that might make his testimony "boring." For someone such as Baron, the consummate scholar who had built a sweeping history of Jewish civilization by weaving together myriad details, this apparently was too much. As a chaired professor at Columbia University and with a legion of publications to his name, he was certainly unaccustomed to being told, particularly by a commercial lawyer, how to present his historical material. Hausner's and Robinson's suggestion that his depiction of the world that had been decimated might be boring outraged him. Addressing Hausner as he might an audacious undergraduate who suggested that he make his classroom lectures more scintillating, Baron declared, "Boredom is relative and very often depends on the manner in which the facts are presented." Then, taking a swipe at Hausner, Baron referred to the trial proceedings of the previous few days. "Anyway, nothing was more boring than the testimony of the Yad Vashem representative regarding the validity of certificates and documents, and yet you accepted this testimony as being essential to the trial."

Hausner, apparently recognizing that he had overstepped his bounds and upset his witness on the eve of his testimony, immediately backed down, writing, "You will of course express your opinions on historical issues as you see fit." Then groveling just, a bit, he assured Baron, "your unique scientific standing and your publications are sufficient guarantee that the picture you present will be accurate and enthralling."[19]

In fact, Hausner's concerns were not entirely misplaced. His inelegant suggestion to Baron came while the trial was already under way. His fears about boredom might have been prompted by what had been happening in the courtroom. As soon as the trial opened, Servatius raised a number of objections concerning the legality of the trial. In his response, Hausner, anxious to demonstrate that Israel's decision to try Eichmann was sanctioned by international law, spoke for "hour after hour" over two days. He refuted Servatius's challenges by citing numerous cases from Great Britain and throughout the United States, including Idaho. By this point the gallery, both the sections reserved for the general public and the press, were "half empty," as the trial seemed, one spectator wrote in his diary, poised to "sink into the boredom of citations."[20] Most reporters, who had come to describe a genocide trial, were bored. Some were hanging out in the snack bar. There were those, however, who praised Hausner's demonstration that "scrupulous justice is [being] observed." Even those who had previously questioned the ability of Israel to conduct a fair trial reversed their opinions. Professor Hugh Trevor-Roper, covering the trial for a British newspaper, acknowledged that after listening to Hausner cite these British and American precedents, he was now convinced, as he had not been previously, that this legal proceeding would rest "unmistakable on the established theory and practice of civilized nations."[21] After deliberating, the judges, not surprisingly, rejected the defense's objections.

Finally the essence of the trial could commence. Hausner opened with a ten-hour speech, the first paragraph of which many Israelis, certainly those who were in school at that time and for a decade thereafter, can still recite by heart.

> When I stand before you here, Judges of Israel, to lead the Prosecution of Adolf Eichmann, I am not standing alone. With me are six million accusers. But they cannot rise to their feet and point an accusing finger towards him who sits in the dock and cry: "I accuse." For their ashes are piled up on the hills of Auschwitz and the fields of Treblinka and are strewn in the forests of Poland. Their graves are scattered throughout the length and breadth of Europe. Their blood cries out, but their voice is not heard. Therefore, I will be their spokesman and, in their name, I will unfold the terrible indictment.

He then proceeded to lay out the terrible path of destruction that had cut across the European continent and beyond. The intensity of his presentation was followed by the more technical and tedious testimony by a police inspector, who explained in great and precise detail how those working to prepare the case determined the authenticity of the documents that had been submitted to the court. It was this that prompted Baron to say, in his retort to Hausner's admonition that he keep the audience interested, "nothing was more boring than that." A bit kindlier, one journalist noted that it was "purely technical and uninteresting . . . but required to offer a solid basis to the evidence introduced by the prosecutor."[22]

Finally, almost two weeks after the trial began, Baron entered the witness box. He had decided that out of deference to the state of Israel, he would testify in Hebrew, a language he knew well but that he spoke in a somewhat stilted and rather formal manner with an accent. For the Israeli audience, the accent, which was not at all uncommon in Israel, with its multitude of immigrants, was probably less problematic than the stilted, formal, professorial style.

At the request of the judge that he cover his head in order to take the oath, Baron placed his *kippah* on his head and his hand on the Hebrew Bible.[23] As soon as he finished, he removed it and slipped it back into his pocket. When the judge asked him to identify himself, he did so first in Hebrew, Shalom Baron, and then in English, Salo Wittmayer Baron. When Hausner asked him to give a "cross-section of the situation of the Jewish people before the Holocaust," Baron paused for a moment and offered the court an apology for his Hebrew, which he acknowledged was "not fluent, as I do not use it every day." He noted that "from time to time words may escape" him and asked that when that happened, he be allowed to use English or another language.[24]

Then, speaking, as one Israeli journalist described it, "softly, in professorial tones, as if lecturing his students," Baron delivered a sweeping survey of European Jewish life. In recent years, his testimony has been properly described as a "masterly summation" of the history of nineteenth- and twentieth-century European Jewish history. It was rich in both detail—descriptions of synagogues, archives, libraries, and philanthropic, social, and professional organizations—and in broader developments—the impact of emancipation and the enlightenment. Addressing the demographic impact of the Holocaust, he estimated that but for the destruction, the world Jewish population would be twenty million.[25] He stressed the resourcefulness and ingenuity of European Jewry and its ability to both respond to the physical, legal, and social oppression and to take advantage of new opportunities offered by legal and social emancipation.[26]

Baron also noted the extraordinary impact that European Jewry had on the societies in which they lived. There was no field—science, art, music, architecture, or literature—that did not have the imprint of Jews on it. He spoke of the genius of Franz Kafka, Franz Werfel, Stefan Zweig, Marc Chagall, Amedeo Modigliani, Albert Einstein, Sigmund Freud, Emile Durkheim, and a host of others. He praised Jewish communities for their remarkable adaptability to new and emerging conditions.[27]

He stressed that even as some Jews took advantage of the new opportunities that were offered to them, others nurtured their age-old religious traditions. Jewish learning flourished. He acknowledged that the Jewish community had its share of "sinners and idiots, thieves and lunatics." Nonetheless, he contended, in a somewhat hyperbolic tone, one could legitimately describe the "first third of the 20th century [as] the golden age of Ashkenazi Jewry in Europe." There was virtually no aspect of Jewish life upon which he did not touch. He described a uniquely vital, thriving, and creative community, one that reveled in the new even as it embraced its rich past.[28] It was a masterful and sweeping summary of Jewish life. Few historians were capable of such a historical *tour de force*.

Most of what Baron said in court regarding the contours of Jewish history and communal life was contained in the memorandum he prepared in anticipation of testifying and which has been republished. There were, however, a few moments of personal digression.[29] Early in his testimony, right after apologizing for his less-than-perfect Hebrew, he told the court that he stood before it "not as an eye-witness or a jurist, but as a historian."[30] His disclaimer about not being an eyewitness notwithstanding, he was, in many respects, precisely that. This became starkly clear when, at one point in his testimony, while describing the impact of the Holocaust, Baron asked for permission to take a "personal" detour. He told the court that after leaving his hometown of Tarnów, Poland, as a young student, he had returned twice to visit, once in 1937 and again in 1958. On his first visit, he found "a flourishing community of some 20,000 Jews, with all their outstanding institutions, a synagogue that had existed there for about 600 years, and so on." When he returned a second time, he discovered a radically different scene. "I found about twenty Jews there and only a few of them were natives of Tarnów." This, he testified, was "typical" of towns throughout Poland and neighboring countries.[31] In forensic terms, he was not an eyewitness to the destruction. Yet, he was an eyewitness to precisely what had been destroyed. At that moment, when he recalled his visit to his hometown, journalists Shlomo Ginossar and Gabriel Stern observed, "this historical and academic testimony was elevated to a personal testimony." He was not describing just a world that was no more. He was describing *his* world, which was no more. It is noteworthy that it was this one segment that was most quoted by journalists and contemporary historians, myself included, when writing of his testimony.[32]

Baron answered Hausner's questions for close to a session and a half. When Hausner finished, Servatius rose for the defense. If the first portion of Baron's testimony had been, as journalist Haim Gouri described it, "devoted to the marvelous panorama of European Jewish life as it had been," this portion of his testimony was "devoted to the ashes."[33] Servatius immediately threw down the gauntlet. Noting that Baron had referred to the persecution that had been directed at the Jewish people and "with all these evils [that] befell it," he then asked, "if throughout these times it had only done good, can you ... detail the reason for the negative attitude ... against the Jewish people?" Although on the surface it might have appeared to be a benign inquiry, it was not. (Nothing a good defense attorney does in court is ever without thought.) It was akin to asking women to explain why men rape, or battered wives why men abuse them. Though Servatius would probably have denied it, there were three implicit suggestions in his query. First, the victims—in this case, Jews—were responsible for causing their persecution. Second, there was a rational explanation for anti-Semitism, and it was to be found in their behavior. Finally, if there was such a long historical arc of anti-Semitism, then people such as Eichmann were innocent pawns in the inevitable sweep of history.

Recognizing the trap Servatius had set for him, Baron argued that it was the perpetrators' "dislike of the unlike," and not Jews' behavior, that was the cause of Jew-hatred. They were considered "unbelievers ... heretics. ... People who did not believe in what the majority in the country believed, whether Christian, Moslem or otherwise." Moreover, Baron declared, the anti-Semitism of the Nazis was qualitatively different from what had preceded it. Previous acts of persecution, including the most heinous, were "trivial in comparison to what happened in the 1940s." The more recent events had "no precedent."[34]

Matters took an even more bizarre turn when Servatius posed what he called "a question of philosophy of history." Citing Hegel and Spengler and the theory of "idealistic determinism," Servatius asked about the nature of free will and historical determinism. Servatius was clearly proposing that Eichmann was just playing the role history had inevitably determined for him. In what might well be described as an intellectual exchange taking place in the shadow of a killing field, Baron rejected the lawyer's suggestion and argued that people are "responsible for what they do and cannot plead that they are only carrying out what history demands of them."[35]

Mercifully, that exchange, which was probably distasteful to those who understood its nuance and exceptionally mind-numbing to those who did not, soon came to an end. After answering some questions from the judges regarding the *Protocols of the Elders of Zion*, Baron stepped down.[36]

There was a decidedly mixed reaction to Baron's testimony. Some observers were disturbed by this panoramic survey of excursion into great Jewish achievements. Although, it should be noted, that this was precisely what Hausner asked Baron to do. Harry Mulisch, a Dutch writer, who attended the trial on a daily basis, argued that it bore no connection to Eichmann's crimes: "Had the Jews been a cultureless tribe . . . something like the . . . Gypsies, would their deaths have been any less terrible? Is Eichmann on trial as a killer of people or as an annihilator of culture? Is a murderer guiltier if a culture got lost in the process?"[37] At lunch on the first day of Baron's testimony, Mulisch asked these questions of Hausner. "He thinks so," Mulisch wrote in his diary. "I don't."[38]

Others were apparently overwhelmed, or possibly bored, by the detail and put off by Baron's professorial style. Two well-known foreign journalists told Ben Gurion that the testimony had not really helped them grasp the nature of anti-Semitism. The correspondent from *Frankfurter Allgemeine Zeitung* disparaged the choice of Baron and attributed it to the influence of American Zionists.[39] Other journalists were annoyed because of the length of Baron's testimony. One observer noted, "the dramatic tension that reached its climax during Hausner's indictment was almost completely diluted by Baron's sociological considerations."[40]

In what was the most scathing critique of all, Ben-Gurion subsequently declared at a gathering of Israeli officials, "He embarrassed us all." This negative assessment was shared by others, including some from the Foreign Ministry. Nahum Ester, the trial coordinator for that ministry, observed that Baron's "testimony did not leave the desired impression and caused differences of opinion." Robinson claimed that Baron's testimony was full of inaccuracies and errors. He prepared a long memorandum that accused Baron of "fragmentary and inaccurate" answers replete with "historical errors" and "faulty statistics." His testimony also exhibited, Robinson claimed, a "conspicuous lack of thought and preparation." Though Robinson, an experienced lawyer, might have disagreed with some of Baron's conclusions, his attack on this consummate scholar for lack of thought and preparation seemed wildly off the mark. Anyone, even someone who thought the testimony was completely off the mark, would have recognized the extensive research and preparation on which it was founded. In addition to knowing that Israeli officials were upset with the testimony, could Robinson possibly have been beset by a pique of professional competition or disturbed that he was not the one giving this testimony in the gaze of the world press and the television cameras? Ironically and revealingly, what seemed to bother him more were the "autobiographical elements" of Baron's testimony, including his reference visits to Tarnów, which, as I have previously noted, was one of the most oft-quoted portions of his testimony. Some journalists highlighted that particular sentence alone.[41]

But Ben-Gurion's biting comments—"embarrassed us"—about Baron may have also been prompted by the fact that he did not want Baron in the first place. According to Hausner, Ben-Gurion had another candidate. He proposed Zalman Shazar, his long-time compatriot in the leadership of Mapai and the Histadrut, someone who was well versed in Jewish history and a future president of the state. When journalists complained to the prime minister about the testimony, he wrote in his diary, "Just as I feared." Ben-Gurion's annoyance at the selection of Baron was evident when, after declaring that Baron had embarrassed them, he added that in selecting Baron, "we had failed miserably." Then, as if to refuse to shoulder any of the responsibility for this choice, he added, "I was against it."[42]

Hannah Yablonka, who has studied Israeli's involvement in the trial, speculates that there was yet another factor. She believes the prime minister was wary of Baron's Zionist credentials.[43] Yablonka might well be correct. Ben-Gurion and his fellow political Zionists believed that the Holocaust marked not only the end of European Jewish civilization but confirmation that it had been doomed for many centuries. In contrast to this perspective, Baron celebrated its achievements. Baron's extensive scholarly work depicted, analyzed, and reveled in the towering significance and magisterial accomplishments of Diaspora Jewish civilization. Ben-Gurion might well have wanted someone who, while celebrating what had once been, would engage in what was then the dominant Israeli national perspective, *shelilat hagolah*, denigration of the Diaspora. And, if not denigrating the Diaspora, he might, at the least, have wanted a witness who would refrain from raising it as a towering example of Jewish achievement. The prime minister may well have wanted someone who would tell the court and, by extension, the youth of Israel, that had Jews only shed the blinders from their eyes, they would have seen disaster looming. They would have done what prescient Zionists, among them Ben-Gurion, Shazar, and many of their colleagues, did: leave for the *Yishuv*.

If these were the Israelis' expectations, they picked the wrong person. Baron's Zionism was not Ben-Gurion's political Zionism. Though a great supporter of Israel, Baron was, as his student Herzberg described it, an adherent of Ahad Ha'am's cultural Zionism. Israel, as a cultural center and place of ingathering for Jews, was of pivotal importance for him. But so was the Diaspora. In contrast to the *idée fixe* then extant in Israel, that Israel was the center, Baron believed that Israel and the Diaspora coexisted as two equal nexuses of Jewish life. As a consequence of the Holocaust, the Diaspora center had shifted from a decimated Europe to America.[44]

Apparently, Baron did make some adjustments to his testimony to accommodate Ben-Gurion's expectations. In his enumeration of Jews with "extraordinary minds," he included Hebrew poet Chaim Nachman Bialik and Zionist leader and stateman Chaim Weizmann. When he had met with Ben-Gurion, the prime minister had told him, "we must present [Jewry's] outstanding personalities, [such as] Einstein, Bialik." (Notably, Ben-Gurion did not mention Weizmann, with whom he differed during the Mandate period and whom he relegated to the ceremonial office of president.) Both Weizmann and Bialik made incalculable contributions to Zionism and Israeli politics and culture. But his references to them seemed, as Baron's biographer, Robert Liberles, observes, "out of place in his presentation." They came in the midst of a discussion of Jewish contributions, such as those of Einstein's, to the world at large.[45] Although Baron might have made this accommodation to satisfy Ben-Gurion, he was not about to repudiate his views on the incalculable value of Diaspora civilization.

In retrospect, Baron's testimony was a professional triumph—if one can use that term when speaking of utter destruction—summarizing and analyzing the expanse of European history in a nuanced and analytical fashion. However, it was, as both journalists and Israeli officials recognized, also a forensic failure. A trial is always part theater. Depending on the situation, there are different audiences that must be satisfied, including judges, juries, spectators, and journalists. In this case, there were two additional audiences: Israeli youth and the world at large. Baron was the wrong person to expect to play to these or, for that matter, any gallery. He was the epitome of a scholar, one who probably knew more details about European Jewish civilization than any of his colleagues worldwide. However, what the trial needed was a storyteller, one who could provide both the accurate detail and the sweep, but do so in a fashion that those who were not students of history could grasp.

I write this critique with some trepidation. Not only did Baron prepare for this task with great conviction and seriousness, but his analysis of European Jewish history has profoundly influenced my education, *weltanschauung*, and pedagogy. But I also write this based not just on my study of the Eichmann trial in general, and his testimony in particular, but from personal experience. In 1993, I published a book that analyzed Holocaust denial. In it, I made brief mention of David Irving, then arguably one of the world's leading Holocaust deniers. When the book appeared in the United Kingdom, Irving sued me for libel by calling him a denier. He had waited until he could bring the case in the UK, where libel laws place the burden of proof on the defendant. In the United States, Irving would have had to prove the falsehood of what I said. In the UK, the onus was on me to prove the truth of what I wrote. In addition, in the United States, there is the "public figure defense," which emanates from a Supreme Court decision that a public figure (this would include authors) must prove "malicious intent" in order to win a libel suit. In other words, they must prove that the author of the words knew or should have known that they were false. After a ten-week trial, we won a stunning victory, one that decimated Irving's claims and affirmed mine. It left Irving's reputation in tatters.[46]

Many people drew direct parallels between the Eichmann trial and my legal proceedings, including the British press. The *Daily Telegraph* declared in its lead editorial, "This trial has done for the new century what the Nuremberg tribunals or the Eichmann trial did for earlier generations."[47] This response may well be categorized as an example of media hyperbole. There is clearly no comparing the Eichmann trial to mine. Eichmann's misdeeds incalculably overshadow Irving's. One man saw to the killing of people, millions of them; the other to the killing of their history.

There were contrasting structural differences as well. At *Beit Ha'am*, the Nazi was the defendant. In London, it was the Holocaust historian. In Jerusalem, the testimony by close to one hundred eyewitnesses was the centerpiece. Their personal recounting of their experiences helped to put the Holocaust in front of the world. In contrast, in London, we called no survivors. We did so for forensic and strategic reasons. The myriad documents about the Holocaust, together with material evidence and existing testimonies, constitute overwhelming evidence of its historicity. We did not want to suggest to the judge, who would render a decision in the case, that anything more, including eyewitnesses, was needed. Moreover, we did not want the centerpiece of this case to become "did the Holocaust happen?"[48]

But there were things linked to these two events. During the trial, in response to a request from my lawyers, the Israeli government released a memoir that Eichmann had written while his appeal was being heard by the Israeli Supreme (High) Court. From the time of his execution in 1962, the manuscript had sat in the Israeli government archives. In the late 1990s, one of Eichmann's children asked that it be released. Israel debated the matter, but nothing happened. At the time of my trial, I thought there might be something in the manuscript that would help us further expose Irving's claims as lies. A few weeks later, retired Israeli High Court Justice Gabriel Bach, who had served as Hausner's first assistant during the Eichmann trial, called me to inform me that after consulting with high-ranking jurists and historians, the current Israeli attorney general had decided to release the manuscript to me. (I was later told by then Prime Minister Barak that he, too, supported the release.)

Another, more amorphous link, but one that brings us back to Baron's testimony, is that both trials were premised on bringing history into the courtroom. Our objective was to prove that Irving was a liar, that he made claims for which he lacked any evidence. We made him the defendant. Our primary tool for doing so was the testimony and reports of leading historians. They followed his footnotes back to the sources and fully demonstrated that his claims were a tissue of lies.[49]

Similar to the Eichmann trial, my trial had three distinct aspects: historical, forensic, and public. I knew that on certain days the testimony would be tedious, difficult for anyone not versed in the details of a gas chamber or Nazi hierarchy to fully grasp. As I listened to our historical experts try to unpack a complicated aspect of Irving's twisting of the truth, I thought back to Baron's testimony and reflected on the predicament he had faced. (Although, it is doubtful that he thought of it as a predicament.)

History is a nuanced enterprise. Historians look for trends. They rarely speak in unequivocal terms. The courtroom is often perplexed, if not frustrated, by the historian's shades of gray. It wants definitive statements. It wants pithy, easily grasped conclusions.

I thought—and still do—that the comparisons of my trial to Nuremberg and Eichmann were extreme. However, I was in full agreement with the comment made by the London *Times* on the morning after the verdict in my case, "history has had its day in court and scored a crushing victory." This is what happened in Jerusalem in 1961 and in London in 2000. One victory, the more recent one, was recognized as such immediately. The other has taken longer to be recognized as such. That delay, however, does not diminish its magnitude.

NOTES

1. Sergio Minerbi, *The Eichmann Trial Diary: An Eyewitness Account* (New York: Enigma, 2011), 7.
2. Lawrence Douglas, *The Memory of Judgment: Making Law and History in the Trials of the Holocaust* (New Haven, CT: Yale University Press 2005), 60, 66, 72, 78–80.
3. "Public to Get Access to Nuremberg Trials Digital Recordings," *AP News*, October 14, 2019, https://gvwire.com/2019/10/14/public-to-get-access-to-nuremberg-trials-digital-recordings/.
4. Gideon Hausner, *Justice in Jerusalem* (New York: Harper & Row, 1966), 307.
5. Pnina Lahav, *Judgment in Jerusalem: Chief Justice Simon Agranat and the Zionist Century* (Berkeley: University of California Press,1997), 122–25.
6. Hausner, *Justice in* Jerusalem, 290.
7. Hausner, *Justice in* Jerusalem, 291, emphasis added.
8. Stephan Landsman, "The Eichmann Case and the Invention of the Witness-Driven Atrocity Trial," *Columbia Journal of Transactional Law* 51, no. 1 (January 2012): 69, http://blogs2.law.columbia.edu/jtl/wp-content/uploads/sites/4/2014/05/51ColumJTransnatlL69_%EF%BF%BCThe-Eichmann-Case-and-the-Invention-of-the-Witness-Driven-Atrocity-Trial.pdf; Samuel D. Kassow, *Who Will Write Our History?: Emanuel Ringelblum, the Warsaw Ghetto, and the Oyneg Shabes Archive* (Bloomington: Indiana University Press, 2007); Hannah Yablonka, *The State of Israel* (New York: Schocken, 2004), 73–74; Boaz Cohen, "Rachel Auerbach, Yad Vashem, and Israeli Holocaust Memory," *Polin*, 20 (2008): 213–15; and Yablonka, "Preparing the Eichmann Trial: Who Really Did the Job?" *Theoretical Inquiries in Law* 1, no. 2 (July 2000): 13–15.
9. *The Trial of Adolf Eichmann: Record of Proceedings in the District Court of Jerusalem* (Jerusalem: Israel Ministry of Justice, 1992) (hereafter *TAE*), 1–8.
10. Yablonka, *State of Israel*, 100.
11. Yablonka, *State of Israel*, 100.

12. Among the names of people who were considered but rejected for a variety of reasons were Shaul Esh and Eric Kulka, two men who would become much-respected historians. Yablonka, *State of Israel*, 100.
13. Hausner adopted *in toto* Robinson's work on the aspects of the trial that dealt with international law. Hausner, *Justice in* Jerusalem, 303, 313; Jacob Robinson, *And the Crooked Shall Be Made Straight: A New Look at the Eichmann Trial* (New York: Macmillan, 1965).
14. Pinchas Rosen to Benjamin Eliav, December 20, 1960; Benjamin Eliav to Salo W. Baron, February 7, 1961; in *Salo W. Baron Papers, Stanford Special Collections*, Box 54, as cited in Robert Liberles, *Salo Wittmayer Baron: Architect of Jewish History* (New York: New York University Press, 1995), 400n88. Haim Yahil to Benjamin Eliav, January 11, 1961, as cited in Yablonka, *State of Israel*, 271n38.
15. Natalia Aleksiun, "Salo Baron and Jewish Historiography in Galicia," in *The Enduring Legacy of Salo W. Baron*, ed. Hava Tirosh-Samuelson and Edward Dabrowa (Kraków: Jagiellonian University Press, 2017), 116.
16. The subtitle of Liberles's biography of Baron, "architect of Jewish history"; and Liberles, *Salo Wittmayer Baron*, 323.
17. Hausner to Baron, March 20, 1961, as cited in Yablonka, *State of Israel*, 102, 271n41.B.
18. Deborah Lipstadt, *The Eichmann Trial* (New York: Schocken, 2011), 63; Tom Segev, *The Seventh Million* (New York: Henry Holt, 1991), 346.
19. Hausner to Baron, April 22, 1961; Baron to Hausner, April 23, 1961; Hausner to Baron, April 23, 1961; as cited in Yablonka, *State of Israel*, 103.
20. Haim Gouri, *Facing the Glass Booth* (Detroit: Wayne State University Press, 2004), 4; Minerbi, *Eichmann Trial Diary*, 15.
21. Hugh Trevor-Roper, "The Nuremburg of the Jewish People," *Sunday Times* (London), April 16, 1961; Hausner, *Justice in* Jerusalem, 320–21.
22. Minerbi, *The Eichmann Trial Diary*, 28.
23. Baron's testimony begins at 16:50, United States Holocaust Museum, "Eichmann Trial," accessed July 28, 2021, https://collections.ushmm.org/search/catalog/irn1001039.
24. *TAE*, 169.
25. *TAE*, 170ff., 184.
26. Liberles, *Salo Wittmayer Baron*, 323–33, provides an extensive and comprehensive summary of this testimony. The testimony was subsequently published as "European Jewry Before and After Hitler," in both *The American Jewish Year Book* 63 (New York/Philadelphia: American Jewish Committee/Jewish Publication Society, 1962) and *The Catastrophe of European Jewry* (Jerusalem: Yad Vashem, 1976), (hereafter cited as *Baron*), 173–259.
27. *TAE*, 178ff.; *Baron*, 194.
28. *TAE*, 177–81; *Baron*, 215.
29. See note 23.
30. *TAE*, 169.
31. *TAE*, 183.
32. "Trial Diary," *Al Hasmishmar*, April 25, 1961, as cited in Yablonka, *State of Israel*, 105. See also Lipstadt, *Eichmann Trial*, 68, and Gouri, *Facing the Glass Booth*, 23.
33. Gouri, *Facing the Glass Booth*, 25.

34. *TAE*, 187–88.
35. *TAE*, 188–89; Peter Papadatos, *The Eichmann Trial* (London: Stevens & Son, 1964), 106.
36. *TAE*, 189–90.
37. Harry Mulisch, *Criminal Case 40/61, the Trial of Adolf Eichmann: An Eyewitness Account* (Philadelphia: University of Pennsylvania Press, 2005), 63.
38. Minerbi, *Eichmann Trial Diary*, 36.
39. I have found no evidence to support this contention.
40. Minerbi, *Eichmann Trial Diary*, 36.
41. One of the things that troubled ministry officials was Baron's comment that Draja Mihajlovic's forces, rather than Marshall Tito's, had liberated Yugoslavia. Baron was asked to retract his comments, which he did. Nahum Ester to Yahil, re Eichmann Trial from April 11–14, 1961, Israel State Archives, as cited in Yablonka, *State of Israel*, 104, 271n54.
42. Protocol of conversations in the president's residence, on the publication of Ben-Zvi's *The History of the Jewish People in the Land*, November 11, 1961, Ben-Gurion Archives, Meetings, as cited in Yablonka, *State of Israel*, 271n55; Gideon Hausner, *The Jerusalem Trial*, vols. A and B, as cited in Yablonka, *State of Israel*, 104.
43. Gouri, *Facing the Glass Booth*, 23; Yablonka, *State of Israel*, 101.
44. Liberles, *Salo Wittmayer Baron*, 215–16.
45. *TAE*, 178ff.; Liberles, *Salo Wittmayer Baron*, 328.
46. For the judgment in *Irving v. Penguin Books and Lipstadt*, see https://www.hdot.org/judge/#.
47. *Daily Telegraph* (London), April 12, 2000.
48. This what happened during the trials of Ernst Zündel in Canada, something we were intent on avoiding.
49. For historical reports entered into evidence in the trial, see https://www.hdot.org/trial-materials/witness-statements-and-documents/.

Chapter Seven

BUILDING THE FOUNDATIONS OF SCHOLARSHIP AT HOME

Salo Baron and the Judaica Collections at Columbia University Libraries

MICHELLE MARGOLIS CHESNER

Salo Baron's impact on Judaic scholarship in the twentieth century is hardly unknown. Moreover, his leadership of the Jewish Cultural Reconstruction Project, which dealt with the thorny problem of Nazi-looted books and Judaica after World War II, solidly places him in the annals of the history of bibliography as well. Less well known, however, is the outsized impact Baron had on the collections at his home institution. This chapter will discuss how Baron's connections to and scholarship within the Judaica library collections at Columbia University ensured the library's place as a one of the most important Judaica collections in the United States.

When Linda Miller approached Nicholas Murray Butler regarding an endowed chair of Jewish history at Columbia, Butler crunched the numbers and decided that $200,000 was a reasonable amount to allow for a salary of $9,000–$10,000 per year. However, he went a step further before offering his recommendation to Mrs. Miller. As described in Robert Liberles's opus on Salo Baron's life, "*in order to make available additional funds for the library* and for research assistance, Butler requested a total endowment of $250,000."[1] From its inception, the Miller Chair was indicated to provide some support for acquiring Jewish studies collections—after all, how could one endow a chair in a new subject at a university without ensuring adequate resources for research? Butler's expectations were fully realized.

With the chair's first incumbent came a library champion who built a collection that would be used extensively by himself, his students, and the broader world of Jewish scholarship.

BEGINNINGS: HEBRAICA AND JUDAICA AT COLUMBIA

Even before Baron's tenure, Columbia had been collecting Judaica in some form or another for almost two centuries. Its founder, Samuel Johnson, taught Hebrew at the fledgling Kings' College from its inception in 1754, and Hebrew studies remained important throughout the eighteenth century.[2] Even though the American Revolutionary War was waging during its production, the monumental Kennicott Bible of 1774–76 lists three New York subscribers: Kings College (the only American colonial institution on the subscription list) and two fellows of the college (Rev. Mr. Inglis and Rev. Dr. Ogilvie; fig. 7.1).[3] Throughout the nineteenth century, Columbia's was among the largest collections of Hebraica in the United States. In 1859, when William J. Rhees published his *Manual of Public Libraries*, the list of top libraries for Hebraica collections placed Columbia third (with one hundred items). First place went to Union Theological Seminary (with two hundred fifty items), whose collection was incorporated into Columbia's in 2004.[4]

The first major donation of Judaica to Columbia, by Temple Emanu-El in 1892, has been well documented.[5] The temple established a chair in rabbinic literature at Columbia University in 1887, which was filled by Richard James Horatio Gottheil, son of Temple Emanu-El's rabbi, Gustav Gottheil.[6] Within a few years of Gottheil's hire, donors began stepping forward with Judaica donations for the university. Notable donors included Oscar Straus, who was instrumental in acquiring one hundred thirty-five manuscripts from Ephraim Deinard by 1890.[7] In May 1892, the Temple Emanu-El Trustees gifted "the library of the Temple to Columbia College of this City."[8] This collection consisted of twenty-five hundred printed books and forty-five manuscripts, which the temple had purchased in 1872.[9] Additional important donations came to Columbia over the course of the following decade, including a collection of forty-seven manuscripts from Mr. J. N. Hazard, Mr. Benjamin Stern, and Mr. Charles A. Dunn. In 1900, Stephen S. Wise donated about "six or seven hundred volumes," mostly printed books but also some significant manuscripts, from his father, Aaron's, library.[10]

xii   SUBSCRIBERS

Hodge, Rev. Dr	C		
Hoghton, Sir Henry, Bart	C	P	E
Holdſworth, Arthur, Eſq; Mount Galpin, Dartmouth			E
Home, Rt Honble and Rev. The Earl of	C		
Honywood, Fraſer, Eſq;	C		
Howard, John, Eſq;	C	P	
Hughes, Rev. Mr, Vice-Preſident of Queen's College, Cambridge			E
Hume, Rt Rev. The Lord Biſhop of Saliſbury	C		E
Hunt, Rev. Dr, Canon of Chriſt Church, and Regius Profeſſor of Hebrew	C	P	E
Hunt, Henry, Eſq;		P	
Hunter, Dr William, F. R. & A. SS. Phyſician Extraordinary to Her Majeſty	C	P	E
Hutchinſon, Rt Rev. The Lord Biſhop of Killala			E
Hutchinſon, Francis, Eſq;	C	P	
Jackſon, Cyril, Eſq;			E
Jane, Rev. Mr		P	E
Jebb, Rev. Mr, Cambridge			E
Jeffreys, Rev. Dr, Canon of Chriſt Church			
Jenkinſon, Rt Honourable Charles	C	P	E
Jennens, Charles, Eſq;			E
Jennings, Rev. Dr, London	C		
Jeſus College, Oxford	C		
Jeſus College, Cambridge			E
Inglis, Rev. Mr, Fellow of King's College, New York			E
Innys, John, Eſq;	C	P	E
John's St College, Cambridge			E
Johnſon, Rt Rev. The Lord Biſhop of Worceſter	C	P	E
Jones, Mrs Mary, Oxford	C		
Jones, Thomas, Eſq;		P	E
Iremonger, Joſhua, Eſq;			E
Jubb, Rev. Dr	C	P	E
Kaye, Rev. Dr, F. R. & A. SS. Sub-Almoner to His Majeſty	C	P	E
Kearney, Rev. Dr, Profeſſor Hiſtory, Trinity College, Dublin		P	E
Kearney, Rev. Mr, Aſſiſtant to King's Prof. Greek, Trin. Coll. Dublin		P	
Keene, Rt Rev. The Lord Biſhop of Ely	C	P	E
King, Rev. Dr		P	
King's College, Cambridge	C	P	E
King's College, Aberdeen			E
King's College, New York			E
Kinnoull, Rt Honble Earl			E
Kippis, Rev. Dr	C		
Krauter, Rev. Dr, Bath			E
Kynaſton, Thomas, Eſq;	C		
Lambe, James, Eſq;	C		
Lane, John, Eſq; Fellow of Queen's College, Cambridge			E
Laugher, Rev. Mr	C		
Lawſon, Rev. Mr	C	P	
Lee, Matthew, Eſq; Ebford	C	P	E
Lee, Thomas Huckel, Eſq; Exeter			E
Leeds, His Grace, The Duke of			E
Legge, Rt Honble Henry Bilſon	C		

FIGURE 7.1. Benjamin Kennicott, *Vetus Testamentum Hebraicum: cum variis lectionibus* (Oxford, 1774-76), vol. 1, "Subscribers: Great Britain, Ireland, America," xii.
Image from Internet Archive, courtesy University of Toronto.

The early twentieth century included a flurry of activity around the building of Judaica collections in the United States, especially in the New York area.[11] Philanthropists such as Jacob Schiff and Mayer Sulzberger were working closely with institutions in New York and other areas to build substantial collections in the United States, and they donated collections to various Jewish and non-Jewish institutions, especially the Jewish Theological Seminary and the New York Public Library. After Schiff acquired the library of Dr. Mortiz Steinschneider in 1898, he corresponded with Sulzberger about the most appropriate recipient for this important collection, and Columbia was included, along with Hebrew Union College, the Jewish Theological Seminary, and the New York Public Library, on his shortlist.[12]

SALO BARON AT THE LIBRARY

By the time Baron arrived at the university, there was thus a strong foundation of Judaica collecting for him to build on—and it was expected that he would build the collection. President Butler's letter offering Baron the position, on December 14, 1930, included, if not a mandate, an expectation: "We should hope that you would guide the University in building up its collection of books and other research material in the field."[13] Baron took this recommendation seriously. Within a few years of his arrival at Columbia, he had clearly established a strong relationship with the library. The following statement in the 1933 Report of the Librarian shows Baron's commitment to building its collections:

> Since the establishment of the Chair for Jewish History, Literature, and Institutions on the Miller Foundation in 1930, the Library has considerably increased its collections in the field of Jewish studies, including Hebraica as well as Judaica. Professor Baron has spent a great deal of time and thought in deciding on questions of scope and policy. *His aim has been a double one: to increase the existing Hebrew collections so as to accumulate a good working library for research students, and to develop the facilities of the Library for scholars doing research work in specific fields through the acquisition of manuscripts and rare prints.*[14]

Baron was completely dedicated to creating a world-class Judaica collection—building on the foundation that Gottheil and others had laid—to ensure that both "research students" and "scholars" could actively and successfully do their work. Various correspondence between Baron and university administrators consistently show the allocation of excess funds from the Miller endowment "for the purchase of Hebrew books for the library" and "to be used by the University libraries for the acquisition of books and journals of Jewish interest."[15] (Interestingly, Baron would use the phrase "Jewish interest," which was interpreted by the university administration as "Hebrew."[16]) In later years, as expenses against the Miller fund increased, and with limited funds for library acquisitions, Baron explicitly requested "the Trustees to allot to the Library $300 from general University funds."[17]

Baron actively worked with bookdealers and collectors to build strong and up-to-date collections. The same librarian's report from 1933 describing Baron's plans for the collections also cites an acquisition of more than three thousand Jewish studies books, including rare imprints from the fifteenth and sixteenth centuries.

It is clear that the library respected and sought Baron's opinions and advice relating to the collections. Roger Howson (university librarian, 1926–40) reached out to Baron about duplicate books and how to dispose of them,[18] and Baron sent regular messages to Howson indicating that sums from the Miller fund could be used to purchase books that Baron would select for the collections. When Columbia built a new library on the South Lawn of its campus, Baron reached out to Howson, expressing his hope that the Hebraica and Judaica would remain in Low Library with the other special and distinctive collections. Howson had anticipated the request, having written to Director of Libraries Charles Williamson a few days earlier to confirm the same thing. He swiftly reassured Baron that the collections would remain in Low Library.[19] Baron also secured a "cubicle" at the newly built South Hall (which would be renamed Butler Library in 1946), and both he and his wife, Jeannette, used it extensively.[20]

Howson's successors in the library continued to correspond with Baron regarding acquisitions in Jewish studies for the libraries throughout the years of his tenure at Columbia.[21] Among the important decisions deferred to Baron was the question of microfilming Hebrew manuscripts from the collections, along with approvals for acquisition requests from other users to the library.[22] Additionally, Baron took full advantage of his connections with the library to secure access for some of his colleagues, such as Aron Freimann and Shalom Spiegel.[23]

THE BARON/FRAENKEL COLLECTION
OF HEBREW MANUSCRIPTS

Baron was well aware that the acquisition of materials was not very useful if the items acquired were not processed and cataloged so they could be found by researchers. A mere two years after his hire, the relatively new professor thus reached out to Howson and suggested that the library hire a young student who was looking for work, Isaac Mendelsohn. Backing up his words with funding, Baron offered to pay half of Mendelsohn's salary out of the Miller chair if the library would cover the other half. The library accepted the offer.[24] It would prove increasingly valuable the following year, when Baron would make the deal of a lifetime, firmly establishing Columbia University's library as a leading player among Judaica collections.

According to Baron's own account many years later, upon his arrival, Columbia's Judaica collection was "valuable from an antiquarian standpoint, but could hardly be of any use to a class of predominantly unprepared students." Baron thus set out to establish a teaching and research collection for his new home institution. In his words, "because all this took place during the Great Depression, when prices generally were going down, I was confident that the amount set aside out of the Miller fund would suffice for a presentable Jewish collection."[25]

In early 1933, Baron met with Viennese bookdealer David Fraenkel[26] to discuss possible acquisitions for the library. In February, Fraenkel sent a letter to Baron with a list of various options, including a "big collection of 600 manuscripts on different subjects" and "more than 80" relating to "the Study of Jewish History of Greece."[27] After much negotiation, the initial asking price of $15,000 was reduced to $7,500, and the deal was made. On May 1, 1933, University Secretary Frank D. Fackenthal wrote to Baron to congratulate him—the trustees had approved $2,000 from the Miller fund for the initial purchase of manuscripts.[28] The librarian's letter came four days later with a note congratulating Baron on a fine bargaining job.[29] A few months later, the Committee on Finance approved a "sum of $5500, chargeable to the accumulated income of the Miller (Nathan J.) Fund, [to] be made available for the purchase for the library of a collection of important Hebrew manuscripts and rare prints."[30] This was likely a second payment for the collection from Fraenkel.

The acquisition was celebrated in the Report of the Librarian for that year:

> A large collection of Hebrew manuscripts has been recently purchased from Rabbi David Fraenkel of Vienna. In addition to 650 manuscripts in Hebrew characters, over twenty manuscripts written in Arabic, Persian, Turkish, Spanish, Italian, and Greek furnish information, hitherto unavailable, as to various phases of Jewish history and literature.... One special part of the Miller collection that has its own interest is a section that covers Jewish communal life in Greece from the seventeenth to the nineteenth century. The printed catalogue of this section lists eighty manuscripts and forty printed volumes.[31]

Notwithstanding the huge importance of the collection, there was no notice of the acquisition within the Columbia press. The timing definitely played a part, as the world was transfixed by events in Europe. Indeed, there was a mention of Hebrew books in May 1933 in the *Columbia Spectator*, but for a very different story: the Jewish student adviser had tried to donate to the library copies of books that were burned by the Nazis as a "symbolic and significant answer to the Hitler demonstration." Howson turned down the offer, claiming that the Nazis were just burning Marxist materials and that they would be shown to be fools for acting like "a spoiled child" and should be ignored.[32]

The following year, however, the acquisition was duly noted in the the *New York Times*, indicating a collection of "650 manuscripts in Hebrew characters, more than twenty manuscripts in Arabic, Perisian, Turkish, Spanish, Italian and Greek . . . from Babylon, Baghdad, Greece, Italy, Spain, Turkey and Yemen."[33]

Hiring Mendelsohn in 1932 turned out to be a prescient plan. The archives show that his contract was continually renewed, and updates to his work are scattered throughout library correspondence and reports. By the late 1940s, Mendelsohn had produced the two-volume *Descriptive Catalogue of Semitic Manuscripts (mostly Hebrew) in the Libraries of Columbia University*, which described about 650 of the codex manuscripts (fig. 7.2). Volume One was typescript, but Volume Two remained handwritten. Both volumes were mimeographed, but only a few copies were made.[34]

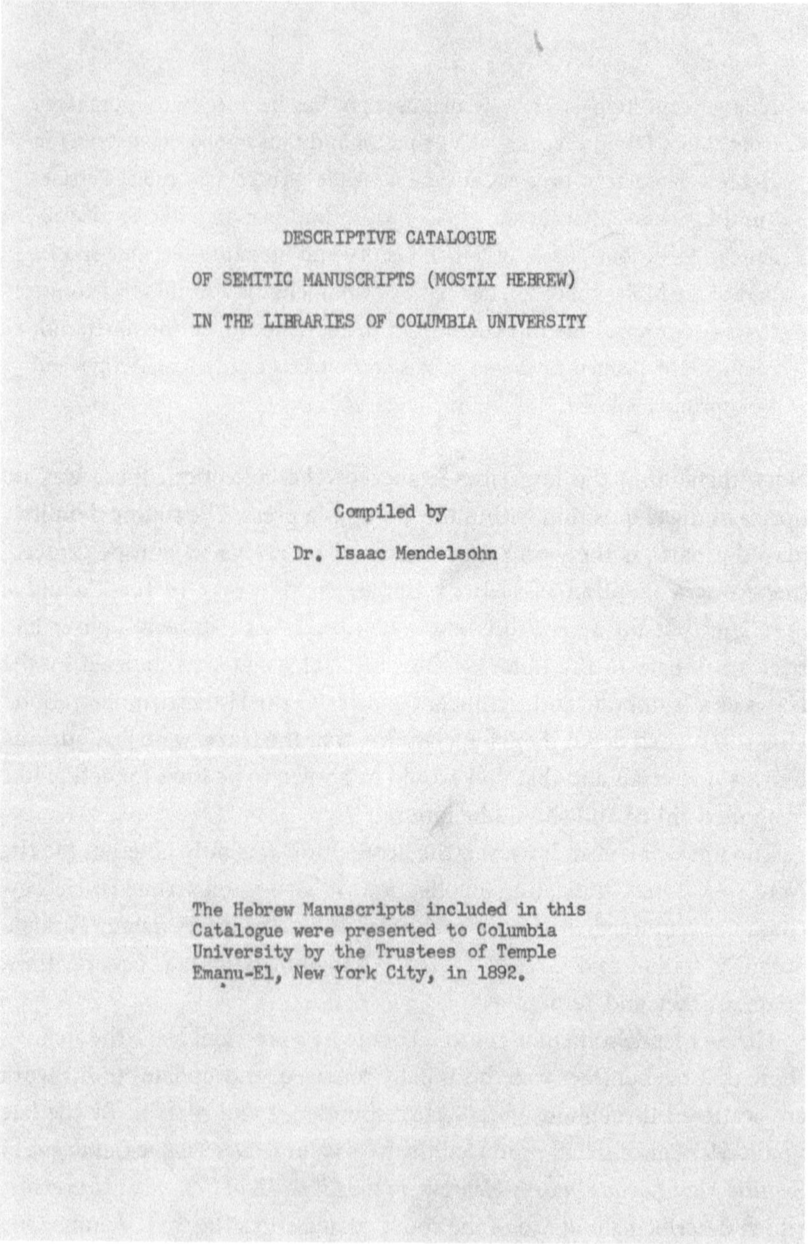

DESCRIPTIVE CATALOGUE

OF SEMITIC MANUSCRIPTS (MOSTLY HEBREW)

IN THE LIBRARIES OF COLUMBIA UNIVERSITY

Compiled by

Dr. Isaac Mendelsohn

The Hebrew Manuscripts included in this
Catalogue were presented to Columbia
University by the Trustees of Temple
Emanu-El, New York City, in 1892.

FIGURE 7.2. Isaac Mendelsohn's *Descriptive Catalogue of Semitic Manuscripts (mostly Hebrew) in the Libraries of Columbia University* (circa 1940s).
Image Courtesy Columbia University Libraries.

USING THE COLLECTION, OLD AND NEW[35]

Once the manuscripts arrived, Baron wasted no time in delving into their contents. As early as 1937, he published an article in the festschrift for Samuel Kraus dealing with a dispute between the Sephardi and Ashkenazi congregations in Verona.[36] The dispute was documented in manuscript by Rabbi Ḥizkiyah Mordekhai Basan, who was asked to adjudicate between the aggrieved parties. The disagreement began when the Sephardic community opened a new synagogue in 1653, in opposition to the legislation of the community from 1630 not to do so. Baron's carefully researched article uses the Columbia manuscript[37] as a starting point, but it also cites sources from collections around the world, including the Kauffman collection in Budapest, the Oppenheim collection in Oxford, and the collection of the Jewish Theological Seminary (whose librarian, Alexander Marx, was a familiar correspondent and friend of Baron). Baron's first footnote on the article proudly identifies the new manuscript as "from the collection of manuscripts that were acquired from Rabbi David Fraenkel in the year 1932."[38]

Baron's writings show that his interest was not just in the collection that he brought to the Columbia libraries but in all Judaica found in the collection. In 1940, he reviewed a book by Ralph L. Rusk, *Letters to Emma Lazarus in the Columbia University Library* for *Jewish Social Studies*.[39] The review took a distinctly Jewish angle, as would be appropriate for the journal, and described, as Baron put it, the "unique position of Emma Lazarus in the history of American-Jewish letters."

The most prolific area of Baron's scholarship from Columbia's collections focused on the books and documents relating to the Jews of Greece. The Greek manuscripts were described separately in Howson's librarian's report cited earlier, noted for both their uniqueness and scholarly value. Baron published a series of articles describing various aspects of the Greek communities, especially that of Corfu (e.g., fig. 7.3). The year 1942 saw a piece[40] on *pidyon shevuyim*, the purchase (and thus redemption) of Jewish captives by the Jews of Corfu, as part of a larger discussion of various communal activities detailed in a community record book[41] that was included in the collection that he had acquired for Columbia. In the body of this article, Baron noted that "a few years ago I had the opportunity to acquire a collection of rare manuscripts for this [Columbia's] library, from

FIGURE 7.3. Ketubah Corfu, February 23, 1820, Marriage of Avraham ben Hayyim de Brugnato and Esther bat Ya'akov Kiridi, Columbia MS X893 K51991.
Image Courtesy Columbia University Libraries.

David Fraenkel, who has a reputation for acquiring unique rare Judaica."[42] Additional articles followed in 1944[43] and 1953,[44] which focused on the communal disputes between the dwindling native Greek Jewish population and the Italian emigre community in Corfu (fig. 7.4).[45]

BUILDING THE FOUNDATIONS OF SCHOLARSHIP AT HOME

FIGURE 7.4. Opening leaves to *Universita' Italiana della Sinagoga Corfiota Aborigine contro Universita' della Sinagoga Corfiota Grecu* (Corfu, 1665–81), Columbia X893 78 vol. 3 no. 6.
Image Courtesy Columbia University Libraries.

Baron's larger monographs also show that he worked extensively with the Columbia collections for his broader research. A passing line in *The Jewish Community: Its History and Structure to the American Revolution* refers to the sale of a fourteenth-century manuscript ("now in the Columbia University Library")[46] for twenty-six gold ducats as part of a discussion on the cost of manuscripts in the medieval period. It is noteworthy that this particular manuscript,[47] an important collection of pre-Lurianic kabbalah, had also been explicitly mentioned in the librarian's report of the Fraenkel acquisition back in 1933: "For example, a large manuscript on vellum containing a collection of Kabbalistic works was written, according to two colophons, which appear to be authentic, by one Moses Barzilai in the years 5085–5105 (1325–45). Curiously, it contains at the end a contract, dated 5165 (1405) which states that this volume was sold by one Jacob Alkbakar for twenty-six gold ducats."[48]

Another important aspect of this manuscript is the light it sheds on the history of scribal practices. Malachi Beit-Arié was the first to note that the earlier of two colophons in the manuscript, from 1325, was copied

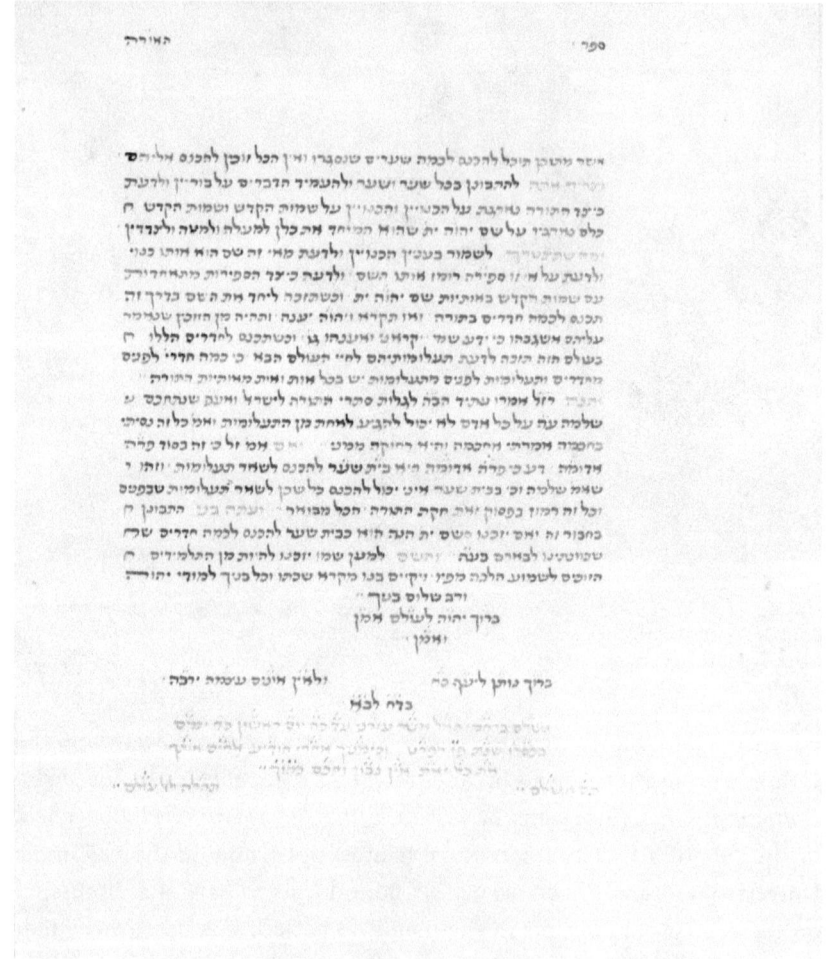

FIGURE 7.5. Kabbalistic miscellany, 1405, leaf 109v. Note that this colophon indicates a completion year of 1325, as copied directly from *Biblioteca Laurenziana Plut. II 41*. Columbia MS X893 G363. Image Courtesy Columbia University Libraries.

exactly from a manuscript at the Biblioteca Laurenziana[49] in (as the second colophon indicates) 1405 (fig. 7.5). Beit-Arié has also identified additional works by the same fifteenth century scribe.[50]

In 1953, Baron published an article on the thought of Shemu'el David Luzzatto (known as Shadal), a prominent Paduan rabbi and scholar, using a manuscript[51] of Shadal's lectures as part of a discussion on Shadal's perspective on the Revolution of 1848.[52]

There are many more instances in which Baron might have consulted Columbia's Judaica collections and did not cite them explicitly, especially in his magnum opus, *A Social and Religious History of the Jews*. The bibliography for this monumental work intersperses early printed works from the fifteenth or sixteenth century with recent publications from his time. Were the early prints the ones that he acquired for the Columbia Library, or those from his extensive personal collections?[53] Many reminiscences of Baron center him in Butler Library,[54] and he certainly remained involved in its activities throughout his tenure there.[55] To cite one of many examples, Baron was asked to serve on the committee in 1951 to "work out plans" for an "Archive of Russian and East European History and Culture."[56] The resulting Bakhmeteff Archive is now the largest collection of Russian émigré materials outside of Russia.

Baron's work for the Jewish Cultural Reconstruction project likely influenced the decision for Columbia to receive more than two thousand items when those heirless books were distributed in the late 1940s.[57] Perhaps ironically, considering Baron's involvement in JCR, the library "insisted that they could not accept the policy of returning books to JCR because the cost of making books available to readers prevented their simply giving back volumes."[58] Unfortunately, the JCR books received by Columbia cannot be identified today because they were not marked with the iconic bookplate as mandated by the restitution organization, but several have been identified as coming from Nazi-occupied Europe.

BARON'S SUCCESSORS AND THE COLUMBIA COLLECTIONS

Baron's students followed their teacher in using Columbia manuscripts in their research. Abraham Berger's chapter in a festschrift to Baron cites an important manuscript of Abraham Abulafia that describes the unity of mankind in the messianic era.[59] Gerson D. Cohen received his doctorate under Arthur Jeffrey in the Semitics Department but no doubt was influenced by Baron as well. Cohen was appointed associate professor of Jewish history on Baron's retirement, and the year he was promoted to full professor, he published an article on Abraham

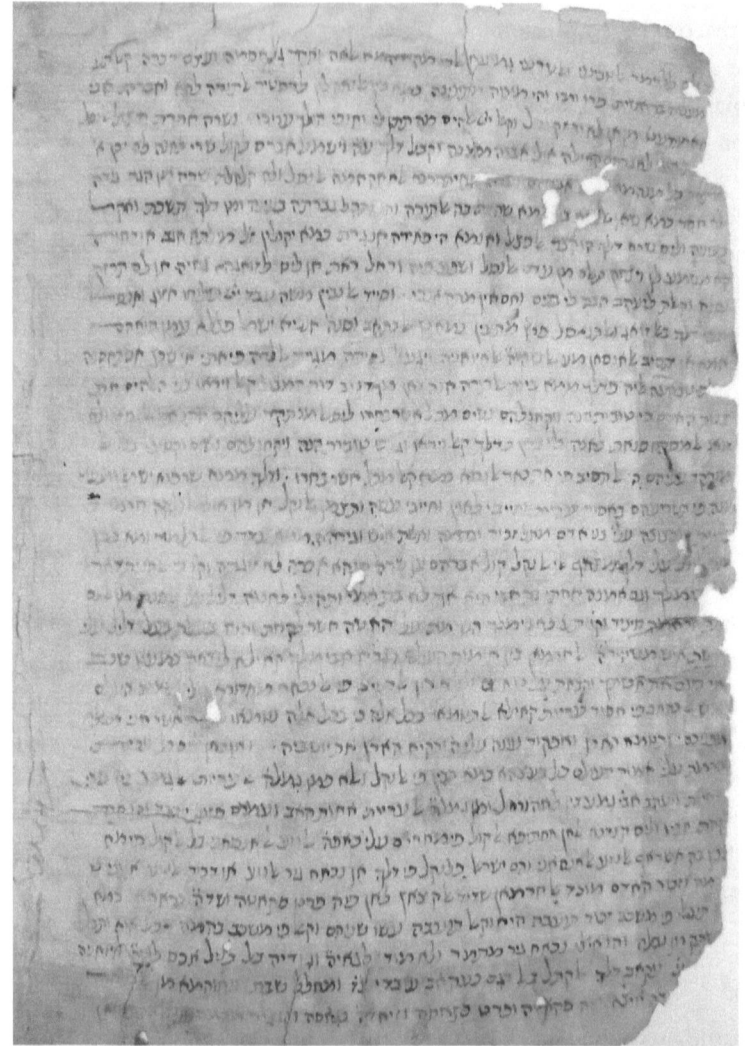

FIGURE 7.6. *Kifdyat al-'Abidin*, by Abraham Maimuni, 14th century (fragment). Columbia Rare Book & Manuscript Library, MS X893.15 M28, no. 26.

Maimuni, which would cite a fragment held at Columbia that was part of Maimuni's *Kifdyat al-'Abidin,* much of which is lost today (fig. 7.6).[60] The portion at Columbia described by Cohen contains a portion from part II of this work, including "a section on the obligation to procreate children."[61]

Baron's retirement in 1963 by no means indicated a cessation of work—either scholarly or pedagogical. A 1976 dissertation by Morris B. Margolies[62] focusing on the life, thought, and oeuvre of Shemu'el David Luzzatto (Shadal), citing no less than five Columbia manuscripts,[63] "acknowledges his debt to his teacher, Professor Salo W. Baron, who encouraged this project from its inception and who supplied many constructive suggestions which have proved most helpful to the work."[64] Decades later, another student, and Baron's successor at Columbia, Yosef Yerushalmi, would also engage deeply with the manuscripts. In 1981, Yerushalmi produced an exhibition called *Perspectives on Jewish Messianism*.[65] Additionally, the Judaic collections were featured prominently in a pamphlet for a fundraising campaign for the Center for Jewish Studies in 1976, which included the following statement: "Of particular importance are manuscripts in the collection on history and sociology. For example, in a mid-16th Century petition to a Venetian doge, Christian councilors ask for repeal of a decree ordering expulsion of Jews.[66] Another relates a plague in the Ghetto of Padua in 1630.[67] Another relates Robespierre's attitude to the Jewish religion.[68] The collection also contains six responsa and a ban promulgated by rabbis of Hamburg in the 1920's against use of any language but Hebrew in religious services and against organ playing in synagogues."[69]

It is notable that the same pamphlet, which requests support for various aspects of the center, such as funded chairs and fellowships, includes a recommended $550,000 for an endowment for library collections.[70] A sizable library endowment would not come until 2008, when the Norman E. Alexander Foundation donated $4 million to support collections and a dedicated librarian for Judaica.

CONCLUSION

In 1998, Robert Singerman wrote a history of Judaica collections in the United States from the mid-eighteenth century to the present. The title of his article, "Books Weeping for Someone to Visit and Admire Them," referred to the Temple Emanu-El collection before it was donated to Columbia in 1892.[71] The history of Judaica collections in the United States in the twentieth century has yet to be fully written, but when it does, Salo Baron will feature prominently within it. Over the course of more than thirty years as a professor at Columbia, Baron was actively involved in building library collections for research and scholarship in the field that he shaped in America, that of Jewish history. His deep commitment to Judaica collections continued well into his retirement—a 1973 proposal for a survey of Judaica collections in American archives and research libraries listed Dr. Salo W. Baron foremost on the "Panel of Experts," specifically "to serve as an expert on scholarly needs in the archival and library field."[72] And unlike the collection that preceded him, the books that he acquired for the collection had no chance to "weep." On the contrary, they were used extensively in research and scholarship by Baron, his students, and his successors, both at Columbia and in the broader field of Jewish studies.

NOTES

Writing an archives-based paper during a global pandemic, when a critical collection is across the country, can be incredibly difficult. This paper could not have been written without the generous assistance of Eitan Kensky and Anna Levia at the Stanford University, and the Department of Special Collections at Stanford University Libraries, who helped me to access the necessary documents in a timely manner. I am grateful to the Baron Estate for providing me permission to publish documents from the Salo Baron Papers. Many thanks as well to Jocelyn Wilk, Columbia University Archivist, who patiently answered many questions and provided sources I would otherwise never have seen. Jane Siegel has been sending me citations about Columbia's Judaica collection for a decade now, and this work would be severely lacking without her generous and kind assistance.

1. Robert Liberles, *Salo Wittmayer Baron: Architect of Jewish History* (New York: New York University Press, 1959), 59, emphasis added; cf. Columbia University Archives, Central Files, Miller File, Linda Miller to Nicholas Butler, May 9, 1928; Butler's response of May 11.
2. Samuel Johnson's letters include correspondence with Judah Monis, the first printer to use Hebrew movable type in the Americas. See "Samuel Johnson and Hebrew at Columbia," *Jewish Studies at CUL* (blog), https://blogs.cul.columbia.edu/jewishstudiesatcul/2019/01/16/samuel-johnson-and-hebrew-at-columbia.
3. Benjamin Kennicott, *Vetus Testamentum Hebraicum: cum variis lectionibus* (Oxford: Clarendon Press, 1774–76), vol. 1, Subscribers: Great Britain, Ireland, America, xii, xiv.
4. William J. Rhees, *Manual of Public Libraries, Institutions, and Societies, in the United States, and British Provinces of North America* (Philadelphia: J. B. Lippencott & Co., 1859), as cited in Robert Singerman, "Books Weeping for Someone to Visit and Admire Them: Jewish Library Culture in the United States, 1850–1910," *Studies in Bibliography and Booklore* 20 (1998): 110.
5. Richard J. H. Gotthheil, *Life of Gustav Gottheil: Memoir of a Priest in Israel* (Williamsport, CT: Bayard, 1936), 208–11.

6. For more information on the establishment of the chair and Temple Emanu-El's motivation for it, see the Minutes of Temple Emanu-el, "Special Meeting of the Board held March 15, 1887," 312, at the Temple Emanu-El Archives, New York, NY.
7. See Ephraim Deinard, *Devir Ephraim* (St. Louis, MO: Moinester Printing Co., 1926), 1. Note that Deinard claims this happened in 1888, whereas the Columbia trustee minutes list the donation was made in 1890. It is possible that the final donation did not take place until the later date. A list of twenty-eight manuscripts is included in the Columbia College Library Report, list of additions (sixteen), May 1890, 16-17.
8. Columbia University Archives, trustee minutes, June 5, 1892, 173.
9. The collection was put up for sale in Amsterdam by Frederick Muller in 1868 and included parts of the libraries of Giuseppe Almanzi, Jacob Emden, and S. D. Lewenstein. The entire collection is described in Meijer Roest, *Bet Ha-Sefer: Catalog der Reichhaltigen Sammlungen Hebraischer und Judischer Bucher, Handschriften, Kupferstiche, Portraits etc:... Giuseppe Almanzi...* (Amsterdam: F. Müller, 1868).
10. Columbia University Archives, Central Files, Richard Gottheil file, box 327, folder 4, November 19, 1900.
11. A few histories of Judaica collections in the United States exist: Menahem Schmelzer on JTS, "Building a Great Judaica Library—At What Price?" in *Tradition Renewed: A History of the Jewish Theological Seminary of America, vol.1, The Making of an Institution of Jewish Higher Learning*, ed. Jack Wertheimer (New York: Jewish Theological Seminary of America, 1997), 677–715; Charles Berlin on Harvard, "The Judaica Collection at Harvard," *Jewish Book Annual* 26 (1968–69): 58–63; and Arthur Kiron on Dropsie-Annenberg-Penn, "The Professionalization of Wisdom: The Legacy of Dropsie College and Its Library," in *The Penn Library Collections at 250: From Franklin to the Web* (Philadelphia: University of Pennsylvania Library, 2000), 182–201. But there is still work to be done on a comprehensive history of Judaica collecting in the United States during the first part of the twentieth century.
12. Schmelzer, "Building a Great Judaica Library," 686, 711n36. It might not be a coincidence that the collection was ultimately granted to JTS in 1907, shortly after Schiff wrote a strongly worded letter to Butler decrying the genteel anti-Semitism at Columbia that prevented the university from appointing a Jewish trustee, something that Schiff had been decrying since the late 1890s. See Columbia University Archives, Central Files, Jacob H. Schiff file, 1891–1917, box 338, folder 18.
13. Columbia University Archives, Central Files, Linda R. Miller file, box 667, folder 31.
14. Columbia University Libraries, Report of the Librarian, 1933, 17; emphasis added.
15. In Columbia University Archives, Central Files, Salo Wittmayer Baron file, box 407, folder 20, see, e.g., Frank Fackenthal to Baron, October 7, 1940 ($300); income statement for 1948–49 ($600) and 1949–50 ($300); Baron to Grayson Kirk, November 28, 1950 ($300); and W. Emerson Gentzler to Baron, May 9, 1951 (request for $300 deferred to the following year). See also Stanford University Libraries, M0580, Baron Papers, box 55, folder 13, and correspondence between Baron and Library director Richard Logsdon regarding funding for the collections.

16. In Columbia University Archives, Central Files, box 22, Ba 1938–39, see, e.g., Baron to Fackenthal, September 30, 1938; and Fackenthal's handwritten note of "Hebrew?" next to Baron's text indicating "Jewish interest," and the subsequent response from Fackenthal on October 3 indicating $1,000 from the Miller fund "for the purchase of Hebrew books for the Library."
17. Columbia University Archives, Central Files, box 25, Ba 1946–47, Baron to Fackenthal, March 16, 1947. Baron's letter notes that "we began with an allocation of $2,000 annually . . . reduced to $300 . . . in recent years."
18. Stanford University Libraries, M0580, Baron Papers, box 9, folder 1, March 13, 1933 (Baron to Howson). Shockingly, perhaps, to today's sensibilities, the duplicates the library was looking to discard were incunabula.
19. Columbia University Archives, Library Office Files, box 35 (series 2), Hebrew Manuscripts, correspondence between Charles Williamson and Howson, April 21 and 23, 1934.
20. Stanford University Libraries, M0580, Baron Papers, box 26, folder 7, Baron to Williamson regarding "Study 732," February 12, 1941; box 38, folder 2, Baron to Williamson, February 8, 1938; and others.
21. See, e.g., Baron to library director Logsdon regarding funding for Jewish studies collections in Stanford University Libraries, M0580, Baron Papers, "Center for Israel Studies, Library, 1954," box 215, folder 4. The same file also includes fairly detailed correspondence with Williamson regarding specific acquisitions in Jewish studies from around the world.
22. "Center for Israel Studies, Library, 1954"; Williamson to Baron, October 27, 1955, regarding acquisition of microfilm of a Latin (!) manuscript for a user, and Longsdon to Baron, June 7, 1955 regarding the Gitelson project to microfilm important Hebrew manuscripts at Columbia and other institutions.
23. Stanford University Libraries, M0580, Baron Papers, box 26, folder 7, Baron to Williamson, June 30, 1939 and December 26 1939, as well as box 38, folder 2, Baron to Williamson (multiple dates).
24. Columbia University Archives, Central Files, box 351, Howson to Fackenthal, December 16, 1932. Note that A. S. Halkin had done some previous work cataloging "Semitic" manuscripts under a grant secured by Richard Gottheil. Mendelsohn was also a student of Gottheil's, and Gottheil had recommended him earlier for cataloging. It appears that the decision was made to hire Mendelsohn only after Baron offered additional funding for the job.
25. David L. Langenberg, ed., *Of Many Generations: Judaica and Hebraica from the Taube/Baron Collection* (Stanford, CA: Stanford University Libraries, 1989), 17.
26. Baron knew Fraenkel from Vienna, and Fraenkel reached out to him for assistance in many areas, including selling additional books to others. More important, perhaps, was Baron's assistance to Fraenkel in helping him with emigration to the United States prior to World War II. For more on Baron's assistance of Fraenkel and others, see Evelyn Adunka, "Salo W. Baron's Efforts to Rescue Austrian Colleagues and Students," in *The Enduring Legacy of Salo Baron*, ed. Hava Tirosh-Samuelson and Edward Dabrowa (Kraków: Jagiellonian University Press, 2017), 311.
27. Stanford University Libraries, M0580, Baron Papers, box 9, folder 1, February 17, 1933, David Fraenkel to Salo Baron, two letters in both Hebrew and English. Interestingly, the Hebrew letter asks Baron to check his English and make sure it is

accurate. It seems that Baron had asked Fraenkel for a description of the collection in English to bring to the library as a proposal for purchase.

28. In Fraenkel's previously cited letter, he hoped "that you will kindly take into consideration the opportunity of purchasing such rare and most valuable collections for such incomparable low quotations" and cited the "present economic conditions" as a factor.
29. Stanford University Libraries, M0580, Baron Papers, May 5, 1933, box 6, folder 2, Howson to Baron.
30. Columbia University Archives, Trustee Minutes, Report of the Committee on Finance, October 2, 1933.
31. Columbia University Libraries, Report of the Librarian, 1933, 17–18.
32. "Rabbi Cancels Gift of Books," *Columbia Spectator*, May 11, 1933, 1.
33. "Columbia Library Gets Hebrew MSS: Collection of a Vienna Rabbi Reveals new Light on Jewish History," *New York Times*, January 4, 1934, 17.
34. The *Descriptive Catalogue* is now freely available online, via the Internet Archive, at https://archive.org/details/ldpd_12138657_001.
35. Portions of this section were published in the Institute for Israel and Jewish Studies magazine, fall 2020. This section is indebted to Jeanette M. Baron's "A Bibliography of the Printed Writings of Salo Wittmayer Baron," *Salo Wittmayer Baron Jubilee Volume on the Occasion of his Eightieth Birthday* (Jerusalem: American Academy for Jewish Research, 1974), English Section, I:1–38. As noted in the introduction to the bibliography, Baron had "none other than his wife who has been his principal research assistant throughout the years."
36. Salo Baron, Salo Sakhsukh kehilot be-verona ap"y teshuvat R. Mordekhai Bashan be-sof ha-me'ah ha-sheva' 'esreh" in *Sefer ha-yovel le-profesor Shemu'el Kroys* (Jerusalem, 1937), 217–54.
37. Columbia MS X893.19 B29.
38. Columbia MS X893.19 B29, 247n1; my translation.
39. Salo Baron, "Review of Letters to Emma Lazarus in the Columbia University Library by Ralph L. Rusk," *Jewish Social Studies* 2, no. 1 (Jan. 1940): 108–9.
40. Salo Baron, Salo, "Le-toledot ha-halukah u-fidyon ha-shevuyim be-me'ah ha-17," *American Hebrew Year Book* 6 (1942): 167–79.
41. Columbia MS X893.19 P653, leaf 3 for *pidyon shevuyim*.
42. Salo Baron, "Le-toledot ha-halukah u-fidyon ha-shevuyim be-me'ah ha-17," 167; my translation. Note here how Baron continuously supported Fraenkel's business—even in published articles!
43. Salo Baron, "On the History of the Corfu Community and Their Organization," [In Hebrew], in *Kovets mada 'i le-zekher Mosheh Shor*, ed. Louis Ginsberg and Abraham Weiss (New York: Hotsa'at Va'adat Zikaron Mosheh Shor, 1945), 25–41.
44. Salo Baron, "Jewish Immigration and Communal Conflicts in Seventeenth-Century Corfu," in *The Joshua Starr Memorial Volume; Studies in History and Philology* (New York: Conference on Jewish Relations, 1953), 169–82.
45. Cited in these articles were Columbia MS X893 Z8 03, no. 06; Columbia MS X893.19 D35; and Columbia MS X893.19 P653.
46. Salo Baron, *The Jewish Community: Its History and Structure to the American Revolution* (Philadelphia: Jewish Publication Society of America, 1942), 2:200.
47. Columbia MS X893 G363.

48. Columbia University Libraries, Report of the Librarian, 1933, 18.
49. [Kabbalistic Miscellany], 1325. Biblioteca Laurenziana Plut. II. 41. A full list of the items in the miscellany can be found on KTIV: The International Collection of Digitized Hebrew Manuscripts: https://web.nli.org.il/sites/nlis/en/manuscript/pages/results.aspx#query=lsr01,contains,all&query=any,contains,Biblioteca%20Laurenziana%20Plut.II.41
50. Malachi Beit-Arié, "Transmissions of Texts by Scribes and Copyists: Unconscious and Critical Interferences," *Bulletin of the John Rylands University Library of Manchester* 75, no. 3 (1993): 41–42.
51. Columbia MS X893 L9767. For more on Shadal manuscripts at Columbia, see "The Luzzatto Family at Columbia," *Jewish Studies at CUL* (blog), October 12, 202, https://blogs.cul.columbia.edu/jewishstudiesatcul/2020/10/12/the-luzzatto-family-at-columbia/. . For an important dissertation on Shadal and his works by a student of Baron, see notes 64–65.
52. Baron, Salo, "Shadal ve-ha-mahapekha be-shenot ha-608-9"in *Sefer Assaf: Simha Assaf Jubilee Volume*, ed. Umberto Cassutto et al. (Jerusalem: Mossad HaRav Kook, 1953), 44.
53. Baron's vast personal library collection was acquired by Stanford University in 1985. See Langenberg, *Of Many Generations*.
54. See, for example, Michael Stanislavski, "Salo Wittmayer Baron: Demystifying Jewish History," *Columbia* Magazine, January 15, 2005, https://magazine.columbia.edu/article/salo-wittmayer-baron-demystifying-jewish-history; and Robert Chazan, "Salo Wittmayer Baron," *Proceedings of the American Academy for Jewish Research* 58 (1992): 7–13.
55. It is not clear whether Baron was involved in the acquisition of the Oko-Gebhardt Spinoza collection (1947), but he was on the guest list for the reception honoring the gift. He declined, possibly because he was deeply involved with work for the Jewish Cultural Reconstruction at that time.
56. Columbia University Archives, Central Files, Baron file, box 407, folder 20–21, Grayson Kirk (vice president and provost) to Baron, May 2, 1951.
57. Dana Herman, "*Hashavat Avedah:* A History of Jewish Cultural Reconstruction, Inc." (PhD thesis, McGill University, 2008), 262.
58. Herman, *Hashavat Avedah*, 239.
59. Abraham Berger, "The Messianic Self-Consciousness of Abraham Abulafia: A Tentative Evaluation," in *Essays in Jewish Life and Thought Presented in Honor of Salo W. Baron*, ed. Joseph L. Blau, Philip Friedman, Arthur Hertzberg, and Isaac Mendelsohn (New York: Columbia University Press, 1959), 55–61. The call number of the manuscript cited is Columbia MS X893 Ab92 (footnote 19). Note that this manuscript was not part of the Fraenkel/Baron acquisition; it had been at Columbia since at least 1922.
60. Gerson D. Cohen, "The Soteriology of R. Abraham Maimuni," in *Proceedings of the American Academy for Jewish Research* 35 (1967): 75–98. The manuscript cited is Columbia MS X893.15 M28.
61. Cohen, "The Soteriology of R. Abraham Maimuni," 95.
62. Morris B. Margolies, "Samuel David Luzzatto: Traditionalist Scholar" (PhD diss., Columbia University, 1976).

63. Margolies, "Samuel David Luzzatto," 322. Columbia MSS X893 L9764, X893 L9766, X893 L9736, X893 L9767, and (erroneously labeled Hebrew Union College) X893.1BC L979.
64. Margolies, "Samuel David Luzzatto," ii–iii.
65. *Perspectives on Jewish Messianism. An Exhibition of Rare Books and Manuscripts from the Judaica Collections of the Columbia University Libraries*, April 13–24, 1981. The catalogue was produced under the auspices of the Center for Jewish Studies.
66. Columbia MS X893.19 C684.
67. Columbia MS X893 Ab8.
68. Columbia MS X893 H62.
69. The manuscript is Columbia MS X893 C26. The quote cited here is from Columbia University Archives, Columbia University Library Office Files, box 405, Center for Israel and Jewish Studies, "The Professionalization of Judaica: Columbia and Jewish Studies," draft, 10, 1976. The draft was sent to the libraries for review.
70. Center for Israel and Jewish Studies, "The Professionalization of Judaica," 13.
71. Singerman, "Books Weeping for Someone to Visit and Admire Them."
72. Columbia University Archives, Columbia University Library Office Files, box 314, "Jewish Studies."

Chapter Eight

FROM EUROPE TO PITTSBURGH

Salo W. Baron and Yosef H. Yerushalmi Between the Lachrymose Theory and the End of the Vertical Alliance

PIERRE BIRNBAUM

In 1930, Salo Baron was appointed professor of Jewish studies in the Department of History at Columbia University, a first in the Western world. Baron soon became the most important and prolific Jewish historian of the twentieth century, confident about the future of the Jewish people in America. According to Baron, the United States was becoming the permanent domicile of the Jewish people, a place where they could, at long last, have a normal life, a life without tears. Thus, surrounded by many talented students writing their doctoral dissertations, Baron struggled against the notion of despair. He thought that Jews, whatever might be the dangers of their emancipation, could have a decent collective life in exile.

Fifty years later, Yosef Haim Yerushalmi, one of Baron's best pupils, was also hired to teach in the Department of History at Columbia. Following the Shoah, Yerushalmi was less certain; hope was fading. The fact that the Jewish people, in exile, had had to rely on the fragility of royal alliance demonstrated the permanent weakness of exile, from Spain to modern Germany. Could the Jewish people really find a permanent domicile in exile, or perhaps in Israel?

This discussion began in 1928, when Salo Baron ended his famous article, "Ghetto and Emancipation," with the following sentence: "it is time to break with the lachrymose theory of the pre-Revolutionary woe and to adopt a view more in accord with historical truth."[1] A few months before obtaining this prestigious position in the New World, Baron had nevertheless argued against the virtues of Emancipation and, paradoxically, described the Middle Ages as a world in which Jews lived a more peaceful life. Therefore, "at any rate, it is clear that Emancipation has not brought the Golden Age."[2] In this incredible paper, the French Revolution is seen not as the awakening of liberty for Jews, which is the conventionally accepted vision of 1789, but as evil, marking the birth of a world in which Jews lost their privileges, their autonomy, their well-being and, most important, their specific position vis-à-vis the state. Baron argued against Heinrich Graetz's interpretation of the French Revolution. For Graetz, "the Revolution was a judgment which in one day atoned for the sins of a thousand years.... For the Jews, the most abject and despised people in European society, the day of redemption and liberty was to dawn after their long slavery among the nations of Europe."[3] Baron did not want to see this kind of emancipation as the "dawn of a new day after a nightmare of the deepest horror." According to him, there was no "complete contrast between the black of the Middle Ages and the White of the Post-Emancipation period."[4] After all, "the gains of the Revolution" have been overestimated, and its "miracles were not so great as we supposed."[5]

At the core of Baron's argument is the notion that the lachrymose theory of Jewish history prior to the French Revolution, dear to Graetz, does not accurately depict the historical reality of this time, during which Jews had a peaceful life. They enjoyed a specific status as *servi camerae*, which protected them from their neighbors' anti-Semitism, a protection that was lost in the period of emancipation during which a wild, modern anti-Semitism was invented.

For Baron, "the peasants were really serfs in civil law, that is, they belonged to a private owner as a kind of private property. The Jews were so to speak, serfs in public law, and as such belonged to the ruler as representative or embodiment of the State, and they were inherited by his successor in office through public law.... The difference in the legal status between Jew and peasant was what David Hume, writing in that period on the condition of ancient slaves, called the difference between 'domestic slavery' and 'civil subjection.'" The first, he recognized, "is more cruel and oppressive than any civil subjection whatsoever."[6]

For Baron, therefore, if the Middle Ages were not a dark period for the Jews, if the ghetto was a voluntary kind of community, a moment of relative happiness compared, for instance, to the harsh destiny of the peasants, if it was not a moment of intense Jewish suffering and persecutions, if the lachrymose vision of Jewish history does not describe those centuries as everyone believed, it might be because this specific status of *servi camerae* bestowed on them a specific relationship to the state. They therefore had a quasi-privileged position compared with others, such as the peasants. For most of his life, Baron adhered to this iconoclastic view of the Middle Ages, which implied more or less openly that, on the contrary, the modern period had come to be a time of suffering. More explicitly, in 1937, Baron stated that in the Middle Ages, "the government always tried to protect the lives of the Jews. In contrast to Czarist Russia, for instance, no medieval government ever countenanced pogroms."[7] The same interpretation applied to the Soviet revolution, during which persecutions against the Jews were as severe as during the czarist regime.[8] And, almost thirty years later, when he testified at the Eichmann prosecution, in describing the savage persecution of the *Kristallnacht* (Night of Broken Glass) in Germany, Baron argued that "the government itself, instead of protecting the synagogues, caused their destruction. This was an unusual step, since there had been nothing like it throughout the history of the darkest Middle Ages and throughout modern times."[9] Nazism, in modern times, appeared to be the opposite of the Middle Ages, during which "Emperors and Princes, Bishops and municipal authorities usually tried to stave off mob attacks upon their Jewish subjects." For Baron, "there is no evidence of any important medieval ruler engineering riots against his Jewish subjects. With the Nazis, however, nearly every attack on the Jews was planned in advance by the authorities and executed by government and party officials."[10]

Ultimately, the lachrymose vision of Jewish history does not describe the way in which the Jews were living during the Middle Ages as most historians have claimed; on the contrary, it is the modern period that is best described as such. The tzar and the Nazi state, for instance, planned violent riots against the Jews. Moreover, the main reason for this unprecedented behavior was the failure of the Vertical Alliance with the state, an alliance described a long time ago by Ibn Verga and carefully studied by Baron. In a way, Baron gives a more positive appreciation of this alliance than Verga, who knew that the kind King Manuel did not, in fact, protect the Jews from the mob, that the alliance was more of a myth than a real or effective policy.

One should also stress that Baron had an equally negative view of the French Revolution and of a modern royal alliance within the context of a secular state. From one article to the next, he denounces the famous phrase of the Count of Clermont-Tonnerre, which describes the harshness of this revolution against the Jews: "The Jews should be denied everything as a nation, but granted everything as individuals," making them citizens cut off from their community. The count added, "if they do not accept, let them be banished."[11] According to Baron, "the traditional medieval solution of the Jewish question through conversion or expulsion was here modified only by the secular alternative of national assimilation or banishment."[12] Baron outlined the "negativistic, anti-religious crusade of such great leaders of the French Enlightenment as Voltaire and the encyclopedists which, though principally aimed at Catholic dogma, ritual and history, has serious repercussions for their Jewish counterparts."[13] He argued that "the modern egalitarian state could no longer tolerate the existence of such a self-governing corporate body."[14] He lamented "the dissolution reached by the ghetto community under the impact of Emancipation"[15] and considered the consistory organized by Napoleon as "serving the state's purposes rather than those of the Jews."[16] Moreover, the main illustration of modern Emancipation tells us again that for Baron, the lachrymose vision of Jewish history does not concern the Middle Ages but modern times, from revolutionary France to Germany under Hitler or Russia, where "total assimilation" under the Soviets destroyed the "pillars" of the Jewish community.[17]

If, during the Middle Ages the state protected its Jews, today the modern nation-state betrays them, whatever its logic and its ideology. And for some of Baron's students, such as Arthur Herzberg, there is not even a difference between the French Revolution and Nazism, the latter seen as the consequence of the former.[18] As David Engel noticed, "Baron viewed modern European Jewish history, unlike the history of Jewry in the Middle Ages, as a story of continuous upheaval engendered by ubiquitous deep ruptures in the fabric of Jewish society, culture and relations with others. . . . Such a perspective permitted him to produce works on the modern period that were hardly free of lachrymosity as he defined it."[19]

To summarize Baron's argument, one could argue that, indeed, he should have said more explicitly that the lachrymose theory of Jewish history had value at least for the modern period, during Emancipation, if not for the Middle Ages and life in the ghetto. Had he expressed it so, most contemporary historians dealing with modern European societies would not criticize his theories by underscoring the intensity of these persecutions and anti-Semitic riots, in effect demonstrating how meaningful the lachrymose vision of modern Jewish history is. In fact, they agree with the explicit—or, at the very least, implicit—aspects of Baron's argument.

Moreover, if Baron more or less endorsed this vision throughout his life, if, without saying it explicitly, he looked at the modern period—in its pathological dimension (Nazism, Soviet power, and so on), but also in its more rationalist dimension (like the French Revolution)—as a context of pain and suffering for Jews, one can also see here an unexpected extension of the lachrymose theory to which he was opposed; for instance, when Baron, after the Eichmann trial, wrote,

> All my life I have been struggling against the hitherto dominant "lachrymose conception of Jewish history"—a term that I have been using for more than forty years—because I have felt that, by overemphasizing Jewish sufferings, it distorted the total picture of the Jewish historic evolution and at the same time, it served badly a generation which has become impatient with the "nightmare" of endless persecutions and massacres. However, just as we must not misunderstand the true realities of life among the still predominant orthodox and traditionalist East-European Jewish masses during the Nazi era, so we must not overlook the inherent tragedies of Jewish life during two millennia of dispersion.[20]

Suddenly, the lachrymose theory extends itself to "the inherent tragedies of Jewish life during two millennia of dispersion," which, for the first time, includes the Middle Ages. Occasionally, Baron's opposition is less clear. And for the first time also, it is the idea of "dispersion," therefore of diaspora seen as *galut*, that appears to be responsible for those tragedies. For once, it seems that Baron was sharing Yitzah Baer's ideas on *galut*, interpreted as the inherent betrayal of Jewish life, whatever its period and place.[21] Strangely, Baron, the laudator of diaspora Jewishness, seems to agree with Baer's judgment: "All that we did on foreign soil was a betrayal of our own spirit."[22] What a paradox! "Theoretically, at least, Baron was a diaspora-oriented historian. . . . In an age of anti-*galut* trends, he became one of the authoritative spokesmen of a pro-*galut* philosophy . . . he also declared *galut* a permanent feature of Jewish existence and destiny."[23] But from time to time, Baron had a more negative vision of the "inherent tragedies" of *galut*, practically sharing Baer's harsh words.

In the 1960s, Baron at last found a diaspora without tears, without persecution or anti-Semitic riots. Its evolutionary interpretation, from the ghetto to Emancipation, suddenly vanished. Evil can emerge in different times and places, but hope is nevertheless shaping one society, innocent of any Jewish persecution: the United States, where Baron himself found a suitable haven at Columbia University. For numerous Eastern European Jewish scholars between the two world wars, leaving the old continent, crossing the Atlantic, and finding a new home in America was like a dream. At last, a peaceful place, far from Russian pogroms; extreme-right mobilization; mass mobilization in Germany, Austria, Romania and so on; and anti-Semitic behavior at the university! Many sociologists, anthropologists, and historians left Eastern Europe, Germany, or Austria, such as Franz Boas, Edward Sapir, Karl Deutsch, Hans Kelsen, Ernst Kantorowicz, Hans Kohn, Erich Fromm, and Albert Hirschman. Baron was among them and shared their sociological and historical approaches of their new home.

If one could draw a "geography of hope," the United States would be the main part of it.[24] In their new "home,"[25] most Jewish immigrant scholars enjoyed a peaceful life, free from tears. They became vibrant advocates of the American way of life, its pluralism, liberalism, and tolerance; they left—for good—their ancient ideological world full of hatred and political passions and invested their energy in the knowledge of the logic of their new sociological environment. Surrounded by numerous pupils who received their PhD under his supervision and who later became important scholars primarily of American Judaism, Baron created a rich and innovative field of study in his new home. Far from Spain in the Middle Ages, far from any ghetto environment within old Europe, Baron, in this new period of his life, wrote about many aspects of American Judaism: its cultural but also socioeconomic aspect, demography, and history since the foundation of the republic. He gave many talks showing the specificity of American society and the way in which Jews could improve their conditions in their new environment. He became the leader of various Jewish institutions and gave many speeches in various philanthropic Jewish structures: "Baron increasingly saw American Jewish history as an ideal research site for his theories of the mutual influence of social and religious trends in Jewish history."[26] He was full of confidence in the future of American Judaism. "American Jewry, I am certain," wrote Baron, "will also give unprecedented pioneering answers to its present challenges of creating a novel American Jewish culture."[27]

Baron's "love affair with America" is without limits. In the end, his "rosy" description of his new home looks like a kind of utopia, a modern emancipated society in which the new ghetto, the community, protects Jews and allows them to build strong collective networks, efficient bonds, and, therefore, a lively cultural and religious life.

His book *The Jewish Community, Its History and Structure to the American Revolution* tells us how far he departed from "Ghetto and emancipation": ghetto metamorphosed into a vibrant community is the perfect environment within an emancipated society for a lively Jewish life, even if, "in the New World," they had "to adjust themselves to the sectarian conflicts and animosities carried over from the European mother lands by their Christian neighbors."[28] Whatever those difficulties, Baron outlined the fact that during the last decade, Jewish congregations had increased their membership, and the attendance at synagogues had grown.[29] In the United States, Jews don't need the protection of the state: the vertical alliance loses its efficiency in such a society with a weak decentralized state. And as a non–nation-state, the state cannot attempt, as in France, to assimilate the Jews by shaping their values and destroying their collective bonds. Indeed, the royal alliance vanishes in a context in which Jews share the same status as their fellow citizens.

Turmoil in Baron's vision of the lachrymose theory! In the United States, Jews don't need the protection of the state, as they did in the Middle Age, nor are they threatened by the state, as in the Emancipation period. They live a quiet life in their suburbs; they freely join their community at the local level. Far from "the inherent tragedies of Jewish life during two millennia of dispersion," hope is finally a feeling shared by most American Jews, who are immersed in their community, far from the weak state. The main evidence for this state of happiness is the low level of anti-Semitism. The lachrymose theory of Jewish life must therefore be for the first time abandoned: for Baron, "American Jewish history, unable to produce a succession of riots and discriminatory laws, could hardly fit into this traditional pattern."[30]

Obviously, Baron knew and even described some low level of anti-Semitism in the United States: the fact that Jews were excluded from some hotels, the quotas against them within the Ivy League, the reluctance of white Anglo-Saxon Protestant society to accept them in a deeply Protestant culture, and so on. He even mentioned Father Coughlin's anti-Semitic mobilization against the "Jew Deal," Ford, and the *Protocols of the Elders of Zion*, and other anti-Semitic manifestations during McCarthyism.

But, in the end, America was free of pogroms, riots, and killings of Jews as in the ghetto period or, more important, the period of Emancipation, during which the modern state itself and not the mob launched the pogroms. Far from the Vienna of his childhood, from Berlin but also Paris, from the secular messianism of the Soviet Union but also from the beloved old Spain, America became the lost paradise, the new "center" of Jewish life. In this home, exile had, at last, become a "normal" life.

Yosef Yerushalmi, Baron's pupil, also enjoyed a normal life in New York, where he was appointed to Baron's chair at Columbia after having received his doctorate under Baron's supervision (fig. 8.1). Throughout his

FIGURE 8.1. Yosef Hayim Yerushalmi, flanked by his parents, Hava and Leon Yerushalmi, in front of Low Library on the day he received his PhD from Salo Baron, June 1, 1966.
Courtesy of the Columbia University Archives.

life, Yerushalmi maintained an intense admiration for Baron's pathbreaking work, quoting his books and articles in most of his own work. However, it seems to me that despair rather than hope remained at the core of his life. If Yerushalmi navigated his entire life between despair and hope, his gloom, depression, and loneliness were much stronger than any optimistic vision of Jewish history. Having spent many hours talking with him—in his apartment, in his country house, where we both spent three long days talking and recording the conversation, in various downtown cafes, walking with him in the Upper West side, and in the sunny streets of Paris—may I say that neither messianism nor hope was deeply molded in his thoughts. Whatever his Baronian background and his own reluctance to agree with the lachrymose theory of history, Yerushalmi had, perhaps, no real hope for the fallen Jews. Even if he once wrote that "Jewish history is fraught with tragedy but it is not a history of despair,"[31] he acknowledged also that "my people now as in the past are in grave peril for their life."[32] And no radical revolution can save the Jews: "the revolution that claims to be the 'final' one, such revolution will not hesitate to create a hell and call it paradise."[33]

Although Yerushalmi never wrote any specific article on "Ghetto and Emancipation," he might have disagreed with this quasi-evolutionist vision of Jewish history. One can even assert that his main research dealt only with the modern or premodern period, whereas the contemporary moment is practically absent from his work, contrary to Baron's approach. Furthermore, he was less interested than his master in any sociological turn, and unlike Baron, he never built any quantitative study based on twentieth-century statistics dealing with any kind of socioeconomic behavior. One could even claim that, contrary to Baron, contemporary societies related to the process of Emancipation were not at the core of his research.

Yerushalmi's pathbreaking book, *From Spanish Court to Italian Ghetto*, was published in 1971. Baron wrote a foreword, saying that "Professor Yerushalmi's excellent biography of Isaac Cardoso is an important landmark in this field . . . a fascinating contribution to learning."[34] In many respects, one could claim that this fabulous book is a perfect case study of applying Baron's vision of Jewish history. His main character, Isaac Cardoso, a physician, was able to rise through the ranks of the royal state. His career in Spain is an example that would have fit perfectly with the strategy of vertical alliance during this period: Cardoso, protected by Count Olivares, climbed to the heights of power "under his patronage."[35]

However, Cardoso prefers to abandon this strategy, leaving the vertical alliance, choosing in its stead exile and a return to the Italian ghetto, his new "home in Verona."³⁶ At last, unexpectedly leaving the brilliant court of Madrid, Cardoso "had come to the end of all his journeys. For the next thirty years he lived and worked in the Ghetto of Verona, an honored member of the Sephardic community . . . in peace."³⁷

This could be a perfect illustration of Baron's vision: instead of being deeply honored as a non-Jew at the court, where science and a kind of emancipation are revered, Cardoso flees the world that is undergoing a process of modernization and decides to lock himself within the ghetto, where he can "live as a Jew."³⁸ There, in his appeal to the princes, with "pride," Cardoso wrote, "The Jews are not the serfs of the nations, but a Republic apart. . . . The Jews who live today are not really the slaves of the princes in whose territories they reside."³⁹

Yerushalmi followed Baron's logic, outlining the merits of the Middle Ages. Three years after *From Spanish Court to Italian Ghetto*, his 1974 lecture, "Response to Rosemary Ruether," could have been written by Baron. Like his mentor, Yerushalmi insists on the fact that "Jews were not enslaved under Christendom. . . . Medieval Jewry had an entire gamut of well-defined rights which, on the whole, made the socio-economic status of the Jews superior to that of the Christian peasantry who often constituted the bulk of the population."⁴⁰ This sentence could have been written by Baron. The following one as well: mentioning explicitly the *Shevet Yehudah* perhaps for the first time, he wrote that for Ibn Verga, in the church during the Middle Ages, " it was the lower clergy who were the true enemies of the Jews. . . . The King and the Pope were at least committed to the rule of law and were thus pillars of whatever stability the Jews enjoyed."⁴¹ Yerushalmi, like Baron, shows in this crucial lecture that in modern times, anti-Semitism is not "merely a metamorphosed medieval Christian anti-Semitism." Now, for the first time, "The issue *is* physical extermination. Not reprobation, discrimination or any variety of opprobrium, but genocide. . . . The Holocaust took place in our secular century and *not* in the Middle Ages. Moreover, medieval anti-Jewish massacres were the work of the mob and the rabble. State-inspired pogroms of the type that took place in Czarist Russia, State-instigated genocide of the Nazi type—these are entirely modern phenomena. . . . The Holocaust was the work of a thoroughly modern, neopagan state."⁴²

So, for Yerushalmi, as for Baron, huge tears are to be found within the modern period, and the lachrymose vision of Jewish history fits much more with this period than with the "dark" Middle Ages. Like Baron, he insists, "the slaughter of Jews by the State was not part of the medieval Christian world-order."[43] Therefore, if the *Shevet Yehuda* was strangely absent from his doctoral dissertation, where it might have illustrated a kind of brief royal alliance between Cardoso and the king, it is clearly becoming a key in Yerushalmi's work. It was for him, as for Baron, a permanent obsession almost from the beginning of his academic career until the very end, and we long waited for his English translation.[44]

If there was no Holocaust in the Middle Ages, if the state was not responsible for the various persecutions of the Jews, if Baron's vision of an almost peaceful Middle Ages is accepted by Yerushalmi, in fact, he is not quite as sure about the good intentions of the state. It seems to me that he is much more pessimistic than Baron: Jews might have a dream of being protected by the state during the Middle Ages, but they face real and terrible slaughter during the modern period. For instance, in 1976, Yerushalmi published his *Lisbon Massacre of 1506 and the Royal Image in the Shevet Yehudah*, a marvelous book in which he describes how Ibn Verga tried to exonerate Don Manuel, the "gracious king" of Portugal, even after he failed to protect the Jews. For Yerushalmi, the royal alliance became "a guiding myth which gripped many of the Hispano-Jewish elite down to the very eve of the Expulsion."[45] And in the very last line of this brilliant study, he insisted: "In a real sense, Spanish Jews had been, from the very outset, prisoners of their own archetypes."[46] What kind of hope might they have expected from Ibn Verga's analysis based on a new "science of history," a book that Yerushalmi read in seventeen different editions?[47] At the beginning of *Lisbon Massacre*, Yerushalmi describes Baron's work "on the Jewish alliance with the State in the Middle Ages"[48] but immediately adds that this alliance was "a dream," "an archetype." His interpretation of the *Shevet Yehudah* is one of hopelessness:

> Jews sought a direct vertical alliance ... [which] was forged at the expense of a horizontal alliance with other segments or classes of the general population.... If the central authority was prone to regard Jews as allies, by that very token they further aroused the resentment of an already hostile population. The more the Jews sought the protection of the former, the

more they found themselves in tension with the latter and so each trend reinforced the other in a seemingly endless spiral. It was, on the whole, one of the more tragic aspects of the dialectics of Jewish existence among the nations.[49]

Far from Baron's optimistic analysis, Yerushalmi looks at the royal alliance as a "tragic" moment within Jewish history. Certainly not as tragic as the Holocaust in the modern period, but nevertheless full of tears. Even if he wrote that "the Inquisition for all its excesses, was not the Gestapo," he added that "the student of modern German Jewry who turns to the history of Spanish New Christian will find characteristics that are familiar to him, and may feel an inverted sense of *déjà vu*. The ambiguity and insecurity of assimilated Jews, the anxiety of hovering between acceptance and rejection, integration and marginality, the *jüdischer Selbsthass*, all are present there."[50]

This pessimism remains more or less the same throughout his life. For instance, forty years after his *Lisbon Massacre*, Yerushalmi wrote what might have been his most famous article: "Servants of the Kings and Not Servants of Servants. Some Political Aspects of the Political History of the Jews." Quoting again the *Shevet Yehudah*, he acknowledges that the vertical alliance was "generally the more favorable for them," and outlines again, like Baron, that during this period there was "no slaughter."[51] The royal alliance in medieval Europe is seen again as an "ideal model" that has been "mythologized."[52] But now he sees this royal alliance through a much more critical lens: Jews had "an excessive reliance on and faith in the state," which has "purposely sought the destruction of the Jews"; and at the end of the day, this royal alliance has "finally been demythologized."[53] Henceforth, whatever the persecutions and the myths of the Middle Ages, a return to this era when "the highest level of power still knew limits"[54] remains desirable.

Nowadays, Jews can no more be confident in the royal alliance, which has brought only disillusion and despair. Therefore, it seems difficult to establish a correlation between Yerushalmi's vision of the state's vertical alliance with the Jews and the question of hope. Can we really assume, as Lois Dubin does, that "for Yerushalmi himself, the royal alliance inspired hope," that for him, "the myth of the royal alliance" was "emblematic of Jewish agency and resiliency over the long term," and that it "was one factor that helped sustain diaspora Jewish hope"?[55] This alliance was supposed to protect them from despair, to give them hope, to steer them away from the lachrymose theory of history, but at different times, during the Middle Ages as in the twentieth century, it failed.

It is quite striking, it seems to me, that the word *hope* is never or seldom mentioned as such in Yerushalmi's numerous books and pages on Ibn Verga. The connection between the two dimensions, hope and alliance, was never made explicit. On the contrary, in his only and last study of hope, the vertical alliance is nowhere taken as a key issue, not even mentioned. One could draw a correlation between the alliance and hope, but Yerushalmi never made it openly himself. Furthermore, if he acknowledged the fact that the royal alliance, seen through Ibn Verga's study, is only an "archetype," a "myth," how can it have led to any real hope in Spain, Germany or elsewhere? It looks like a kind of secular messianism, but is full of dangers, engendering false hopes soon to be disappointed, turned into illusions and, in fact, into despair.

In this article, Yerushalmi begins by outlining that "we cannot explore the history of Jewish hope without at the same time exploring the history of Jewish despair"; and he adds, quoting Joshua ben Hananiah, "Not to mourn at all is impossible. . . . But to mourn too much is also impossible."[56] But then, he notices that "from where we stand after the Shoah, in terms of numbers, methods, and the motivations of the persecutors, the Iberian catastrophe may seem, objectively, a lesser event. Yet all our texts testify that, *subjectively*, for the generation that experienced within a mere twenty years the expulsion from Spain, Sicily and Sardinia, the total conversion in Portugal, the expulsions from Navarre, Provence and the Kingdom of Naples, all links in a terrible chain, the trauma may well have been comparable."[57]

"The small step toward hope itself,"[58] described in this last study, does not provide any real secular or messianic hope. Perhaps after all, Yerushalmi might have accepted a revisionist interpretation of the lachrymose theory of Jewish history, which seems to describe the miseries suffered by the Jews during both the Middle Ages and the modern period. We know that Yerushalmi does not agree with Yitzak Baer's extremely negative interpretation of the *galout*, of exile, that he does not accept his judgment that the *galout* was always "an extraordinary tragedy," a "betrayal" of our spirit. In his preface to Baer's book published in France, which has not yet been translated into English, he uses the word "excessive" several times to qualify Baer's vision of the Jewish exile from Palestine.[59]

But, after all, it might be that Yerushalmi's vision of Jewish history is even more tragic than Baer's, who was hoping that the way back to Palestine would, at last, give permanent hope to the Jewish people. The statement that does not console Yerushalmi, who wrote that "in the mind of the mass contemporary Jews everywhere, there is only one state upon which they can utterly rely, the Jewish state with all its imperfections. The nightmare that haunts the Jewish imagination is not merely the recollection of what happened but the possibility, however remote, that the Jewish state might itself be destroyed."[60] Furthermore, in 2005, when, for the first time, Yerushalmi gave a series of lectures on the Israeli state, he underlined that Israel, this "human hope," remained nowadays in a "grim situation."[61] Hope is a necessity, but it might not necessarily materialize. Yerushalmi worried that Israel might "be destroyed," and in Europe, "could the horror be repeated? In 1945 I thought it impossible. By now I have lost that absolute certainty."[62] Moreover, if he felt "at home" in the United States, he never had, like Baron, the same love affair with the "nation of nations," with its long-term history, its democratic roots, and the richness of its local community. He even wrote, "When the East European Jewish immigrants flocked to America, their expectations too were nothing if not Aquarian, for America was indeed to be the scene of the Millennium, *die goldene medineh*, where the Jewish past belonged to Russia, Poland or Galicia and had no place in the Aquarian leap from the tenement to the suburbs. We understand why it is that the memory of so many American Jews extends at best to some vestigial images of a grandmother."[63] Such a feeling almost contemptuous of American Jewry, so different from Baron's visions,[64] led Yerushalmi to write that "nowadays, the Diaspora is no more in Babylon than in Alexandria. Some interesting creations can be seen among American Jews in the United States or elsewhere but the heart of Jewish life beats in Israel. . . . In that sense, I can almost say that I am an Israeli. My decision to stay in the U.S was not based on ideological reasons but on various circumstances of life."[65]

Finally, for Yerushalmi, real hope being so fragile and uncertain, the lachrymose theory of Jewish history almost seems to make sense. Perhaps nowadays Baron, too, would have joined those who, like Baer and somehow Yerushalmi himself,[66] ultimately saw *galut* as a contemporary "vale of tears."[67] After Charlottesville (August 12, 2017) and the alt-right anti-Semitic mobilization, after Pittsburgh (October 27, 2018) and its massacre when, for the first time in American history, eleven Jews were brutally killed and many others were injured, after this first American pogrom remembering Kishinev and the "City of Slaughter,"[68] after so many deadly attacks on American Jews by mostly white nationalist anti-Semitic radicals, would Baron still be confident in the exceptional benevolence of American society toward the Jews? How would Yerushalmi have reacted?[69] Will the lachrymose theory of Jewish history today reach the American shores? Is it coming to the United States? Is Philip Roth's novel *The Plot Against America* becoming an awful and frightening reality bringing despair and "death for the Jews," a dramatic moment that could have threatened Salo Baron's or Yosef Yerushalmi's quiet life in the Upper West Side, so familiar to Saul Bellow?

NOTES

1. Salo W. Baron, "Ghetto and Emancipation," in *The Menorah Treasury Harvest of Half a Century*, ed. Leo Schwarz (Philadelphia: Jewish Publication Society of America, 1964), 63.
2. Baron, "Ghetto and Emancipation," 63.
3. Heinrich Graetz, *History of the Jews*, 6 vols. (Philadelphia: Jewish Publication Society of America, 1949), V:429–30.
4. Baron, "Ghetto and Emancipation," 50–51.
5. Baron, "Ghetto and Emancipation," 51.
6. Baron, "Ghetto and Emancipation," 53–54.
7. Salo W. Baron, *A Social and Religious History of the Jews*, vol. 2 (New York: Columbia University Press, 1937), 36.
8. Salo W. Baron, *The Russians Jews Under Tsars and Soviets* (New York: Macmillan, 1964), xxii.
9. The Nizkor Project, "The Trial of Adolf Eichmann," 12th sess., pts. 5–7, 16, http://www.nizkor.com/hweb/people/e/eichmann-adolf/transcripts/Sessions/.
10. Nizkor Project, "The Trial of Adolf Eichmann." See Claude Klein, *Le cas Eichmann, vu de Jérusalem* (Paris: Gallimard, 2012).
11. Clermont-Tonnerre, quoted by Yosef H. Yerushalmi in "From Expulsion to Emancipation. Texts and Documents on Jewish Rights, 16th–18th Centuries," Coursepacks, Columbia University, n.d., 229.
12. Salo Baron, "Changing Patterns of Antisemitism: A Survey," *Jewish Social Studies* 38, no. 1 (Winter 1976): 16. In numerous works, Baron uses Comte de Clermont-Tonnerre's words as the example of the deep negative consequences of assimilation related to the process of Emancipation organized by the nation-state. See, for instance, "Civil Versus Political Emancipation," in *Studies in Jewish Religious and Intellectual History, Presented to Alexander Altman on the Occasion of His Seventieth Birthday*, ed. Siegfried Stein and Raphael Loewe (University, AL: University of Alabama Press, 1979), 34.

13. Salo Baron, *The Jewish Community, Its History and Structure to the American Revolution*, 3 vols. (Philadelphia: Jewish Publication Society of America, 1945), 2:360. At first, Baron wanted to call this book *The Ghetto Community: A History of the Jewish Community from the Babylonian Exile to the Emancipation*. See Robert Liberles, *Salo W. Baron, Architect of Jewish History* (New York: New York University Press, 1995).
14. Salo Baron, "The Jewish Question in the Nineteenth Century," *Journal of Modern History* 10, no. 1 (March 1938):: 59.
15. *Jewish Community, Its History and Structure*, 1:8.
16. *Jewish Community, Its History and Structure*, 1:13.
17. *Jewish Community, Its History and Structure*, 1:16.
18. Arthur Herzberg, *The French Enlightenment and the Jews* (New York: Columbia University Press, 1966).
19. David Engel, "Crisis and Lachrymosity: On Salo Baron, Neobaronianism, and the Study in Jewish History," *Jewish History* 20, nos. 3-4 (December 2006): 250. Engel also wrote that "Baron displayed little conviction that the Holocaust demanded a new approach to writing the history of the Jews," in *Historians of the Jews and the Holocaust* (Stanford, CA: Stanford University Press, 2010), 50.
20. Salo Baron, "Newer Emphasis in Jewish History," *Jewish Social Studies* 25, no. 4 (October 1963): 240.
21. Yitzak Baer, *Galut* (New York: Schocken, 1947).
22. Baer, *Galut*, 122.
23. Isaac Barzilay, "Yishaq Baer and Salo W. Baron: Two Contemporary Interpreters of Jewish History," *Proceedings of the American Academy for Jewish Research* 60: 20, 38, 45. On the relationship between Baron and Baer, see Eleazar Gutwirth, "Mourning, Melancholy and Hexis: Towards a Context for Fritz Yshaq Baer," *European Journal of Jewish Studies* 9, no. 2 (2015): 9.
24. Pierre Birnbaum, *Geography of Hope. Exile, the Enlightenment, Disassimilation* (Stanford, CA: Stanford University Press, 2004).
25. Deborah Dash Moore, *At Home in America* (New York: Columbia University Press, 1983).
26. Debra Dash Moore, "Review of *Salo Wittmayer Baron: Architect of Jewish History*, by Robert Liberles," *AJS Review* 22, no. 1 (1997): 149.
27. Salo W. Baron, "Can American Jewry Be Culturally Creative?" in *Steeled by Adversity: Essays and Addresses on American Jewish Life*, ed. Jeannette Meisel Baron (Philadelphia: Jewish Publication Society, 1971), 549-51. See also Beth Wenger, "Salo Baron and the Vitality of American Jewish Life," in *The Enduring Legacy of Salo Baron*, ed. Hava Tirosh-Samuelson and Edward Dąbrowa (Kraków: Jagiellonian University Press, 2017), 263-65.
28. Baron, *Jewish Community, Its History and Structure*, 2:365.
29. Baron, *Jewish Community, Its History and Structure*, 1:6.
30. Baron, "American Jewish History," 32.
31. Yosef H. Yerushalmi, "Between Amsterdam and New Amsterdam: The Place of Curaçao and the Caribbean in Early Modern Jewish History," *American Jewish History* 2 (December 1982): 192.
32. Yosef H. Yerushalmi, "Response to Rosemary Ruether," in *Auschwitz: Beginning of a New Era? Reflections on the Holocaust*, ed. Eva Fleischer (Brooklyn, NY: Ktav., 1977), 107.

33. Yosef H. Yerushalmi, *A Jewish Historian in the "Age of Aquarius* (Brookline, MA: Hebrew College, June 1970), 9.
34. Yosef H. Yerushalmi, *From Spanish Court to Italian Ghetto: Isaac Cardoso: A Study in Seventeenth-Century Marranism and Jewish Apologetics* (New York: Columbia University Press, 1971), x–xi.
35. Yerushalmi, *From Spanish Court to Italian Ghetto*, 164.
36. Yerushalmi, *From Spanish Court to Italian Ghetto*, 206.
37. Yerushalmi, *From Spanish Court to Italian Ghetto*, 214–15.
38. Yerushalmi, *From Spanish Court to Italian Ghetto*, 477.
39. Yerushalmi, *From Spanish Court to Italian Ghetto*, 469.
40. Yerushalmi, "Response to Rosemary Ruether," 99–100.
41. Yerushalmi, "Response to Rosemary Ruether," 102.
42. Yerushalmi, "Response to Rosemary Ruether," 103.
43. Yerushalmi, "Response to Rosemary Ruether," 104.
44. Years ago, Yerushalmi started to translate what, in his eyes, was seminal work; but dissatisfied with it, he never published it.
45. Yosef H. Yerushalmi, *Lisbon Massacre of 1506 and the Royal Image in the Shebet Yehudah* (Cincinnati: Hebrew Union College, 1976), 30.
46. Yerushalmi, *Lisbon Massacre of 1506*, 66.
47. Yosef H. Yerushalmi, "Clio and Minerva: Reflections on Jewish Historiography in the Sixteenth Century," *Proceedings of the American Academy for Jewish Research* 46–47 (1979–80): 627, 630, https://www.jstor.org/stable/3622374.
48. Yerushalmi, *Lisbon Massacre of 1506*, xii.
49. Yerushalmi, *Lisbon Massacre of 1506*, xi. See Birnbaum, *Geography of Hope*, chap. 8.
50. Yosef H. Yerushalmi, *Assimilation and Racial Antisemitism: The Iberian and the German Models* (New York: Leo Baeck Institute, 1982), 26.
51. Yosef H. Yerushalmi, "Servants of the Kings and Not Servants of Servants: Some Political Aspects of the Political History of the Jews," in *The Faith of Fallen Jews: Yosef Yerushalmi and the Writing of Jewish History*, ed. David Myers and Alexander Kaye (Waltham, MA: Brandeis University Press, 2014), 260.
52. Yerushalmi, "Servants of the Kings," 257, 260. See Maurice Kriegel, " *L'alliance royale, le mythe et le mythe du mythe*," Critique (January–February 2000): 28. Pierre Birnbaum, *Prier pour l'Etat. Les Juifs, l'Alliance royale et la démocratie* (Paris: Calmann-Lévy, 2005).
53. Yerushalmi, "Servants of the Kings," 264, 266.
54. Yerushalmi, "Servants of the Kings," 268–69.
55. See Lois Dubin's brilliant article, "Yosef Yerushalmi, the Royal Alliance and Jewish Political Theory," *Jewish History* 28, no. 1 (2014): 74–75.
56. See Yosef H. Yerushalmi, "Toward a History of Jewish Hope," in *The Faith of Fallen Jews*, 303, 315.
57. Yerushalmi, "Toward a History of Jewish Hope," 306.
58. Yerushalmi, "Toward a History of Jewish Hope," 315.
59. Yosef H. Yerushalmi, "Preface," in Yitzhak Baer, *Galout, L'imaginaire de l'exil dans le judaïsme* (Paris: Calmann-Lévy, 2000), 46–47.
60. Yerushalmi, "Servants of the King," 268.
61. Yosef H. Yerushalmi, *Israel, the Unexpected State: Messianism, Sectarianism, and the Zionist Revolution* (Tübingen, Germany: Mohr Siebeck, 2006), 72.

62. Yerushalmi, "Servants of the King," 268.
63. Yerushalmi, *A Jewish Historian in the "Age of Aquarius,"* 10.
64. Yerushalmi once told a student working on a Jewish-American thinker's ideas, "Why do you work on the history of American Judaism? Is it so crucial if you compare it with Europe or Asia or even Africa?" Baron was listening to the conversation; he got angry and told Yerushalmi, "You are talking of the greatest Jewish community in the world!" Yosef Hayim Yerushalmi, *Transmettre l'histoire juive. Entretiens avec Sylvie-Anne Goldberg* (Paris: Albin Michel, 2012), 40.
65. Yosef H. Yerushalmi, "Entretien à Jérusalem," with Dominique Bourel, postface to *Zakhor, Histoire juive et mémoire juive* (Paris: La Découverte, 1984), 154–55.
66. Lois Dubin thinks the contrary. For her, "Yerushalmi's response to the Shoah with a history of hope rather than despair reinforced his commitment to Baron's antilachrymose views." "Yosef Yerushalmi, the Royal Alliance and Jewish Political theory," 78.
67. Joseph Ha-Cohen, *The Vale of Tears* (Hague, Netherlands: Nijhoff, 1971).
68. Matthew Fridman, "American Pogrom," *Politics/Letters Live* (November 5, 2018), http://politicsslashletters.org/commentary/american-pogrom/. See also "Forward" (October 4, 2020). On Donald Trump and the rise of anti-Semitism, see Brett Ashley Kaplan, "'Grotesquery to the Surface': The Leo Frank Case and Philip Roth's *The Plot Against America* Revisited in Trump's Alt-Right America," *Studies in American Jewish Literature* 39, no. 1 (2020).
69. In April 2005, during an Israel and Jewish studies seminar at Columbia led by Yosef Yerushalmi, we were listening to David Weiss-Halivni's lecture, "Sixty Years After the Liberation: Are we Going back?" Professor Halivni was retiring from Columbia and going to settle in Israel, to leave the *galut*. Though he no longer feared being inspected by Dr. Mengele, he insisted, in his moving lecture, that anti-Semitism is still growing, Jews are again becoming a pariah people. To conclude his talk, he said, "I am more on the pessimistic side. . . . It is my duty to warn and your duty to listen and evaluate." To close the collective discussion that followed, Yerushalmi underlined that "there are many different anti-Semitisms. . . . The entire world does not hate the Jews. . . . There is no inevitability to antisemitism." Would he hold the same position today? How would he cope with Pittsburgh, a breaking point in American Jewish history?

Chapter Nine

SALO BARON AND HIS INNOVATIVE RECONSTRUCTION OF THE JEWISH PAST

ROBERT CHAZAN

Salo Baron altered perceptions and presentations of the history of the Jews for fellow scholars and lay readers around the globe. This achievement was grounded in Baron's unusual intellectual abilities, which facilitated his control of many languages and literatures and of rich bodies of primary data and secondary literature. Anyone familiar with Baron's footnotes cannot but be impressed with his mastery of so much data. Baron kept up assiduously with the ever-expanding body of research on the various periods of the Jewish past. Those of us fortunate enough to have studied with him were used to seeing him regularly at the card catalogues of the Columbia University library in the morning and in the stacks during the afternoon, and emerging toward the end of the day with arms full of books. Baron's ability to master the increasingly rich literature on the Jewish past and to engage in formulating his own conclusions on that past was remarkable.

To be sure, more was involved in Baron's achievements than simply his unusual intellectual ability. Also notable were his energy and personal experience of a wide range of cultural and intellectual environments. Baron lived a long, healthy, and robust life and exhibited, almost until the end, a high level of energy. This energy was yet another factor in his enormous body of scholarly creativity. Additionally, Baron was exposed to a number of stimulating environments. He was initially shaped by his birth area of northeastern Europe, did his graduate work (a rabbinical degree and three doctorates, which is most unusual and in fact amazing) in Austria, and ended up living most of his life in the New World. His immersion in all three environments was intense and served to broaden his intellectual and emotional horizons. I recall attending a memorial service after his death and hearing one of Baron's grandsons speak warmly of sharing with his grandfather his fascination with American baseball. Not surprisingly, the grandson indicated that his grandfather possessed remarkable command of baseball history and statistics.[1]

Less tangible than Baron's intellectual powers and his familiarity with multiple environments was his willingness to embrace new positions. We are all familiar, of course, with scholars who delight in exhibiting their personal prowess by criticizing the conventional and the accepted. Baron was utterly uninterested in this kind of self-aggrandizement, as I shall indicate shortly. He was, however, fully willing to engage accepted positions and challenge them. It was not out of a desire for self-aggrandizement or a basic cantankerousness that Baron was prepared to engage accepted perspectives and challenge them. This willingness reflects, rather, a commitment to truth and the conviction that acceptance of erroneous positions is costly to human knowledge and progress.

Baron's recoiling from self-aggrandizement was evident in his teaching and remains obvious in his voluminous writings. Let me begin with his teaching. Baron's classes hewed very closely to topic and involved the presentation of his conclusions on whatever the topic might have been. There was no one-upmanship in citing the work of others and destroying it, in the process establishing the superiority of the presenter. Baron eschewed such antics. The same is true in his writing as well. Baron's written work by and large involves straightforward presentation of the conclusions his studies had reached. His personal voice is muted, and this was obviously intended. Though in fact much of his work was groundbreaking (as we shall shortly see), he did not highlight these innovations; he simply presented then as the conclusions to which his research had led him.

I have portrayed Baron's self-effacement as a virtue, and it surely was. Virtues, however, often have negative consequences along with the positive. Baron's presentation style in both the classroom and his writing had two negative consequences. The first was a lack of drama. Highlighting the struggle with prior views introduces an element of drama into both teaching and writing. As a result of his self-effacement, Baron sacrificed this appealing and useful element of drama. There was a monotony to the Baron classroom; to the extent that students might have been aware of the prior stances that Baron's conclusions negated, they might have been able to introduce the drama themselves, but few students were in such a position. The same is true for readers of the Baron oeuvre. It does not elicit excitement; it is, of course, recognized as authoritative, but it does not draw the reader in. I have long suspected that few readers of the second edition of *A Social and Religious History of the Jews* open the first page of a given volume and read consecutively through it; rather, the tendency is to identify the pages in which a given issue is treated, read those pages and their attendant notes, elicit the desired information, and close the volume.[2]

There was a second and weightier negative consequence to Baron's presentational style, and that involves training in historical methodology. Students in the Baron classroom were there to imbibe wisdom about aspects of the Jewish past; they were also there to learn about historical methodology. The same is true for his readers. Baron's laudatory self-effacement meant that students and readers were not exposed to his historical methodology, which is what moved him to his most influential innovations in the writing of Jewish history. But his modesty precluded sharing that methodology with his students and readers, to the detriment of both.

In order to understand the innovations in Baron's historical methodology, it is necessary to go back to the earliest stages of his career. Early on, Baron published a fairly brief and uncharacteristic essay in a semi-popular journal—an essay that was both exciting in terms of drama and illuminating in terms of methodology. This brief and uncharacteristic essay has remained very popular and is widely read and regularly cited. It is exciting to read, overtly offers major reflections on historical methodology, and lays the groundwork for a number of the innovative aspects of Baron's later work. "Ghetto and Emancipation: Shall We Revise the Traditional View?" appeared in the 1928 volume of *The Menorah Journal*, a serious publication but not formally a scholarly journal.[3]

At this time, Baron was a fairly young thirty-three years old and had been in the United States for only two years. It was a rather brash statement by the young scholar, not at all in tune with the more self-effacing stance of the older Salo Baron. What occasioned this introduction of self constitutes yet another central theme in the Baron persona. From his early years, Baron had been deeply involved in the issues of contemporary Jewish life. As he matured into a distinguished scholar, he continued his involvement in the issues of Jewish life, using his knowledge of the Jewish past to illuminate the present. His 1928 essay did not appear in a scholarly journal because it was not directly addressed to fellow scholars. The intended audience for this essay was the leadership of the contemporary Jewish community. In Baron's 1928 view, early twentieth-century Jewish leaders—rabbis and professional and lay Jewish leaders—were being led astray by the reigning scholarship on premodern Jewish history and the shift to modernity. Baron argues that this reigning scholarship portrays premodern Jewish history as an unending sequence of persecution and suffering and the onset of modernity as the longed-for improvement in Jewish circumstances. Indeed, there was a scholarly and popular sense that the French Revolution ushered in a new, different, and excitingly positive phase in the lengthy and previously dolorous history of the Jewish people.

Baron's 1928 essay set out to challenge this simplistic contrast between the persecution and suffering of prerevolutionary Jewish life and the exhilarating new circumstances that dawned during the late eighteenth century. The essay itself was brief—a mere dozen pages—and almost free of notes. In fact, it addressed only prerevolutionary Jewish history in any detail, not making a serious case for balancing perceptions of postrevolutionary Jewish life, an issue that Baron would subsequently address at great length. The essay ended with a memorable sentence: "Surely it is time to break with the lachrymose theory of pre-Revolutionary woe, and to adopt a view more in accord with historical truth."[4] The notion of an erroneous emphasis on the lachrymose in prerevolutionary Jewish history was emphasized throughout Baron's subsequent scholarship and has been strongly associated with him. At the same time, it is noteworthy that this memorable closing sentence focuses on the prerevolutionary only, without suggesting that the essay had addressed the error of undue enthusiasm for the changes in Jewish life introduced by the French Revolution.

Given that this 1928 essay is a polemical piece, Baron had to construct an argument, and he did so brilliantly, in the process revealing some of the core elements in his historical methodology. The first step in making his case for an alternative and more positive perspective on prerevolutionary

Jewish life was to narrow the vast expanse of Jewish history prior to the revolution. The Baron ploy constituted excellent polemical strategy—and in fact more. Rather than treat the long and confusing trajectory of the Jewish past, he elected to focus on a relatively brief period, the seemingly bleak sixteenth through eighteenth centuries in Europe. If these few centuries—generally viewed as the nadir of premodern Jewish experience—could be shown to have been less horrendous than generally portrayed, then the case for reconceptualizing overall prerevolutionary Jewish life would have been effectively made.

Baron moved carefully to make his case for reconceptualizing Jewish life in Europe during the sixteenth through eighteenth centuries. His first step was to examine and criticize the regnant scholarly perception of a number of broad theoretical and legal aspects of Jewish life during this allegedly dark period. The very first negative view cited by Baron is that during this period, Jews did not enjoy equality. This negative perspective clearly reflects the modern Enlightenment value of human equality. Baron's rejection of this critique of premodern Jewish life was quick and decisive, while at the same time introducing a major methodological consideration. Baron's response was relatively straightforward: premodern European life did not involve equality as an ideal. Societies were not organized on the basis of individual citizens; rather, they were corporate—that is, organized around clusters of people. Individual equality was a reality for no one, and thus lack of equality for Jews in effect meant nothing.

For Baron, the broad question to be asked about Jewish circumstances during the sixteenth through eighteenth centuries was the relative standing of the Jewish cluster. What was its position in society? Baron's answer to this reformulated question was complex. On the one hand, the Jewish cluster was clearly inferior to a number of other clusters, for example, the nobility and the clergy; at the same time, Jews enjoyed far higher status than the rural peasantry. The cluster closest to the Jews in status and rights was the urban burgher group, and the status and rights of these two groups—Jews and urban Christians—was in large measure parallel. The standing of the Jewish cluster on the European scene during the sixteenth through eighteenth centuries thus tells us little about Jewish circumstances.

In this approach to the issue of societal status and rights, Baron was introducing a broad methodological principle that was core to his scholarly research. Key to his rejection of the notion of the lack of equality for prerevolutionary Jews was his awareness of the underlying structures of societal life during this period. The ideal of individual equality was nonexistent in Europe in those centuries. This awareness made the assessment of prerevolutionary Jewish life as deficient for its lack of equality appear to be misguided. Throughout his subsequent oeuvre, Baron was insistent on and demonstrated regularly a full grasp of broad societal structures and issues, and he evaluated Jewish circumstances in term of his knowledge of the larger societal setting in which a particular segment of the Jewish past took place.

Rejection of the notion of prerevolutionary Jews as disadvantaged by virtue of inequality was succeeded by consideration of a number of well-known features of medieval European Jewish life. These features began with Jewish serfdom, which was widely documented and suggested to many modern observers the lowest possible Jewish status on the prerevolutionary scene. Baron acknowledged the reality of the legal definition of many prerevolutionary European Jews as serfs of one or another ruler—barons, monarchs, and emperors. He insisted, however, that the status of Jews as serfs of a given ruler was by no means the same as the status of European non-Jews legally defined as serfs. Jews metaphorically defined as serfs did not suffer the grievous disabilities of European non-Jewish serfs. Indeed, Jewish serfdom actually included, according to Baron, both negatives and positives. Among the positives were the protections carefully provided by the baronial, royal, and imperial masters of Jewish serfs and the internal autonomy for Jewish life that they provided. This autonomy included Jewish legal, educational, and social welfare systems; for Baron, this autonomy was a significant and positive element in prerevolutionary Jewish circumstances.

Yet another reality of prerevolutionary European Jewish life was legal ghettoization of the Jews—the insistence that Jews live their lives within a specified sector of prerevolutionary European towns. Again, to modern sensibilities, ghettoization was a jarring reflection of painful Jewish circumstances. Once again, Baron begins with his broad knowledge of medieval realities. He points out that medieval towns included a wide range of neighborhoods populated by one or another group—economic groups such as builders or bakers, or ethnic groups like immigrants. Indeed, many of the medieval neighborhood names—including names identifying the neighborhood or street as populated by Jews—have survived down to the present. Also, Baron once more presents this separatism as an advantage to premodern Jewish life, enabling Jews to maintain their identity effectively.

Finally, Baron notes the imagery of prerevolutionary Jewish life as constantly threatened by the dangers of prosecution and persecution by the powerful institution of the Inquisition. As the notion of religious coercion became increasingly distasteful to Enlightenment thinkers, the Inquisition became the arch-symbol of unacceptable coercion in the name of faith. Thus, Jewish suffering at the hands of the Inquisition was regularly highlighted in citations of the panoply of persecutions of prerevolutionary Jews. Baron does not, of course, defend inquisitorial cruelty. What he does, however, is to indicate with precision the nature of the institution. In fact, insists Baron, the Inquisition—despite its fearfulness—was a well-defined ecclesiastical court charged with identifying and punishing Christians who were guilty of heretical thinking. Thus, in point of fact, the Inquisition was unconcerned directly with Jews. To be sure, many of those haled before the Inquisition during its heyday were former Jews who had converted and were now Christians suspected of backsliding to their former Jewish faith. Although this was in many ways lamentable for these Christian victims of inquisitorial cruelty, the Inquisition was not directly involved in persecution of Jews.

Baron's responses to these popular allegations of prerevolutionary Jewish suffering involved essentially dismissal of the allegations in one of a number of ways. After countering these widespread perceptions, Baron took a more positive, audacious, and innovative position on the circumstances of prerevolutionary European Jews, moving from the theoretical and legal status of these Jews to the practical detail of their lives. To cite Baron's own formulation, "Legally and in theory, we have seen, the status of the Jews was by means an inferior one. But did actual events—persecutions, riots, pogroms, monetary extortions—reduce their theoretical legal privileges to fictions in practice? Even here the traditional answers of historians do not square with the facts."[5]

How might Baron have addressed the realities of prerevolutionary Jewish life? The notion is daunting. Might it have been possible to create some kind of comparative scale of anti-Jewish violence or monetary extortion? How might such a scale comparing anti-Jewish with internal anti-Christian violence and monetary extortion have been constructed? The difficulties seem insurmountable. The Baron response was striking. Baron sought quantitative data that were difficult, but not impossible, to assemble. He focused on the growth of the European Jewish population during this purportedly bleak period. What can be said of the change in Jewish population during these dark centuries? During this period, there is no evidence of significant immigration of Jews. Thus, change in Jewish population can reflect only internal growth or decline.

Baron claimed that from the sixteenth through the eighteenth centuries, the Jewish population of Christian Europe grew markedly. Such marked population growth indicates that despite the realities of physical violence and economic despoliation, there was enough stability in Jews' circumstances to allow for families to bring children into the world, raise them to adulthood and childbearing age, and see the emergence of another generation and a larger number of progeny. Indeed, Baron goes further. He claims that from the sixteenth through the nineteenth century, the Jewish population increased at four times the rate of the general population. He does not identify all the elements in this striking disparity. He does claim, however, that the widely documented anti-Jewish violence and economic despoliation cannot have been, in the aggregate, as horrendous as generally portrayed if Jewish population was expanding at such a rapid rate. Methodologically, the movement from absorption in the qualitative intensity of the depiction of violence and despoliation to the dispassionate immersion in quantitative data constitutes a striking innovation that was to typify many of Baron's most important findings.

Baron also addresses the issue of the well-known limitations on Jewish economic activities. Jews were highly restricted in their economic pursuits during the sixteenth through eighteenth centuries. Baron does not challenge the realities. Rather, he reinterprets these realities. In his own formulation, "The very restrictive legislation [endured by Jews] proved in the long run beneficial to Jewish economic development. It forced them into the money trade, and throughout the Middle Ages trained them in individual enterprise without guild backing, compelled them to set up international contacts, . . . and equipped them with vast sums of ready cash. With the dawn of early capitalism, and the need for ready money for the new manufactures and international trading ventures, the Jew fitted readily into the new economic structure."[6] Here Baron does not actually refute the portrayal of prerevolutionary Jewish circumstances as in fact very difficult; rather, he suggests that these difficult circumstances eventually bore positive results.

As noted, in this brief but important essay, Baron challenged the reigning bleak view of Jewish circumstances during the sixteenth through eighteenth centuries. He did not challenge what he felt was an overly positive view of postrevolutionary Jewish circumstances, although he would subsequently do this as well. Viewed in retrospect, Baron's challenge to the starkly negative perspectives on prerevolutionary Jewish circumstances was overall limited. He dismissed as meaningless the sense that Jews did not enjoy equal rights in the face of the reality that equal individual rights were not a feature of the prerevolutionary period. Rather, societies were organized in clusters. Though this certainly makes sense and would be emphasized effectively in Baron's subsequent research and writing, he did not convincingly show that the Jewish cluster was not significantly disadvantaged. His investigation of the realities of Jewish serfdom, ghettoization of the Jews, and the impact of the Inquisition mitigated somewhat the sense that these realities were deeply harmful; Baron's investigation did not, however, fully dismiss the sense of baneful circumstances.

Baron's movement from broad imagery and specific motifs to the realities of Jewish life was extremely significant. It signaled a focus on Jewish circumstances as lived by Jews. Once again, the results—viewed retrospectively—were limited. Impressive Jewish population growth is an important overall reality, but it does not cancel out the lived effect of recurrent persecution and despoliation. The fact that eventually the limitations placed on Jewish economic activity produced positive results for later Jews does not efface the negative experiences of the Jews who were economically limited.

The sense I have expressed as to the limited successes of Baron's reconsiderations of prerevolutionary Jewish life does not detract—to my mind—from the significance of the 1928 essay. In a number of ways, "Ghetto and Emancipation" cleared the path to Baron's later innovative perspectives on the Jewish past. This path-clearing included, first, willingness to break with well-established paradigms. Readiness to challenge widely accepted views constitutes a difficult but necessary step in scholarly creativity. Baron's essay helped him to take this vital step. Second, the essay shows awareness of the need to break down the lengthy span of Jewish history into meaningful and coherent segments. I have previously depicted Baron's focus on the sixteenth through eighteenth centuries as an effective polemical ploy. It was, in fact, much more. Early in the essay Baron noted disparate elements in what is generally described as medieval Jewish history. He indicates a period of the Middle Ages during which "Jews lived under Islamic rule under relatively good circumstances"; he further claims that during these early centuries of the Middle Ages, "even Western Jewry was far superior to its Christian neighbors in culture and means." Segmentation of Jewish history into coherent periods emerges as critical to meaningful analysis of Jewish circumstances, and this emphasis appears prominently in the essay.

A third important emphasis that emerges in the essay is the need to master broad historical patterns in order to grasp Jewish experience properly. Jews have, after all, historically constituted a rather small human community; although they arguably contributed disproportionately to many cultural and spiritual features of the West, they did not shape in any important ways the broad Western settings in which they found themselves. Without understanding of the broad context in which differing segments of the Jewish people found themselves, proper comprehension of the experience of these Jews is impossible. A final emphasis that emerges from "Ghetto and Emancipation" is the effort to probe beyond convenient theoretical and legal categories into the lived experience of the Jews under study.

Much changed in Baron's life not long after publication of the essay. At that time, Columbia University accepted a gift for the creation of the Miller Chair in Jewish History, Literature and Institutions, a chair that ultimately had a major influence on the development of Jewish studies in American academia. This chair constituted a major innovation and created difficult circumstances for those entrusted with responsibility for filling this entirely new position. Eventually, Salo Baron was invited to become the first Miller Professor.[7] As such, he had to adapt to new circumstances for a Jewish history scholar. Talented and productive historians of the Jews much predated the Miller chair, but those historians of the Jewish past were generally lodged in Jewish institutions, most commonly rabbinical seminaries. These settings provided almost none of the knowledge of the general backdrop of Jewish life—which Baron showed in his 1928 essay was necessary for proper knowledge of the Jews—and often required sensitivity to major Jewish theological principles, including the conviction that Jewish history was shaped by divine response to Jewish fulfillment or nonfulfillment of the divine-human covenant. The Columbia University setting posed new and different challenges.

Baron's 1928 essay proves that in many ways, he was well suited to meet these challenges. The essay indicates clearly that Baron had broken with the theological perspectives that portrayed Jewish history as shaped by the interactions of God and Israel. He obviously saw no reason to articulate this departure from traditional Jewish historical thinking, but his acceptance of the modern humanistic approach toward history was a prerequisite to filling the Columbia position. Moreover, as we have seen, Baron insisted, even before his appointment to the university's history faculty, that reconstructing Jewish history required full grasp of the general setting in which Jews found themselves. Thus, the essay suggests that Baron would have welcomed a position such as the Miller Chair as salutary for his historical research and writing.

Baron began his tenure in the Miller chair in 1931, an occasion that is being celebrated appropriately in this collection. Not long thereafter, he presented ten Schermerhorn lectures under the title "Jewish Society and Religion in Their Historical Interrelation." The title is significant from a number of perspectives. It indicates that these lectures would be of interest to a broad audience, one whose interests went beyond straightforward Jewish history. Moreover, the title tackles the difficult and divisive issue of the nature of Jewishness. With the onset of the modern reorganization of Western governance and the abandonment of the corporate premodern governance that we have noted, Jews could no longer present themselves as a separate cluster in society that involved both national/ethnic and religious identity. In order to secure citizenship in the new European states, Jews had to renounce separate Jewish national and ethnic identity and identify Jewishness as religious identity only. Baron's Schermerhorn lectures skirted this contentious issue by addressing the relationship of Jewish societies— a rather amorphous term—and spirituality.

The Schermerhorn lectures led fairly quickly to Baron's initial masterpiece, the first edition of *A Social and Religious History of the Jews*.[8] The relationship of the lectures to the book is patent, but so are the differences. Whereas the lectures involved analysis of the relationship between society and religion, which would be interesting to Jews on the one hand

and students of such relationships on the other, the book directs itself unabashedly to the history of the Jews. There is nothing untoward in this more specific focus on Jewish history—the history of the Jews is one of the topics of the Miller chair, after all. Indeed, most of the members of the history faculty of Columbia University were focused on the past of one or another human community. Writing histories of these diverse human communities was a central responsibility of the members of the Columbia history faculty.

The first edition of *A Social and Religious History of the Jews* is an unfortunately neglected segment of the Baron oeuvre. Once Baron decided to embark on what he perceived to be an expanded second edition, he in effect doomed the first edition to irrelevance. Whenever there is a second edition of any work, there would seem to be no point in consulting the first edition any further. In fact, however, this is not at all the case with *A Social and Religious History of the Jews*. Had the second edition been given a different title (perhaps something like *Major Aspects of the Jewish Past*), readers would have continued to immerse themselves in the three volumes of Baron's 1937 achievement, to their enormous benefit.

The two versions of the book are, in fact, quite different from one another. The earlier work covered, in two volumes of text and one volume of notes, the total trajectory of the Jewish past, laying bare a creative reconceptualization of that lengthy history. The later work addressed in infinitely greater detail much—but not all—of Jewish history in eighteen volumes. The rich detail in what Baron dubbed the second edition obscured the forest in favor of the very many trees. Had he not made this unfortunate titling choice, I am convinced that both achievements would be regularly consulted for different purposes. I have already suggested that few readers of the second work will open a particular volume and read sequentially from beginning to end. This would not have been the case with the first work. My experience is that it can usefully be read from beginning to end and that the reader can emerge with a valuable new sense of the broad organization of the Jewish past.

Let us note briefly some of the important innovations of the 1937 edition. Throughout the ages, Jews had adopted the tripartite scheme popular among many peoples—a period of distinction, a period of decline, and a period of return to achievement and glory. For Jews, the initial period in their history involved a series of high points: the fashioning of a covenant with the one and only God in the universe, conquest of the land promised by that God as the special inheritance of Israel, and distinguished rulers such as King David. The crucial turning point in traditional Jewish historical thinking came in the year 70, when the Romans purportedly exiled the Jews from their promised land after suppressing the Jewish rebellion that had begun four years earlier. It is traditionally claimed that after 70, Jews became a diaspora people, subject to all the pain and suffering that Moses associated with diaspora existence. The end to this period of decline has been projected in a number of ways. For the very traditional, it will take place in the miraculous style of the redemption that brought the Jews out of Egyptian servitude. For many modern Western Jews, the anticipated change took place with the transformation of Europe and the granting of equality to the Jews of the West. And for the nationalistically inclined Jews of eastern Europe, deliverance took place with the growing Jewish population of Palestine and the emergence of the state of Israel in 1948.

Baron rejected totally this traditional tripartite division of Jewish history. Emblematic of this rejection was his utter dismissal of the importance of the year 70 CE. This date, which loomed so large in the traditional scheme, was accorded a scant four pages in the 1937 version of *A Social and Religious History of the Jews*. Baron also effaced the distinction between Jewish experience within and outside the Land of Israel. For him, this distinction was grounded in theology rather than history. Patterns of Jewish suffering and well-being are readily observable in all sites of Jewish habitation, and no clear distinction can be drawn between the Land of Israel and elsewhere in terms of these patterns.

Baron's periodization of Jewish history was new and complex, light-years beyond the traditional and simplistic three-stage distinction. In his preface, Baron indicated that his twelve chapters fell into four broad periods: "After an introductory chapter, Chapters II-IV deal with the history of ancient Israel down to the Restoration; Chapters V-VII treat the period between Alexander and Mohammed; Chapters VIII-X discuss the medieval period from the rise of Islam to the seventeenth century; while Chapters XI, XII, and the Epilogue are devoted to modern Jewish history."[9] This is a striking departure from prior Jewish—and Christian—thinking. Baron's insistence, announced in the 1928 essay, on the importance of setting Jewish history within its broader context is patent. Key to this periodization of Jewish history are Alexander, Mohammed, the rise of Islam, and the seventeenth century. Major alterations in Jewish circumstances are no longer associated with the covenant between God and Israel or even simply with prominent events among the Jews themselves. In effect, evolving circumstances among Jews themselves are projected as the results of broad changes on the world scene. The requirement that Jewish history be seen this way was expressed clearly in the 1928 essay, as we have seen.

This innovative segmentation of the Jewish past represents a broader assault than, in 1928, on the regnant emphasis on the lachrymose in Jewish history. Simple removal of the year 70 from periodization of Jewish history constituted a decisive blow against the lachrymose. More positively, none of the factors projected as defining periods in Jewish history has any tinge of the lachrymose about it. There is nothing lachrymose about the Restoration, Alexander, Mohammed, the rise of Islam, or the seventeenth century.

Baron's departure from his normal reticence in 1928 resulted in an unusual and helpful glimpse into the thinking process and methodological convictions that undergirded his later magisterial works. These methodological convictions made him especially appropriate for the pathbreaking Columbia position and found clear expression in his first great but underappreciated masterpiece, the 1937 version of *A Social and Religious History of the Jews*. Baron's tenure in the Miller chair—like his research and writing—had enormous impact. Just as his research and writing changed perspectives on the long and complex trajectory of Jewish history, so, too, did his service in the Columbia history department alter perspectives on the field of Jewish studies. The simple reality of full acceptance onto the faculty of one of America's premier history departments heightened the sense of Jewish history and Jewish studies more generally as serious academic fields. As the remarkable Baron corpus evolved, convictions as to the seriousness of the fields of Jewish history and Jewish studies intensified. When new positions in Jewish studies began to proliferate in the 1960s, many of the new positions were filled by Baron students. Also, importantly, university departments that might have been skittish about absorbing the seemingly new field of Jewish studies were reassured by the Baron presence at Columbia and by his prodigious scholarship, which was widely known and respected.[10]

NOTES

1. Robert Liberles has published a valuable biography of Baron, *Salo Baron: Architect of Jewish History* (New York: New York University Press, 1995).
2. Salo Wittmayer Baron, *A Social and Religious History of the Jews*, 2nd ed., 18 vols. (New York: Columbia University Press, 1952–83).
3. Salo Baron, "Ghetto and Emancipation: Shall We Revise the Traditional View?" *Menorah Journal* 14 (1928): 515–26.
4. "Ghetto and Emancipation," 526.
5. "Ghetto and Emancipation," 521.
6. "Ghetto and Emancipation," 522.
7. On this innovative search and appointment, see Paul Ritterband and Harold S. Wechsler, *Jewish Learning in American Universities: The First Century* (Bloomington: Indiana University Press, 1994), chap. 7.
8. Salo Wittmayer Baron, *A Social and Religious History of the Jews*, 3 vols. (New York: Columbia University Press, 1937).
9. *Social and Religious History of the Jews*, 1:vi.
10. At a few points in this essay, I have introduced recollections drawn from my experiences of Salo Baron, the Columbia professor. Let me close with a recollection of the influence of Salo Baron across American academia. On completion of my doctorate at Columbia in 1967, I was invited to apply for a new junior position in Jewish history in the Department of History at Ohio State University. In my initial interview, I found members of the department struggling—very politely—with the new field. Those convinced of its place in their department regularly cited Salo Baron, his longtime place in the Columbia Department of History, and his prodigious scholarship.

Chapter Ten

REMEMBERING PROFESSOR SALO BARON
Personal Recollections of a Former Student

JANE S. GERBER

Salo Baron was a familiar sight on Riverside Drive, regardless of the weather. I could tell the precise time of day by the resolute stride of his stout figure on Broadway or Riverside Drive, reminiscent of an Alpine hiker. Even when blustering winds would whip off the Hudson River and the streets were almost deserted, Baron would pass by on his daily constitutional en route to the Columbia University campus.

I was one of the last group of doctoral students to enter the Jewish history program he headed when I transferred to Columbia in the fall of 1962. He continued giving classes after his retirement in 1963, and I continued to audit them after my orals. I was also his sole female doctoral student at the time. I got to know him in several other contexts as well: I served as book review editor at the journal *Jewish Social Studies* from 1969 to 1989 while Professor Baron and his wife, Jeannette, actively headed the parent organization of the journal (the Conference on Jewish Relations) and his daughter Tobey Gitelle served as the journal's managing editor for part of that time. He also served on my orals and doctoral defense committee after his retirement.

Our encounters took place in both formal and informal settings. The required doctoral seminar met weekly in the evening in his home on Claremont Avenue. *Jewish Social Studies* staff would meet monthly in successive offices on Broadway and 113th Street, West 57th Street, and Broadway and West 73rd Street, or in the dining room of his apartment. Professor Baron usually chaired the editorial meetings and engaged actively in discussions and the planning of its public events and conferences. He was personally connected with members of the journal's larger board, one of whom was his cousin, another his personal accountant. Over the years I observed his involvement with undergraduate and graduate students, his family, and his colleagues in a variety of contexts. I even had the honor of spending a weekend at his home in Connecticut with my husband. Although we interacted in many contexts, it was always as teacher and student. Although he suggested after I completed my doctoral defense that I call him Salo, I never could manage that. Not too many of his former students called him by his first name.

Transferring from Harvard to Columbia in 1962, I planned to do my PhD on some aspect of the history of the Jews in the Muslim world. I had taken several courses in Jewish history at the Hebrew University of Jerusalem and earned an MA in Middle Eastern studies at Harvard—a program with a heavy emphasis on Arabic language, and more as a training ground for the State Department and Aramco upper echelons than as preparation for academic study. I had a formal but friendly relationship with Professor Isadore Twersky at Harvard, but I vacillated about entering his doctoral program because I lacked the requisite training in rabbinics and Judaic texts. My interview with Professor Baron allayed my fears about the gap in my Judaica background as preparation for the program. I wasn't yet aware of the fact that I would be one of the few in the program who was not a rabbi or a rabbinical student and that my selected field of study was not of major scholarly interest to Baron even though he was characteristically interested in Jewish life everywhere. I was also unaware of the fact that I was the only female student in the program. Only later did these issues become apparent.

Professor Baron was willing to meet, have me audit a class of his, and discuss my transfer to Columbia. In our meeting in his office, I recall that his questions about my educational background were straightforward. He was particularly interested in my foreign language preparation, history training, and undergraduate courses taken at Wellesley College and my graduate training up to that time. He did not seem particularly concerned about my Judaica training; perhaps it was obvious to him that a woman in the 1960s who had gone to Wellesley would probably lack training in classical Hebrew sources. He suggested almost offhandedly that I take a few courses at the Jewish Theological Seminary when I entered the Columbia Department of History and implied that this would be adequate. Only later did I realize that his broad approach to Jewish history, encompassing a wide variety of fields and requiring a multiplicity of languages (I was required to show proficiency in four languages), enabled him to train students from a variety of backgrounds and disciplinary approaches.

I recall his inquiring at the interview where my parents were born. My response that my father's birthplace was Yekatrinaslav in the Ukraine elicited an animated and somewhat detailed response from Baron on Jewish population movements and demographics in the Russian Pale of Settlement in the early twentieth century. His follow-up question on my parents' education at Hunter and City Colleges and their occupations stimulated him to muse about the quotas Jews faced in the professions in the United States as well as the role that access to New York's free public higher education played in the remarkable story of American Jewish mobility. His interest in data, economics, and broad trends in society often animated his discussions in our encounters. His demeanor at this initial meeting was welcoming, gracious, and supportive; these were personal traits that I would see repeatedly over more than twenty years of our association. Armed with his support, I began an unanticipated decades-long journey and a lifelong career teaching at the City University of New York Graduate Center.

The doctoral seminar, a requirement of first- and second-year Jewish history doctoral students at Columbia, was customarily held weekly in the evening at the dining room table in Professor Baron's apartment on Claremont Avenue. The table was, if I recall correctly, a large, bulky European one that seated eight people and occupied most of the dining room. The walls of the room were covered with impressive European diplomas, framed citations, awards, commendations, and honorary degrees. It was daunting wallpaper for a twenty-four-year-old to gaze at on a weekly basis: three doctoral degrees with elaborate seals from the University of Vienna in history (1917), political science (1922), and jurisprudence (1923); a diploma from the Rabbinical Seminary in Vienna (Israelitisch-Theologischen Lehranstalt); and citations from various Jewish institutions, such as the Jewish Institute of Religion-Hebrew Union College and the American Jewish Committee. An air of Old World scholarship, redolent with the names of great institutions of European learning, pervaded the apartment. Baron faced us, his back to these framed degrees, and we therefore would read them repeatedly as we looked at him attentively or as our attention wandered from the student presentations. Those presentations spanned the broadest geographic terrain and chronological eras; nineteenth-century Polish and Russian Jewish social history, nineteenth-century German anti-Semitism, the Chofetz Chaim, the career of Rabbi Leo Baeck, medieval Gerona, medieval Jewish polemics, the synagogues of Hellenistic Palestine, and facets of American Jewish communal history. My paper was on Moroccan Jewry in the sixteenth century.

While the graduate students were delivering their works in progress at his dining room table, Professor Baron would listen attentively, unexpectedly interjecting a reference now and then to an article in an obscure journal in any number of languages. In contrast to his vigor in the classroom, he often seemed somewhat tired in the evening, but this appearance was deceptive. He would occasionally interject and cite an additional reference, which might well be in Arabic, German, Yiddish, Hebrew, French, Polish, Czech or even Turkish. The students received these comments with a sense of excitement. The references spanned all continents and centuries and demonstrated his inclusion of several disciplines in his understanding of the craft of the historian.

The professor's comments were usually sparing but always pertinent and sometimes personal. When they turned personal, he would preface his remarks with "Excuse me for being personal but. . . ." Occasionally he would reminisce about a particular personality or event in sharp detail. I recall that his blend of the personal and professional often related to the historical roles played by European Jewish personalities and a nuance of the contexts in which they acted. Despite the awe with which we regarded him, I never detected any sense of intimidation on the part of the students. Rather, we all deeply respected him.

Salo Baron was not a hands-on mentor. For a student relatively new to Jewish history, this entailed being an autodidact. I was concentrating on the Jews of Muslim lands and found him removed from the subject. He was most helpful to those students (usually rabbinical students enrolled in the History program who had advanced knowledge of source material) who had already precisely delineated the areas that they wanted to explore and were presenting research they had already begun. He was especially kind toward students who were older and European, particularly if they were postwar refugees. After his retirement, his successors almost immediately eliminated some of these men from the doctoral program, and they usually completed their doctorates at other New York institutions. Baron's bond with refugee scholars was longstanding. Starting in the 1920s and into the '30s and '40s, he extended a helping hand to many European refugee scholars seeking gainful employment at Jewish institutions in America. Some of them were probably given small tasks, for which I suspect Baron obtained modest stipends from private philanthropists or funds from his chair at Columbia.

Many years after our first meeting, as I was describing my experiences teaching about the Sephardic crypto-Jewish experience in a refusenik seminar in Moscow and Leningrad in 1976, Baron listened to my account attentively, especially when I described the heavy KGB presence that was palpable in a car parked downstairs in the street. He suddenly began to describe in elaborate and minute detail his research trip to the Soviet Union in 1937, replete with observations about the weather aboard ship as it departed Odessa in the Black Sea, the time of day and activities on the wharf, the conditions of the Jews in Odessa, and the specific documents that the librarian in Leningrad reluctantly produced while hovering over Baron as he read them in the brief time he had been allotted. His detailed recollections from forty years prior to this conversation included the name of the ship, the exact time of its departure, the sources he examined in the Leningrad *genizah* archives, as well as wide-ranging comments on the Firkovich collection and the idiosyncrasies of the collector. Only later did Jeannette relate that the months-long trip to Europe and Palestine occurred when their infant daughter was only a few months old and had remained with Jeannette's mother in New York. Most of Professor Baron's personal anecdotes related to his research trips to archives or to his lectures in various Jewish communities. He spoke more than once about his speaking tour in South Africa and the particulars of its Jewish community.

Along one wall in his dining room were overflowing bookshelves, specially built, three layers deep and stuffed with foreign-language journals. He once mentioned how many of the volumes were acquired in Europe after the war while he served as chairperson, alongside executive secretary Hannah Arendt, of the organization known as the Jewish Cultural Reconstruction. He explained that the vast repository of Jewish libraries and ceremonial artifacts that was looted by the Nazis had been assembled in Germany at the close of the war by the American military governor of occupied Germany, General Lucius Clay, at the urging of Baron and others. The organization for Jewish Cultural Reconstruction was authorized to catalog and distribute this enormous warehouse of confiscated Jewish treasures on behalf of world Jewry. Its contents were slated to be donated to surviving or fledgling Jewish communities. When the group was organized during the latter part of the war, the scope of destruction of European Jewry was not yet known. The repository contained approximately half a million books and thousands of rare manuscripts and overflowed with multiple copies of journals and ritual objects from the private and communal libraries and institutions of the murdered Jewish communities of Europe. About forty percent of its treasures were distributed to institutions in Palestine and the United States, the remainder going to surviving Jewish communities in Europe and South Africa and those individual owners still living. Some of these volumes and manuscripts would form the kernel of the National Library in Jerusalem.

For Baron, the question of the rehabilitation of what he optimistically hoped would be a surviving remnant community in Europe was complex. He became preoccupied with the passing of the baton of Jewish learning from the embers of Europe to America and the Yishuv. Baron once reminisced in an uncustomarily personal fashion about going through the inventory of the treasures of the destroyed European Jewish civilization together with Arendt, Gershom Scholem, and other scholars. On another occasion, Baron berated me for smoking too much and unexpectedly mentioned that he was conversing with Arendt when she lit a cigarette and had her fatal heart attack in their presence in 1975. As an aside, Jeannette also smoked, using a long cigarette holder.

Baron was not religiously observant, although he mentioned that he had come from a traditional home. He once explained that his apartment in New York was kosher in deference to the many European guests and JTS faculty members, including Saul Lieberman, Louis Ginzberg, and Alexander Marx, who would visit on shabbat. In his Connecticut home, he was not kosher. He did speak of holiday observance, mentioning that Arendt attended a Passover Seder at their apartment. It was known that he spent the Jewish holidays in isolation in Connecticut, working in his retreat on their property. His books all identified his Connecticut estate, Yifat Shalom (the combination of his and Jeannette's Hebrew names), as the site of his most creative work. I don't recall any other discussion of observance or tradition. When one particularly frequent visitor and friend (Arthur Hertzberg) referred to his own Chassidic youth in Europe, or another (Abraham Duker) spoke in detail of prewar Poland, while yet another (Zosa Szajkowski) recounted an anti-Semitic incident he had experienced in the French Foreign Legion, Baron would relate to the accounts with what appeared to be some personal familiarity of their context. I never heard Baron speak Yiddish, although Hertzberg would sprinkle his conversation with Yiddish expressions, and Baron obviously understood them.

Professor Baron was an engaging teacher. It was never clear whether he prepared his class lectures beforehand. He would come to class directly from his office, sit at a desk, and take one small note card or envelope out of his pocket and deliver a flawless lecture. In the course of the lecture, he would refer to the small note card, which contained a quote written in the tiniest handwriting imaginable.. His lectures were wide ranging yet well organized and perfectly crafted. He sometimes took a break in the middle of class but always engaged with students, undergraduates as well as graduates. Unlike many of the Columbia faculty of that era, Professor Baron was not aloof. He would inquire about former students, many of whom had assumed pulpits in various parts of the country in an era when PhDs in Jewish history could not find employment in a university. He seemed to delight in the presence of some of their children, undergraduates at Columbia, who attended his classes. Students were not discouraged from asking questions during his lectures. I never saw him distracted by the interruption. I don't recall ever seeing him stand up in the classroom or write on the blackboard.

Professor Baron didn't give written final exams in his history lecture classes; rather, he would administer an oral exam to the entire class at his final meeting of the semester. He would have the students seated in two or three rows and go around the room posing questions that appeared to be randomly selected. Sometimes he would proceed to offer an extended answer to a question he posed if no one could answer it. Sometimes he would ask one student several questions that were increasingly specialized in nature. I recall that he specifically asked me about the Picciotto family of Italian (Livornese) background, who served as Jewish diplomats in European consulates in nineteenth-century Syria. He was visibly pleased when I began to explain the significance of the Francos (families of Italian origin in the Near East) and the phenomenon of extraterritorial rights exercised by Jews in the Ottoman Empire. These weren't "trick" questions that he pulled out of a hat. They were his method of using the particular case to distill and explicate a broader phenomenon. I think that is what made him a popular figure on the lecture circuit in the broader Jewish community. He could translate his scholarship for a general audience and bring his own current research naturally into his discussion on a more general topic. Unlike some members of the Jewish studies profession in its infancy in the 1970s, Baron had no disdain for community audiences, even if he was more elitist by temperament.

I once asked Professor Baron how he acquired his English language skills. With a somewhat sheepish smile, he described how he would listen avidly to the radio when he arrived in America in the late 1920s. When he encountered a word that he didn't understand on the radio or in the newspapers, he would write it in a small notebook, look it up in the dictionary, and make sure to use the word in conversation or writing thereafter. He confessed that he especially enjoyed typically American popular culture of his era, such as Westerns featuring Gene Autry or the Lone Ranger, and suggested that he continued to enjoy listening to the radio. Although his accent remained thick, he was never at a loss for words. I once asked Jeannette when Professor Baron stopped using German. She replied that it occurred after the war, when a former foreman of the Baron property informed them of the murder of his parents and sister in 1942 and the destruction of the 25,000 Jews of Tarnów (who constituted 55 percent of the prewar population of that Galician city). "He never spoke a word of German again," Jeannette succinctly replied.

As the sole female student in the cohort of graduate students, I confronted a dilemma. Although Jeannette Baron was not present in the room during the seminar in their home, she would enter at its conclusion to serve tea or coffee and cookies. I think that she was generally listening in the kitchen, which adjoined the room where the seminar was being held. It was expected that I, as the only other woman present, would help her serve and clean up. I never saw outside help in their home and did try to lend a helping hand—reluctantly, since all the male students remained seated and were not expected to participate in this female role.

Over the many years of our encounters, especially at *Jewish Social Studies*, Jeanette invited me to participate in other "female" activities, including shopping at discount stores on Broadway (at one lingerie store in particular), which I declined as politely as I could without insulting her. She was deeply involved in *Jewish Social Studies* as president of the Conference of Jewish Relations; her calls to my home occurred almost daily, invariably at supper time, when my three young children were especially demanding. I didn't want to assume the role of a daughter or confidant, especially as I was beleaguered by child-rearing and academic and tenure responsibilities. Jeannette would discuss the journal but also wanted to know more about what was going on at Columbia and how her husbands' successors were doing.

The *Jewish Social Studies* journal was a pet project of Professor Baron. It was an outgrowth of the Conference on Jewish Relations that he had founded in the 1930s with Professor Morris Raphael Cohen of City College as a response to the growing threat that Nazism posed to American Jewry and the mounting anti-Jewish discrimination in America in the 1930s. Baron became president of the Conference on Jewish Relations right before Pearl Harbor. From the outset, he insisted that policy formation in the Jewish community be based on accurate knowledge of the state of the Jews. He defined that knowledge broadly to include studies of the demographic, mortality, morbidity, occupational, and communal structures of American Jewry. Jewish population studies assumed a high priority for him, given the urgency of immigrant absorption in the 1930s. Baron's approach differed from that of the traditional Jewish defense organizations in this respect. His concerns included the need for broad studies of the nature of attitudes toward Jews, including on college campuses and questions of quotas in higher education. These concerns shaped the orientation and activities of the journal when it was founded by the conference in 1937. During its independent existence in New York, its boards included former students, colleagues, relatives (his daughter and wife were especially active), and some businessmen and lawyers. He was deeply involved in all the journal's activities, including soliciting articles, defining topics for special conferences (such as its conference on anti-Semitism), recruiting membership, raising funds, and establishing a monograph series. Over the years there were many discussions about the finances of the journal. The amounts discussed were small, and there seemed to be repeated negotiations with its publisher of long standing (Ktav). I don't recall any general call to younger scholars to submit their articles to the journal. The same attitude of turning to his inner circle of friends and former students prevailed in the conference program planning that occurred.

Baron nurtured optimistic hopes for the American Jewish community and was very familiar with its panoply of organizations and institutions. Unlike many of the Judaica scholars of the 1970s and 1980s who self-consciously sought to separate their Jewish community involvement from their professional identities and harbored insecurities about being too closely associated with the surrounding Jewish community, Baron, although unaffiliated in his personal life, never evinced either ambivalence or hostility toward the wider community. His upbringing in Tarnów had included the positive figure of his businessman father as a head of the Jewish community. Although Baron once proudly mentioned that Jeannette was a scion of the Meisel banking family of Prague, he showed no snobbery. All aspects of American Jewish life—be they summer camps, synagogue activities, sisterhoods and men's clubs, and adult education of the Jewishly illiterate—were subjects he seemed to see as subjects worthy of study. Just as his definition of the history of the Jews was expansive, the totality of American Jewish experiences and expressions intrigued him.

My relationship with the Barons was not solely formal. My husband and I were invited to spend a weekend at the Baron home in Connecticut in 1971. I was excited by the prospect. The house in Canaan had a large plot of land (about a hundred acres) but was within walking distance of town. On Saturday morning, my husband and the professor walked into town to pick up the Baron's newspapers—the *New York Times*, *Wall Street Journal*, and *Value Line*. Much to my surprise at the time, I realized that Professor Baron avidly followed the stock market. Perhaps that interest was a manifestation of his family background of bankers and property owners in western Galicia. That evening a member of the *Jewish Social Studies* board of directors who summered nearby came for dinner with his wife. Baron was at ease, garrulous and animated in his reminiscences, although never overbearing or bragging in any way.

The Baron house in Canaan was not far from a small summer music festival, and the Barons planned to attend the matinee concert with us. During intermission Baron invited me to take a stroll. He seemed to have something on his mind and finally blurted out, "I am worried about you." Somewhat taken aback, I inquired why. He replied that I had taken three maternity leaves, my dissertation had been completed two years earlier but not submitted, and he felt it was time to hand it in so that I could obtain the credential and move on. He suggested that my life would not allow further revisions and those that I felt necessary could be done later. It was time to move on, he stated matter-of-factly. He also volunteered to come out of retirement (he had retired several years before this incident) and to sit on my defense committee. I was stunned by the generosity of his offer and could barely respond. I later thought it through and focused on submission and completion. At that point, my Columbia adviser agreed on final revisions and set up the committee for the defense. Looking back at this incident and my personal career teaching in a graduate school program for more than four decades, I realize anew how attuned Baron was to the lives of his students, all the while composing his magisterial *Social and Religious History of the Jews* and also securing the foundations for the teaching of Jewish studies in the United States.

In 1978, the Barons came to Boston to the annual meeting of the Association for Jewish Studies. Most of the senior scholars, including Baron, did not typically attend the annual gathering of younger scholars, which was held at the Copley Plaza Hotel in its early years. Baron was being honored by the association at its Sunday evening banquet. The weather that weekend was worse than the usual New England snowstorms that regularly plagued the annual December meetings, and the Barons were taking the train from New York. People were dramatically arriving all day from around the Northeast after spending hours on the road. A group of participants celebrated each bedraggled traveler in the hotel's lobby as he or she arrived. As chair of the banquet (I was the program vice president of the Association for Jewish Studies and soon to be elected its first female president), I was particularly anxious about whether the Barons would arrive. When they finally appeared, Professor Baron immediately wanted to see a relative who was attending the conference as well as a former student who held a pulpit in New England. He asked that they come to his hotel suite, despite his harrowing trip and advanced age.

At the banquet that evening, I was seated next to Baron on the dais in the ornate hotel ballroom. He was very quiet and seemed distracted and pensive. When he got up to give his address after dinner, it was evident that he was visibly moved and said something to the effect that he was not only honored to be there but also quite relieved, as he looked out at the large audience, that "the future of the Jewish people which had hung in the balance was assured. When there are 500 Jewish artists and writers, 500 Jewish journalists, 500 rabbis, and 500 Judaic scholars in America," he continued, "the future was secure." As he looked out at the ballroom filled with a new generation of doctoral students, I think I caught a special glimmer in his eye. His optimism, despite living through the twentieth century, was vindicated. As both participant and observer, he mused on the shift in the mantle of leadership from Europe to America, a shift in which his own presence was such a vital factor.

Chapter Eleven

RECOLLECTIONS FROM THE BARON DAUGHTERS

SHOSHANA B. TANCER AND TOBEY B. GITELLE

Dad was already teaching at Columbia when he met Mother, a graduate student of economics. She had been advised to see him about a proposed dissertation topic on Jewish banking in Europe. The meeting did not go well. Mother was very upset that he grilled her on the number of languages she knew and ended the conversation, in his heavy German accent, with "I assume you know English." Nonetheless, when they accidentally met in the stacks of the New York Public Library a few weeks later, she accepted his invitation to join him for tea and a little more than a year later, in June 1934, they eloped.

Their backgrounds were similar but strikingly different. Dad came from an Orthodox Jewish family, the richest in the city of his birth in 1895, Tarnów, Austria where, in addition to their beautiful city home, they owned a country estate and Romanian oil wells. Mother was American-born in 1911 to a very comfortable Conservative Jewish family. Her father was a haberdasher, and her mother's family was in real estate. She was an only child, a "daddy's girl" and was devastated by his death when she was seventeen. She was still able to attend New York University and then enroll at Columbia. She would tell us that in her youth she enjoyed parties, dining out, dancing, theater, and concerts. It appears that her life changed after she married, for with the exception of concerts, we were not aware of our parents having much of a social life or taking advantage of New York City's vast cultural scene.

By mutual agreement, instead of an engagement ring, they bought an abandoned farm in northwestern Connecticut shortly before their marriage. It was in the town of Canaan, a rural community that had the advantage of not being on the route to anywhere, at least until Tanglewood was established. It also had the advantage of being a stop on the New York, New Haven, and Hartford train line. The farm was located on Honey Hill Road, and one of their neighbors raised bees and goats, so it was indeed the land of milk and honey. They combined their names and called the property Yifat Shalom, Mother's Hebrew name being Yaffa and Dad's, Shalom. This was their summer home from that time forward, even though neither knew how to drive a car then. It was to this home that they retreated after our mother's mother died in their New York apartment in March 1941. Dad was able to teach his classes in New York by taking the train one morning a week and returning the next afternoon. We spent our early childhood in this environment, coming back to New York City in September 1945 so that Dad would be able to do more research and we would be exposed to other Jews, there being none in Canaan. We also would be able to take advantage of all the city had to offer. It all happened just as planned. After junior high, Shoshana went to the Bronx High Science of Science and Barnard; Tobey went to Hunter Junior High and followed to the same high school and college.

When Dad accepted his position at Columbia, he made two requests prior to his acceptance: first, that he be placed in the History Department rather than either the Religion or Language Departments, and, second, that he have a full-time secretary, not realizing that in the United States typewriters were cheap and staff was expensive, the reverse of the situation in Europe. It was the task of his secretary, until his official retirement from Columbia in 1963, to type and retype his manuscripts as well as his correspondence. Dad, a perfectionist, would revise his work over and over, and with each iteration, a new manuscript had to be typed. This was before the days of computers, printers, and copiers, which have given us the ability to cut and paste rather than retype an entire page or pages. Dad was also engaged in voluminous correspondence, always keeping a carbon copy of what he sent as well as the originals received. Stanford University Library, which received Dad's papers after his death, informed us that his correspondence alone took up some seventy-two linear feet of shelving. His secretaries were never idle.

Dad was a traditional man of his time. He believed in the division of labor between spouses, up to a point. He was to work and earn money; she was to take care of the household and the children. However, we always knew that Mother also helped him with his work. To be clear, she never assisted with the research and initial writing—that was always exclusively his domain—but with the typing, editing, and collating. We were too young to know what Mother did when we lived in New York before 1941, but when we lived in Canaan full-time, she had a very active communal life in addition to being the proofreader of manuscripts, galleys, and page proofs. Every evening after dinner, for as long as we can remember, our parents would sit at a table across from each other, one reading and the other checking to make sure that all of the corrections and no errors had been made in the most recent version. In addition, Mother would sometimes suggest different wording so that a sentence would not be as convoluted as German sentences frequently are. Dad would graciously accept her alternative, and then they would return to the proofreading. After we returned to New York, from 1945 to the summer of 1963, she continued her involvement with the larger community in the city.

After 1963, Dad no longer had a secretary. As a result, the task of typing was added to that of proofreading, and Mother no longer had time to devote to other causes. To the best of our knowledge, she saw her role as providing Dad with as much assistance as she could so that he could work in peace and comfort. It probably was for this reason that she had previously turned down an offer to work for the Office of Price Administration. Another factor might have been that the out-of-pocket expenses to maintain our family in her absence would have been greater than her salary. It is interesting that only upon Mother's insistence as a result of the women's movement, did Dad acknowledge her contribution to his work.

During the war and while in Connecticut, Mother had the added responsibilities of child care, cooking, and housekeeping. Women were replacing men in the factories, and maids and cooks were nowhere to be found. She had not been raised to do this work, and we believe that she found it difficult and exhausting. Nonetheless, she did her part as an air raid warden and an instructor in first aid for the Red Cross, and she knitted for the military. We had a gigantic Victory Garden, some one hundred yards square, which Dad tended with our "help" (Shoshana was six and Tobey three when the war broke out). We did not get too much produce from this plot thanks to the woodchucks and rabbits, which Dad would not disturb from their natural habitat. Mother took to canning the apples and pears from the trees on our property. Dad went with us to harvest ripened milkweed pods, which contained a fluffy substance used by the military for life vests, and we combed the property for scrap metal, which, in addition to flattened cans, were picked up by the Boy Scouts.

When we returned to New York, Mother became active in many organizations. She participated in Columbia University Teas, a group of women who offered tea and cookies to students, which was funded by the sale of daffodils and apple blossom branches that they harvested from a Columbia botanical facility in Westchester. She suggested and created a small fund for indigent students at Bronx Science who needed money for travel or books, a fund we believe is still in existence, and she raised money for the Visiting Nurses Association. Mother also was president of the Jewish Music Council, the purpose of which was to define and support that field.

Dad had a very definite schedule. Although a workaholic, as one would guess from the quantity of publications under his name, he also believed in exercise. Right after breakfast, he would take a long walk. When in New York, he preferred strolling down Riverside Drive, unless one of us was at Bronx Science, at which time he would walk us to the subway station at 125th Street and 8th Avenue in Harlem. When in Connecticut in the summer, he would often take a scythe with him to clear the path on his way to the boathouse, which was approximately half a mile away. When finished with his morning academic work, he would then swim across the Housatonic and return for lunch at 1:00 p.m. He claimed that he needed the walks to clear his mind and prepare for the day's work. After lunch, time would be spent with correspondence and reading the newspapers, including the financial ones, before he would return to his office in New York or study in Canaan at 3:00, only to rejoin the family to hear the 6:00 news. During the war this was very important to him, as he did not know the fate of his parents and older sister, Gisella, who had been caught in Poland because their parents had not left for the United States and she had not returned to Palestine a week before Poland was invaded. Unfortunately, as he was later to learn, all three were killed rather early in the war, and he never overcame his sense of guilt for not having persuaded his parents to accompany him and Mother when they returned to America in the fall of 1937. Dinner would be at 7:00, followed by the ritual of reading manuscripts until 11:00.

Then came tea and something sweet. Dad would go to bed and Mother would stay awake reading mystery stories.

In addition to teaching at Columbia, Dad would frequently travel throughout the United States giving lectures. In this way, he was able to learn about the Jewish communities, their interests and concerns as well as the role they played in the broader society. At the same time, and as he was the son of a banker, this was a way to increase his income. Being very frugal, the lectures enabled him, with the assistance of Mother's advice, to develop a large portfolio before his death.

But Dad did not just teach at Columbia. Prior to his appointment and for the first year thereafter, he continued to teach at the Jewish Institute of Religion. His contract there was for an additional year, and he probably wanted to assure himself of an alternative were he to discover that the students at Columbia would not be interested in enrolling in his courses. He taught at the Jewish Theological Seminary after Alexander Marx's death and following his official retirement. He also taught at Rutgers and Brown while still giving classes at Columbia, as an emeritus, until 1978. He thought it historic that he, a naturalized citizen, was teaching at three universities created before our country was born.

Dad was very proud to be an American. This pride manifested itself in many ways. It was, we believe, one of the reasons he thought the time had come to have U.S. Jewish history written. This opinion was not shared by many, who thought it was too early for such investigations, but he fought for it. His affiliation with this country was also reflected in his comment when, after having seen a bust that had been made of him which he refused to buy, that were that sculpture to be found as if in Pompeii, it would be called the bust of some American. Among his proudest honors was being named one of ten Connecticut Patriots by Governor Ella Grasso in the 1976 Bicentennial. Another was receiving an honorary doctorate from the university at which he had taught for so many years. This was just one of thirteen honorary degrees awarded to him.

On a more personal level, growing up in our home was special. We spent some Saturday afternoons at the homes of Sol Lieberman, Louis Ginzburg, and Alexander Marx, looking quietly at picture books of the Holy Land while our parents discussed important topics. For us, these visits were boring, for at home we were not Sabbath observers and could do more to entertain ourselves. We also met many other famous people, Jewish and non-Jewish, from all over the world whom our parents hosted. We grew up in an environment, unusual at that time, in which we could become anything we wanted and converse comfortably with anyone we met. Dad was a "walking encyclopedia" and was most helpful with suggestions in doing our homework, including essays while we were in college. Mother taught us the household arts and manners, which were very important to her. As their children, we did not realize how much of a contribution to Jewish history and institutions our father had made. It is only in retrospect that we can appreciate what a giant he was and how much the entire field of Jewish studies and the centers of Jewish studies owe to him.

BIBLIOGRAPHY OF THE PUBLICATIONS OF PROFESSOR SALO WITTMAYER BARON (1895-1989)

MENACHEM BUTLER

This bibliography is an updated and expanded version of Jeanette M. Baron, "A Bibliography of the Printed Writings of Salo Wittmayer Baron," in *Salo Wittmayer Baron Jubilee Volume on the Occasion of His Eightieth Birthday*, vol. 1, ed. Saul Lieberman and Arthur Hyman (Jerusalem: American Academy for Jewish Research, 1975), 1–37. I am grateful to Dr. Charles Berlin, Professor Elisheva Carlebach, Mr. Charles Knapp, and Dr. Adina Yoffie for their assistance and guidance in the preparation of this bibliography.

FESTSCHRIFTEN

1. Blau, Joseph L., Philip Friedman, Arthur Hertzberg, and Isaac Mendelsohn, eds. *Essays on Jewish Life and Thought: Presented in Honor of Salo Wittmayer Baron*. New York: Columbia University Press, 1959.
2. Lieberman, Saul, and Arthur Hyman, eds. *Salo Wittmayer Baron Jubilee Volume on the Occasion of His Eightieth Birthday*. 4 vols. Jerusalem: American Academy for Jewish Research, 1975.
3. Kirshenblatt-Gimblett, Barbara, ed. *Writing a Modern Jewish History: Essays in Honor of Salo W. Baron*. New Haven, CT: Yale University Press, 2006.
4. Tirosh-Samuelson, Hava, and Edward Dąbrowa, eds. *The Enduring Legacy of Salo W. Baron*. Kraków: Jagiellonian University Press, 2017.

BOOKS

1. Baron, Salo W. *Die Judenfrage auf dem Wiener Kongress: Auf Grund von zum Teil ungedruckten Quellen dargestellt*. Vienna: Löwit, 1920.

BIBLIOGRAPHY

2. Baron, Salo W. *Die politische Theorie Ferdinand Lassalles.* Leipzig: C. L. Hirschfeld, 1923.
3. Baron, Salo W., and Alexander Marx, eds. *Jewish Studies in Memory of George A. Kohut.* New York: Bloch, 1935.
4. Baron, Salo W. *A Social and Religious History of the Jews.* Vol. 1. New York: Columbia University Press, 1937.
5. Baron, Salo W. *A Social and Religious History of the Jews.* Vol. 2. New York: Columbia University Press, 1937.
6. Baron, Salo W. *A Social and Religious History of the Jews.* Vol. 3. New York: Columbia University Press, 1937.
7. Baron, Salo W. *Bibliography of Jewish Social Studies, 1938-39.* New York: Conference on Jewish Relations, 1941.
8. Baron, Salo W., ed. *Essays on Maimonides: An Octocentennial Volume.* New York: Columbia University Press, 1941.
9. Baron, Salo W. *The Jewish Community: Its History and Structure to the American Revolution.* Vol. 1. Philadelphia: Jewish Publication Society, 1942.
10. Baron, Salo W. *The Jewish Community: Its History and Structure to the American Revolution.* Vol. 2. Philadelphia: Jewish Publication Society of America, 1942.
11. Baron, Salo W. *The Jewish Community: Its History and Structure to the American Revolution.* Vol. 3. Philadelphia: Jewish Publication Society of America, 1942.
12. Baron, Salo W. *President's Report, 1940-1943.* New York: Conference on Jewish Relations, 1943.
13. Baron, Salo W. *President's Report, 1943-1946.* New York: Conference on Jewish Relations, 1946.
14. Baron, Salo W. *Modern Nationalism and Religion.* New York: Harper and Brothers, 1947.
15. Baron, Salo W. *The Jewish Community and Jewish Education.* New York: American Association for Jewish Education, 1948.
16. Baron, Salo W., Ernest Nagel, and Koppel S. Pinson, eds. *Freedom and Reason Studies in Philosophy and Jewish Culture: In Memory of Morris Raphael Cohen.* New York: Conference on Jewish Relations, 1951.
17. Baron, Salo W. *A Social and Religious History of the Jews.* Vol. 1, *Ancient Times.* 2nd ed. Philadelphia: Jewish Publication Society, 1952.
18. Baron, Salo W. *A Social and Religious History of the Jews.* Vol. 2, *Ancient Times.* 2nd ed. Philadelphia: Jewish Publication Society, 1952.
19. Baron, Salo W., and Joseph L. Blau, eds. *Judaism, Postbiblical and Talmudic Period.* New York: Liberal Arts Press, 1954.
20. Baron, Salo W. *A Social and Religious History of the Jews.* Vol. 1. [In Hebrew.] Trans. I. M. Grintz. Tel Aviv: Massada, 1955.
21. Baron, Salo W. *Great Ages and Ideas of the Jewish People.* New York: Random House, 1956.
22. Baron, Salo W. *Histoire d'Israël vie sociale et religieuse.* Vol. 1. Paris: Presses Universitaires de France, 1956.
23. Baron, Salo W. *A Social and Religious History of the Jews.* Vol. 2. [In Hebrew.] Trans. I. M. Grintz. Tel Aviv: Massada, 1956.
24. Baron, Salo W. *A Social and Religious History of the Jews.* Vol. 3, *Heirs of Rome and Persia.* 2nd ed. Philadelphia: Jewish Publication Society, 1957.

BIBLIOGRAPHY

25. Baron, Salo W. *A Social and Religious History of the Jews.* Vol. 4, *Meeting of East and West.* 2nd ed. Philadelphia: Jewish Publication Society, 1957.
26. Baron, Salo W. *A Social and Religious History of the Jews.* Vol. 5, *Religious Controls and Dissensions.* 2nd ed. Philadelphia: Jewish Publication Society, 1957.
27. Baron, Salo W. *Histoire d'Israël vie sociale et religieuse.* Vol. 2. Paris: Presses Universitaires de France, 1957.
28. Baron, Salo W. *A Social and Religious History of the Jews.* Vol. 2. [In Hebrew.] Trans. I. M. Grintz. Tel Aviv: Massada, 1957.
29. Baron, Salo W. *A Social and Religious History of the Jews.* Vol. 6, *Laws, Homilies, and the Bible.* 2nd ed. Philadelphia: Jewish Publication Society, 1957.
30. Baron, Salo W. *A Social and Religious History of the Jews.* Vol. 7, *Hebrew Language and Letters.* 2nd ed. Philadelphia: Jewish Publication Society, 1957.
31. Baron, Salo W. *A Social and Religious History of the Jews.* Vol. 8, *Philosophy and Science.* 2nd ed. Philadelphia: Jewish Publication Society, 1957.
32. Baron, Salo W. *Modern Nationalism and Religion.* 2nd ed. New York: Meridian, 1960.
33. Baron, Salo W. *A Social and Religious History of the Jews: Index to vols. 1–8.* 2nd ed. Philadelphia: Jewish Publication Society, 1960.
34. Baron, Salo W., Benzion Dinur, Shmuel Ettinger, and Israel Halpern, eds. *Yitzhak F. Baer Jubilee Volume: On the Occasion of his Seventieth Birthday.* [In Hebrew.] Jerusalem: Historical Society of Israel, 1960.
35. Salo W. Baron, *Histoire d'Israël vie sociale et religieuse.* Vol. 3. Paris: Presses Universitaires de France, 1961.
36. Baron, Salo W. *Histoire d'Israël vie sociale et religieuse.* Vol. 4. Paris: Presses Universitaires de France, 1961.
37. Baron, Salo W., and Joseph L. Blau, eds. *Judaism: Postbiblical and Talmudic Period.* New York: Liberal Arts Press, 1962.
38. Baron, Salo W. *Últimas Crônicas do Judaismo Europeu.* Rio de Janeiro: Instituto Brasileiro-Judaico de Cultura, 1962.
39. Blau, Joseph L., and Salo W. Baron, eds. *The Jews of the United States, 1790–1840: A Documentary History.* New York: Columbia University Press, 1963.
40. Baron, Salo W. *Histoire d'Israël vie sociale et religieuse.* Vol. 5. Paris: Presses Universitaires de France, 1964.
41. Baron, Salo W. *History and Jewish Historians: Essays and Addresses.* Ed. Arthur Hertzberg and Leon A. Feldman. Philadelphia: Jewish Publication Society, 1964.
42. Baron, Salo W. *The Russian Jew Under Tsars and Soviets.* New York: Macmillan, 1964.
43. Baron, Salo W. *A Social and Religious History of the Jews.* Vol. 4. [In Hebrew.] Trans. Zvi Ankori. Tel Aviv: Massada, 1965.
44. Baron, Salo W. *La epoca moderna.* Buenos Aires: Paídos, 1965.
45. Baron, Salo W. *A Social and Religious History of the Jews.* Vol. 7. [In Hebrew]. Trans. Yehoshua Amir. Tel Aviv: Massada, 1965.
46. Baron, Salo W. *A Social and Religious History of the Jews: Late Middle Ages and Era of Expansion, 1200–1650.* Vol. 9, *Under Church and Empire.* 2nd ed. Philadelphia: Jewish Publication Society, 1965.
47. Baron, Salo W. *A Social and Religious History of the Jews: Late Middle Ages and Era of Expansion, 1200–1650.* Vol. 10, *On the Empire's Periphery.* 2nd ed. Philadelphia: Jewish Publication Society, 1965.

48. Baron, Salo W. *Deutsche und Juden*. Frankfurt am Main: Suhrkamp, 1967.
49. Baron, Salo W. *A Social and Religious History of the Jews: Late Middle Ages and Era of Expansion, 1200–1650*. Vol. 11, *Citizen or Alien Conjurer*. 2nd ed. Philadelphia: Jewish Publication Society, 1967.
50. Baron, Salo W. *A Social and Religious History of the Jews: Late Middle Ages and Era of Expansion, 1200–1650*. Vol. 12, *Economic Catalyst*, 2nd ed. Philadelphia: Jewish Publication Society, 1967.
51. Baron, Salo W. *Historia social y religiosa del pueblo judío*. Vol. 1. Buenos Aires: Paidós, 1968.
52. Baron, Salo W. *Historia social y religiosa del pueblo judío*. Vol. 2. Buenos Aires: Paidós, 1968.
53. Baron, Salo W. *Historia social y religiosa del pueblo judío*. Vol. 3. Buenos Aires: Paidós, 1968.
54. Baron, Salo W. *Historia social y religiosa del pueblo judío*. Vol. 4. Buenos Aires: Paidós, 1968.
55. Baron, Salo W *Historia social y religiosa del pueblo judío*. Vol. 5. Buenos Aires: Paidós, 1968.
56. Baron, Salo W. *Historia social y religiosa del pueblo judío*. Vol. 6. Buenos Aires: Paidós, 1968.
57. Baron, Salo W. *Historia social y religiosa del pueblo judío*. Vol. 7. Buenos Aires: Paidós, 1968.
58. Baron, Salo W. *Historia social y religiosa del pueblo judío*. Vol. 8. Buenos Aires: Paidós, 1968.
59. Baron, Salo W. *A Social and Religious History of the Jews: Late Middle Ages and Era of Expansion, 1200–1650*. Vol. 13, *Inquisition, Renaissance, and Reformation*. 2nd ed. Philadelphia: Jewish Publication Society, 1969.
60. Baron, Salo W. *A Social and Religious History of the Jews: Late Middle Ages and Era of Expansion, 1200–1650*. Vol. 14, *Catholic Restoration and Wars of Religion*. 2nd ed. Philadelphia: Jewish Publication Society, 1969.
61. Baron, Salo W. *Modern Nationalism and Religion*. Freeport, NY: Books for Library Press, 1971.
62. Baron, Salo W. *Steeled by Adversity: Essays and Addresses on American Jewish Life*. Ed. Jeannette Meisel Baron. Philadelphia: Jewish Publication Society, 1971.
63. Baron, Salo W. *Ancient and Medieval Jewish History: Essays*. Ed. Leon A. Feldman. New Brunswick, NJ: Rutgers University Press, 1972.
64. Baron, Salo W. "*Halom she-nitgashem* (A Dream Come True)." Inaugural lecture delivered at the opening of the Chaim Rosenberg School of Jewish Studies. Tel Aviv: Tel Aviv University, 1972.
65. Baron, Salo W. *The Jewish Community: Its History and Structure to the American Revolution*. Vol. 1. Westport, CT: Greenwood, 1972.
66. Baron, Salo W. *The Jewish Community: Its History and Structure to the American Revolution*. Vol. 2. Westport, CT: Greenwood, 1972.
67. Baron, Salo W. *The Jewish Community: Its History and Structure to the American Revolution*. Vol. 3. Westport, CT: Greenwood, 1972.
68. Baron, Salo W. *A Social and Religious History of the Jews*. Vol. 1, *Ancient Times*. 2nd ed. (6th printing). New York: Columbia University Press, 1972.

BIBLIOGRAPHY

69. Baron, Salo W. *A Social and Religious History of the Jews.* Vol. 5. [In Hebrew.] Trans. Zvi Baras. Tel Aviv: Massada, 1972.
70. Baron, Salo W. *A Social and Religious History of the Jews.* Vol. 6. [In Hebrew.] Trans. Joseph Nedava. Tel Aviv: Massada, 1972.
71. Baron, Salo W. *A Social and Religious History of the Jews: Late Middle Ages and Era of Expansion, 1200–1650.* Vol. 15, *Resettlement and European Expansion.* 2nd ed. Philadelphia: Jewish Publication Society, 1973.
72. Baron, Salo W. *Émancipation civile versus émancipation politique.* Montréal: Institut Jacob Blaustein pour le développement des droits de l'homme, 1974.
73. Baron, Salo W. *História e historiografia do povo judeu.* São Paulo, Brazil: Perspectiva, 1974.
74. Baron, Salo W., and Arcadius Kahan. *Economic History of the Jews.* Ed. Nachum Gross. New York: Schocken, 1975.
75. Baron, Salo W. *Quelques pages des carnets d'un historien: Le Judaïsme européen avant et après Hitler.* Brussels: Institut universitaire d'Êtudes du Judaïsme Martin Buber, 1975.
76. Baron, Salo W. *The Russian Jew Under Tsars and Soviets.* 2nd ed. New York: Macmillan, 1976.
77. Baron, Salo W. *A Social and Religious History of the Jews: Late Middle Ages and Era of Expansion, 1200–1650.* Vol. 16, *Poland-Lithuania 1500–1650.* 2nd ed. Philadelphia: Jewish Publication Society, 1976.
78. Baron, Salo W. *Palestinian Messengers in America, 1849–79: A Record of Four Journeys.* New York: Arno, 1977.
79. Baron, Salo W. *Steeled by Adversity: Essays and Addresses on American Jewish Life.* [In Hebrew.] Jerusalem: Schocken, 1977.
80. Baron, Salo W., and George S. Wise. *Violence and Defense in the Jewish Experience.* Philadelphia: Jewish Publication Society, 1977.
81. Baron, Salo W., and Isaac E. Barzilay. *American Academy for Jewish Research: Jubilee Volume.* Jerusalem: American Academy for Jewish Research, 1980.
82. Baron, Salo W. *A Social and Religious History of the Jews: Late Middle Ages and Era of Expansion, 1200–1650.* Vol. 17, *Byzantines, Mamelukes, and Maghribians.* 2nd ed. Philadelphia: Jewish Publication Society, 1980.
83. Baron, Salo W. *The Contemporary Relevance of History: A Study in Approaches and Methods.* New York: Columbia University Press, 1986.
84. Baron, Salo W. *Under Two Civilizations: Tarnów, 1895–1914.* Stanford, CA: Stanford University Press, 1990.
85. Baron, Salo W. *The World Dimensions of Jewish History.* [In Hebrew.] Jerusalem: Shazar, 1996.

ARTICLES AND REVIEWS

1. S. B. A. [Salo W. Baron]. "A Sad Phenomenon." [In Hebrew.] *ha-Mizpeh* 9, no. 43 (November 8, 1912): 3.
2. S. B. A. [Salo W. Baron]. "Financial Crisis." [In Hebrew.] *ha-Mizpeh* 9, no. 44 (November 15, 1912): 2–3.

3. S. B. A. [Salo W. Baron]. "The Problem of Social Welfare and Its Reforms." [In Hebrew.] *ha-Mizpeh* 9, no. 46 (November 29, 1912): 1-2.
4. S. B. A. [Salo W. Baron]. "Reform of the Electoral System for the Galician Diet." [In Hebrew.] *ha-Mizpeh* 9, no. 49 (December 20, 1912): 1-2
5. Baron, Salo W. "Portents of the Day." [In Hebrew.] *ha-Mizpeh* 10, no. 27 (July 11, 1913): 2-3.
6. S. B. A. [Salo W. Baron]. "The Polish Boycott." [In Hebrew.] *ha-Mizpeh* 10, no. 7 (February 14, 1913): 2-3.
7. S. B. A. [Salo W. Baron]. "The Polish Boycott." [In Hebrew.] *ha-Mizpeh* 10, no. 8 (February 21, 1913): 1-2.
8. S. B. A. [Salo W. Baron]. "The Polish Boycott." [In Hebrew.] *ha-Mizpeh* 10, no. 9 (February 28, 1913): 3-4.
9. S. B. A. [Salo W. Baron]. "The Polish Boycott." [In Hebrew.] *ha-Mizpeh* 10, no. 10 (March 7, 1913): 2-3.
10. S. B. A. [Salo W. Baron]. "The Polish Boycott." [In Hebrew.] *ha-Mizpeh* 10, no. 11 (March 14, 1913): 3-4.
11. S. B. A. [Salo W. Baron]. "On the Threshold of a New Period." [In Hebrew.] *ha-Mizpeh* 10, no. 36 (September 12, 1913): 4-5.
12. Baron, Salo W. "The Problem of the Day." [In Hebrew.] *ha-Mizpeh* 11, no. 3 (January 16, 1914): 2-3.
13. Baron, Salo W. "The Problem of the Day." [In Hebrew.] *ha-Mizpeh* 11, no. 4 (January 23, 1914): 2-3.
14. Baron, Salo W. "On the Anniversary of the *ha-Mizpeh*." [In Hebrew.] *ha-Mizpeh* 11, no. 17 (April 24, 1914): 2-3.
15. Baron, Salo W. "On the Anniversary of the *ha-Mizpeh*." [In Hebrew.] *ha-Mizpeh* 11, no. 18 (May 1, 1914): 3.
16. Baron, Salo W. "In Honor of Mordecai David Brandstaetter on the Occasion of His Seventieth Birthday." [In Hebrew.] *ha-Tsefirah* 40, no. 94 (May 7, 1914): 1.
17. Baron, Salo W. "In Honor of Mordecai David Brandstaetter on the Occasion of His Seventieth Birthday." [In Hebrew.] *ha-Tsefirah* 40, no. 95 (May 8, 1914): 4.
18. Baron, Salo W. "In Honor of Mordecai David Brandstaetter on the Occasion of His Seventieth Birthday." [In Hebrew.] *ha-Tsefirah* 40, no. 97 (May 11, 1914): 1-2.
19 Baron, Salo W. "*Nation oder Sprache?*" *Die Wage* 21, no. 18 (May 4, 1918): 276-80.
20. Baron, Salo W. "*Graetzens Geschichtsschreibung: Eine methodologische Untersuchung.*" *Monatsschrift für die Geschichte und Wissenschaft des Judenthums* 62, no. 1 (1918): 5-15.
21. Baron, Salo W. "The Situation of the Jews in Roumania." *Jewish Tribune* 97, no. 17 (October 24, 1924): 4.
22. Baron, Salo W. "Ferdinand Lasselle, the Jew." [In Hebrew.] *ha-Tekufah* 23 (1925): 347-62.
23. Baron, Salo W. "*Jewish People and World Peace.*" [In Japanese.] *Revue Internationale* (1925-26): 106-7.
24. Baron, Salo W. "Review of *History of Israel, Vols. 2-4*, by Josef Klausner." [In Hebrew.] *Literarische Wochenschrift* 27 (December 5, 1925): 840-41.
25. Baron, Salo W. "Review of *Weltgeschichte des jüdischen volkes, vol. 1*." *Literarische Wochenschrift* 3-4 (January 20, 1926): 72-73.

BIBLIOGRAPHY

26. Baron, Salo W. "Review of *Aus zwei Jahrhunderten*, by N. M. Gelber, and *Die Juden und der polnische Aufstand 1863*, by N. M. Gelber." *Monatsschrift für Geschichte und Wissenschaft des Judentums* 70, nos. 3-4 (March–April 1926): 134–35.
27. Baron, Salo W. "Dur den Schutz der Minderheiten: Der Kongress der Volkerbundligen." *Wiener Morgenzeitung* 8, no. 2644 (July 4, 1926): 2.
28. Baron, Salo W. "Eine Palastinadebatte auf dem Kongress der Volkerbundligen." *Wiener Morgenzeitung* 8, no. 2646 (July 6, 1926): 2.
29. Baron, Salo W. "Jüdische und Palästina Fragen auf dem Zehnten Kongress der Internationalen Union der Volkerbundligen." *Zionistische Korrespondence* 6, no. 27 (July 9, 1926): 1–5.
30. Baron, Salo W. "Eine Palastinadebatte auf dem Kongress der Volkerbundligen." *Wiener Morgenzeitung* 8, no. 2650 (July 10, 1926): 2.
31. Baron, Salo W. "Unveröffentlichte Aktenstücke zur Judenfrage auf dem Wiener Kongreß (1814–15)." *Monatsschrift für Geschichte und Wissenschaft des Judentums* 70, nos. 11–12 (November–December 1926): 457–75.
32. Baron, Salo W. "Azariah de Rossi." [In Hebrew.] In *Hebrew Encyclopedia: Brochure*, 28–29. Berlin: Eshkol, 1926.
33. Baron, Salo W. "Review of *Nachgelassene Briefe und Schriften*, by Ferdinand Lassalle." *Archiv für die Geschichte des Sozialismus und der Arbeiterbewegung* 12 (1926): 449–50.
34. Baron, Salo W. "Review of *Geschichte der Juden in Frankfurt am Main (1150–1824)*, vol. 1." *Literarische Wochenschrift* 7 (February 13, 1927): 166–67.
35. Marx, Alexander, and Salo W. Baron. "In Memoriam: Zvi Peretz Chajes." [In Hebrew.] *ha-Doar* 8, no. 8 (December 23, 1927): 114–16.
36. Baron, Salo W. "Azariah de Rossi's Attitude to Life (Weltanschauung)." In *Jewish Studies in Memory of Israel Abrahams*, ed. George Alexander Kohut, 15–52. New York: Jewish Institute of Religion, 1927.
37. Baron, Salo W. "Freedom and Constraint in the Jewish Community: A Historic Episode." In *Essays and Studies in Memory of Linda R. Miller*, ed. Israel Davidson, 9–23. New York: Jewish Theological Seminary of America, 1927.
38. Baron, Salo W. "Isacco Artom." In *Jüdisches Lexikon*, vol. 1 (cols. 486–87). Berlin: Jüdischer Verlag, 1927.
39. Baron, Salo W. "The Study of Jewish History." *Jewish Institute Quarterly* 4, no. 2 (January 1928): 7–14.
40. Baron, Salo W. "Rabbi H.P. Chajes as Scholar and Teacher." [In Hebrew.] *Shevilei Ha-Hinukh* 4, no. 1 (March 1928): 37–45.
41. Baron, Salo W. "Research in Jewish History." *Jewish Institute Quarterly* 4, no. 4 (May 1928): 3–5.
42. Baron, Salo W. "In Memoriam: Mordecai David Brandstadter." [In Hebrew.] *ha-Doar* 8, no. 28 (June 3, 1928): 438–41.
43. Baron, Salo W. "Ghetto and Emancipation: Shall We Revise the Traditional View?" *Menorah Journal* 14, no. 6 (June 1928): 515–26.
44. Baron, Salo W. "Review of *The Legacy of Israel*, ed. Edwyn R. Bevan and Charles Singer." *Journal of Religion* 8, no. 3 (July 1928): 477–79.
45. Baron, Salo W. "Adolf (Abraham) Fischhof." In *Jüdisches Lexikon*, vol. 2., cols. 673–74. Berlin: Jüdischer Verlag, 1928.

46. Baron, Salo W. "Bernhard Freiherr von Eskeles." In *Jüdisches Lexikon*, vol. 2., col. 513. Berlin: Jüdischer Verlag, 1928.
47. Baron, Salo W. "Heinrich Friedjung." In *Jüdisches Lexikon*, vol. 2., cols. 822–23. Berlin: Jüdischer Verlag, 1928.
48. Baron, Salo W. "La méthode historique d'Azaria de' Rossi." *Revue des Études Juives* 86 (1928): 151–75.
49. Baron, Salo W. "Nationalism and Intolerance: Part 1. Babylon to the Seventeenth Century." *Menorah Journal* 16, no. 6 (June 1929): 503–15.
50. Baron, Salo W. "Nationalism and Intolerance: Part 2. From the Seventeenth Century to the Twentieth." *Menorah Journal* 17, no. 2 (November 1929): 148–58.
51. Baron, Salo W. "Azariah de Rossi." In *Hebrew Encyclopedia*, vol. 1, cols. 689–63. Berlin: Eshkol, 1929.
52. Baron, Salo W. "An Italian Responsum of Abraham Graziano." [In Hebrew.] In *Studies in Jewish Bibliography and Related Subjects in Memory of Abraham Solomon Freidus*, ed. Louis Ginzberg et al., 122–37. New York: Alexander Kohut Memorial Foundation, 1929.
53. Baron, Salo W. "La méthode historique d'Azaria de' Rossi." *Revue des Études Juives*, 87 (1929): 43–78.
54. Baron, Salo W. "The Authenticity of the Numbers in the Historical Books of Old Testament." *Journal of Biblical Literature* 49, no. 3 (January 1930): 287–91.
55. Askowith, Dora. "Prof. Salo Baron Is Interviewed on Teaching Jewish History." *Jewish Tribune*, February 14, 1930, 2, 7.
56. Baron, Salo W. "Teaching Jewish History." [In Polish.] *Chwila* (May 4, 1930): 9–10.
57. Baron, Salo W. "Abraham Berliner (1833–1915)." In *Encyclopaedia of the Social Sciences*, vol. 6, 418–19. New York: Macmillan, 1930.
58. Baron, Salo W. "I. M. Jost the Historian." *Proceedings of the American Academy for Jewish Research* 1 (1930): 7–32.
59. Baron, Salo W. Introduction to *Die galizischen Juden im Kampfe um ihre Gleichberechtigung (1848–1868)*, by Philip Friedman, v–vi. Frankfurt am Main: J. Kauffmann, 1930.
60. Baron, Salo W. "Zydzi w Rumunii." *Miesięcznik Żydowski* 1, no. 4 (March 1931): 322–25.
61. Baron, Salo W. "Review of *A History of the Hebrew People from the Earliest Times to the Year 70 A.D.*, by George A. Barton." *Historical Outlook* 21, no. 6 (October 1931): 304–5.
62. Baron, Salo W. "Zur ostjüdischen Einwanderung in Preußen: Aktenstücke." *Zeitschrift für die Geschichte der Juden in Deutschland*, n.s. 3, no. 2–3 (1931): 193–203.
63. Baron, Salo W. "Heinrich Graetz." In *Encyclopedia Judaica*, vol. 7, 645–52. Berlin: Eshkol, 1931.
64. Baron, Salo W. "Zecharias Frankel." In *Encyclopaedia of the Social Sciences*, vol. 6, 418–19. New York: Macmillan, 1931.
65. Baron, Salo W. "Interview." *Der Wiener Tag*, July 3, 1932.
66. Baron, Salo W. "Jewish Emancipation." In *Encyclopaedia of the Social Sciences*, vol. 8, 394–99. New York: Macmillan, 1932.
67. Baron, Salo W. "Joseph Karo." In *Encyclopaedia of the Social Sciences*, vol. 8, 547–48. New York: Macmillan, 1932.

BIBLIOGRAPHY

68. Baron, Salo W. "Review of *The Holy Land under Mandate*, by Fannie A. Andrews, and *History of Palestine*, by Angelo S. Rappoport." *Historical Outlook* 24, no. 3 (March 1933): 160–61.
69. Baron, Salo W. "Jewish Influence on Christian Reform Movements." *Jewish Quarterly Review* 23, no. 4 (April 1933): 405–10.
70. Baron, Salo W. "Germany's Ghetto, Past and Present: A Perspective on Nazi Laws Against Jews." *Independent Journal of Columbia University* 3, no. 3 (November 15, 1933): 3–4.
71. Baron, Salo W. "Żydzi a żydostwo." *Miesięcznik Żydowski* 3, part 2, nos. 11–12 (November–December 1933): 193–207.
72. Baron, Salo W. "The Israelite Population Under the Kings." [In Hebrew.] In *Abhandlungen zur Erinnerung an Hirsch Perez Chajes*, ed. Victor Aptowitzer and Arthur Zacharias Schwarz, 73–136. Vienna: Alexander Kohut Memorial Foundation, 1933.
73. Baron, Salo W. "The Jews and the Syrian Massacres of 1860." *Proceedings of the American Academy for Jewish Research* 4 (1933): 3–31.
74. Baron, Salo W. "Résumés des Communications présentées au Congrès." In *VIIe Congrès International des Sciences Historiques*, vol. 2, 455. Warsaw: Comité organisateur du congrès, 1933.
75. Baron, Salo W. "Profile." In *Galician Jewish Celebrities*, by Gershom Bader, 23. [In Hebrew.] New York: National Booksellers, 1934.
76. Baron, Salo W. "Review of *Berthold Auerbachs sozial politischer und ethischer Liberalismus*, by M. I. Zwick." *Germanic Review* 10, no. 1 (January 1935): 50–51.
77. Baron, Salo W. "Review of *Palestine the Last Two Thousand Years*, by Jacob de Haas." *Annals of the American Academy of Political and Social Science* 178 (March 1935): 235–36.
78. Baron, Salo W. "Review of *Palestine: The Last Two Thousand Years*, by Jacob de Haas." *American Historical Review* 40, no. 3 (April 1935): 545–46.
79. Baron, Salo W. "Maimonides, guia y legislador de su pueblo." *Revista Hispánica Moderna* 1, no. 4 (July 1935): 303–7.
80. Baron, Salo W. "An Historical Critique of the Jewish Community." *Jewish Education* 8, no. 1 (September 1935): 2–8.
81. Baron, Salo W. "An Historical Critique of the Jewish Community." *Jewish Social Service Quarterly* 12, no. 1 (September 1935): 44–49.
82. Baron, Salo W. "Abraham Benisch's Project for Jewish Colonization in Palestine (1842)." In *Jewish Studies in Memory of George A. Kohut*, ed. Salo W. Baron and Alexander Marx, 72–85. New York: Bloch, 1935.
83. Baron, Salo W. "The Historical Outlook of Maimonides." *Proceedings of the American Academy for Jewish Research* 6 (1935): 5–113.
84. Baron, Salo W. "The History of German Jews in Palestine." [In Hebrew.] In *Minha le-David: Jubilee Volume in Honor of David Yellin* [In Hebrew], 113–28. Jerusalem: Rubin Mass, 1935.
85. Baron, Salo W. "Review of *Le Scorpion*, by Marcel Bulard." *American Historical Review* 41, no. 2 (January 1936): 412–13.
86. Baron, Salo W. "Answer to Review of *A Social and Religious History of the Jews*, by Solomon Zeitlin." *Revue des Études Juives*, n.s. 2, no. 2 (July–December 1937): 141–43.

87. Baron, Salo W. "Review of *Die Juden im christlichen Spanien*, by Fritz Baer." *American Historical Review* 43, no. 1 (October 1937): 101–3.
88. Baron, Salo W. "Review of *Das Judentum und die geistigen Strömungen des 19. Jahrhunderts*, by Albert Lewkowitz." *Review of Religion* 2, no. 1 (November 1937): 80–83.
89. Baron, Salo W. "A Communal Controversy in Verona." [In Hebrew.] In *Jubilee Volume for Professor Samuel Krauss on His Seventieth Birthday* [In Hebrew], 217–54. Jerusalem: Rubin Mass, 1937.
90. Baron, Salo W. "From the History of the Jewish Settlement in Jerusalem." [In Hebrew.] In *Sefer Klausner: A Collection of Science and Belles-Lettres Gathered for Professor Joseph Klausner on His Sixtieth Jubilee*, ed. Naftali H. Tur et al., 302–12. Tel Aviv: Va'ad ha-Yovel, 1937.
91. Baron, Salo W. "Democracy and Judaism." *Hadassah Newsletter* 18, no. 4 (January 1938): 66–67.
92. Baron, Salo W. "The Jewish Question in the Nineteenth Century." *Journal of Modern History* 10, no. 1 (March 1938): 51–65.
93. Baron, Salo W. "Review of *Noble Families Among the Sephardic Jews*, by Isaac Da Costa." *American Historical Review* 43, no. 3 (April 1938): 608–10.
94. Baron, Salo W. "Socioreligious Research in Jewish History: A Lecture." [In Yiddish.] *Di Tsukunft* 43, no. 5 (June 1938): 341–47.
95. Baron, Salo W. "*A propos de Mon A Social and Religious History of the Jews*." *Revue des Études Juives*, n.s. 4, nos. 1–2 (July–December 1938): 139–46.
96. Baron, Salo W. "Review of *Juden und Judentum in deutschen Briefen aus drei Jahrhunderten*, by Franz Kobler." *Historia Judaica* 1, no. 1 (November 1938): 74–75.
97. Baron, Salo W. "A Bibliography on Palestine and the Refugee Problem." *Bulletin of the Story Behind the Headlines* 2, no. 8 (December 6, 1938): 21–23.
98. Baron, Salo W. "Emphases in Jewish History." *Jewish Social Service Quarterly* 15, no. 2 (December 1938): 219–35.
99. Baron, Salo W. "A Study in the History of Jewish Enlightenment and Education in Vienna." [In Hebrew.] In *Sefer Touroff: Festschrift for Nisson Touroff*, ed. Isaac Silberschlag and Yohanan Twersky, 167–83, 374–79. Boston: Teachers' Training Institutes, 1938.
100. Baron, Salo W. "Emphases in Jewish History." *Jewish Social Studies* 1, no. 1 (January 1939): 15–38.
101. Baron, Salo W. "Review of *The Jew in the Medieval World: A Sourcebook, 315–1791*, by Jacob Rader Marcus." *American Historical Review* 44, no. 2 (January 1939): 421–22.
102. Baron, Salo W. " 'In Medieval Europe.' Review of *The Jew in the Medieval Community*, by James Parkes." *Menorah Journal* 27, no. 1 (January–March 1939): 102–7.
103. Baron, Salo W. "Emphases in Jewish History." *Jewish Education* 11, no. 1 (April 1939): 8–22.
104. Baron, Salo W. "Review of *Studien zur jüdischen Selbstverwaltung im Altertum*, by Hans Zucker." *Jewish Social Studies* 1, no. 2 (April 1939): 264–65.
105. Baron, Salo W. "Cultural Problems of American Jewry." *Jewish Center* 17, no. 2 (June 1939): 7–11.

106. Baron, Salo W. "*Review of Occident and Orient: Moses Gaster Anniversary Volume*, edited by Bruno Schindler and Arthur Marmorstein." *Jewish Social Studies* 1, no. 3 (July 1939): 370–73.
107. Baron, Salo W. "Booknote on *Early Hebrew Printing in Spain and Portugal*, by Joshua Bloch." *Jewish Social Studies* 1, no. 3 (July 1939): 391–92.
108. Baron, Salo W. "Booknote on *Die jüdische Auswanderung aus Deutschland*, by Michael Traub." *Jewish Social Studies* 1, no. 3 (July 1939): 392.
109. Baron, Salo W. "Booknote on *Die Liebe zu Gott bei Moses Ben Maimon*, by Ernst Hoffman." *Jewish Social Studies* 1, no. 3 (July 1939): 391.
110. Baron, Salo W. "Booknote on *Sacrifices in Ancient Israel*, by W. O. E. Oesterley." *Jewish Social Studies* 1, no. 3 (July 1939): 389–90.
111. Baron, Salo W. "*Un iluminista sefardí de la época napoleónica*." *Judaica* 7, nos. 73–75 (July–September 1939): 68–77.
112. Baron, Salo W. "Moses Cohen Belinfante, a Maskil of Napoleon's Times." [In Yiddish.] *YIVO Bleter* 13, nos. 5–6 (September–October 1939): 429–59.
113. Baron, Salo W. "Review of *Jacob Emden: A Man of Controversy*, by Mortimer J. Cohen." *Jewish Social Studies* 1, no. 4 (October 1939): 483–87.
114. Baron, Salo W. "Review of *Transactions of the Jewish Historical Society of England*, vol. 13; and *Miscellanies*, vol. 3." *Jewish Social Studies* 1, no. 4 (October 1939): 467–69.
115. Baron, Salo W. "Review of *Moses and Monotheism*, by Sigmund Freud." *American Journal of Sociology* 45, no. 3 (November 1939): 471–77.
116. Baron, Salo W. "Cultural Problems of American Jewry." In *Harry L. Glucksman Annual Lectures 1: The Cultural Basis of American Life*, 16–26. New York: Jewish Welfare Board, 1939.
117. Baron, Salo W. "Booknote on *Asher ha-Levi's Book of Travels Written by Himself*, edited by Avraham Yaari." *Jewish Social Studies* 2, no. 1 (January 1940): 114.
118. Baron, Salo W. "Booknote on *De Gabirol à Abravanel*, by Saül Mézan." *Jewish Social Studies* 2, no. 1 (January 1940): 113.
119. Baron, Salo W. "Booknote on *Quelques portraits de nos maîtres des études sémitiques*, by David Sidersky." *Jewish Social Studies* 2, no. 1 (January 1940): 112–13.
120. Baron, Salo W. "Review of *Judaism and Christianity* by W. O. E. Oesterley, Herbert Loewe, Erwin I. J. Rosenthal." *American Historical Review* 45, no. 2 (January 1940): 358–61.
121. Baron, Salo W. "Review of *Letters to Emma Lazarus in the Columbia University Library*, by Ralph L. Rusk." *Jewish Social Studies* 2, no. 1 (January 1940): 108–9.
122. Baron, Salo W. "Review of *Magna Bibliotheca Anglo-Judaica*, by Cecil Roth." *Jewish Social Studies* 2, no. 1 (January 1940): 97–99.
123. Baron, Salo W. "Review of *The Pharisees: The Sociological Background of Their Faith*, by Louis Finkelstein." *Review of Religion* 4, no. 2 (January 1940): 196–99.
124. Baron, Salo W. "Review of *The Pharisees: The Sociological Background of Their Faith*, by Louis Finkelstein." *Journal of Biblical Literature* 59, no. 1 (March 1940): 60–67.
125. Baron, Salo W. "Great Britain and Damascus Jewry in 1860–61: An Archival Study." *Jewish Social Studies* 2, no. 2 (April 1940): 179–208.
126. Baron, Salo W. "Review of *Ausgewählte historische Schriften: Dokumenten-sammlung*, by Manfred Reifer." *Jewish Social Studies* 2, no. 2 (April 1940): 220.

127. Baron, Salo W. "Review of *Hayyim Habshush, Travels in Yemen*, edited by S. D. Goitein." *Jewish Social Studies* 2, no. 2 (April 1940): 226–27.
128. Baron, Salo W. "Review of *Scritti in onore di Dante Lattes*, edited by Guido Bedarisa." *Jewish Social Studies* 2, no. 2 (April 1940): 223–26.
129. Baron, Salo W. "*Jewish Social Studies*, 1938–39: A Selected Bibliography." *Jewish Social Studies* 2, no. 3 (July 1940): 305–88.
130. Baron, Salo W. "Reflections on the Future of the Jews of Europe." *Contemporary Jewish Record* 3 (July–August 1940): 355–69.
131. Baron, Salo W. "The Future of European Jewry." *Sentinel* 119, no. 5 (August 1, 1940): 6, 27–29.
132. Baron, Salo W. "The Future of European Jewry." *Sentinel* 119, no. 6 (August 8, 1940): 6, 22.
133. Baron, Salo W. "The Future of European Jewry." *Sentinel* 119, no. 7 (August 15, 1940): 6, 22.
134. Baron, Salo W. "Reflections on the Future." *Canadian Jewish Chronicle*, August 9, 1940: 8, 12.
135. Baron, Salo W. "Reflections on the Future." *Canadian Jewish Chronicle*, August 16, 1940: 8, 12.
136. Baron, Salo W. "The Future of European Jewry." *Jewish Forum* 23, no. 9 (October 1940): 164–65.
137. Baron, Salo W. "In Memoriam: Zevi Diesendruck." *American Historical Review* 46, no. 1 (October 1940): 255–56.
138. Baron, Salo W. "*Jewish Social Studies*, 1938–39: A Selected Bibliography (Concluded)." *Jewish Social Studies* 2, no. 4 (October 1940): 481–605.
139. Baron, Salo W. "Review of *Zur Zeit- und Geistesgeschichte des Judentums*, by Oskar Wolfsberg." *Historia Judaica* 2, no. 2 (October 1940): 119–20.
140. Baron, Salo W. "The Future of European Jewry [part I]." *Israel's Messenger* 37, no. 9 (December 20, 1940): 4, 21.
141. Baron, Salo W. "Simon Dubnow's Historical Method." [In Hebrew.] *Bitsaron* 2, no. 3 (December 1940): 212–15.
142. Baron, Salo W., and Shalom Spiegel. "In Memoriam: Zevi Diesendruck." *Proceedings of the American Academy for Jewish Research* 10 (1940): 3–4.
143. Baron, Salo W. Introduction to *The Cooperative Credit Movement in Palestine*, by Manoah L. Bialik, v. Ann Arbor, MI: Edwards Brothers, 1940.
144. Baron, Salo W. "Reflections on the Future of the Jews of Europe." *Jewish Social Service Quarterly* 17, no. 1 (1940): 5–19.
145. Cohen, Mortimer J., and Salo W. Baron. "Communications." *Jewish Social Studies* 2, no. 1 (January 1940): 117–23.
146. Baron, Salo W. "Bookplate on *Great Britain and Palestine, 1915–39*, and *Rebuilding Palestine*." *Jewish Social Studies* 3, no. 1 (January 1941): 121–22.
147. Baron, Salo W. "Bookplate on *The History of Israel*, by H. Wheeler Robinson." *Jewish Social Studies* 3, no. 1 (January 1941): 118–19.
148. Baron, Salo W. "The Future of European Jewry [part II]." *Israel's Messenger* 37, no. 10 (January 24, 1941): 4, 6.
149. Baron, Salo W. "Review of *The Jewish Theological Seminary of America: Semi-Centennial Volume*, edited by Cyrus Adler; and *The Hebrew University, Jerusalem: Its History and Development*." *Jewish Social Studies* 3, no. 1 (January 1941): 99–102.

BIBLIOGRAPHY

150. Baron, Salo W. "Review of *The Jew in the Contemporary World*, by A. L. Sachar." *American Historical Review* 46, no. 2 (January 1941): 455–56.
151. Baron, Salo W. "Review of *Jewish Fate and Future*, by Arthur Ruppin." *Jewish Digest* (January 1941): 89–92.
152. Baron, Salo W. "The Future of European Jewry [part III]." *Israel's Messenger* 37, no. 11 (February 21, 1941): 3.
153. Baron, Salo W. "Review of *Kaiser Julian und das Judentum*, by Joseph Vogt." *Jewish Social Studies* 3, no. 2 (April 1941): 220.
154. Baron, Salo W. "Yehudah Halevi: An Answer to an Historic Challenge." *Jewish Social Studies* 3, no. 3 (July 1941): 243–72.
155. Baron, Salo W. "Review of *The British Consulate in Jerusalem in Relation to the Jews of Palestine, 1838–1914*, part 1, *1838–1861*, by Albert M. Hyamson." *Jewish Social Studies* 3, no. 3 (July 1941): 343.
156. Baron, Salo W. "Bookplate on *Cultural Approaches to History*, edited by Caroline F. Ware." *Jewish Social Studies* 3, no. 4 (October 1941): 439–40.
157. Baron, Salo W. "Bookplate on *World of Nations: A Study of the National Implications in the Work of Karl Marx*, by Solomon F. Bloom." *Jewish Social Studies* 3, no. 4 (October 1941): 438–39.
158. Baron, Salo W. "Review of *A History of the Jewish Community in Wilno*, vol. 1: *Environment and Communal Organization*, by Israel Klausner." *Jewish Social Studies* 3, no. 4 (October 1941): 419–20.
159. Baron, Salo W. "The Economic Views of Maimonides." In *Essays on Maimonides: An Octocentennial Volume*, ed. Salo W. Baron, 127–264. New York: Columbia University Press, 1941.
160. Baron, Salo W. "Maimonides, the Leader and Lawgiver." In *Essays on Maimonides: An Octocentennial Volume*, ed. Salo W. Baron, 12–18. New York: Columbia University Press, 1941.
161. Baron, Salo W. "Rashi and the Community of Troyes." In *Rashi Anniversary Volume*, ed. H. L. Ginsberg, 47–71. New York: American Academy for Jewish Research, 1941.
162. Baron, Salo W. "Correspondence: Response to Review of *Essays on Maimonides*, by Solomon Zeitlin." *Jewish Quarterly Review* 32, no. 3 (January 1942): 321–25.
163. Baron, Salo W. "In Memoriam: David Yellin (1864–1941)." *Jewish Social Studies* 4, no. 2 (April 1942): 191.
164. Baron, Salo W. "Booknote on *Bohdan, Hetman of Ukraine*, by George Vernadsky." *Jewish Social Studies* 4, no. 3 (July 1942): 286.
165. Baron, Salo W. "Booknote on *Yehuda Halevy*, by David Druck." *Jewish Social Studies* 4, no. 3 (July 1942): 286.
166. Baron, Salo W. "Modern Capitalism and Jewish Fate." *Menorah Journal* 30, no. 2 (July–September 1942): 116–38.
167. Baron, Salo W. "Review of *Transactions of the Jewish Historical Society of England*, vol. 14, and *The British Consulate in Jerusalem*, part II, *1862–1914*, by Albert M. Hyamson." *Jewish Social Studies* 4, no. 4 (October 1942): 403–7.
168. Baron, Salo W. "What War Has Meant to Community Life." *Contemporary Jewish Record* 5, no. 5 (October 1942): 493–507.
169. Baron, Salo W. "Juda Levi: Respuesta a un desafío histórico." *Judaica* 10, nos. 112–14 (October–December 1942): 165–83.

BIBLIOGRAPHY

170. Baron, Salo W. "Review of *A History of the Jews in England*, by Cecil Roth." *Journal of Modern History* 14, no. 4 (December 1942): 522–23.
171. Baron, Salo W. "American and Jewish Destiny: A Semimillennial Experience." Address delivered under the auspices of the Synagogue Council of America on Monday Evening, October 12, 1942. New York: Spanish and Portuguese Congregation Shearith Israel, 1942.
172. Baron, Salo W. "A Contribution to the History of Palestine Relief and the Ransom of Captives in the Seventeenth Century." [In Hebrew.] *American Hebrew Year Book* 6 (1942): 167–79.
173. Baron, Salo W. "The Effect of the War on Jewish Community Life," Harry L. Glucksman Memorial Lecture for 1942. New York: Harry L. Glucksman Memorial Committee, 1942.
174. Baron, Salo W. Foreword to *Essays on Antisemitism*, ed. Koppel S. Pinson, vii–x. New York: Conference on Jewish Relations, 1942.
175. Baron, Salo W. "The Jewish Factor in Medieval Civilization." *Proceedings of the American Academy for Jewish Research* 12 (1942): 1–48.
176. Baron, Salo W. "Moses Cohen Belinfante: A Leader of Dutch-Jewish Enlightenment." *Historia Judaica* 5, no. 1 (April 1943): 1–26.
177. Baron, Salo W. "Review of *A History of the Jews in England*, by Cecil Roth." *Jewish Social Studies* 5, no. 1 (January 1943): 61–63.
178. Baron, Salo W. "Review of *The Jews in France*, by Elias Tcherikower." *Jewish Social Studies* 5, no. 1 (January 1943): 67–70.
179. Baron, Salo W. "Migration Speeds Progress." *Rescue: Information Bulletin of the HIAS* 1, no. 3–4 (March–April 1944): 3, 15–16.
180. Baron, Salo W., and Jeannette M. Baron. "Palestinian Messengers in America, 1849–79: A Record of Four Journeys." *Jewish Social Studies* 5, no. 2 (April 1943): 115–62.
181. Baron, Salo W., and Jeannette M. Baron. "Palestinian Messengers in America, 1849–79: A Record of Four Journeys (Concluded)." *Jewish Social Studies* 5, no. 3 (July 1943): 225–92.
182. Baron, Salo W. "Booknote on *The Graphic Historical Atlas of Palestine*, vol. 1, by F. A. Telihaber." *Jewish Social Studies* 5, no. 4 (October 1943): 407–8.
183. Baron, Salo W. "Booknote on *The Jewish Quarterly Review*, vol. 33, no. 2–3: Saadia Anniversary Issue." *Jewish Social Studies* 5, no. 4 (October 1943): 408.
184. Baron, Salo W., and Alexander Marx. "In Memoriam: Ismar Elbogen." *Proceedings of the American Academy for Jewish Research* 13 (1943): xxiv–xxvi.
185. Baron, Salo W., and Michael Higger. "In Memoriam: Viktor Aptowitzer." *Proceedings of the American Academy for Jewish Research* 13 (1943): xii–xiii.
186. Baron, Salo W. "Israel's Present: In Man's Faith and This Crisis," 78–82. New York: Council of Union of American Hebrew Congregations, 1943.
187. Baron, Salo W. "On the History of the Jewish Settlement in Tiberias in 1742–1744." [In Hebrew.] In *Jubilee Volume: A Tribute to Professor Alexander Marx*, ed. David Frankel, 79–88. New York: Jewish Theological Seminary of America, 1943.
188. Baron, Salo W. "Saadia's Communal Activities." In *Saadia Anniversary Volume*, 9–74. New York: American Academy for Jewish Research, 1943.
189. Baron, Salo W. "Vienna, Congress of (1814–1815)." In *The Universal Jewish Encyclopedia*, vol. 10., ed. Isaac Landman, 418–19. New York: Universal Jewish Encyclopedia, 1943.

BIBLIOGRAPHY

190. Baron, Salo W. "In Memoriam: Ismar Elbogen (1874-1943)." *Jewish Social Studies* 6, no. 1 (January 1944): 91-92.
191. Baron, Salo W. "Review of *Studies in Memory of Asher Gulak and Samuel Klein.*" *Jewish Social Studies* 6, no. 3 (July 1944): 275-78.
192. Baron, Salo W. "Review of *The Idea of Nationalism: A Study in Its Origins and Background*, by Hans Kohn." *Jewish Social Studies* 6, no. 4 (October 1944): 408-11.
193. Baron, Salo W. "Herman Bernstein." In *Dictionary of American Biography*, vol. 21, suppl. 1, ed. Harris E. Starr, 77-79. New York: Charles Scribner's Sons, 1944.
194. Baron, Salo W. "On the History of the Corfu Community and Their Organization." [In Hebrew.] In *Studies in Memory of Moses Schorr*, ed. Abraham Weiss and Louis Ginzberg [In Hebrew], 25-41. New York: Professor Moses Schorr Memorial Committee, 1944.
195. Baron, Salo W. "Booknote on *Henry Charles Lea, Minor Historical Writings and Other Essays*, edited by Arthur C. Howland." *Jewish Social Studies* 7, no. 1 (January 1945): 94.
196. Baron, Salo W. "At the Turning-Point." *Menorah Journal* 33, no. 1 (April-June 1945): 1-10.
197. Baron, Salo W. "The Spiritual Reconstruction of European Jewry." *Commentary Magazine* 1, no. 1 (November 1945): 4-12.
198. Baron, Salo W. "The Jewish Community of Tomorrow." In *Moral and Spiritual Foundations for the World of Tomorrow: The Centenary Series*, 75-83. New York: Congregation Emanu-El, 1945.
199. Baron, Salo W. "Levi Herzfeld: The First Jewish Economic Historian." In *Louis Ginzberg Jubilee Volume: On the Occasion of His Seventieth Birthday*, 75-104. New York: American Academy for Jewish Research, 1945.
200. Baron, Salo W. "The Spiritual Reconstruction of European Jewry." *Yearbook of the Central Conference of European Rabbis* 55 (1945): 193-206.
201. Baron, Salo W. "Introductory Statement to *Tentative List of Jewish Cultural Treasures in Axis-Occupied Countries.*" Supplement, *Jewish Social Studies* 8, no. 1 (January 1946): 5-11.
202. Baron, Salo W. Foreword to *Tentative List of Jewish Educational Institutions in Axis-Occupied Countries*. Supplement, *Jewish Social Studies* 8, no. 3 (July 1946): 5-8.
203. Baron, Salo W. Foreword to *Essays on Antisemitism*, 2nd ed., ed. Koppel S. Pinson, vii-ix. New York: Conference on Jewish Relations, 1946.
204. Baron, Salo W. "Booknote on *The Arab Awakening: The Story of the Arab National Movement*, by George Antoninus." *Jewish Social Studies* 9, no. 2 (April 1947): 191-92.
205. Baron, Salo W. "Booknote on *Peoples of the Soviet Union*, by Corliss Lamont." *Jewish Social Studies* 9, no. 2 (April 1947): 190-91.
206. Baron, Salo W. "How South African Jewry Should Plan Its Future." *Jewish Affairs* 2, no. 4 (April 1947): 4-9.
207. Baron, Salo W. "Prospects for the Diaspora." *New Palestine* 37, no. 20 (June 20, 1947): 143-46.
208. Baron, Salo W. "Calls on JWB to Change from Service Agency to Central Guiding Body." *JWB Circle* 2, no. 6 (June-July 1947): 5, 14.
209. Baron, Salo W. Foreword to *Tentative List of Jewish Periodicals in Axis-Occupied Countries*. Supplement, *Jewish Social Studies* 9, no. 3 (July 1947): 7-9.

210. Baron, Salo W. "Booknote on *American Policy Toward Palestine*, by C. J. Friedrich." *Journal of Modern History* 19, no. 3 (September 1947): 286.
211. Baron, Salo W. "Religious Liberty: Area of Investigation." In *Seminar on Religion and Democracy*, 1–6. New York: Columbia University, 1947.
212. Baron, Salo W. "Work Among Our Youth." In *Proceedings of the Plenary Session*, 55, 61–64. Montreal: Canadian Jewish Congress, 1947.
213. Baron, Salo W. "The Year in Retrospect." *American Jewish Year Book* 49 (1947): 103–22.
214. Baron, Salo W. "Booknote on *Biographical Sketch of H. P. Chajes*, by Kuno Trau and Michael Karyan." *Jewish Social Studies* 10, no. 1 (January 1948): 97–98.
215. Baron, Salo W. Foreword to *Papers Given at the Seminar on Religion and Democracy of Columbia University*. *Review of Religion* 12, no. 2 (January 1948): 116.
216. Baron, Salo W. Preface to *Addenda and Corrigenda to Tentative List Jewish Cultural Treasures in Axis-Occupied Countries*. Supplement, *Jewish Social Studies* 10, no. 1 (January 1948): 3–4.
217. Baron, Salo W. "Review of *The Emergence of the Jewish Problem, 1878–1939*, by James Parkes." *Middle East Journal* 2 (January 1948): 96–97.
218. Baron, Salo W. "The Jewish Community and Jewish Education." *Jewish Education* 19, no. 2 (March 1948): 7–13.
219. Baron, Salo W. Introduction to *Tentative List Jewish Publishers of Judaica and Hebraica in Axis-Occupied Countries*. Supplement, *Jewish Social Studies* 10, no. 2 (April 1948): 5–7.
220. Baron, Salo W. "Judaism Tomorrow" [review of *The Future of the American Jew*, by Mordecai Kaplan]. *New York Times Book Review*, May 2, 1948, 12.
221. Baron, Salo W. "Report of the JWB Survey Commission." In *The JWB Survey*, ed. Oscar I. Janowsky, vii–xiii. New York: Dial, 1948.
222. Baron, Salo W. "Weizmann Tells His Own Story" [review of *Trial and Error*, by Chaim Weizmann]. *New York Times Book Review*, January 23, 1949, 1.
223. Baron, Salo W. "Review of *Civilization on Trial*, by Arnold J. Toynbee." *Political Science Quarterly* 64, no. 1 (March 1949): 110–13.
224. Baron, Salo W. "The Impact of the Revolution of 1848 on Jewish Emancipation." *Jewish Social Studies* 11, no. 3 (July 1949): 195–248.
225. Baron, Salo W. "Review of *The American Jewish Year Book 5709 (1948–49)*, edited by Sidney J. Jacobs." *Sentinel* 169, no. 1 (July 7, 1949): 28.
226. Baron, Salo W. "A Diplomatic Episode in the Spanish-Portuguese Community of London (1841)." *Bulletin Congregation Habonim* 9, no. 9 (September 1949): 12–16.
227. Baron, Salo W. "The Revolution of 1848 and Jewish Scholarship, Part I: France, the United States and Italy." *Proceedings of the American Academy for Jewish Research* 18 (1949): 1–66.
228. Baron, Salo W. "Opening Remarks to Conference on Problem of Research in the Study of the Jewish Catastrophe, 1939–1945." *Jewish Social Studies* 12, no. 1 (January 1950): 13–16.
229. Baron, Salo W. "American Jewish History: Problems and Methods." *Publications of the American Jewish Historical Society* 39, no. 3 (March 1950): 207–66.
230. Baron, Salo W. "Community Responsibility for Jewish Education." *B'nai B'rith Messenger* 53, no. 33 (March 31, 1950): 22–23.

BIBLIOGRAPHY

231. Baron, Salo W. "Letter: Rabbi Markowitz Misled on Census Stand." *National Jewish Post and Opinion*, May 19, 1950: 13.
232. Baron, Salo W. "Moritz Steinschneider's Contributions to Jewish Historiography." In *Alexander Marx Jubilee Volume: On the Occasion of His Seventieth Birthday*, ed. Saul Lieberman, 83–148. New York: Jewish Theological Seminary of America, 1950.
233. Baron, Salo W. "Review of *A Documentary History of the Jews in the United States, 1654–1875*, edited by Morris Schappes." *Jewish Social Studies* 13, no. 1 (January 1951): 77–80.
234. Baron, Salo W. "The Choice Is Man's" [review of *The Legacy of Maimonides*, by Ben Zion Bokser]. *New York Times Book Review*, February 18, 1951, 25.
235. Baron, Salo W. "Review of *Les Juifs dans les Pays-Bas au moyen-âge*, by Jean Stengers." *Speculum* 26, no. 2 (April 1951): 407–9.
236. Baron, Salo W. "Booknote on *Dr. Mayer Evner: Ein jüdisches Leben*, by Manfred Reifer." *Jewish Social Studies* 13, no. 3 (July 1951): 284–85.237. Baron, Salo W. "Booknote on *Hitler Directs His War*, edited by Felix Gilbert." *Jewish Social Studies* 13, no. 3 (July 1951): 283.
238. Baron, Salo W. "Booknote on *Nietzsche: Philosopher, Psychologist, Antichrist*, by Walter A. Kaufmann." *Jewish Social Studies* 13, no. 3 (July 1951): 283–84.
239. Baron, Salo W. "Booknote on *The Romance of the Mendelssohns*, by Jacques Petitpierre." *Jewish Social Studies* 13, no. 3 (July 1951): 282.
240. Baron, Salo W. "Booknote on *South African Jews in World War II*." *Jewish Social Studies* 13, no. 3 (July 1951): 285–86.
241. Baron, Salo W. "Booknote on *Understanding History: A Primer of Historical Method*, by Louis Gottschalk." *Jewish Social Studies* 13, no. 3 (July 1951): 280–81.
242. Baron, Salo W. "Review of *The Great Synagogue, London, 1690–1940*, by Cecil Roth." *Jewish Social Studies* 13, no. 3 (July 1951): 261–62.
243. Baron, Salo W. "Thread of Culture" [review of *Hellenism in Jewish Palestine*, by Saul Lieberman]. *New York Times Book Review*, July 29, 1951, 7.
244. Baron, Salo W. "New Horizons in Jewish History." In *Freedom and Reason: Studies in Philosophy and Jewish Culture in Memory of Morris Raphael Cohen*, ed. Salo W. Baron, Ernest Nagel, and Koppel S. Pinson, 337–53. New York: Conference on Jewish Relations, 1951.
245. Baron, Salo W. "Review of *Galen on Jews and Christians*, by Richard Walzer." *Journal of the History of Medicine and Allied Sciences* 6 (1951): 428–29.
246. Baron, Salo W. "The Revolution of 1848 and Jewish Scholarship, Part II: Austria." *Proceedings of the American Academy for Jewish Research* 20 (1951): 1–100.
247. Baron, Salo W. "Guilt and History" [review of *The Foot of Pride*, by Malcolm Hay, and *The American Jew: Character and Destiny*, by Ludwig Lewisohn]. *New Republic*, January 21, 1952, 19–20.
248. Baron, Salo W. "Aspects of the Jewish Communal Crisis in 1848." *Jewish Social Studies* 14, no. 2 (April 1952): 99–144.
249. Baron, Salo W. "History of Zionist Movement" [review of *Fulfillment: The Story of Zionism*, by Rufus Learsi]. *Saturday Review*, April 12, 1952, 37–38.
250. Baron, Salo W. "A Revolutionary Transformation of Jewish Community." *ADL Bulletin* 9, no. 5 (May 1952): 2.
251. Baron, Salo W. "Booknote of *A History of Greek Literature*, and *A History of Latin Literature*, by Moses Hadas." *Jewish Social Studies* 14, no. 3 (July 1952): 277–78.

252. Baron, Salo W. "Impact of Wars on Religion." *Political Science Quarterly* 67, no. 4 (December 1952): 534–72.
253. Baron, Salo W. "Hebrew Civilization." In *Background of the Middle East*, ed. Ernst Jackh, 33–42. Ithaca, NY: Cornell University Press, 1952.
254. Baron, Salo W. "Hebrew Civilization." In *Encyclopedia Americana*, vol. 19, 38k–38n. New York: Americana Corp., 1952.
255. Baron, Salo W. "Booknote on *The Fall of Jerusalem and the Christian Church*, by S. G. F. Brandon." *Jewish Social Studies* 15, no. 1 (January 1953): 83.
256. Baron, Salo W. "Review of *Contemporary Jewry: A Survey of Social, Cultural, Economic and Political Conditions*, by Israel Cohen." *Jewish Social Studies* 15, no. 1 (January 1953): 90–92.
257. Baron, Salo W. "The Cold War and Jewry." *American Zionist* 43, no. 7 (February 5, 1953): 21–24.
258. Baron, Salo W. "Faith and History in the Jewish Past." [In Hebrew.] *Megillot* (March 1953): 5–14.
259. Baron, Salo W. "Review of *Seder R. Amram Gaon*, part 1, by David Hedegard." *Jewish Social Studies* 15, no. 2 (April 1953): 178–79.
260. Baron, Salo W. "Review of *The New State of Israel*, by Gerald de Gaury." *Political Science Quarterly* 68, no. 2 (June 1953): 287–88.
261. Baron, Salo W. "Booknote on *Addresses and Lectures, by Zevi (Hirsch) Perez Chajes*." *Jewish Social Studies* 15, no. 3–4 (July–October 1953): 329.
262. Baron, Salo W. "Booknote on *Handbook of Denominations in the United States*, by Frank S. Mead." *Jewish Social Studies* 15, nos. 3–4 (July–October 1953): 332.
263. Baron, Salo W. "Booknote on *Menschen und Ideen: Erinnerungen*." *Jewish Social Studies* 15, nos. 3–4 (July–October 1953): 329.
264. Baron, Salo W. "Booknote on *The Protestant Crusade 1800–1860: The Growth of Bigotry and the Anti-Catholic Movement in America*, by Ray Allen Billington." *Jewish Social Studies* 15, nos. 3–4 (July–October 1953): 331–32.
265. Baron, Salo W. "Review of *Discourse on the Status of Jews in Venice*, by Simha (Simone) Luzzatto," *Jewish Social Studies* 15, nos. 3–4 (July–October 1953): 313–14.
266. Baron, Salo W. "*Revolutions of 1848: A Social History*, by Priscilla Robertson." *Jewish Social Studies* 15, nos. 3–4 (July–October 1953): 330.
267. Baron, Salo W. "Some Studies of Judaism" [review of *Landmarks and Goals*, by Abraham A. Neuman]. *New York Times Book Review*, October 25, 1953, 46.
268. Baron, Salo W. "Church and State Debates in the Jewish Community of 1848." In *Mordecai M. Kaplan Jubilee Volume*, ed. Moshe Davis, 49–72. New York: Jewish Theological Seminary, 1953.
269. Baron, Salo W., and Ralph Marcus. "In Memoriam: Eugen Täubler." *Proceedings of the American Academy for Jewish Research* 22 (1953): xxxi–xxxiv.
270. Baron, Salo W. "Jewish Immigration and Communal Conflicts in Seventeenth-Century Corfu." In *The Joshua Starr Memorial Volume: Studies in History and Philosophy*, 169–82. New York: Conference on Jewish Relations, 1953.
271. Baron, Salo W. "Samuel David Luzzatto (Shadal) and the Revolution of 1848." [In Hebrew.] In *Sefer Assaf: Simha Assaf Jubilee Volume*, ed. Umberto Cassutto et al., 40–63. Jerusalem: Mosad ha-Rav Kook, 1953.
272. Baron, Salo W. "American Jewish Communal Pioneering." *Publications of the American Jewish Historical Quarterly* 43, no. 3 (March 1954): 133–50.

BIBLIOGRAPHY

273. Baron, Salo W. "Report of the President, 1953–1955." *Publications of the American Jewish Historical Society* 44, no. 4 (June 1954): 243–47.
274. Baron, Salo W. "Some of the Tercentenary's Historic Lessons." *Publications of the American Jewish Historical Society* 44, no. 4 (June 1954): 199–209.
275. Baron, Salo W. "Booknote on *David Kimhi's Hebrew Grammar (Mikhlol): Systematically Presented and Critically Arranged*, by William Chomsky." *Jewish Social Studies* 15, nos. 3–4 (July–October 1954): 328.
276. Baron, Salo W. "Three Hundred Years of American Jewry." *300* (September 1954): 3, 5.
277. Baron, Salo W. "The Three Centuries of Jewish Experience in America." *New York Times Book Review*, September 12, 1954, 5.
278. Baron, Salo W. "Three Hundred Years of American Jewry." *Greater St. Louis Jewish Star*, October 11, 1954, 5.
279. Baron, Salo W. "Trescientos años de vida judia en los Estados Unitos." *Tribuna israelita* 120 (November 1954): 26–27.
280. Baron, Salo W. "American Jewish History: Problems and Methods." [In Hebrew.] *ha-Doar* 35, no. 2 (November 12, 1954): 25.
281. Baron, Salo W. "American Jewish Communal Pioneering." [In Yiddish.] *Di Tsukunft* 59 (1954): 251–59.
282. Baron, Salo W. "The Future of American Jewry." [In Hebrew.] *Gesher* 2–3 (1954): 9–17.
283. Baron, Salo W. Foreword to *The Jewish Community in Westchester, 1843–1925*, by Stuart E. Rosenberg, 1. New York: Columbia University Press, 1954.
284. Baron, Salo W. Foreword to *The Records of the Earliest Jewish Community in the New World*, by Arnold Wiznitzer, vii–viii. New York: American Jewish Historical Society, 1954.
285. Baron, Salo W. "Historic Jerusalem: City, Holy and Eternal." In *Historic Jerusalem: City, Holy and Eternal*, 11–32. New York: Hemisphere, 1954.
286. Baron, Salo W., and Joseph L. Blau. Introduction to *Judaism, Postbiblical and Talmudic Period*, ed. Salo W. Baron and Joseph L. Blau, xi–xxvi. New York: Liberal Arts Press, 1954.
287. Baron, Salo W. "Report on Israel." In *Evolution in the Middle East: Reform, Revolt and Change*, ed. Sydney Nettleton Fisher, 77–85. Washington, DC: Middle East Institute, 1954.
288. Baron, Salo W. "Newly-Published Book Bares Nazis' Sadistic Cruelties Against Millions of Europe's Jews" [review of *Harvest of Hate: The Nazi Program for the Extermination of the Jews in Europe*, by Leon Poliakov]. *Sentinel* 191, no. 3 (February 3, 1955): 26.
289. Baron, Salo W. "Communal Responsibility for Jewish Social Research." *Jewish Social Studies* 17, no. 3 (July 1955): 242–45.
290. Baron, Salo W. "Opening Statement at the Tercentenary Conference on American Jewish Sociology." *Jewish Social Studies* 17, no. 3 (July 1955): 175–76.
291. Baron, Salo W. "Review of *Jewish Symbols in the Greco-Roman Period*, vols. 1–2, by Erwin R. Goodenough." *Journal of Biblical Literature* 74, no. 3 (September 1955): 196–99.
292. Baron, Salo W. "Review of *Third and Fourth Books of the Maccabees*, by Moses Hadas." *Journal of Biblical Literature* 74, no. 3 (September 1955): 280–81.

293. Baron, Salo W. "Booknote on *The Age of Reformation*, by E. Harris Harrison." *Jewish Social Studies* 17, no. 4 (October 1955): 359.
294. Baron, Salo W. "Are the Jews Still the People of the Book?" Oscar Hillel Plotkin Lecture, 1–20. Glencoe, IL: Oscar Hillel Plotkin Library, 1955.
295. Baron, Salo W. "Conference Theme on the Writing of American Jewish History." *Publications of the American Jewish Historical Society* 46, no. 3 (March 1956): 137–40.
296. Baron, Salo W. "Tireless Fighter" [review of *The Personal Letters of Stephen Wise*, by Justine Wise Polier, and James Waterman Wise]. *New York Times Book Review*, July 8, 1956, 18.
297. Baron, Salo W. "One Hundred Years [of] Jewish History in America." *B'nai B'rith Messenger* 59, no. 49 (July 13, 1956): 8, 20.
298. Baron, Salo W. "Review of *Eretz Israel under Ottoman Rule*, by Itzhak Ben-Zvi." *Middle Eastern Affairs* 7, nos. 8–9 (August–September 1956): 302–3.
299. Baron, Salo W. "A Vilna Excommunication and the Great Powers." *Horeb* 12 (September 1956): 62–69.
300. Baron, Salo W. "Review of *An Old Faith in the New World: Portrait of Shearith Israel, 1654-1954*, by David and Tamar de Sola Pool." *American Historical Review* 62, no. 1 (October 1956): 246–47.
301. Baron, Salo W. "The Emancipation Movement and American Jewry." [In Hebrew.] *Eretz Israel* 4 (1956): 205–14.
302. Baron, Salo W. Foreword to *Monumental Inscriptions in the Burial Ground of the Jewish Synagogue at Bridgetown, Barbados*, by E. M. Shilstone, i–ii. London: University College London, 1956.
303. Baron, Salo W. "In Memoriam: Jacob Shatzky (1893-1956)." [In Yiddish.] *YIVO Bleter* 40 (1956): 234–37.
304. Baron, Salo W. "*En lisant Maimonide*." in *Dix ans après la chute de Hitler, 1945-1955*, ed. Jonah M. Machover, 67–76. Paris: Éditions du Centre, 1956.
305. Baron, Salo W. "Maimonides' Significance to Our Generation." In *Maimonides: His Teachings and Personality. Essays on the Occasion of the 750th Anniversary of His Death*, ed. Simon Federbush, 7–16. New York: Cultural Department of the World Jewish Congress, 1956.
306. Baron, Salo W. "Second and Third Commonwealth: Parallels and Differences." In *Israel: Its Role in Civilization*, ed. Moshe Davis, 58–66. New York: Harper & Brothers, 1956.
307. Baron, Salo W. "Tempered by Hardship" [review of *Louis Marshall: Champion of Liberty*, edited by Charles Reznikoff]. *New York Times Magazine*, July 21, 1957, 8.
308. Baron, Salo W. "Palestine, History, the New Settlement, 1800–1882, part 2: The Jewish Settlement." [In Hebrew.] In *Encyclopedia ha-Ivrit*, vol. 6, cols. 504–508 (1957).
309. Baron, Salo W. "Basic Problems of the Dispersions in the Free World." [In Hebrew.] *Hazit* 4 (1957–58): 230–36.
310. Baron, Salo W. "The Place of American Jewry in Jewish History." [In Hebrew.] *ha-Doar* 37, no. 17 (February 21, 1958): 303–4.
311. Baron, Salo W. "The Place of American Jewry in Jewish History." [In Hebrew.] *ha-Doar* 38, no. 18 (February 28, 1958): 323–24.

BIBLIOGRAPHY

312. Baron, Salo W. "Can American Jewry Be Culturally Creative?" *Jewish Heritage* 1, no. 2 (Spring 1958): 11–14, 58.
313. Bernstein, Edgar. "Salo Baron's Impact on South African Jewry." *Jewish Affairs* 13, no. 4 (April 1958): 20–23.
314. Baron, Salo W. "An Historian Looks at South African Jewry." *Jewish Affairs* 13, no. 5 (May 1958): 4–8.
315. Baron, Salo W. "An Historian Looks at South African Jewry." *Jewish Affairs* 13, no. 6 (June 1958): 13–16.
316. Baron, Salo W. "Diaspora and Zion." *Jewish Frontier* 25, no. 7 (July 1958): 7–12.
317. Baron, Salo W. "U.S. Jewry's Cultural Future." *B'nai B'rith Messenger* 62, no. 7 (September 19, 1958): 24.
318. Baron, Salo W. Foreword to *Max Nordau, Philosopher of Human Solidarity*, by Meir Ben-Horin, ix–x. New York: Conference on Jewish Social Studies, 1958.
319. Baron, Salo W. "Concluding Remarks to the Joint Conference on the Impact of Israel on the American Jewish Community." *Jewish Social Studies* 21, no. 1 (January 1959): 87–88.
320. Baron, Salo W. "The Dialogue Between Israel and the Diaspora." *Forum for the Problems of Zionism, Jewry and the State of Israel* 4 (Spring 1959): 236–44.
321. Baron, Salo W. "Bookplate on *Demographic Yearbook 1957*." *Jewish Social Studies* 21, no. 3 (July 1959): 214.
322. Baron, Salo W. "The Israel-Diaspora Dialogue." *World Jewry* 6, no. 11 (September 1959): 7–8.
323. Baron, Salo W. "*Le Dialogue entre Israel et la Diaspora.*" *L'Arche* 36 (December 1959): 26–30.
324. Baron, Salo W. Foreword to *Karaites in Byzantium: The Formative Years, 970–1100*, by Zvi Ankori, vii–viii. New York: Columbia University Press, 1959.
325. Baron, Salo W. "The Jewish State and the Jewish People from the Historic Perspective." In *Proceedings of the Fourth Plenary Assembly of the World Jewish Congress*, 148–164. Geneva: World Jewish Congress, 1959.
326. Baron, Salo W. "Moses Maimonides (1135–1204)." In *Great Jewish Personalities in Ancient and Medieval Times*, vol. 1, ed. Simon Noveck, 204–30. New York: B'nai B'rith Great Books, 1959.
327. Baron, Salo W. "*Etapas de la emancipacion judia.*" *Diogenes* 29 (March 1960): 65–94.
328. Baron, Salo W. "*Etapas de la emancipacion judia.*" *Diogenes* 29 (March 1960): 71–101.
329. Baron, Salo W. "New Approaches to Jewish Emancipation." *Diogenes* 29 (Spring 1960): 56–81.
330. Baron, Salo W. "Who Is a Jew? Some Historical Reflections." *Midstream* 6, no. 2 (Spring 1960): 5–16.
331. Baron, Salo W., and Cecil Roth. "Communications." *Jewish Social Studies* 22, no. 2 (April 1960): 125–27.
332. Baron, Salo W. "Review of *Josel von Rosheim*, by Selma Stern." *American Historical Review* 65, no. 3 (April 1960): 670.
333. Baron, Salo W. "Who Is A Jew? Some Historical Reflections." [In Hebrew.] *ha-Doar* 40, no. 24 (May 6, 1960): 457–58.

334. Baron, Salo W. "Who Is A Jew? Some Historical Reflections." [In Hebrew.] *ha-Doar* 40, no. 25 (May 13, 1960): 475–77.
335. Baron, Salo W. "*Que est Juif? Quelques considérations historiques*." *L'Arche* 46 (November 1960): 48–51.
336. Baron, Salo W. Foreword to *Guide to Jewish History Under Nazi Impact*, by Jacob Robinson and Philip Friedman, xix–xxi. New York: YIVO, 1960.
337. Baron, Salo W. "The Image of the Rabbi in Traditional Literature." *Proceedings of the Rabbinical Assembly of America* 24 (1960): 84–92.
338. Baron, Salo W. "In Memoriam: Philip Friedman." *Proceedings of the American Academy for Jewish Research* 29 (1960): 1–7.
339. Baron, Salo W. "Introductory Remarks." *Herzl Year Book* 3 (1960): 11–14.
340. Baron, Salo W. "Plenitude of Apostolic Powers and Medieval Jewish Serfdom." [In Hebrew.] In *Yitzhak F. Baer Jubilee Volume: On the Occasion of his Seventieth Birthday*, ed. Salo W. Baron, Benzion Dinur, Shmuel Ettinger, and Israel Halpern, 102–24. Jerusalem: Historical Society of Israel, 1960.
341. Baron, Salo W. "The Long Road That Led to Israel" [review of *The Idea of the Jewish State*, by Ben Halpern]. *New York Times Book Review*, January 22, 1961, 7, 35.
342. Baron, Salo W. "In Memoriam: Isaiah Sonne (1887–1960)." *Jewish Social Studies* 23, no. 2 (April 1961): 130–32.
343. Baron, Salo W. "Testimony at the Eichmann Trial." [In Hebrew.] *ha-Doar* 41, no. 25 (May 5, 1961): 434–35.
344. Baron, Salo W. "*Der Hass auf den Anderen: Aussagen im Eichmann–Prozess in Jerusalem*." *Frankfurter Allgemeine Zeitung*, May 17, 1961, 13.
345. Baron, Salo W. "The Image of the Rabbi in Traditional Literature." [In Hebrew.] *ha-Doar* 41, no. 27 (May 19, 1961): 476–78.
346. Baron, Salo W. "In Memoriam: Koppel Shub Pinson." *Jewish Social Studies* 23, no. 3 (July 1961): 138–42.
347. Baron, Salo W. "*Interdependencia judia y la Alianza*." *Revista de la Alliance* 35 (October 1961): 25–31.
348. Baron, Salo W. "Jewish Interdependence and the Alliance." *Alliance Review* 15, no. 35 (Winter 1961): 23–29.
349. Schultz, Andrew B. "Interview: Baron and Jewish History." *Columbia Daily Spectator*, December 13, 1961, 4.
350. Baron, Salo W. "*Quien es Judio*: Who is a Jew? Some Historical Reflections." *Davar* 92 (January–March 1962): 64–82.
351. Baron, Salo W. "World Dimensions of Jewish History." [In Hebrew.] *ha-Doar* 42, no. 24 (April 13, 1962): 382–84.
352. Baron, Salo W. "Introductory Remarks to *Papers and Proceedings on the Emergence of New African States and World Jewry*." *Jewish Social Studies* 24, no. 2 (April 1962): 67–68.
353. Baron, Salo W. "World Dimensions of Jewish History." [In Hebrew.] *ha-Doar* 42, no. 25 (May 4, 1962): 416–18.
354. Baron, Salo W. "*Berichtigung*." *Zeitschrift der Savigny-Stiftung für Rechtsgeschichte* 79, no. 1 (August 1962): 547–48.
355. Baron, Salo W. "*Trois siècles d'esprit pionnier dans le communautés juives*." *L'Arche* 67–68 (August–September 1962): 58–62.
356. Baron, Salo W. "Anti-Semitism." In *Encyclopaedia Britannica*, vol. 2 (1962): 75–78.

BIBLIOGRAPHY

357. Baron, Salo W. "Exilarch." In *Encyclopaedia Britannica*, vol. 8 (1962): 967–68.
358. Baron, Salo W. "From a Historian's Notebook: European Jewry Before and After Hitler." *American Jewish Year Book* 63 (1962): 3–53.
359. Baron, Salo W. "The Future of Jewish Culture in the United States." *JPS Bookmark* 9, no. 2 (1962): 7–9.
360. Baron, Salo W. "The Jewish Commonwealth and the Dispersions." In *The Ethic of Power: The Interplay of Religion, Philosophy and Politics*, ed. Harold D. Lasswell and Harlan Cleveland, 3–25. New York: Harper, 1962.
361. Baron, Salo W. "Josel of Rosheim." In *Encyclopaedia Britannica*, vol. 13 (1962): 150.
362. Baron, Salo W. "Medieval Nationalism and Jewish Serfdom." In *Studies and Essays in Honor of Abraham A. Neuman*, ed. Meir Ben-Horin, Bernard D. Weinryb, and Solomon Zeitlin, 17–48. Leiden: Brill, 1962.
363. Baron, Salo W. "Pharisees." In *Encyclopaedia Britannica*, vol. 17 (1962): 689–90.
364. Baron, Salo W. "Some Recent Literature on the History of the Jews in the Pre-Emancipation Era (1300–1800)." *Journal of World History* 7, no. 1 (1962): 137–71.
365. Baron, Salo W. "World Dimensions of Jewish History." Leo Baeck Memorial Lecture 5, 1–26. New York: Leo Baeck Institute, 1962.
366. Baron, Salo W. "Booknote on *Der Parlamentarier Eduard Lasker und die parlamentarische Stilentwicklung der Jahre 1867–1884*, by Richard W. Wiel." *Jewish Social Studies* 25, no. 1 (January 1963): 93–94.
367. Baron, Salo W. "Booknote on *A Study in Austrian Intellectual History: From Late Baroque to Romanticism*, by Robert A. Kann." *Jewish Social Studies* 25, no. 1 (January 1963): 93.
368. Baron, Salo W. "Interview: Jewish College Students Are More Religious." *National Jewish Post and Opinion* 18, no. 26 (March 1, 1963): 4–5.
369. Baron, Salo W. "The Problem of Teaching Religion." *Columbia College Today* 10, no. 3 (Spring–Summer 1963): 25–27.
370. Baron, Salo W. "In Memoriam: Israel Spanier Wechsler (1886–1962)." *Jewish Social Studies* 25, no. 2 (April 1963): 100–01.
371. Baron, Salo W. "American Jewish Scholarship and World Jewry." *American Jewish Historical Quarterly* 52, no. 4 (June 1963): 274–82.
372. Baron, Salo W. " 'A Reply' Upon Receiving the Lee M. Friedman Award." *American Jewish Historical Quarterly* 52, no. 4 (June 1963): 332–33.
373. Baron, Salo W. "In Memoriam: David Rosenstein (1895–1963)." *Jewish Social Studies* 25, no. 3 (July 1963): 172–73.
374. Baron, Salo W. "Newer Emphases in Jewish History." *Jewish Social Studies* 25, no. 4 (October 1963): 235–48.
375. Baron, Salo W. "The Dialogue Between Israel and the Diaspora." In *Mission of Israel*, ed. Jacob Baal-Teshuva, 306–20. New York: Robert Speller & Sons, 1963.
376. Baron, Salo W. "The Problem of Teaching Religion." *Bulletin of the National Foundation for Jewish Culture* 3, no. 1 (1963).
377. Baron, Salo W. "Testimonies at the Eichmann Trial." In *The State Against Adolf Eichmann*, vol. 1., 306–20. Jerusalem: Israel Ministry of Justice, 1963.
378. Baron, Salo W. "World Dimensions of Jewish History." In *Simon Dubnow: The Man and His Work*, ed. Aaron Steinberg, 26–40. Paris: World Jewish Congress, 1963.
379. Baron, Salo W. "The Cultural Potential of American Jewry." *Hadassah Magazine* 45, no. 6 (February 1964): 6, 28.

BIBLIOGRAPHY

380. Baron, Salo W. "Medieval Folklore and Jewish Fate." *Jewish Heritage* 6, no. 4 (Spring 1964): 13–18.
381. Baron, Salo W. "Action Through Knowledge." *Torch* 23, no. 3 (Summer 1964): 5–7.
382. Baron, Salo W. "Whither American Jews? Can Faith and Tradition Continue to Flourish in the World's Richest Democracy?" *London Jewish Chronicle*, September 4, 1964, 49–50.
383. Baron, Salo W. Foreword to *The Meaning of Jewish History*, vol. 1, by Jacob Agus, vii–viii. New York: Abelard-Shuman, 1964.
384. Baron, Salo W. "From Colonial Mansion to Skyscraper: An Emerging Pattern of Hebraic Studies." *Rutgers Hebraic Studies* 1 (1964): 3–24.
385. Baron, Salo W. "Ghetto and Emancipation." In *The Menorah Treasury: Harvest of Half a Century*, ed. Leo W. Schwarz, 50–63. Philadelphia: Jewish Publication Society, 1964.
386. Baron, Salo W. "The Nazi Impact on European Jewry." In *Exhibition: Life, Struggle and Uprising in the Warsaw Ghetto*, 10–11. New York: YIVO, 1964.
387. Baron, Salo W. "Newer Emphases in Jewish History." [In Hebrew.] *ha-Doar* 45, no. 27 (May 28, 1965): 485–88.
388. Baron, Salo W. "Interview." *Reconstructionist* 21, no. 9 (June 11, 1965): 12–21.
389. Baron, Salo W. "Millennial Heritage." *World Jewry* 9, no. 5 (September–October 1965): 19–20.
390. Baron, Salo W. "Can American Jewry Be Culturally Creative?" In *Jewish Heritage Reader*, ed. Lily Edelman, 301–5. New York: Taplinger, 1965.
391. Baron, Salo W. Foreword to *America Is Different: The Search for Jewish Identity*, by Stuart E. Rosenberg, vii–ix. New York: Thomas Nelson, 1965.
392. Baron, Salo W. Foreword to *A History of Jewish Crafts and Guilds*, by Mark Wischnitzer, vii–viii. New York: Jonathan David, 1965.
393. Baron, Salo W. "Introduction: Georg Brandes and Lord Beaconsfield." In *Lord Beaconsfield: A Study in Benjamin Disraeli*, by Georg Brandes, v–xiv. New York: Thomas Y. Crowell 1965.
394. Baron, Salo W. "Jewish Community." In *Standard Jewish Encyclopedia*, 469–75. New ed. Garden City, NY: Doubleday, 1965.
395. Baron, Salo W. "John Calvin and the Jews." In *Harry Austryn Wolfson Jubilee Volume: On the Occasion of His Seventy-Fifth Birthday*, vol. 1, 141–63. Jerusalem: American Academy for Jewish Research, 1965.
396. Baron, Salo W. "Medieval Folklore and Jewish Fate." In *Jewish Heritage Reader*, ed. Lily Edelman, 13–18. New York: Taplinger, 1965.
397. Baron, Salo W. "Moses Maimonides (1135–1204)." In *Molders of the Jewish Mind*, 75–101. Washington, DC: B'nai B'rith Department of Adult Jewish Education, 1966.
398. Baron, Salo W. "Some Historical Lessons for Jewish Philanthropy." In *The Critical Challenges to Philanthropy*, 2–9. New York: Federation of Jewish Philanthropies, 1965.
399. Baron, Salo W. "An Incurable Disease." *Alliance Review* 20, no. 40 (Spring 1966): 11–13.
400. Baron, Salo W. "In Historic Perspective." *Our Age* 2, no. 2 (October 31, 1966): 1–3.
401. Baron, Salo W. "The Jewish Community and Jewish Education." In *Judaism and the Jewish School*, ed. Judah Pilch and Meir Ben-Horin, 11–13. New York: Bloch, 1966.

BIBLIOGRAPHY

402. Baron, Salo W. "Jews and Germans: A Millennial Heritage." *Midstream* 13, no. 1 (January 1967): 3–13.
403. Baron, Salo W. "*Una Enfermedad Incurable*." *Tribuna Israelita* (July–August 1967): 24–26.
404. Baron, Salo W. "Anti-Semitism." In *Encyclopaedia Britannica*, vol. 2 (1967): 81–90.
405. Baron, Salo W. "*Comunidade Judia*." In *Encyclopaedia Judaica* (1967): 343–50.
406. Baron, Salo W. "Exilarch," in *Encyclopaedia Britannica*, vol. 8 (1967): 965.
407. Baron, Salo W. "*Graetzens Geschichtsschreibung: Eine methodologische Untersuchung*." In *Wissenschaft des Judentums im deutschen Sprachbereich: Ein Querschnitt*, vol. 1, ed. Kurt Wilhelm, 353–360. Tübingen: Mohr Siebeck, 1967.
408. Baron, Salo W. "Josel of Rosheim." In *Encyclopaedia Britannica*, vol. 13 (1967): 86–87.
409. Baron, Salo W. "Pharisees." In *Encyclopaedia Britannica*, vol. 17 (1967): 794.
410. Baron, Salo W. "*Herencia medieval y realidades modernas en las relaciones entre judios y Protestantes*." *Diogenes* 16, no. 61 (January–March 1968): 31–48.
411. Baron, Salo W. "*Heritage medieval et realites modernes dans les relations entre juifs et protestants*." *Diogenes* 61 (January–March 1968): 36–58.
412. Baron, Salo W. "Medieval Heritage and Modern Realities in Protestant-Jewish Relations." *Diogenes* 61 (Spring 1968): 32–51.
413. Baron, Salo W. "From a Historian's Notebook: European Jewry Before and After Hitler." In *Out of the Whirlwind: A Reader of Holocaust Literature*, ed. Albert H. Friedlander, 133–54. New York: UAHC Press, 1968.
414. Baron, Salo W. "Hirsch Perez Chajes." [In Hebrew.] In *Encyclopedia ha-Ivrit* 17 (1968), cols. 351–53.
415. Baron, Salo W. "Symposium: Nationalism in the Middle East." In *The Middle East in the Contemporary World*, 35–37. New York: American Professors for Peace in the Middle East, 1968.
416. Baron, Salo W. "An Unusual Excommunication Formula from Frankfurt." [In Hebrew.] In *Studies in Mysticism and Religion Presented to Gershom G. Scholem*, ed. E. E. Urbach, R. J. Zwi Werblowski, and Ch. Wirszubski, 29–34. Jerusalem: Magnes, 1968.
417. Baron, Salo W. "Medieval Folklore and Jewish Fate." *Jewish Affairs* 25, no. 3 (March 1970): 14–19.
418. Baron, Salo W. "Jewish Pioneering: A Lesson of Jewish History." *Jewish Heritage* 11, no. 4 (Summer 1969): 53–55.
419. Baron, Salo W. "Impact of Nationalism." In *Readings in English for Students of the Social Sciences and Humanities*, ed. N. A. Berkoff, Batya Ariel, and Jane Falk, 50–51. Jerusalem: Hebrew University Press, 1969.
420. Baron, Salo W. "Jewish Community." [In Hebrew.] In *Jewish Encyclopedia*. Ramat-Gan: Massada, 1969.
421. Baron, Salo W. "Jewish Communal Pioneering." In *The Jewish Experience in America*, vol. 1, ed. Abraham J. Karp, 1–18. New York: American Jewish Historical Society, 1969.
422. Baron, Salo W. "Patterns of Survival." In *The Judaic Tradition*, ed. Nahum M. Glatzer, 733–38. Boston: Beacon, 1969.
423. Baron, Salo W. "A Review of Freud." In *Monotheism and Moses*, ed. Robert J. Christen and Harold E. Hazelton, 39–43. Lexington, MA: D. C. Heath, 1969.

424. Baron, Salo W. "Who Is a Jew? Some Historical Reflections." In *Readings in English for Students of the Social Sciences and Humanities*, ed. N. A. Berkoff, Batya Ariel, and Jane Falk, 142–49. Jerusalem: Hebrew University Press, 1969.
425. Baron, Salo W. "*Rachi et la Communaute de Troyes*." L'Arche 162–163 (September 16–25, October 1970): 61–68.
426. Baron, Salo W. "Optimistic, But for New Priorities." *National Jewish Post and Opinion*, December 25, 1970, 8.
427. Baron, Salo W. "Reflections on Ancient and Medieval Jewish Historical Demography." [In Hebrew.] In *Aryeh Tartakower Jubilee Volume* [In Hebrew], ed. Yosef Shapiro, 31–45. Tel Aviv: Brit Ivrit Olamit, 1970.
428. Baron, Salo W. "In Memoriam: Cecil Roth." *American Historical Review* 76, no. 2 (April 1971): 591–92.
429. Baron, Salo W. "*Nationalismus und Religion in der heutigen Welt*." Saeculum 22, no. 2–3 (1971): 305–16.
430. Baron, Salo W. "Cultural Reconstruction of Russian Jewry." *JPS Bookmark* 18, no. 2 (June 1971): 4–5, 10.
431. Baron, Salo W. "Review of *The Letters and Papers of Chaim Weizmann*, ed. Leonard Stein and Gedalia Yogev." *Political Science Quarterly* 86, no. 2 (June 1971): 359–62.
432. Baron, Salo W. "Transmitting and Enriching the Heritage of Judaism." Address delivered at the 39th General Assembly of the Council of Jewish Federations, November 14, 1971.
433. Baron, Salo W. "Anti-Semitism." In *Encyclopaedia Britannica*, vol. 2 (1971): 81–90
434. Baron, Salo W. "A Collection of Hebrew-Latin Aphorisms by a Christian Hebraist." In *Studies in Jewish Bibliography, History and Literature in Honor of I. Edward Kiev*, ed. Charles Berlin, 1–10. New York: Ktav, 1971.
435. Baron, Salo W. "Cultural Reconstruction of Russian Jewry." The 1971 Allan Bronfman Lecture, 3–27. Westmount, Quebec: Congregation Shaar Hashomayim, 1971.
436. Baron, Salo W. Foreword to *From Spanish Court to Italian Ghetto*, by Yosef Hayim Yerushalmi, ix–xi. Seattle: University of Washington Press, 1971.
437. Baron, Salo W. Introduction to *Union Catalog of Hebrew Manuscripts and Their Location*, by Aron Freimann, iii–v. New York: American Academy for Jewish Research, 1971.
438. Baron, Salo W. "Moses and Monotheism." In *Psychoanalysis and History*, ed. Bruce Mazlish, 50–55. New York: Grosset and Dunlop, 1971.
439. Baron, Salo W. "Conference on Jewish Social Studies." In *Encyclopedia Judaica*, vol. 5 (1972): col. 874.
440. Baron, Salo W. "Economic History." In *Encyclopedia Judaica*, vol. 16 (1972): cols. 1266–96.
441. Baron, Salo W. Foreword to *A Jewish Princedom in Feudal France, 768–900*, by Arthur J. Zuckerman, vii–vii. New York: Columbia University Press, 1972.
442. Baron, Salo W. "Hirsch (Zevi) Peretz Chajes." In *Encyclopedia Judaica*, vol. 5 (1972): cols. 325–26.
443. Baron, Salo W. Introduction to *Ancient and Medieval Jewish History: Essays by Salo Wittmayer Baron*, ed. Leon A. Feldman, xv–xxiii. New Brunswick, NJ: Rutgers University Press, 1972.

BIBLIOGRAPHY

444. Baron, Salo W. Introduction to *Not Free to Desist: The American Jewish Committee, 1906–1966*, by Naomi W. Cohen, xi–xiii. Philadelphia: Jewish Publication Society, 1972.
445. Baron, Salo W. "Israelitisch-Theologische Lehranstalt, Vienna." In *Encyclopedia Judaica*, vol. 9 (1972): cols. 1067–68.
446. Baron, Salo W. "John Calvin." In *Encyclopedia Judaica*, vol. 5 (1972): cols. 66–68.
447. Baron, Salo W. "Population." In *Encyclopedia Judaica*, vol. 9 (1972): cols. 866–903.
448. Baron, Salo W. "The Council of Trent and Rabbinic Literature." In *Ancient and Medieval Jewish History: Essays by Salo Wittmayer Baron*, ed. Leon A. Feldman, 353–71, 555–64. New Brunswick, NJ: Rutgers University Press, 1972.
449. Baron, Salo W. "A Definitive Mendelssohn Biography" [review of *Moses Mendelssohn: A Biographical Study*, by Alexander Altmann]. *Jerusalem Post Magazine*, July 27, 1973, 18.
450. Baron, Salo W. Foreword to *The Alexander Kohut Memorial Foundation: A Review of Activities (1915–1972)*, by Tovia Preschel, 3–4. New York: American Academy for Jewish Research, 1973.
451. Baron, Salo W. Preface to *Die hebräischen Handschriften in Österreich*, vol. 4, ed. Arthur Zacharias Schwarz, D. S. Loewinger, and E. Roth. New York: American Academy for Jewish Research, 1973.
452. Baron, Salo W. "In Memoriam: Benzion Dinur (1884–1973)." *Proceedings of the American Academy for Jewish Research* 41–42 (1973–1974): xix–xxiv.
453. Baron, Salo W. "Review of *Moses Mendelssohn: A Biographical Study*, by Alexander Altmann." *Journal of the History of Philosophy* 12, no. 2 (April 1974): 264–65.
454. Baron, Salo W. "Can American Jewry Be Culturally Creative?" [In Hebrew.] In *Hagut Ivrit be–Europah, vol. 3: Studies on Jewish Themes by Contemporary European Scholars*, 471–75. Tel Aviv: Yavneh, 1974.
455. Baron, Salo W. "The Impact of the Revolution of 1848 on Jewish Emancipation." In *Emancipation and Counter-Emancipation: Selected Essays from Jewish Social Studies*, ed. Abraham G. Duker and Meir Ben-Horin, 141–204. New York: Ktav, 1974.
456. Baron, Salo W. "The Journal and the Conference of Jewish Social Studies." In *Emancipation and Counter-Emancipation: Selected Essays from Jewish Social Studies*, ed. Abraham G. Duker and Meir Ben-Horin, 1–11. New York: Ktav, 1974.
457. Baron, Salo W. "A Noteworthy Letter from Heinrich Graetz." In *Studies in Jewish History: Presented to Professor Raphael Mahler on his Seventy-Fifth Birthday*, ed. by Shlomo Yeivin, 77–82. Tel Aviv: Merhavia, 1974.
458. Baron, Salo W. "Solomon Ibn Ya'ish and Sultan Suleiman the Magnificent." In *Joshua Finkel Festschrift: In Honor of Dr. Joshua Finkel*, ed. Sidney B. Hoenig and Leon D. Stitskin, 29–36. New York: Yeshiva University Press, 1974.
459. Baron, Salo W. "Review of *Jews, Wars, and Communism*, by Zosa Szajkowski, *The Jews in Soviet Russia Since 1917*, by Lionel Kochan, and *The Last Exodus*, by Leonard Schroeter." *Jewish Social Studies* 37, no. 2 (Spring 1975): 170–73.
460. Baron, Salo W. "Review of *The Jews of Poland: A Social and Economic History of the Jewish Community in Poland from 1100 to 1800*, by Bernard D. Weinryb." *American Historical Review* 80, no. 3 (June 1975): 685.

BIBLIOGRAPHY

461. Baron, Salo W. "Jewish Studies at Universities: An Early Project." *Hebrew Union College Annual* 46 (1975): 357–76.
462. Baron, Salo W. "Judaism, a History of: General Observations." In *Encyclopaedia Britannica* (1975).
463. Baron, Salo W. "Personal Notes: Hannah Arendt (1906–1975)." *Jewish Social Studies* 38, no. 2 (Spring 1976): 187–89.
464. Baron, Salo W. "Nationalism and Religion in the Contemporary World." *Journal of Ecumenical Studies* 13, no. 4 (Fall 1976): 633–51.
465. Baron, Salo W. "Changing Patterns of Antisemitism: A Survey." *Jewish Social Studies* 38, no. 1 (Winter 1976): 5–38.
466. Baron, Salo W. "Changing Patterns of Antisemitism." [In Hebrew.] *be-Tefutsoth ha-Golah* 18, no. 79–80 (Winter 1976): 125–52.
467. Baron, Salo W. "European Jewry Before and After Hitler." In *The Catastrophe of European Jewry: Antecedents, History, Reflections*, ed. Yisrael Gutman and Livia Rothkirchen, 175–239. Jerusalem: Yad Vashem, 1976.
468. Baron, Salo W. "The Jewishness of Culture." [In Hebrew.] *Forum on the Jewish People, Zionism, and Israel* 2, no. 25 (1976): 71.
469. Baron, Salo W. "Nationalism and Religion in the Contemporary World." *Journal of Ecumenical Studies* 13, no. 4 (1976): 117–35.
470. Baron, Salo W. "The Ancient and Medieval Period: Review of the History." In *Violence and Defense in the Jewish Experience*, by Salo W. Baron and George S. Wise, 17–35. Philadelphia: Jewish Publication Society, 1977.
471. Baron, Salo W. "Discussion." In *World Jewry and the State of Israel*, ed. Moshe Davis, 109–10. New York: Arno, 1977.
472. Baron, Salo W. Introduction to *Violence and Defense in the Jewish Experience*, by Salo W. Baron and George S. Wise, 3–14. Philadelphia: Jewish Publication Society 1977.
473. Baron, Salo W. "The Modern and Contemporary Periods: Review of the History." In *Violence and Defense in the Jewish Experience*, by Salo W. Baron and George S. Wise, 163–90. Philadelphia: Jewish Publication Society, 1977.
474. Baron, Salo W. "Introduction" [In Hebrew] in *The Jewish Philosophy in the Middle Ages: Essays* [In Hebrew], by Harry Austryn Wolfson, 7. Jerusalem: Mosad Bialik, 1978.
475. Baron, Salo W. "Introduction: Reflections on the Achievements and Prospects of Jewish Social Studies." *Jewish Social Studies* 41, no. 1 (Winter 1979): 1–8.
476. Baron, Salo W. "Civil Versus Political Emancipation." In *Studies in Jewish Religious and Intellectual History: Alexander Altmann Jubilee Volume*, ed. Siegfried Stein and Raphael Loewe, 29–49. University, AL: University of Alabama Press, 1979.
477. Baron, Salo W. "The Evolution of Equal Rights: Civil and Political." In *Essays on Human Rights: Contemporary Issues and Jewish Perspectives*, ed. David Sidorsky, 267–81. Philadelphia: Jewish Publication Society, 1979.
478. Baron, Salo W. "Problems of Jewish Identity from an Historical Perspective: A Survey." *Proceedings of the American Academy for Jewish Research* 46–47, Jubilee Volume (1928–29 to 1978–79) [Part 1] (1979–80): 33–67.
479. Baron, Salo W. Preface to *Art et archéologie des juifs en France médiévale*, ed. Bernhard Blumenkranz, 5–8. Toulouse: Privat, 1980.

BIBLIOGRAPHY

480. Baron, Salo W. "Joseph L. Blau: In Appreciation." In *History, Religion, and Spiritual Democracy: Essays in Honor of Joseph L. Blau*, xv–xvii. New York: Columbia University Press, 1980.
481. Baron, Salo W., and Benzion Netanyahu. "In Memoriam: Francisco Cantera y Burgos." *Proceedings of the American Academy for Jewish Research* 48 (1981): xxxii–xxxvi.
482. Baron, Salo W. "Reply to Professor Abraham Karp's Address." *American Jewish History* 71, no. 4 (June 1982): 497–506.
483. Baron, Salo W. "A New Outlook for Israel and the Diaspora." In *Diaspora: Exile and the Jewish Condition*, ed. Étan Levine, 199–209. New York: Jason Aronson, 1983.
484. Baron, Salo W. "Is America Ready for Ethnic Minority Rights?" *Jewish Social Studies* 46, nos. 3–4 (Summer–Autumn 1984): 189–214.
485. Baron, Salo W. Preface to *Les Juifs au regard de l'histoire: Mélanges en l'honneur de Bernhard Blumenkranz*, ed. Gilbert Dahan, 7–8. Paris: Picard, 1985.
486. Baron, Salo W. "Ethnic Minority Rights: Some Older and Newer Trends." The Tenth Sacks Lecture, May 26, 1983, 3–47. Oxford: Oxford Centre for Postgraduate Hebrew Studies, 1985.
487. Baron, Salo W. "Moses Maimonides (1135–1204)." In *Creators of the Jewish Experience in Ancient and Medieval Times*, ed. Simon Noveck, 204–30. Washington, DC: B'nai B'rith, 1985.
488. Baron, Salo W. et al. "Letter: Polish-Jewish Studies." *New York Review of Books* 33, no. 1, January 30, 1986, 44.
489. Baron, Salo W. "In Memoriam: Joseph L. Blau (6 May 1909–28 December 1986)." *Jewish Social Studies* 49, no. 2 (Spring 1987): 95–98.
490. Baron, Salo W. "European Jewry Before and After Hitler." In *The Nazi Holocaust: Perspectives on the Holocaust*, vol. 1, ed. Michael R. Marrus, 3–67. Westport, CT: Meckler, 1989.
491. Baron, Salo W. "A Memoir of My Library." In *Of Many Generations: Judaica and Hebraica from the Taube/Baron Collection*, ed. David L. Langenberg, 17–21. Stanford: Stanford University Libraries, 1989.
492. Baron, Salo W. "John Calvin and the Jews." In *Essential Papers on Judaism and Christianity in Conflict*, ed. Jeremy Cohen, 380–400. New York: New York University Press, 1991. [posthumously published]
493. Baron, Salo W. "Messianic and Sectarian Movements." In *Essential Papers on Messianic Movement and Personalities in Jewish History*, ed. Marc Saperstein, 162–86. New York: New York University Press, 1992. [posthumously published]
494. Baron, Salo W. "Testimony at the Eichmann Trial." In *The Trial of Adolf Eichmann: Record of Proceedings*, vol. 1, 169–90. Jerusalem: Israel Ministry of Justice, 1992. [posthumously published]
495. Baron, Salo W. "Jews in Russia: The First World War and the Revolutionary Period." In *Hostages of Modernization: Studies on Modern Antisemitism, 1870–1933/39*, vol. 2, ed. Herbert A. Strauss, 1291–1311. Berlin: de Gruyter, 1993. [posthumously published]
496. Baron, Salo W. "Social and Economic Changes Among Soviet Jews." In *Hostages of Modernization: Studies on Modern Antisemitism, 1870–1933/39*, vol. 2, ed. Herbert A. Strauss, 1342–56. Berlin: de Gruyter, 1993. [posthumously published]

497. Baron, Salo W. "The Jewish People Before and After the Holocaust." [In Hebrew.] *Mahanayim* 9 (November 1994): 216–26. [posthumously published]
498. Baron, Salo W. "The Golden Age of Poland." [In Hebrew.] In *The Broken Chain: Polish Jewry Through the Ages* [In Hebrew], vol. 1, ed. Israel Bartal and Israel Gutman, 83–113. Jerusalem: Shazar, 1997. [posthumously published]
499. Baron, Salo W. "*Sozial- und Religionsgeschichte der Juden.*" In *Jüdische Geschichte lesen: Texte der jüdischen Geschichtsschreibung im 19. und 20. Jahrhundert*, ed. Michael Brenner, 74–79. Munich: C. H. Beck, 2003. [posthumously published]
500. Baron, Salo W. "*Weltdimensionen der jüdischen Geschichte.*" In *Jüdische Geschichte lesen: Texte der jüdischen Geschichtsschreibung im 19. und 20. Jahrhundert*, ed. Michael Brenner, 151–54. Munich: C. H. Beck, 2003. [posthumously published]
501. Baron, Salo W. "*Ghetto und Emanzipation.*" In *Jüdische Geschichte lesen: Texte der jüdischen Geschichtsschreibung im 19. und 20. Jahrhundert*, ed. Michael Brenner, 229–41. Munich: C. H. Beck, 2003. [posthumously published]
502. Baron, Salo W. "A Memoir of My Library." *Tablet Magazine*, September 8, 2015. [posthumously published]

ACKNOWLEDGMENTS

This volume was both ninety years in the making and the product of recent events no one could have ever predicted. When Nicholas Butler, Columbia University's president, wrote to Salo Wittmayer Baron in 1929 to invite him to assume a chair in Jewish History, Literature and Institutions, he had no idea of the impact that this young scholar from Eastern Europe would have on the university or the larger academic study of the Jewish past in the United States. How could he have known that the appointment of this prolific and erudite scholar would fundamentally alter the course of Jewish studies in the United States, as Baron's writings, teaching, mentorship and development of numerous scholarly organizations inspired many and continues to shape the field to this very day?

Assessing the historical significance of Butler's decision and Baron's arrival at Columbia was the goal of a conference planned for November 2020. But the effort to mark and reflect on Baron's appointment was shaped by another historic event, a once-in-a-century global pandemic that canceled every social event and postponed every face-to-face conference. To stay safe, the notable scholars we had assembled to reflect on the changes wrought to both Columbia and Jewish studies by Baron's arrival in Morningside Heights would have to occur on a page and not in a room. This volume reflects those scholars' continued commitment to sharing their insights, evaluations, and reminiscences of this man and his life's work, despite never being able to descend on Morningside Heights in November 2020 like Baron had done ninety years earlier.

In transforming a conference that never took place into a volume, I must thank the small village of people who enabled this book to see the light of day. I want to begin by thanking my colleagues in Columbia's history department, who have always engaged me in thinking about how Jewish history can force scholars in other fields to contemplate new questions about the past and the historian's craft. I also must thank the directors of the Institute for Israel and Jewish Studies, which Baron founded in 1950, who have supported me since I arrived at Columbia: Michael Stanislawski, who transformed the Center for Israel and Jewish Studies into one of Columbia's revered academic institutes, and Jeremy Dauber, who engineered the Institute's move to its new home in Kent Hall. With much gratitude I recognize Professor Elisheva Carlebach, my present codirector at the Institute for Israel and Jewish Studies. One of the great fortunes of my life has been the opportunity to work with her. It was she, as the director of the Institute for Israel and Jewish Studies, who originally conceived of a conference to mark Baron's arrival at Columbia, while some of his students could still speak to his role in shaping their approach to Jewish history. She also organized another conference, dedicated to the life and work of Yosef Hayim Yerushalmi (convened in 2018 at Columbia), which first made me realize the critical role Baron and his students played in training a generation of scholars in Jewish studies in the United States. As I looked around the room during the Yerushalmi event in 2018, as one of the few people not trained by Baron or one of his students, I comprehended how important Salo Baron was for the development of Jewish studies in the United States as he had shaped a generation of scholars who were dedicated to studying the Jewish past. Many of the speakers at that lively conference pushed me to begin to think about Baron (and Yerushalmi) as not merely historians but historical subjects who remade Columbia University into a center for the training of scholars in Jewish studies as they molded how both laypeople and scholars theorized, conceptualized, and narrated the Jewish past.

This volume would have never been published if not for Dana Kresel at the Institute for Israel and Jewish Studies, who always made sure that the financial and technical aspects of publishing this collection ran smoothly. She, along with Dina Mann, also facilitated the hiring of Lotte Houwink ten Cate, whose attention to detail, unparalleled organizational skills, and

ACKNOWLEDGMENTS

dedication to this project were essential to keeping the volume on track and moving it forward. Karen Santos da Silva helped to create seamless translations. Michelle Chesner, Columbia's Norman E. Alexander Librarian for Jewish Studies, not only helped to find and scan documents from the Columbia archives when no one else could go there but also facilitated contact with Eitan Kensky, at Stanford University Archives, who also looked through and scanned elements of the Baron collection there. Most remarkably, when I realized that Columbia kept no records of who it trained in Jewish history or Jewish studies in general, the indefatigable Michelle Chesner helped find every dissertation that thanked Salo Baron for his advising so that my lists of the students would be as complete as possible. I was helped by colleagues as I tried to piece together all the students who worked with Baron and those he trained. I am extremely grateful to Marsha Rozenblit, Ismar Schorsch, Bob Chazan, Deborah Dash Moore, Scott Ury, Kalman Weiser, and Jeffrey Gurock for their time and expertise. I also want to thank Shoshana Tancer for her priceless personal family photographs and for the words she penned with her sister. I can never adequately express my gratitude to Charlie Knapp for his help with this project, along with his support for the Institute for Israel and Jewish Studies over the years. Through his generosity as the President of the Knapp Family Foundation and of the Salo W. and Jeannette M. Baron Foundation, he is furthering Salo Baron's vision of expanding the world's engagement with the Jewish past.

Finally, I thank all the contributors and the three anonymous reviewers who worked on rigid deadlines to make this volume better. My deep appreciation also goes to Jonathan Sarna, Eric Goldstein, and Beth Wenger for their perspectives on the pivotal role played by Baron within the annals of American Jewish history and the development of Jewish studies in the United States. Connie Xu made possible the digital rendering of Baron's impact on the field of Jewish studies in the United States. My embarking on charting all the students trained by Baron and his students during a pandemic when the university and all its archival repositories were closed was challenging, and, thus, I am sure that I have left people out. I apologize for any oversight, errors, or mistakes, which are all my own and hope to inspire others to look further into Columbia's archives for a full accounting of all those whose lives and scholarship were shaped by Baron.

ACKNOWLEDGMENTS

It has been a pleasure working with Stephen Wesley at Columbia University Press and his excellent team. From the moment I proposed this volume, his exceptional professionalism, strategic thinking, and great kindness proved crucial in getting this book published. To my dear friends who helped me through the crazy year in which this volume was pulled together, Marjorie Lehman allowed me to join her pod during this historic time, and her family of doctors indulged all my queries; Amanda Gordon, Tal Kastner, and Michal Lemberger read through my drafts and have seen me through this project and the ups and downs of life with sage advice and unconditional support.

On a rainy morning before handing in this manuscript, I went to pick up some donuts to celebrate my son's birthday. The person behind the counter asked if my purchase sought to brighten the day of my coworkers. I laughed as the only "coworkers" I have interacted with face to face for the past year have been Ariela, Simone, and Eitan Feinblum, my beloved children, to whom I dedicate this book. Indeed, this entire book project was conceived and executed as I shared my "office" space with my children while they went to school, took tests, baked cookies, and mixed chemicals for labs while I taught my classes, engaged the authors of this volume, and imagined its contents. As we settled into our new home on Claremont Avenue just a few doors down from where Salo Baron lived, worked, and convened his graduate seminars, we learned how to work, go to school, build race tracks, cook three meals a day, study, exercise, and block out one another's noisy interactions with others on Zoom, during what seemed like a never-ending period distinct from any other time we had ever experienced. For the months of the pandemic, as we sat together in our respites from Zoom to eat together, my children humored me, joined my office hours, asked my students about their lives, and kept me laughing. As I bring this book to its conclusion, I feel nothing but gratitude and love for them, as they are models of resilience and teach me each day what truly matters. Like Baron, who always thought of the future despite being immersed in centuries-old historic texts, they prevent me from becoming mired in the past and help me to look forward to the future they will create.

CONTRIBUTORS

Pierre Birnbaum is an emeritus professor at the Sorbonne. He published several books on the state and on relations between the state and the Jews, including *Paths of Emancipation: Jews, States and Citizenship* (with Ira Katznelson) eds., 1995; *Geography of Hope. Exile, the Enlightenment, Disassimilation* (2008); and *Leon Blum. Prime Minister, Socialist, Zionist* (2015). Most recently, he published *La leçon de Vichy. Une histoire personnelle* (2019).

Menachem Butler is program fellow at the Julis–Rabinowitz Program on Jewish and Israeli Law at Harvard Law School and contributing editor at *Tablet* magazine.

Robert Chazan has served as Scheuer Professor of Hebrew and Judaic Studies at New York University for the past three decades. The focus of Chazan's research has been the history of the Jews in medieval western Christendom. His most recent books are *From Anti-Judaism to Anti-Semitism* (2016) and *Refugees or Migrants: Pre-Modern Jewish Population Movement* (2018).

Michelle Margolis Chesner is the Norman E. Alexander Librarian for Jewish Studies at Columbia University. She codirects the project "Footprints: Jewish Books Through Time and Place," is the creator of "Codex Conquest: Jewish Edition," and has curated various library exhibitions, both physical and virtual. She serves as vice president/president-elect of the Association of Jewish Libraries. Michelle's research includes early Jewish printing and the history of Jewish collecting and collections, as well as the intersection of Jewish studies and the digital humanities. Her degrees are from University of Maryland, Long Island University, and New York University.

Bernard Dov Cooperman holds the Louis L. Kaplan Chair in Jewish History at the University of Maryland, where he has served as director of the Joseph & Rebecca Meyerhoff Center for Jewish Studies and the Nathan Miller Center for Historical Studies. Cooperman's research focuses on early modern Italy. His comparison of Salo Baron and Cecil Roth, "Reframing Time to Save the Nation: The Jewish Historian as Cultural Trickster," will appear in a forthcoming volume edited by Barbara Mittler and Thomas Maissen through the University of Heidelberg Press. He is working on a project entitled *The Right to Exclude* on Jewish legal traditions of communal self-government and preference.

David Engel holds the Greenberg Chair in Holocaust Studies at New York University, where he has taught history for over thirty years in the Skirball Department of Hebrew and Judaic Studies. He served as chair of the Skirball Department from 2011 through 2018. From 1985 through 2016 Professor Engel edited the journal *Gal-Ed: On the History and Culture of Polish Jews*, published by Tel Aviv University. A member of the Academic Committee of the United States Holocaust Memorial Museum, and the American Academy of Jewish Research, he has written, lectured, and taught widely about various aspects of East European Jewish history.

Jane Gerber is professor emerita of history and founder and director of the Institute for Sephardic Studies at the Graduate Center of the City University of New York. She is the author and editor of six books, including *The Jews of Spain* (National Jewish Book Award winner), *Cities of Splendour in the Shaping of Sephardi History*, and the forthcoming *Jews and Muslims in Morocco: Their Intersecting Worlds*.

Rebecca Kobrin is the Russell and Bettina Knapp Associate Professor of American Jewish History at Columbia University, where she is also codirector of Columbia's Institute for Israel and Jewish Studies. Her book *Jewish Bialystok and Its Diaspora* (2010) was awarded the Jordan Schnitzer prize. She is the editor of *Chosen Capital: The Jewish Encounter with American Capitalism* (2012) and is coeditor with Adam Teller of *Purchasing Power: The Economics of Jewish History* (2015). Her forthcoming book, *A Credit to the Nation: East European Immigrant Bankers and American Finance, 1870–1930* will be published by Harvard University Press.

Deborah Lipstadt is Dorot Professor of Holocaust Studies at Emory University in Atlanta. Her 2006 *History on Trial: My Day in Court with a Holocaust Denier*

CONTRIBUTORS

was awarded the National Jewish Book Award. Other publications include *The Eichmann Trial* and *Denying the Holocaust: The Growing Assault on Truth and Memory* (1993).

Jason Lustig is a lecturer and Israel Institute Teaching Fellow at the Schusterman Center for Jewish Studies at the University of Texas at Austin. His forthcoming book, *A Time to Gather: Archives and the Control of Jewish Culture*, traces the twentieth-century struggle over who might "own" Jewish history, especially after the Nazi looting of Jewish archives. He received his PhD in history from the University of California, Los Angeles, and was a Harry Starr Fellow in Judaica at Harvard University's Center for Jewish Studies and a Gerald Westheimer Early Career Fellow at the Leo Baeck Institute.

David Sorkin is Lucy G. Moses Professor of History at Yale University. Among his most recent books are *The Religious Enlightenment: Protestants, Jews and Catholics from London to Vienna* (2008) and *Jewish Emancipation: A History Across Five Centuries* (2019).

Francesca Trivellato is Andrew W. Mellon Professor in the School of Historical Studies at the Institute for Advanced Study in Princeton, New Jersey. Her monographs include *The Promise and Peril of Credit: What a Forgotten Legend About Jews and Finance Tells Us About the Making of European Commercial Society* (2019) and *The Familiarity of Strangers: The Sephardic Diaspora, Livorno, and Cross-Cultural Trade in the Early Modern Period* (2009). With Jonathan Karp, she coedited *Jews in Early Modern Europe*, which is forthcoming from Routledge in the Variorum series Classic Essays in Jewish History.

INDEX

Adler, Cyrus, 9
Agudat Israel, 39
American Academy of Jewish Research, 4
American Historical Association, 57, 61, 66
American Jewish Historical Society, 5, 27, 30
American Jewry, 13, 32, 180, 187, 215
Amsterdam, Holland, 89, 91–92, 106
Ankori, Zvi, 38, 48
Anti-Semitism, 16, 101–3, 115, 144–45, 175, 180, 215; modern, 125, 175
Arendt, Hannah, 139, 211–12
Argentina, 132–33
Association for Jewish Studies, 217
Auschwitz, 137, 141
Austria, 12, 45, 50, 86, 118, 193, 219

Baer, Yitzah, 178, 186, 187
Balaban, Meyer, 85
Baron, Jeannette Meisel, 5, 20, 65, 157, 207, 211–12, 214, 216
Baron, Salo: *Economic History of the Jews*, 97; "Ghetto and Emancipation," 13, 26, 28–29, 31, 83, 174, 180, 182, 194, 200–201; *The Jewish Community,*

Its History and Structure, 180; "The Jewish Factor in Medieval Civilization," 101; *Russian Jew Under Tsars and Soviets: A Social and Religious History of the Jews*, 20, 27–28, 30, 61–62, 64, 67, 85, 100, 105, 120–21, 123, 165, 194, 202–5, 217; as teacher, 14, 30, 165, 167, 174–77, 193–94, 207–18
Barzun, Jacques, 58
Bauer, Fritz, 133
Beard, Charles, 58
Ben-Gurion, David, 133, 135, 137, 139, 145–47
Berlin, Germany, 45, 49, 54, 56, 181
Bevis Marks, synagogue, 91
Bialik, Hayim Nahman, 43, 60, 139, 147
Bloch, Joshua, 61
Bloch, Marc, 98, 105
Bonaparte, Napoleon, 107, 177
Brandstätter, Mordechai David, 40, 43
Brawer, Abraham J., 46, 49, 51
Buchholz, Carl August, 82, 83,
Bund movement, 87
Butler, Nicholas Murray, 1, 56, 57–60, 153, 156

INDEX

Cairo Geniza, 46
capitalism, 87, 98, 102, 104, 106
Cardoso, Isaac, 182–184
catholicism, 57, 90
Chajes, Tzvi Peretz, 52
Chazan, Robert, 3, 18, 19
christianity, 61–63, 90, 118
citizenship, 88, 90, 202
Cohen, Gershon D., 18, 165, 166
Columbia University, 1–3, 8–9, 15–17, 20, 28, 37–38, 53–55, 58, 60–62, 65–67, 97, 109, 127, 139–40, 153, 156–58, 161, 165, 167–68, 174, 179, 192, 201–2, 205, 207–9, 211, 213, 215, 217, 219, 222–23
Center for Israel and Jewish Studies, 5, 18; Department of History, 56–58, 174, 209, 220; Judaica collections, 17, 153–54, 156, 161, 163, 165, 167
Conference on Jewish Relations, 215
Congress of Vienna, 51, 81–82, 88

diaspora, 146–47, 178
Dubnow, Simon, 21, 28–29, 81–82, 107, 139
Duker, Abraham, 15

Eichmann, Adolf, 16, 103, 126, 132–33, 135–37, 140–41, 144, 149
Eichmann Trial, 17, 27, 148–50, 176, 178
Einstein, Albert, 139, 142, 147
Eisenbach, Artur, 85
Eisenbeth, Maurice, 107
Elbogen, Ismar, 56
Eliach, Yaffa, 14
Eliav, Benjamin, 138, 139
Emancipation, 14, 16, 81–89, 91–92, 107, 118, 142, 174, 175–77, 179–82
Enelow, Hyman, 10, 55
Engel, David, 85, 177
Enlightenment, 87, 142, 177, 198

Febvre, Lucien, 98, 105–6
Final Solution, 138
Fournier, August, 51
Fraenkel, David, 158, 161–63
French Revolution, 81, 98, 175–78, 195
Friedman, Philip, 85

Galicia, 39–40, 51, 84–85, 107, 187, 216
Gelber, Natan, 85
Ginzberg, Louis, 212, 223
Gitelle, Tobey, 207, 219–224
Glueck, Nelson, 33
Gottheil, Richard, 9, 54, 56, 61, 66, 154, 156
Gottheil, Gustav, 54, 154
Graetz, Heinrich, 21, 28–29, 52, 81–82, 103, 175
Great Depression, 53, 158
Grünberg, Carl, 51

Habsburg Empire, 11, 51, 84, 87
Hausner, Gideon, 135, 137–38, 139–41, 144–46, 149
Halbeachs, Maurice, 106
Halevy, Binyamin, 136–37
Handlin, Oscar, 31
Harvard University, 10, 15, 25, 30, 55, 66, 105, 208
Hasidism, 40–41
Haskalah movement, 40, 86
Hayes, Carlton, 57–58
Hebrew Union College, 31–32, 55, 156, 209
Hebrew University, 49, 208
Hegel, G. W. F., 118, 144
Hertz, Joseph, 55
Hertzberg, Arthur, 64, 66, 139, 147, 177, 213
Herzfeld, Levi, 102, 103
Hirsh, Emil G., 9
Hitler, Adolf, 177
Holocaust, 27, 31–33, 92, 126, 132, 136, 138–39, 142, 146, 148–49, 174, 184–85; denial of, 148
Holy Roman Empire, 82, 117
Howson, Roger, 157–59
Hume, David, 83, 175

Inquisition, 123, 198, 200
international law, 88, 136, 138, 140
Irving, David, 148–49
Islam, 62–63, 101, 204, 205
Israel, 16, 33, 132–34, 136, 138–41, 149, 187; Knesset, 132–33, 136–37, 174, 204
Israel/Palestine, 32

INDEX

Israelitisch-Theologischen Lehranstalt, 11, 45–46, 48–49, 85

Jackson, Robert, 138
Jastrow, Morris, 9
Jerusalem, 52, 126, 134–35, 148, 150, 212
Jewish Cultural Reconstruction, 4, 27, 32, 153, 165, 211–12
Jewish Institute for Religion (JIR) 13, 52–53, 55, 59–61, 89, 97, 209, 223
Jewish Social Studies, 5, 32, 66, 207, 215–16; Conference of Jewish Social Studies, 4–5
Jewish Studies, 1, 2, 4–6, 8–9, 11, 13–18, 21, 25–33, 44, 53–57, 61, 67, 108, 153, 157, 168, 174, 201, 205, 214, 217, 224
Jewish Theological Seminary, 10, 18, 49, 55–56, 156, 161, 209, 212, 223
Judaica, 85, 153, 208, 216; collection of, 3, 153, 156, 158, 168

Kabbalah, 47–48, 163
Kastner, Rudolf, 136–37
Kelsen, Hans, 51
Knapp, Russell, 5
Knapp, Charlie, 20
Kohut, George Alexander, 59
Kraków, Poland, 40, 44, 85, 120

Lachrymose conception of Jewish history, 13, 18, 26, 28, 175–78, 180, 182, 184, 186–88, 195, 205
Landau, Moshe, 137
Lassalle, Ferdinand, 51
League of Nations, 50
Liberles, Robert, 44, 61, 67, 99, 109, 147, 153
Lieberman, Saul, 212, 223
Littauer, Lucius, 10, 55
London, 45, 49, 91–92, 100, 148–50
Luzzato, Shemu'l David (Shadal) 164–65, 167

Mahler, Raphael, 52, 85
Marcus, Jacob Reader, 31
Margulis, Samuel Hirsch, 52
Marshall, Louis, 83

Marx, Alexander, 161, 212, 223
Marx, Karl, 104
Menorah Journal, 13, 194
Miller, Linda, 8, 10–11, 55–56, 153
Miller, Nathan
Miller Chair, 4, 37, 55, 56, 61, 109, 153, 201, 202, 203, 295

Nazi Regime, 33, 47, 119, 211
Nazism, 176–78, 215
Nevins, Allan, 58
New School for Historical Research, 58
New York City, 8–9, 38, 52, 55, 57, 108, 156, 181, 211–12, 215, 217, 219, 221–22
New York Public Library, 55, 61, 156, 219
Nuremberg Trials, 17, 133–38, 148, 150

Ottoman Empire, 86, 214

Palestine, 49–50, 186–87, 204, 212, 222; British Mandate, 31, 83, 106; persecution, 100, 176; pogroms, 99, 176, 179, 181, 183, 188, 198
Poland, 86, 121, 187, 222; Congress, 120
Polish-Lithuanian Commonwealth, 11
Postan, Michael, 98, 104, 105
Potok, Chaim, 38
Protocols of the Elders of Zion, 119, 145, 180

Ranke, Leopold von, 27
Ringelblum, Emanuel, 85, 137
Robinson, James Harvey, 48
Robinson, Yaakov (Jacob) 138–40, 145–46
Rosenau, William, 9
Roth, Cecil, 32, 38, 62
Russia, Tsarist Russia, 86, 118, 177, 187

Sartre, Jean-Paul, 101
Schiper, Ignazy, 85
Scholem, Gershom, 47, 212
Schorr, Moses, 85
Schwarz, Adolf (Aryeh) 45, 47, 51
Sephardi Jews, 98, 161, 183
Servatius, Robert, 126, 136, 140, 144
Shazar, Zalman, 146–47
Sklare, Marshall, 14

Smolenskin, Peretz, 44
Sombart, Werner, 98, 100, 102–6, 109
South Africa, 211–12
Soviet Union, 87, 138, 181, 211
Spain, 179, 182, 186; expulsion from, 123, 174
Stanislawski, Michael, 61

Tancer, Shoshana B., 219–224
Talmud, study of, 40, 43–45, 47, 49, 51
Tarnów, Poland, 11, 39, 41, 44, 53, 85, 143, 214, 216, 219
Temple Emanu-El, 8, 53–55, 154, 167
Trachtenberg, Joshua, 14

Umansky, Yosef, 44
United States, 4, 13, 17–18, 25–27, 30, 32–33, 49, 54, 101, 107, 125, 135, 139–40, 148, 153, 167, 174, 179–80, 187, 194, 209, 212, 217, 220, 222–23
University of Chicago, 9, 55
University of Vienna, 11, 44, 49, 53, 56, 209

Van Ranke, Leopold, 27
Vienna, 11, 38, 44–45, 48, 51–53, 56, 85, 88, 181

Warsaw, Poland, 43, 52, 85; ghetto, 137
Weber, Max, 104, 109
Weizmann, Chaim, 147
Wise, Stephen S., 52, 55, 89
Wissenschaft des Judentums, 46, 49, 60
Wittamayer, Hirsch, 39
Wolfson, Harry, 10, 25, 66
World Jewish Congress on Jews, 107
World War I, 45, 50–51, 61, 83, 85, 87
World War II, 33, 101, 153
World Zionist Congress, 52

Yad Vashem, 140
Yerushalmi, Yosef Hayim, 15, 18, 28, 30, 48, 167, 174, 181–85, 188
Yeshiva University, 52
YIVO, 107

Zionism, 44, 50, 54, 83, 147

GPSR Authorized Representative: Easy Access System Europe, Mustamäe tee 50, 10621 Tallinn, Estonia, gpsr.requests@easproject.com

www.ingramcontent.com/pod-product-compliance
Lightning Source LLC
Chambersburg PA
CBHW022043290426
44109CB00014B/968